India

India
Continuity and Change in the Twenty-First Century

JOHN HARRISS, CRAIG JEFFREY
AND TRENT BROWN

polity

First published in 2020 by Polity Press

Polity Press
65 Bridge Street
Cambridge CB2 1UR, UK

Polity Press
101 Station Landing
Suite 300
Medford, MA 02155, USA

ISBN-13: 978-1-5095-3970-3
ISBN-13: 978-1-5095-3971-0 (pb)

A catalogue record for this book is available from the British Library.

Library of Congress Cataloging-in-Publication Data
Names: Harriss, John, author. | Jeffrey, Craig, 1973– author. | Brown, Trent (Research fellow), author.
Title: India : continuity and change in the 21st century / John Harriss, Craig Jeffrey and Trent Brown.
Description: Cambridge, UK ; Medford, MA : Polity, 2020. | Includes bibliographical references and index. | Summary: "New incarnation of the leading introduction to Indian politics, economy and society today"– Provided by publisher.
Identifiers: LCCN 2020000122 (print) | LCCN 2020000123 (ebook) | ISBN 9781509539703 (hardback) | ISBN 9781509539710 (paperback) | ISBN 9781509539727 (epub)
Subjects: LCSH: India–Economic conditions–21st century. | India–Politics and government–21st century. | India–Social conditions–21st century.
Classification: LCC HC435.4 .H37 2020 (print) | LCC HC435.4 (ebook) | DDC 954.05/3–dc23
LC record available at https://lccn.loc.gov/2020000122
LC ebook record available at https://lccn.loc.gov/2020000123

Typeset in 10 on 13 pt Swift by
Servis Filmsetting Ltd, Stockport, Cheshire
Printed and bound in Great Britain by TJ International Limited

For further information on Polity, visit our website: politybooks.com

Contents

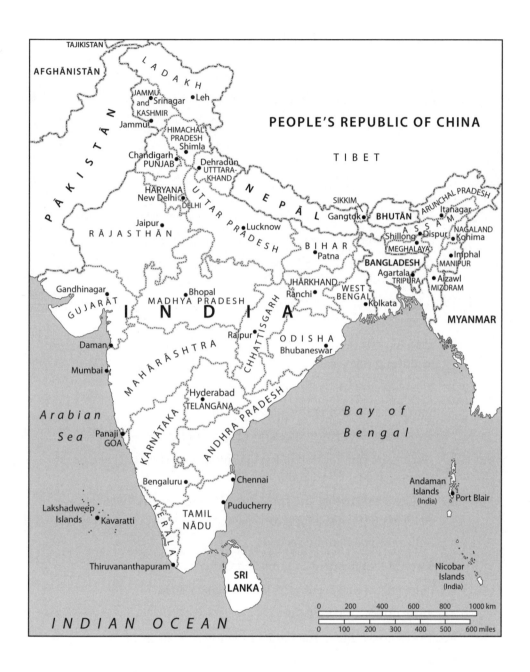

Tables and Figures

Abbreviations

AAP	Aam Aadmi Party
ABVP	Akhil Bharatiya Vidyarthi Parishad
ASER	Annual State of Education Report
BBC	British Broadcasting Corporation
BJP	Bharatiya Janata Party
BJS	Bharatiya Jana Sangh
BIMARU	Bihar, Madhya Pradesh, Rajasthan, Uttar Pradesh
BLD	Bharatiya Lok Dal
BPL	Below the Poverty Line
BPO	Business Process Outsourcing
BRICS	Brazil, Russia, India, China, South Africa
BSP	Bahujan Samaj Party
CAD	Constituent Assembly Debates
CAG	Comptroller and Auditor General
CBI	Central Bureau of Investigation
CEC	Central Empowered Committee
CITU	Centre of Indian Trade Unions
CMP	Common Minimum Programme
CPI	Communist Party of India
CPI(M)/CPM	Communist Party of India (Marxist)
CPI(Maoist)	Communist Party of India (Maoist)
CSO	Central Statistical Office
CSWI	Committee on the Status of Women in India
DBT	Direct Benefits Transfer
DJM	Dharam Jagran Manch
DMK	Dravida Munnetra Kazhagam
DNEP	Draft National Education Policy
DPI	Dalit Panther Iyakkam
EIA	Environmental Impact Assessment
EKC	Environmental Kuznets Curve
EPI	Environmental Performance Index
EPW	*Economic and Political Weekly*
FCRA	Foreign Contributions (Regulation) Act
FDI	Foreign Direct Investment

FERA	Foreign Exchange Regulation Act
FRA	Forest Rights Act
GDP	Gross Domestic Product
GoI	Government of India
GST	Goods and Services Tax
GVA	Gross Value Added
HYV	Hindu Yuva Vahini
IAC	Indians Against Corruption
IAS	Indian Administrative Service
ICDS	Integrated Child Development Services
IDSN	International Dalit Solidarity Network
IIT	Indian Institute of Technology
INC	Indian National Congress
INR	Indian Rupee(s)
IT	Information Technology
JAM	Jan Dhan-Aadhar-Mobile Number
JD	Janata Dal
JNP	Janata Party
JNU	Jawaharlal Nehru University
LGBT	Lesbian, Gay, Bisexual, Transgender
MBC	Most Backward Class/Caste
MGNREGS	Mahatma Gandhi National Rural Employment Guarantee Scheme
MKSS	Mazdur Kisan Shakti Sangathan
MoEF	Ministry of Environment, Forest (and Climate Change)
MLA	Member of the Legislative Assembly
MP	Madhya Pradesh
MPI	Multidimensional Poverty Index
MSDE	Ministry of Skill Development and Entrepreneurship
MSPI	Ministry of Statistics and Programme Implementation
MRTP	Monopolies and Restrictive Trade Practices (Act)
NAC	National Advisory Council
NAPM	National Alliance of People's Movements
NBA	Narmada Bacha Andolan
NCAER	National Council for Applied Economic Research
NCEUS	National Commission for Enterprises in the Unorganised Sector
NDA	National Democratic Alliance
NDTV	New Delhi Television (Limited)
NEET	Not in Employment, Education, or Training
NEP	National Environment Policy
NFHS	National Family Health Survey
NFSA	National Food Security Act
NGO	Non-Governmental Organization

NNPT	Nuclear Non-Proliferation Treaty
NPV	Net Present Value
NREGA/S	National Rural Employment Guarantee Act/Scheme
NRI	Non-Resident Indian
NSS(O)	National Sample Survey (Office)
NWS	Nuclear Weapons States
OBC	Other Backward Class
PDS	Public Distribution System
POTA	Prevention of Terrorism Act
PUCL	People's Union for Civil Liberties
PPP	Purchasing Power Parity
RBI	Reserve Bank of India
RJD	Rashtriya Janata Dal
RSS	Rashtriya Swayamsevak Sangh
RtE	Right to Education (Act)
RTI	Right to Information (Act)
RWA	Resident Welfare Association
SAARC	South Asian Association for Regional Cooperation
SBM	Swachh Bharat Mission
SC	Scheduled Caste
SEZ	Special Economic Zone
SP	Samajwadi Party
SPCB	State Pollution Control Board
SRM	Self-Regulating Market (Economy)
ST	Scheduled Tribe
TFP	Total Factor Productivity
TRAI	Telecommunications Regulatory Authority of India
UAPA	Unlawful Activities (Prevention) Act
UBI	Universal Basic Income
UGC	University Grants Commission
UNDP	United Nations Development Programme
UPA	United Progressive Alliance
UP	Uttar Pradesh
VCK	Viduthalai Chiruthaigal Katchi
VHP	Vishwa Hindu Parishad
WHO	World Health Organization

About the Authors

John Harriss is Professor Emeritus of International Studies at Simon Fraser University, Vancouver. He also taught at the Universities of Cambridge and East Anglia, and at the London School of Economics, and held visiting positions at the National University of Singapore, and in the Centre of Modern Indian Studies at the University of Göttingen. A Fellow of the Royal Society of Canada, John has lived and worked and done research in India over more than four decades, and has written on many different aspects of economy, politics and society in the country.

Craig Jeffrey is Director of the Australia India Institute and Professor of Geography at the University of Melbourne. He has worked on contemporary India and youth for nearly 25 years. Building on long-term social research in north India, he has highlighted the positive contributions of marginalized youth to Indian society, working in Hindi and Urdu, which he speaks fluently. He has written eight books, including *Timepass: Youth, Class and the Politics of Waiting in India* (Stanford University Press, 2010). Professor Jeffrey has advised over thirty PhD researchers in Seattle, Oxford and Melbourne, and is Fellow of the Academy of Social Sciences (UK) and Fellow of the Academy of the Social Sciences (Australia).

Trent Brown is DECRA Research Fellow in the School of Geography at the University of Melbourne. For more than ten years, he has been engaged in research on contemporary India, exploring themes related to rural development, agricultural and environmental education, youth, and civil society. He is the author of *Farmers, Subalterns, and Activists: Social Politics of Sustainable Agriculture in India* (Cambridge University Press, 2018). His current research explores both formal and informal means of agricultural skill development in north India.

Preface and Acknowledgements

This book has its origins in an earlier book that two of us wrote, with Stuart Corbridge, called *India Today: Economy, Politics and Society* (Polity Press, 2013). We began writing that book a decade ago, in 2010, and the writing was mostly completed in mid-2011. In the years that have elapsed since then, there has been a great deal of change in India. Some of it has been associated with the achievement of an absolute majority in the Indian parliament for the first time by the Bharatiya Janata Party (BJP), the political party that is a part of the wider movement of Hindu nationalism, in 2014; but there have been changes too, that are the outcomes of much longer running trends in India's economy and in Indian society. At the same time there are sometimes surprising indications of continuity from the past – in social relationships, for instance, and in the ways in which formally democratic politics works. India has, in many ways, defied the expectations of theorists of 'modernization'. So it has come about, after we responded positively to the suggestion from Polity Press that we should 'update' *India Today*, that we have found ourselves writing a largely new book. Indeed, it has been difficult to draw a line and to stop writing in the late summer of 2019, because of the flurry of policy innovation that has followed from the re-election in April–May of this year, with an increased majority, of the BJP government led by Narendra Modi.

A further reason for this becoming a new book, rather than a second edition of *India Today*, is that our friend Stuart Corbridge found it very difficult to contribute to writing, following his appointment as Vice-Chancellor of the University of Durham in 2015. It is a matter of great regret for us that we have lost the knowledge and insight that Stuart would have brought to this book. At the same time, we want to acknowledge that *India: Continuity and Change in the 21st Century* bears clear marks of the ways in which Stuart designed *India Today*, including its organization around a series of questions about India's economy, politics and society. This book displays its own particular historical path dependency.

We – John Harriss and Craig Jeffrey – were happy that Trent Brown, Craig's colleague in the Australia India Institute at the University of Melbourne, agreed to join us in the writing of this new book, bringing his experience of research on civil society organizations and rural development. None of us is an Indian citizen, so we are writing as sympathetic outsiders, with the disadvantages as well as possible advantages that this status brings. We bring to the book as well the experience of having lived, worked and carried out research in different parts of India for, collectively, very many years – mainly in the south and in West Bengal (Harriss), in western Uttar Pradesh and Uttarakhand (Jeffrey), and in the north-west and Himalayas (Brown), though we have all travelled widely throughout the country. We are able to draw extensively on the excellent research of large numbers of Indian scholars, and in regard to current and recent events, on the work of the many outstanding independent journalists and commentators in the country.

A further reason for our decision to write a new book rather than 'updating' *India Today* is that there is such a large volume of new research and analysis that has been published over the last ten years, both dealing specifically with India, and with the wider questions that are addressed in our book, such as the patterns and determinants of economic growth or trends in democratic politics. We cannot claim to have read everything of note that has been published, but as our bibliography shows, we have drawn extensively on new writing. As in our earlier book, however, we have necessarily referred a good deal to research that has been published in the *Economic and Political Weekly* (EPW). This is a journal that, so far as we are aware, is without parallel elsewhere in the world, publishing each week considered commentary on current events in India, and elsewhere in the world, together with scholarly articles based on high-quality research, across a wide field. The 'EPW' has always encouraged diversity of opinion, and its pages contain vigorous debate. We draw, as well, on the work of the many fine journalists and commentators who write for India's English-language press – the newspapers, *The Hindu*, *The Indian Express* and the *Times of India*; news magazines, including especially *Frontline*, published from Chennai by *The Hindu* group; and independent web-based journalism. We draw in particular on *The Wire* (https://thewire.in), but we have also consulted *Scroll.in* (https://scroll.in) and *The Print* (https://theprint.in). In regard to developments in the Indian economy, the website *Ideas for India* (https://www.ideasforindia.in) lives up to its name, carrying short reports of current research, mainly by economists, and commentary. It, too, encourages diversity of opinion, and debate on policy matters. We have referred, as well, to the Western press, and especially to the *Financial Times* for its coverage of economic affairs, as well as to the *New York Times*, the *Washington Post* and *The Guardian*. All carry thoughtful reporting and commentary.

This book, like *India Today*, is organized around a series of questions, about the Indian economy, politics and society. Each of the chapters can be read independently, and they can be read in any order. This means that there is, necessarily, some overlap in their contents – though we have aimed to reduce this to a minimum. At the same time, the book as a whole does offer what is, we believe, a coherent argument about the changes that have come about in India over the last decade in particular. Careful readers will note that there is some tension in these pages, reflecting the fact that the three authors are not entirely of one mind in their views of the extent and significance of the changes that are associated especially with the dominance that the Bharatiya Janata Party has established in Indian politics. We are confident that this is a strength of our text, because it is of course far too soon to reach a final judgement on contemporary events, and we believe that we have set out evidence and arguments on the basis of which readers can form their own assessments. It is, unashamedly, an academic book, yet one that, we hope – like *India Today* – will be read and referred to by general readers as well as by our colleagues and by students.

In writing the book we have incurred many debts. For gifts variously of inspiration and of critical support and help we would like to thank: Ashwin Subramanian, Neera Chandhoke, Jeff Checkel, Febe De Geest, Chris Gibson, Alf Gunvald Nilsen, Robin Jeffrey, Rob Jenkins, Surinder Jodhka, Jens Lerche, Atul Kohli, Harsh Mander, James Manor, Rahul Mukerji, Johnny Parry, Suhas Palshikar, Amy Piedalue, V. K. Ramachandran, R. Ramakumar, Haripriya Rangan, Nate Roberts, S. Parasuraman, Aruna Roy, Srila Roy, Alpa Shah, Sharada Srinivasan, Olle Tornquist, Gilles Verniers, M. Vijayabaskar and Rupa Viswanath. Special thanks to those who have given us critical comments on one or other of the chapters of the book: Leslie Armijo, Jane Dyson, Chris Fuller, Amanda Gilbertson, K. P. Kannan, Sanjay Ruparelia, N. C. Saxena, Jeff Redding, Kunal Sen and Marcus Taylor. None of these friends is at all responsible for what follows, and most of them disagree with some parts of our text.

Finally, for so much that has nothing to do with writing books, we thank our families, for forbearance, distraction and love.

JH, CJ and TB, Kingston, Ontario; and Melbourne, November 2019

1

Making Sense of Twenty-First-Century India

1.1 Introduction

Early in 2019, the London *Financial Times* announced, 'The Asian Century is set to begin' (Romei and Reed 2019). The grounds on which this pronouncement was based were that whereas in 2000 the Asian economies, all combined, accounted for just one-third of world output, according to calculations based on purchasing power parity (PPP – the method of comparing the currencies of different countries that takes account of differences in standards of living), it was projected that by 2020 they would account for more than half of world output. Among Asian countries, by 2017 China had by far the biggest economy, the biggest in the world according to PPP comparisons, or second to the United States measured in terms of exchange values. According to the first set of calculations (PPP), by 2017 India had the third largest economy in the world, though that of China was two-and-a-half times as big; in terms of the ranking of the gross national income of countries at exchange values, India had only the seventh largest economy in the world and it was only one-fifth as big as that of China, though it was only a little smaller than the economies of the UK and of France – and set to overtake both of them (see tables 1.1 and 1.2).

Looked at historically, however, the world in the twenty-first century is

Table 1.1 Gross National Income (current US$) of Leading Countries, 2017

Country	GNI (US$ billions)
United States	18,980.3
China	12,042.9
Japan	4,888.1
Germany	3,596.6
United Kingdom	2,675.9
France	2,548.3
India	2,405.7
Brazil	1,800.6
Russia	1,355.6

SOURCE: World Bank, *World Development Indicators*

1

Table 1.2 Gross National Income (PPP$) of Leading Countries, 2017

Country	GNI (US$ billions)
China	23,241.5
United States	19,607.6
India	9,448.7
Japan	5,686.3
Germany	4,274.0
Russia	3,721.6
Brazil	3,173.4
France	2,939.3
United Kingdom	2,810.0

SOURCE: World Bank, *World Development Indicators*

returning to the way it was before the 'great divergence' that took place from the later eighteenth century. From about that time, or rather before according to some calculations, the Western European economies that had until then lagged behind the major Asian economies, took off, and their peoples became, on average, very much wealthier than people elsewhere in the world. In the eighteenth century the Indian share of the world economy is reckoned to have been as big as Europe's. With China, India accounted for a very large share of the world's manufactured products. But in the nineteenth century, thanks to European imperialism, 'Asia was transformed from the world's manufacturing centre into classic underdeveloped economies exporting agricultural commodities', in the words of the economic historian, R. C. Allen (cited by Romei and Reed 2019).

India was for long seen as perhaps the archetypal poor developing country, of very little account in the global economy. Latterly, even if it has not experienced quite such a dramatic economic transformation as has China in the last decade or so of the twentieth century and the first twenty years of the present one, India clearly has become a major economic power. According to the World Development Indicators of the World Bank, the average annual growth of GDP in China between 2000 and 2017 was 9.7 per cent, and that of India was 7.5 per cent – both rates much higher than those of comparator countries such as Brazil (2.9 per cent) or Indonesia (5.5 per cent). The average annual growth of GDP in the United States over this period, according to the same data set, was 1.7 per cent, that of the UK 1.5 per cent. In a delicious twist of history, an Indian company, Tata, has become the biggest employer of manufacturing workers in Britain, the former colonial power that ruled over the country for a century and a half. The *Forbes* magazine annual listing of billionaires across the world showed that in 2018 India had 131 of them, the third largest number, behind only the United States and China. There is no doubt that India, with China, will be at the heart of the Asian century.

In other ways, too, a country that was for a long time more or less a back-water in international affairs has thrust itself upon the world's attention, as a state with nuclear weapons, and a very big spender on military equipment. In March 2019 *Reuters* reported, 'Modi hails India as military space power after anti-satellite missile test' (27 March 2019). The country had entered what was called 'an elite space club', with the United States, Russia and China, having successfully blown up a satellite in Low Earth Orbit. The *Reuters* headline reflected, as well, that India's prime minister since 2014, Narendra Modi, had won global recognition, far surpassing the leaders of most other countries. But at the same time some other aspects of contemporary India were being recognized in the international media. On those dollar billionaires, an analysis produced by the NGO Oxfam showed, 'Wealth of 9 richest Indians equivalent to bottom 50% of the country' (NDTV, 21 January 2019). *Aljazeera* reported, 'Seven of the world's worst polluted cities are in India, a new study has revealed' (5 March 2019). The *Washington Post* had the headline, 'India's railroads had 63,000 job openings. 19 million people applied' (4 January 2019). An article in the *New York Times*, about an attack by upper-caste men on a Dalit (the name referring to India's lowest castes, those who used to be called 'untouchable') was titled, '"Tell everyone we scalped you!" How caste still rules in India' (17 November 2018). In July 2018 *BBC News* reported on, 'How WhatsApp helped turn an Indian village into a lynch mob' (19 July 2018), and a day later *The Guardian* carried an article, 'Mobs are killing Muslims in India. Why is no one stopping them?' On the other hand, a writer for the highly respected *Christian Science Monitor* wrote an article, 'Global decline in democracy? The lesson from India may be "Not so fast"' (16 March 2018).

These headlines from some of the leading international news media reflect different aspects of India today. India has changed, quite dramatically, since 2000. It is, in many ways, a very different country. Yet there are also significant elements of continuity, as the *New York Times* story about caste violence suggests. This book is framed around important questions about continuity and change in twenty-first-century India. We draw upon the rich recent scholarship by Indian writers and others to analyse how and why India has changed, and with what consequences, drawing as well upon comparisons with other countries. Why, for example, is Narendra Modi often compared with Recep Erdoğan in Turkey, and even with Donald Trump in the United States? All three leaders are often described as 'populists'. Why? What does it mean? Another comparative question: is it fruitful to make comparisons between race in the United States and the treatment of the lowest castes, the Dalits, or 'untouchables', in India? How has the pursuit of neoliberal economic policy affected India by comparison with other countries, and how effective, in a comparative context, has resistance to it been? In addressing these and other such questions, we will turn to the wider social science literature, and to scholars who study India among other countries, not restricting ourselves only to writing that is focused more or less exclusively on India. For quite some time a great deal of writing about India took little account of work on other countries, treating the country as exceptional, because of its particular complexity – a tendency that led one student of politics, James Manor, to write an article with the title 'What do they know of India who only India know?' (Manor 2010a). Even though this book is about contemporary India, we aim always to refer to experience in other parts of the world, and to comparative research.

1.2 Past and Present

The purpose of this chapter, however, is to address the question of how India in the twenty-first century came to be this India. History matters, of course, and there is a great deal of contemporary scholarship that refers to so-called 'historical path dependency'. Events, or actions, or decisions taken at one moment have repercussions that influence the next. Among economists, for example, as we discuss in the next chapter, there is a body of opinion that the pattern of economic development in all countries is subject to circular and cumulative causation. This means that no country or significant region has had a course of development that is exactly the same as that of another. As Marx once said, in a statement that has been so often quoted that it seems to be a truism, though it is actually profound: 'Men make their own history, but they do not make it as they please'. 'They do not make it', he goes on to say, 'under self-selected circumstances, but under circumstances existing already, given and transmitted from the past' (Marx 1852). Though, as a great contemporary historian, C. A. Bayly – certainly not a 'Marxist' – once wrote, Marx developed the closest that we have to 'a theory of history' (in the author's autobiographical note in Bayly 1998), Marx is quite clear that there are no 'iron laws'. This is because human agency matters, and people can 'make their own history' ('change the course of history', in a conventional phrase) – or, in other words, shift the trajectory of historical path dependency. But then the structures in the context of which they act – 'circumstances transmitted from the past' – greatly influence the possibilities of change at any particular moment. The way that some economic historians perceive historical change is in terms of multiple equilibria. There are historical 'moments' of movement from one equilibrium state to another (Nunn 2009: 75ff). The course of human history is perhaps not so different from the history of life itself, as this was described by Stephen Jay Gould, the evolutionary theorist, as 'a series of stable states punctuated at rare intervals by major events that occur with great rapidity and help to establish the next stable era' (quoted by Castells 1996: 29).

'Circumstances transmitted from the past' include, importantly, what are described as institutions, by which is meant the rules, norms and conventions on which social order, or, putting it somewhat differently, the structure of economies and societies depends. They lead to the establishment of an equilibrium that is maintained over a substantial period of time. The institutional arrangements of a society reflect the interests of those who have power, and they are reproduced over time. But, over time too, economic developments in particular, by shifting the balance of power in society, may change these institutions. It has been argued, for example, that the rise of the triangular trade in the Atlantic between Europe, Africa and the Americas, led to the empowerment of a merchant class against the ruling royal houses in north-western Europe, and that this brought about changes in institutional arrangements that have had profound historical consequences (Acemoglu et al. 2005). But it is not only institutions that matter for long-run patterns of historical change. Culture has an influence, too, and so do knowledge and technology (Nunn 2009).

All these factors enter into the explanation of the 'great divergence'. Institutions certainly played a part, even if we may wish to reject a certain triumphalism about the importance of supposedly 'good' institutions emanating from north-western Europe (Acemoglu et al. 2005; and commentary by Bayly 2008). The significance of cultural values was emphasized by the great sociologist Max Weber, seminally in his work on the role played by the 'protestant ethic' in the development of capitalism. Latterly, the historian David Landes has argued similarly, 'If we learn anything from the history of economic development, it is that culture makes all the difference' – though he also argues that 'culture does not stand alone . . . monocausal explanations will not work' (1998: 516–17). Another scholar, Joel Mokyr, focuses on the importance of knowledge and technology, and the significance of the ferment of public debate and innovation in north-west Europe in the eighteenth and early nineteenth centuries (Mokyr 2016). But there certainly were, also, significant benefits that accrued to the European powers from colonial exploitation. As Kenneth Pomerantz has argued, 'the fruits of overseas coercion . . . help explain the *difference* between European development and what we see in certain other parts of Eurasia (primarily China and Japan)' (2000: 4, emphasis in the original).

The idea of the 'great divergence' is about a very important point of punctuation, or 'moment' of historical change. It was inherently associated with colonialism, and colonial rule certainly 'punctuated' the history of many parts of the world (Nunn 2009). This is true, no doubt, of India. The first moment of historical change that we will consider, therefore, in our discussion of how twenty-first-century India has come to be, is the period of colonial rule, and its impact on India. The second moment is that of the establishment of the post-colonial state, which meant the introduction, as a result of the deliberate decisions of the political elite, of a partially new set of institutions (only 'partially new' because they mostly bear marks of colonial rule). The deliberations of the Constituent Assembly that drew up the Constitution of India mark what was, in a sense, the *invention* of a new India, as a federal, democratic, socialist and secular republic. The Preamble to the Constitution describes India in these terms, as 'democratic', 'socialist' and 'secular' (though it is important to note that the words 'socialist' and 'secular' were only added later, following an amendment passed in 1976), and a fairly large part of the main body of the Constitution is concerned with establishing the particular forms of Indian federalism (though the federal principle was established in the last act passed under colonial rule, in 1935, about the Government of India). The Indian state under the leadership of prime minister Jawaharlal Nehru sought to implement the design of the Constitution, with greater success in some areas than in others. But over time India has been subject to a process of reinvention, as Corbridge and Harriss (2000) described it. This, a third 'moment' in the making of twenty-first-century India, reached a point of culmination with the election of Narendra Modi as prime minister in 2014. Modi's party, the Bharatiya Janata Party (BJP), which won a large majority, is the party-political wing of a 'family' of organizations centred on the Rashtriya Swayamsevak Sangh, which has long been dedicated to making India a 'Hindu rashtra', or Hindu state. It is committed, therefore, to redesigning India, and as we will explain in this book, it has gone a long way towards achieving this goal. Indeed, with the crushing victory of the BJP, led again by Narendra Modi, in the national elections of 2019, it appears to many that the goal has been achieved (see tables 1.3–1.5). The Editorial of *The Hindu* newspaper on 24 May 2019 argued, for example, 'The definitive nature of the Bharatiya Janata Party's victory in the 17th general election marks an unmistakable inflection point in the journey of the Republic ... The outcome must be understood as an electoral endorsement of *Hindutva*, or Hindu nationalism'. Whereas the mainstream of Indian political life and culture was committed to liberal values, it has now been taken over by majoritarian Hindu nationalism. Liberal democracy is in retreat.

1.3 The Impact of Colonialism in India

There is a rich and ever growing literature about the impact of colonial rule in India, and we can only highlight certain themes that seem to us to be particularly significant in regard to India today, and its regional diversity. As we have been writing this chapter, the one hundredth anniversary has passed (on 13 April 2019) of the terrible events in the Jallianwala Bagh, in Amritsar, in Punjab, when Imperial troops fired without warning into a large and peaceful crowd, killing 379 (according to the official enquiry) and injuring more than a thousand. This is a powerful reminder, no matter how reluctant many English people still are to recognize this, that the British, as well as the other

European colonial empires, were based on violence, and on racism. A recent study of British rule in India that makes this point most emphatically is by Wilson, who argues that the reliance on force was, at least in part, a reflection of the weakness of colonial rule, and of the failure of the British to establish long-term relationships in Indian society. 'In practice', he concludes, controversially, 'British actions prolonged and fostered chaos far more than they cultivated security and prosperity' (2016: 498).

Wilson's conclusions can certainly be disputed, and there are other historians who emphasize positive aspects of colonial rule. The economic historian Tirthanka Roy, for example, though he is not an apologist for empire, thinks that openness and integration into the world economy in the nineteenth century helped Indian business to overcome constraints to which it was subject: 'By bringing in knowledge and capital from Britain to India, the open economy enabled huge growth in trade and an off-beat industrialization in the 19th century' (Roy 2018: 261). Roy is critical of the long-established argument that the British effectively 'underdeveloped' India, through the open economy that they encouraged. This was the thesis of Indian economic nationalists in the nineteenth and early twentieth centuries (whose arguments actually influenced the formulation of the idea of 'underdevelopment' by its foremost exponent, A. G. Frank, in the 1960s–70s – see Frank 1967). They emphasized the 'drain' of wealth from India to Britain, through onerous taxation, especially of agriculture, that both paid for the purchase of Indian goods that could then be sold by the colonizers at considerable profit, and for the 'home charges' – payments to Britain for the government of India and for the maintenance of the Indian army (which was deployed to extend and to police other parts of the British empire). Some historians have emphasized, too, both the impoverishment of Indian cultivators by the high levels of tax that they paid on the land (land revenue payments), and the 'deindustrialization' of India by the British, in the interests especially of the British cotton mill industry (and resistance to the purchase of British-made cotton textiles was one of the rallying cries of the struggle for independence from colonial rule). Roy, however, argues that the long-standing focus of scholars of world history on why India fell behind has led them to miss the central paradox of Indian economic history, which he thinks was the coexistence of robust capitalism and stagnant agriculture.

This was the argument, too, of the historian David Washbrook, writing thirty years before Roy (Washbrook 1988). Indians who owned capital, Washbrook thought, had 'never had it so good', because in the context of colonial rule they were able to make very high profits without taking on the risks of entrepreneurship, thanks to the control that they were able to exercise over labour. Roy, however, reckons that capital was generally in short supply in India, likely because of the monsoon climate which caused seasonal boom and slack in the economy 'on a scale not visible in other societies', and that led to large fluctuations in the demand for money and in interest rates within the year. Thus it was that 'The attraction of earning a windfall income in the short-term money market was so great that money was kept idle in the slack season rather than being lent long term' (2018: 12). But Indian capitalism flourished in the colonial period, at least in part because of knowledge and capital that came in from Britain.

Debate will continue about the economic impact of colonialism in India. There is no room for doubt, however, about India's declining share in the global economy in the nineteenth century, and the increasing divergence between India and other countries in Asia and the West. At the same time, as Roy argues, there was a successful Indian capitalist class, and successful Indian-owned industries – cotton mills in Bombay (now Mumbai), for example, and the first steelworks established in Asia, set up in eastern India by the Parsi entrepreneur Jamsetji Tata, founder of the company that now owns such an important share of British manufacturing industry. Roy's argument, too, about 'stagnant agriculture' in colonial India is incontrovertible. Evidence collected by Myrdal for his classic work, *Asian Drama* (1968), shows how poor agricultural productivity was in India, by comparison with much of the rest of Asia, around the time of independence in 1947. Independent India faced a very significant 'agrarian question' – what to do about the productivity of agriculture and the poverty of the mass of the people who continued to live in the villages.

The most significant commercial and industrial development in colonial India took place in and around the colonial port cities – Bombay, Calcutta (now Kolkata), and Madras (now Chennai) – establishing an economic geography that has persisted into the present century. As the economist Bharadwaj noted (1982), the initial advantages of 'Bombay' (the states of Maharashtra and Gujarat) and of 'Madras' (present day Tamil Nadu and the coastal districts of Andhra Pradesh), in regard both to overall economic growth and industrial development have generally been maintained, though those of 'Calcutta' (West Bengal) have not, or at least not to the same extent. Another significant way in which the experience of colonialism may have contributed to the regional disparities that have become ever more pronounced in post-independence India has to do with the long-run effects of the different revenue collection systems used by the British. It has been shown that 'Areas in which proprietary rights were given to landlords [sometimes described as areas of 'zamindari settlement' from the name often given to these tax-collecting landlords] have significantly lower agricultural investments and productivity in the post-independence period than areas where these rights were given to the cultivators [areas of 'ryotwari' settlement]' (Banerjee and Iyer 2005, Abstract; though see also Iversen et al. 2013, for criticism). These differences may have contributed to the disparities in levels of development between northern and eastern India, on the one hand, and the south and the west on the other, that have become increasingly sharp. On most criteria of both economic and social development, the south and west are distinctly more advanced than the north and east (excepting the contemporary states of the north-west – Punjab, Haryana and Himachal Pradesh – which generally compare quite well with the south and west).

But though there was industrialization in colonial India, the great majority of the population and of the labour force remained in the villages and in agriculture. How far, therefore, can there have been the 'social revolution' in India that Marx anticipated in the middle of the nineteenth century? He thought that the 'village system' of India was being dissolved as a result of 'English interference', and that colonialism was producing 'the greatest, and to speak the truth, the only social revolution ever heard of in Asia' (Marx 1853). Marx argued that the development of roads and railways by the British rulers would break down the isolation of India's villages, and that with new irrigation systems and the development of industry, a 'social revolution' would come about. More recently, however, historians have often found reason for arguing that there was considerable continuity, as well as change. The British very largely took over, though they also developed, earlier systems for the taxation of land (discussed by Banerjee and Iyer, whose work is referred to above), and this ensured the reproduction of the power of small numbers of landlords over the very large numbers of small cultivators, under a variety of systems that often made for insecurity of tenure for the actual cultivators of the land. Those with more secure rights, however, and those who held larger amounts of land, became politically powerful in the later part of the colonial period, effectively controlling the local organization of the Indian National Congress, the political party born from the struggle for independence from colonial rule, by the time that India became independent: 'By 1949 conservative coalitions built by dominant landowning castes in alliance with urban businessmen had captured effective control of most [local] Congress Committees' (Frankel 1978: 74). These particular 'circumstances transmitted from the past' severely constrained the possibilities for bringing about social and economic reforms on the part of the national political leadership in the 1950s and 1960s, in particular limiting the prospect of resolving the 'agrarian question' by means of redistributive land reform (which was implemented in some other Asian countries; see chapter 4).

The way the British governed India also enhanced the significance of caste identities. Caste was thought to be a guide to the qualities and the capacities of people, so identifying people by their caste was an important instrument of rule. It was for this reason that the colonizers sought to enumerate people by caste in the decennial census that started to be made in 1871. Those with what were held to be a martial character, for instance, were sought for recruitment into the army: 'by the end of the 18th century there was a general push to identify the "manly races" and to identify the "castes" with appropriate martial qualities' (Michelutti 2008: 73). In this way a process of 'essentialization' of caste (or we might say, a 'hardening' of caste) took place under colonial rule – and their caste identities took on a new meaning for Indians (Dirks 2001; Inden 1990). Some groups started to become organized in caste associations – a particular form of civil society organization (combining ascription and voluntarism) that has been seen as exemplifying 'the modernity of tradition' (Rudolph and Rudolph 1967). In general, there came about an increased awareness of caste identity – and this is another set of 'circumstances transmitted from the past' that is of great importance in contemporary India, when caste communities compete through the process of electoral democracy for shares of state resources (see chapter 8).

One aspect of colonial rule in regard to caste that is of enduring importance is the recognition by the colonial state of the disabilities of those groups, many of them originally agrarian slaves (Viswanath 2014), who came to be described as 'untouchable'. They were deemed by the colonial state to deserve special assistance, or of what has become known generally as affirmative action. The last major piece of legislation passed by the British government concerning the government of India, the Government of India Act 1935, included the reservation of seats in legislative bodies for the so-called 'Depressed Classes', and a government order of 1936 contained a list (or 'schedule') of such caste communities. In 1943 the colonial state decided to combine reservation of seats with reserved jobs in government service for members of the 'Scheduled Castes' ('SCs'), and these practices were then incorporated into the Constitution of independent India. This principle, of providing special privileges to those considered to have suffered from historical disabilities, came to be extended by the post-colonial state to many other caste communities – described officially as 'Other Backward Classes' ('OBCs') – and there continue to be claims being made even by groups that are actually very powerful, for this designation. The reservation of government jobs, and of seats in medical and engineering colleges, for the OBCs, is a powerful incentive for claiming the categorization (see chapter 11) – but it further contributes to the hardening of caste identities that began in the colonial period.

The extent to which colonial rule in India brought 'social revolution', therefore, was quite limited. The development of an urban middle class, albeit small, might be called a 'social revolution'. But unlike the case of some other former colonies (a notable example is that of Vietnam), in which there was an armed struggle for independence, led by a radical political party, the struggle for independence in India was in many ways a conservative one that mainly adhered to the principles of non-violence expounded by Gandhi. There were those in India who took the line of violent resistance to colonial rule – the most notable figure being Bhagat Singh, who is a great folk hero (Maclean 2015) – but the mainstream of the freedom movement generally stuck to Gandhian principles. These included equivocation over caste, and even over untouchability, which Gandhi sought to contest in part by describing people from untouchable groups as 'Harijans', or 'Children of God'. The name, today, is rejected as patronizing by many members of the Scheduled Castes, who call themselves 'Dalits' (meaning, literally, 'broken' or 'oppressed'), though it is still used by others among them. The Congress movement that led the Indian struggle was conservative, too, in the sense that the leadership always sought to control potential radicalism on the parts of both peasants and workers (see, for example, Pandey 1982). As independence approached in the 1940s, another of the great leaders of the Congress, Vallabhai Patel, made sure that the Indian police force, created by the British on the lines of the Royal Irish Constabulary (an occupying force) rather than on those of the Metropolitan Police, and that had been used frequently to oppose the freedom struggle, remained in place – further 'circumstances transmitted from the past' that have contributed to the making of Narendra Modi's India.

The experience of the struggle for independence, however – and it was, probably, the greatest mass movement that the world has yet seen – meant that with the attainment of freedom from colonial rule, there was very little question but that India should be a parliamentary democracy, in line with the liberal ideals that members of the Indian elite had espoused with zeal since quite early in the nineteenth century and had used skilfully against their colonial rulers (see Sarkar 2001 on the historical inheritance of Indian democracy; and on liberalism and India, Bayly 2012). This played a central part in the second moment of historical change that we have distinguished.

1.4 The Invention of Modern India

Democracy

As we suggested earlier, India was the subject of particular acts of invention through the prolonged deliberations of the Constituent Assembly that drew up the Constitution of India – the longest that there is in the world – in 1946–49. Of central importance was that India should be a parliamentary democracy – improbable though this was according to the classic comparative study of Barrington Moore (1966). India, he thought, presents the paradox of the establishment of political democracy without there having first been an industrial revolution. India (in the mid-twentieth century), Moore said, belonged to two worlds: 'Economically it remains in the pre-industrial age . . . There has been no bourgeois revolution . . . But as a political species it does belong to the modern world' (1966: 314). India's democracy was imperfect, but certainly not a sham. Still, many of India's problems, Moore thought, followed from the fact of the unlikely establishment of democracy in a country that, in the later 1940s had only a very small bourgeoisie – the class often credited with being at least the initial driving force behind democratization

– and a very small organized working class, which other scholars find to have been the main social force pushing for the consolidation of democracy. India was still, as we've said, overwhelmingly an agrarian society, in which landlords remained powerful. And landlords, as Moore argued, depend heavily upon labour that is unfree, and so they are generally opposed to democratization.

Yet, for the political elite who were the members of the Constituent Assembly, most of them from the Congress Party that had led the independence struggle, there was no question about it. India must be a democracy. Jawaharlal Nehru – with Gandhi and Patel the third member of the triumvirate that is seen as having led the independence movement, and independent India's first prime minister – in moving the Resolution on Aims and Objects before the Constituent Assembly, in December 1946, declared: 'Obviously we are aiming at democracy and nothing less than democracy . . .' (CAD, 13 December 1946). The Constitution that was finally drawn up lays down that India is a democracy based on universal adult franchise, embracing women as well as men (and we should remember that women in France had been enfranchised only as recently as 1944, and that Swiss women were not to get the vote until 1971). The first national elections were held in 1952, following an extraordinary bureaucratic effort to register 170 million voters. This effort has been described in detail by Ornit Shani, who argues that democracy was effectively made on the ground, 'from wrestling with practical problems of implementing the registration of all adults who would be citizens, as voters' (2018: 252). She explains how the process of operationalizing democracy helped to constitute citizenship, concluding her book with an extended quote from the papers of B. Shiva Rao, who contested one of the parliamentary seats in what was then Madras:

> I did not think the untouchables in the rural areas would attach any great importance to the vote. There again I was in serious error. I visited dozens of polling booths all over the constituency on voting day and found in every queue, whether of men or women voters, untouchables in considerable numbers . . . The experience of standing in the same queue with one's employer, and the consciousness of having the same political right as the high-caste landlords made, I think, a deep impression on many untouchables (quoted by Shani 2018: 257).

Research by anthropologists across India in the twenty-first century shows how very important participation in elections is for poor people, giving them indeed a sense of themselves as equal citizens of the country, in spite of the very considerable inequalities to which they are subject in their daily lives – and which reduce the practical meaning of citizenship for them (Banerjee 2014; and, on the limitations of citizenship, Chatterjee 2004).

Elections at national and provincial/state levels have been held regularly ever since 1952, generally at intervals of five years, with the important exception of the period between 1975 and 1977, when Nehru's daughter, India's third prime minister, Indira Gandhi suspended the Constitution and declared Emergency Rule, using powers that had been taken over from the colonial Government of India Act 1935. The history of India's parliamentary elections, and of the country's political leadership (summarized in tables 1.3 and 1.4), is a story of the long dominance of the Congress Party (INC) – interrupted only by the short periods in office of the Janata coalition government (1977–80), elected following the Emergency, and then of the Janata Dal government headed by V. P. Singh (1989–90) – and subsequently of the rise of the Bharatiya Janata Party (BJP). It was a mark of the failure of the Janata government that Indira Gandhi should have been returned to office, in January 1980, so soon after the end of the Emergency; and Mrs Gandhi's son Rajiv then led the Congress to its greatest electoral victory in December 1984, riding a 'sympathy wave' caused by the assassination of his mother.

Rajiv, however, proved a disappointing prime minister, and the later 1980s also saw the BJP winning support partly through successful political theatre surrounding a dispute over an old mosque, the Babri Masjid, in the city of Ayodhya in Uttar Pradesh. Hindu nationalists claimed that the mosque stood

Table 1.3 Distribution of Votes of Major National Parties, Lok Sabha Elections, 1952–2019

	BJP	BJS	BLD	BSP	CPI	CPM	INC	JD	JNP
1952		3.06			3.29		44.99		
1957		5.97			8.92		47.78		
1962					9.94		44.72		
1967		9.31			5.11	4.28	40.78		
1971		7.35			4.73	5.12	43.68		
1977			41.32		2.82	4.29	34.52		
1980					2.49	6.24	47.97		28.36
1984	7.74				2.71	5.87	49.10		6.89
1989	11.36				2.57	6.55	39.53	17.79	1.01
1991	20.11				2.49	6.16	36.26	11.84	3.37
1996	20.29				1.97	6.12	28.20	8.08	0.19
1998	25.59			4.67	1.75	5.16	25.82	3.24	
1999	23.75			4.16	1.48	5.40	28.30	3.10	
2004	22.16			5.33	1.41	5.66	26.53		
2009	18.80			6.17	1.43	5.33	28.55		
2014	31.34			4.19	0.79	3.28	19.52		
2019	37.40						19.50		

SOURCE: Election Commission of India

KEY: BJP = Bharatiya Janata Party; BJS = Bharatiya Jana Sangh; BLD = Bharatiya Lok Dal; BSP = Bahujan Samaj Party; CPI = Communist Party of India; CPM = Communist Party of India (Marxist); INC = Indian National Congress; JD = Janata Dal; JNP = Janata Party

Table 1.4 Distribution of Seats Won in Lok Sabha Elections, by National Party, 1952–2019

	BJP	BJS	BLD	BSP	CPI	CPM	INC	JD	JNP
1952		3			16		364		
1957		4			27		371		
1962					29		361		
1967		35			23	19	283		
1971		22			23	25	352		
1977			295		7	22	154		
1980					10	37	366		72
1984	2				6	22	404		10
1989	85				12	33	197	143	
1991	120				14	35	232	59	5
1996	161				12	32	140	46	
1998	182			5	9	32	141	6	
1999	182			14	4	33	114	21	
2004	138			19	10	43	145		
2009	116			21	4	16	206		
2014	282				1	9	44		
2019	303			10	2	3	52		

SOURCE: Election Commission of India

KEY: see Table 1.3

on the site of a Hindu temple that marked the birthplace of the god Ram (see chapter 6). This, in our understanding of modern Indian history, was partly instrumental in bringing about a reinvention of India towards the end of the twentieth century, in what we think of as a third moment of historical change. The reinvention of India saw a big shift in economic policy in the direction of neoliberalism, as well as the rise of Hindu nationalism – described by Corbridge and Harriss (2000) as 'elite revolts' – together with what was called a 'second democratic upsurge' with the emergence of a new generation of political leaders from among the OBCs. From 1989 until 2014, no single party won a majority in national elections, and India was ruled by minority or coalition governments, the latter headed by the BJP (in the National Democratic Alliance) between 1998 and 2004, and by the Congress (in the United Progressive Alliance) between 2004 and 2014. The crushing victory of the BJP in the national elections of 2014 marked the ascendancy of the party. Its absolute hegemony, with the effective taking over of the mainstream of Indian politics by Hindu nationalism, and the emphatic shifting of that mainstream to the right (Palshikar 2015), was confirmed by the even more comprehensive victory that the party won in the 2019 elections. The BJP won more than 50 per cent of the vote in 11 of India's major states (or 12 if we

Table 1.5 National Elections 2019, Vote Share and Seats Won, in Major States, by BJP and Congress

	BJP vote share % (seats)	INC vote share % (seats)
Andhra Pradesh	0.96 (0)	—
Assam	36.05 (9)	35.44 (3)
Bihar	23.58 (17)	7.70 (1)
Chhattisgarh	50.70 (9)	40.91 (2)
NCR Delhi	56.56 (7)	22.51 (0)
Goa	51.18 (1)	42.92 (1)
Gujarat	62.21 (26)	32.11 (0)
Haryana	58.02 (10)	28.42 (0)
Himachal Pradesh	69.11 (4)	27.30 (0)
Jammu & Kashmir	46.39 (3)	28.47 (0)
Jharkhand	50.96 (11)	15.63 (1)
Karnataka	51.38 (25)	31.88 (1)
Kerala	12.93 (0)	37.27 (15)
Madhya Pradesh	58.00 (28)	34.50 (1)
Maharashtra	27.59 (23)	16.27 (1)
Odisha	38.37 (8)	13.81 (1)
Punjab	9.63 (2)	40.12 (8)
Rajasthan	58.47 (24)	34.24 (0)
Tamil Nadu	3.66 (0)	12.76 (8)
Telengana	19.45 (4)	29.48 (3)
Uttar Pradesh	49.56 (62)	6.31 (1)
Uttarakhand	61.01 (5)	31.40 (0)
West Bengal	40.25 (18)	5.61 (2)

Source: Election Commission of India

include also Uttar Pradesh in which the BJP came within a whisker of 50 per cent, see table 1.5), and only in Andhra Pradesh, Tamil Nadu and Kerala in the south, and Punjab in the north, was the party not powerfully represented. The elections of 2014 and 2019 can be described, therefore, as a fourth moment of historical change.

But how has democracy worked, in what has remained a country in which the population is largely rural, and in which – in spite of dramatic economic growth since the 1980s – not much less than a half of the labour force is still employed in agriculture? In the 1950s and early 1960s, in the era of what is sometimes referred to as the Nehruvian state, because of the dominance of Jawaharlal Nehru, India had a 'dominant party' system of government, in which one party, the Congress, usually won elections at all levels, even in an open, multi-party democracy. This reflected its authority, as the political party born of the successful movement for independence, and the fact that it had an organization that extended both across the country and from the centre down to local levels. Detailed studies showed, however, that the party mobilized support through intermediaries, at local levels usually from among the dominant landowning communities (as we noted earlier), and that it functioned through a great pyramid of patron–client relations (Manor 1988). The intermediation of political leaders at different levels, and clientelism, have remained highly significant in Indian politics, and the labelling of India as a 'patronage democracy' is a powerful idea (see chapters 7 and 8). The writer most associated with it, Kanchan Chandra, has shown, too, how and why ethnicity plays an important part in Indian politics (Chandra 2004). Many people are most likely to trust someone from their own community. Mobilization has often taken place on the basis of group identities, and the objective of political leaders has often been to win resources from the state for their own people (see chapter 8). Politics has become more and more of a kind of business in which sometimes thuggish individuals with known criminal backgrounds have become increasingly important (as we discuss in chapters 7 and 8). There is, in some parts of the country certainly, where criminal bosses exercise considerable power, what has been called 'mafia raj' (Michelutti et al. 2019). These are problems in the way in which democracy works in the country. They follow from the paradox of India's democratization that Barrington Moore noted.

One of Narendra Modi's claims, following the 2019 elections, was that he and his party had won their great majority because they had successfully transcended caste and community-based voting, and there was support for this argument in the findings of post-poll surveys conducted by the Centre for the Study of Developing Societies. But it was reported (*The Hindu*, 28 May 2019, referring to calculations by the Association of Democratic Reforms) that 43 per cent of the newly elected MPs had criminal records (and that 29 per cent of them had records including serious crimes) compared with 'only' 34 per cent in 2014. The extent to which Modi has really made a difference to the modalities of electoral mobilization in India remains uncertain.

Socialism

Not only was India to be a democracy. It was also intended to be, according to the constitutional design, set on a path towards social democracy. When he moved the Resolution of Aims and Objects before the Constituent Assembly, Nehru made clear his own commitment to socialism – in the sense of economic democracy – even though he said that he and his colleagues had decided not to include the term in the Resolution, given the sentiments of many other members of the Assembly. In practice, Nehru himself and the other important leaders of the Congress equivocated, and were unwilling as well as unable to confront the power either of big business or of the dominant landholders – as Dr Ambedkar, the great leader of India's untouchables, pointed out. In response to Nehru he said, 'I should ... have expected the Resolution to state in the most explicit terms that in order that there may be social and economic justice in the country, that there would be nationalisation of industry and nationalisation of land' (*CAD*, 17 December 1946). Neither was ever seriously contemplated, and – as we discuss in chapter 8 – economic and social rights were relegated in the Constitution to the 'Directive Principles'. These are statements of good intention, enjoined upon the government, but without any force in law. Thus it was that Ambedkar spoke, towards the end of the deliberations of the Constituent Assembly, of the 'life of contradictions' into which India was entering: 'In politics we will have equality and in social and economic life we will have inequality ... How long shall we continue to deny equality in our social and economic life? If we continue to deny it for long, we do so only by putting our political democracy in peril' (*CAD*, 25 November 1949). The later trajectory of Indian democracy bears out his fears.

But Nehru's commitments were not only rhetorical. He had spoken before the Constituent Assembly of its being the responsibility of the members not only 'to free India through a new constitution', but 'to feed the starving people, to clothe the naked masses, and to give every Indian the fullest opportunity to develop himself according to his capacity' (*CAD*, 22 January 1947). Entirely in line with the development theory of the time (Harriss 2014), Nehru and his colleagues in government believed that these objectives, vital to the legitimacy of the new state that came into being in 1947, could best be achieved through economic planning, and a project of development in which the state would play the central role. But Nehru, as he once said, saw India as pursuing a 'third way' between the capitalism of the West and the communism of the Soviet Union and the Eastern Bloc, combining directive planning and accommodative democratic politics (Corbridge and Harriss 2000: 43, 55). The results (as we argue in chapter 2) were not entirely disappointing, but they did lead India, eventually, into a pattern of economic development in which growth barely, if at all, kept pace with population growth, being sacrificed to the special interests of monopolistic big business, rich peasants, and bureaucrats and white-collar professionals. This was the era of what came to be described as the 'licence-permit-quota raj', in which big profits could be made from rents rather than from the improvement of productivity. Agriculture, still by far the most important sector of the economy, was at first rather neglected by the state, and then was sought to be modernized through the application of technology and of improved varieties of wheat and rice (in the 'green revolution'). This did successfully increase the production of cereals, but it left behind the very many cultivators in the large areas of the country lacking in assured irrigation. The environmental impact of the pattern of development, in agriculture and more generally, was accorded scant attention (see chapter 5). But perhaps the most serious failures were the neglect of investment in health and the lack of attention to education. There was a glaring failure to realize the promise in the Constitution that there should be universal primary education within ten years of its promulgation. Given pervasive ill-health and poor educational opportunities, what chance did most Indians have of 'developing themselves according to their capacities'? We discuss these continuing problems in chapters 3, 4 and 13.

It came to be recognized, in the 1970s, that economic development was not bringing about the kind of transformation in the lives of the mass of the Indian people that the country's leaders at the time of independence had looked for. The scale of the problems of poverty in India had to be acknowledged by government, and a number of poverty alleviation programmes were introduced. But there was also eloquent questioning of the model of economic development that was being pursued – and this began to change in the next decade (as we discuss in chapter 2).

Secularism

The birth of independent India brought, as well, the Partition of what had been British India, and the creation of the new state of Pakistan, as a homeland for Indian Muslims (for a fine account of Partition, see Khan 2007). This was the outcome of a long-standing fear of Hindu domination, articulated latterly by the Muslim League, under the leadership of Mohammed Ali Jinnah. Partition took place amid enormous bloodshed (perhaps as many as two million people were killed) and the largest single displacement of people (an estimated 15 million) in history. These events, and the antagonistic relationship between India and Pakistan, often focused on the status of Kashmir, as the only Indian state with a Muslim majority population, have cast an enduring shadow over South Asia (see chapter 14). A very large population of Muslims remained in India (it still has the third largest Muslim population in the world, and not too much smaller than that of Pakistan). But did they belong in India? For Nehru and other liberals in the Congress leadership, it was extremely important that Muslims should be reassured that they did belong. And the Constitution prohibited discrimination on grounds of religion, race, caste, sex or place of birth (Article 15), laid down the freedom of religion (Article 25), and the right among others, of every religious denomination 'to manage its own affairs in matters of religion' (Article 26).

Some of India's leaders were committed to the idea that India should be a secular state. For them, communalism (the antagonism between communities defined by religion) was a product of unreason. Nehru, in particular, who detested religious dogmatism, looked forward to a society in which a scientific temper would prevail. Yet the word 'secular' appeared only once in the Constitution as it was originally drafted, and then only to refer to an aspect of religious practice. As we discuss in chapter 6, the view of secularism that is implicit in the Constitution is not of the radical separation of religion and the affairs of state, as is enjoined in the Constitution of the United States, but rather one of the equality of treatment of different religions. A 'secular state in India', Nehru wrote, 'is a state which honours all faiths equally and gives them equal opportunities' (cited by Madan 1997: 245).

This stance on his part represented a compromise that he was unhappy about. He, and those who thought like him, had to come to terms with the common view among Indians that theirs is a society in which religion has a particularly important place, and the view, too, that Hinduism is a uniquely tolerant religion. The idea of secularism as denoting equality of treatment of religions was a way of reaching a compromise with the currents of Hindu sentiment among even senior Congress leaders, some of whom were also members of the Hindu Mahasabha, the all-India association of Hindus. Though it was the Congress, which had its origins in an association of educated, middle-class professional people, that came to lead the struggle for independence, others had begun to organize as Hindus, against colonial rule, around such issues as that of cow protection, going well back into the nineteenth century. Hindu nationalism has deep historical roots, though the ascendancy in Indian politics of liberal-minded leaders like Nehru in the early years of post-colonial India tended to obscure its significance among many observers. So, the anthropologist T. N. Madan writes, 'Nehru's definition of the secular state in terms of religious pluralism was . . . a compromise, a strategy to deal with an awkward problem, namely the all-pervasive influence of religion in society, that would not go away' (1997: 244).

The compromise exposed the state in the end, however, to accusations of 'pseudo-secularism' – particularly because of the unequal treatment of different religions in the field of personal law – that have helped to fuel the rise of Hindu nationalism. The accusation that the Hindu majority has been discriminated against by the state has provided powerful fuel for Hindu nationalists. Even as we were writing, in the course of the Indian national elections of 2019, the Congress was accused by some BJP politicians of being a party that wants to favour Muslims.

Federalism

The fourth pillar of the post-independence Indian republic was that it should be a union of states, the boundaries of which were an inheritance from the colonial administration. The Congress as a national movement was successful in defining Indianness 'not as a singular or exhaustive identity, but as one which explicitly recognized at least two other aspects. Indian citizens were also members of linguistic and cultural communities: Oriyas or Tamils, Kashmiris or Marathi'. And, 'India's federal arrangements were intended to embody this idea of a layered Indianness' (Khilnani 1997: 175). These federal arrangements are reflected in the way the upper house of the Indian parliament, the Rajya

Sabha, is composed mainly by members elected by the Legislative Assemblies of India's states and Union Territories. In turn, the members of those Assemblies are themselves directly elected, and the Constitution lays down the division of powers, responsibilities and resources between the union government at the centre, and the state governments. The federal principle is relatively weak, however, and the founding fathers were greatly concerned that India should have a strong central government. The powers of the states were curtailed from the outset and the centre has considerable authority in relation to them, including the power of suspending the Legislative Assembly of a state, and of imposing President's Rule – an instrument that has sometimes been used for entirely partisan reasons.

The states of India, as they were inherited from the administrative divisions of British India, were generally multi lingual, and one of the challenges that the Government of India confronted in the 1950s was that of powerful demands from different parts of the country for the recognition of regional cultural groups through the creation of linguistic states. In spite of fears at the time – not least on Nehru's part – that these demands threatened the unity of India, states reorganization did take place. The major states were generally redefined on linguistic lines (though not in the Hindi-speaking heartland of the country), without – as it turned out – endangering national unity. Over time, however, this has helped the rise of significant regional political parties, and in the period of minority and coalition governments between 1989 and 2014, regional parties sometimes exercised considerable influence on the central government. It was thought by some politicians and observers in 2019 that between them the regional parties might win a sufficient number of votes to be able to challenge the BJP in forming the government, but in the event these hopes were dashed by the comprehensive victory that the BJP secured.

The administrative capacities of the different states vary very considerably, including in their abilities to raise revenue. Article 280 of the Constitution requires the Government of India to appoint a Finance Commission every five years to advise on the financial relations between the centre and the states, and one of the problems that these Commissions have to deal with is that of achieving a workable balance between states that are relatively efficient in raising revenues and those that are not. The disparities between the major states in terms of economic and social development have tended to increase over time, and the Finance Commissions have to contend with the concerns of the more efficient states about the extent to which they may be subsidizing those that are more backward.

1.5 The Reinvention of India

The Nehruvian state sought to realize the aims of the Constitution. As we argue in chapter 2, its record in regard to economic development was not quite as poor as has often been suggested, and it succeeded in establishing institutions of liberal democracy – such as, notably, an independent judiciary; an autonomous Election Commission charged with the responsibility of ensuring free and fair elections; and the office of the Comptroller and Auditor General, charged with the audit of the receipts and expenditure of central and state governments – which have served India well. But in the mid-1960s the effort of planned economic development ran into major difficulties, to an important extent because the government was no longer able to raise revenues adequate for sustaining investment. At the same time, and at least partly in consequence, the authority of the Congress Party began to be challenged. Nehru died in May 1964, and was succeeded by Lal Bahadur Shastri, who also died, less than two years later. It was at this juncture that Nehru's daughter Indira Gandhi became prime minister. A split in the Congress Party followed in 1969, and then in the early 1970s – a difficult time in many developing countries, and not just in India – Mrs Gandhi encountered increasing opposition from outside parliament. The more left-wing policies that she was trying to pursue largely failed to deliver. And it was in this context that she declared the Emergency that we referred to earlier.

Change then began to take place in the 1980s, when Mrs Gandhi returned to office after the brief period of the Janata government. First Mrs Gandhi, and then her successor, her son Rajiv, shifted the stance of the government in regard to the private sector. There was a pro-business 'tilt', and in the later 1980s there were tentative moves towards economic liberalization. The pace of economic growth picked up (see chapter 2). But in the same period the Bharatiya Janata Party began to win increasing support, including among business people, professionals, former civil servants and military officers, who had become increasingly frustrated by the Congress government. With the advantage of hindsight, it has seemed to observers of Indian politics that the failures of the Congress government created a kind of a vacuum into which the BJP stepped. From a position of having won only two seats in the 1984 general election, the party took 85 in 1989 and held the balance of power (see tables 1.3 and 1.4). Eventually, in late 1990, the BJP brought down the Janata Dal government led by V. P. Singh, that had taken office in 1989, over its decision to implement the recommendations of a long-shelved report, prepared by a commission headed by B. P. Mandal and that had been appointed by the earlier Janata government. These recommendations were for the considerable expansion of reservations for members of the Other Backward Classes (see chapter 11), and the decision to implement them brought very strong opposition from among members of the higher castes, many of whom were by now BJP supporters.

The early 1990s were momentous years that brought very significant change in India. This was the period of 'Mandal and the Mandir' – of heated controversy over the implementation of the Mandal Commission report, and over the demands of Hindu nationalists for the construction of a temple (the mandir) for Lord Ram on the site of the old mosque at Ayodhya. The latter was advanced in December 1992, when Hindu nationalist volunteers took the law into their own hands, and destroyed the Babri Masjid (though the construction of the temple in its place had still not taken place more than 25 years later). This action was recognized at the time as having shaken the foundations of India's liberal democracy, and with the advantage of hind-sight, it clearly was a major step on the way to the assertion of the Hindu nationalist vision of India as a majoritarian Hindu state. But the beginning of the 1990s also saw a historic change in India's economic policy. A tipping point was reached in 1991 when, as we explain in chapter 2, a crisis over the availability of foreign exchange to pay for imports provided an opportunity for economic liberals in the Indian establishment to make a more decisive move towards neoliberalism. What were known as 'the Economic Reforms' began to be introduced in the first budget of Dr Manmohan Singh, the Finance Minister in a new minority Congress government, in the summer of 1991. We have described the shift in economic policy and the increasing support for Hindu nationalism as 'elite revolts', because both reflected the dissatisfaction of elites with the way India had for long been governed. But there were revolts from below as well, at this time, as the early 1990s saw the emergence of the new generation of 'backward caste' political leaders (from among the 'OBCs'), notably in Uttar Pradesh and Bihar. The political scientist Christophe Jaffrelot was to describe this as a 'silent revolution' (Jaffrelot 2003).

By the end of the twentieth century, therefore, India was being 'reinvented', as a definitely capitalist, 'emerging economy' (rather than a poor 'developing country' with an ostensibly socialist orientation), that was becoming much more integrated into the global economy (our arguments were elaborated by Corbridge and Harriss 2000). Hopes started to build up that India would benefit from its 'demographic dividend' – from the burgeoning numbers of young people entering the labour force (see chapter 13). The middle class was growing, and a new consumerism was becoming evident in Indian society (see chapter 10). The logic behind the description of 'consumer-citizen', used by at least one NGO in Chennai by this time, was apparent. How far rural people and India's poor – and many of India's women (see chapter 12) – were benefit-ing from higher rates of economic growth remained questionable, and the stresses of environmental degradation bore down on them in particular (see chapter 5). The BJP, the political party of the Hindu nationalist movement had effectively challenged the long-running hegemony of the Congress in Indian politics, and it was clearly winning support both from upper caste elites and among many poorer people (albeit more in the north and west than in other parts of the country). At the same time, regionally-based political leaders and parties from lower castes were exercising influence, and there was also abundant evidence of pervasive criminality in Indian politics (and certainly not only among those politicians who came from lower castes). India was no longer remotely 'socialist'; secularism was under severe threat; and for all the strengths of electoral democracy in the country, how much real substance there was to Indian democracy was doubtful.

This is the starting point of the 'new India' that emerged in the early years of the twenty-first century. A new point of punctuation in India's historical trajectory came with the election of Narendra Modi in 2014, and then the completion of the hegemony of the BJP and of Hindu nationalism were marked by the outcome of the national elections of 2019. This book, through the questions that we address in each chapter, aims to tell the story of these years.

PART ONE

ECONOMY AND ENVIRONMENT

2

When and Why Has India's Economic Growth Accelerated?

2.1 Introduction: Thinking About Economic Growth

India's gross domestic product (GDP – the market value of all goods and services made within the country in a given year), grew at an average annual rate of 3.7 per cent from 1950–51 to 1979–80, then at almost 6 per cent a year in the period from 1980–81 to 2000–01 – and at an even higher rate, between 7 and 8 per cent, thereafter, at least until 2009–10, after which the growth rate slowed down significantly (see table 2.1). The assessment of more recent trends has been complicated by controversial changes in the statistical procedures for the measurement of GDP, made by the Government of India (Kazmin 2019a). The authors of a World Bank research paper published late in 2018 conclude, however, that over the period 1991–2003, the annual rate of growth averaged 5.4 per cent; that in 2004–08 the growth rate reached an 'unsustainable' 8.8 per cent, followed by an extended slowdown; and finally that by 2018 growth had returned to around 7 per cent, considered to be the trend rate of growth (Ahmad et al. 2018). After early 2018, however, the rate of economic growth declined considerably, falling below 5 per cent per annum towards the end of 2019 (*The Hindu*, 29 November 2019).

Table 2.1 Independent India's Decadal Growth Rates

Period	Growth rate per annum (%)	Growth rate per capita per annum (%)
1951–52 to 1959–60	3.5	1.7
1960–61 to 1969–70	4.0	1.8
1970–71 to 1979–80	3.0	0.7
1980–81 to 1989–90	5.6	3.4
1990–91 to 1999–2000	5.8	3.7
2000–01 to 2009–10	7.3	5.7
2010–11 to 2014–15	6.1	4.8
1951–52 to 1979–80	**3.5**	**1.4**
1980–81 to 2009–10	**6.2**	**4.3**

SOURCE: Calculations by Joshi (2017, table 2.1)

On the face of it, something must have happened around 1980–81, or just before then, to have caused the economy in India to take off. What might explain the initial acceleration in the growth rate, and then the subsequent surge in the 2000s? Is the later slowing down of the economy only a temporary blip, or might it persist? Can India maintain over twenty years or more the level of 'super-fast' growth (7 per cent per annum and above) that is calculated as being necessary if the country is to achieve standards of living to compare with those among even the lower ranked high-income countries today (Joshi 2017: ch. 1)? To answer these questions, we begin by asking what economic theory suggests.

While it is clear that the supply of factors of production – capital and labour – fundamentally drives growth, it is also well established that whether or not supply materializes is a function of the demand for outputs. Both supply-side and demand-side factors matter. With regard to the supply side, however, empirical research and theorizing have also shown that growth is not explained simply by factor inputs, and that something else, a 'residual', is extremely important. A lot of research has been devoted to opening up the 'residual', and the consensus is that 'the growth of gross domestic product (GDP) and divergences in per capita GDP will be closely tied to individual country performance with regard to productivity' (Yusuf 2014: 55). What is referred to as Total Factor Productivity (TFP) – roughly defined as a measure of efficiency gains in the use of capital and labour – is reckoned to be crucial and to account for a more or less large share of economic growth. Its mainsprings, in turn, include technology and innovation, some of it embodied in equipment, but also organization – for the way in which industrial production, using more or less the same equipment, is organized, can make a great deal of difference to productivity. This was an important reason for the great success of Japanese companies in manufacturing automobiles. Knowledge, therefore, matters, and is now incorporated in economists' growth models. Productivity is seen as depending on the learning and innovation systems of society that produce and determine the quality of human capital (the skills and knowledge that people bring), the capacity to generate ideas, and the ability to absorb and make use of technology.

With particular regard to India, and productivity, one of the more critical constraints that the country now faces is the lack of very basic skills in the labour force, because of the failures of the education system (discussed in detail in chapter 13). This is one of the reasons why later developers, like India, may be unable to benefit from 'catching up' by making use of advanced technologies developed elsewhere. India has, however, gained a great deal over the last years of the twentieth and the early years of the twenty-first century from the supply of people with high skills in regard to information technology – the fruit of early investments in higher education. Kotwal et al. (2011) conclude a survey of the economics literature on India's growth story with the view that it reflects above all the happy coincidence of the availability of new technologies (in the IT sector) and of the skilled manpower to make use of them, thanks to India's early investments in tertiary education (as in the now famous Indian Institutes of Technology) – though they also note that trade liberalization and opening to foreign investment, after 1991, contributed to this. Sustained growth, they argue, would not have been possible without the reforms that were initiated at that time.

Even if the basics of it are quite straightforward, the complexity of the processes of economic growth have made theorizing extremely difficult. Given this complexity, and the dynamic nature of the processes involved, subject as they are – as we explain below – to circular and cumulative causation, there is really no substitute for the specific historical analysis of different cases. This is the conclusion reached by economists Kenny and Williams (2001) in a review of economic growth theory and of empirical analyses of growth based on large-*n* cross-country studies. Another economist, Yusuf, is quite downbeat, in a review of the field, about the achievements of economic growth theory. The limitations of theory and policy are indicated, he suggests, by the fact that between 1960 and 2011 only 8 out of 190 countries averaged growth rates of 7 per cent or more for two decades (Yusuf 2014).

Pritchett and Werker, similarly, argue that 'The principal fact about the growth rates of countries over the medium run (five to ten, to 15 years) is [their] volatility' (2012: 7), and Pritchett and Summers (2014) have shown that episodes of very high growth are usually short-lived and end in slowing back down to the world average. These findings, showing that economic growth is usually episodic, suggest that there are distinct questions that have to be addressed in thinking about growth. What are the factors that bring about growth accelerations? What then causes growth to decelerate? In other words: what initiates higher rates of growth, and then what factors influence whether or not growth is sustained?

Arguments about the Political Economy of Growth

In this chapter we discuss findings in the economics literature about growth episodes in the history of independent India, with a focus on the final years of the twentieth century and the first one-and-a-half decades of the twenty-first. We will explore the proximate factors, notably the trends in savings and investment, and the ways in which they have been allocated, that have influenced the long initial period of modest growth rates, subsequent accelerations and, most recently, in the years after 2010–11, an apparent slowdown with, so far (at the time of writing in 2019), still only an uncertain recovery. But we examine, as well, the social and political determinants of these proximate factors, having in view the dynamic, recursive interactions between institutions and the pattern of economic development. The framework of economic institutions in which development takes place reflects, at a point in time, the power structure of society and the relationships between political and economic elites. What are the bargains struck between them, or, in other words, what is the character of the political settlement? But then the way in which an economy grows and changes influences these power relationships, and over time brings about institutional change (Acemoglu et al. 2005). This helps to explain what we mean when we say that economic growth is subject to circular and cumulative causation. There is an important feedback relationship between the pattern of growth and its political drivers, but this also sets a path of change from which it is difficult to break away.

An example of this from India is that policy decisions taken in the 1950s, the outcome of the relationships that then prevailed between political and economic elites, set the country on a course of industrial development that has favoured capital-intensive industry in spite of India's apparent comparative advantage, given an abundance of cheap labour power, in labour-intensive industry. In 2017 Arvind Panagariya, then the outgoing Deputy Chairman of the Niti Aayog, the body set up in 2014 to replace the old Planning Commission, lamented what he referred to as the 'Brahminical mind-set' of India's big business groups, because of their evident preference for capital-intensive sectors rather than for investing in labour-intensive manufacturing. But in his remarks Panagariya also referred to the significance of the reservations that were instituted early in the history of independent India, restricting the production of many basic consumer goods to small-scale industrial units, so keeping out the big companies: 'We have not been able to shake out of these historical legacies. In a natural way, the future structure of the economy gets a bit driven by the current structure. And our current structure has been determined by . . . the old licence permit, small-scale reservation period' (reported in *The Hindu*, 13 August 2017).

This history accounts for the pronounced dualism that distinguishes Indian manufacturing, and the economy as a whole, given the size and significance of the unorganized sector (or 'informal sector', as it is sometimes described). This is estimated to account for 58 per cent of all domestic product, and 45 per cent of non-farm domestic product; and for 83 per cent of all non-farm employment (Kotwal et al. 2011). In manufacturing there is, it is argued, a 'missing middle'. In India, according to data from the Asian Development Bank (Joshi 2017: table 5.3), 84 per cent of all manufacturing employment is in micro-sized and small units, employing up to 49 workers, and only 5.5 per cent in medium-sized firms (employing 50–199 workers). By comparison, in East Asian economies, the distribution is much more even across firm sizes (or in China it is weighted towards the largest units). This matters because there is a close relationship between firm size, labour productivity and wages, and it is argued that in India growth is held back by the high proportion of workers in very small firms. Generally, successful manufacturing of consumer goods such as garments and shoes, for export, is carried on in factories employing large numbers. And, as Joshi has it, in common with Panagariya, 'In India, one of the obstacles to the formation of such companies was the reservation of hundreds of labour-intensive products for exclusive production by small firms. Small-scale industry reservations have been drastically pruned in recent years. But many obstacles to the growth of labour-intensive activities still remain' (Joshi 2017: 72). These include constraints on credit supply: even medium-sized firms experience difficulty in securing credit (Kotwal et al. 2011).

Research shows, therefore, that institutions (which include regulations such as those restricting the production of a range of commodities to small industrial units, as well as, for example, those that define property rights) exert an important influence on patterns and rates of economic development. But we also have to recognize that there may be a big gap between what institutions lay down, and what actually happens. Pritchett and Werker, for instance, refer to the rules regarding the issue of a driving licence in Delhi. These state that everyone should take a driving test, but research showed that only 12 per cent of those who had employed a tout, an intermediary, ended up taking the test. The touts, for a 'fee', found ways around the rules. In practice, the two authors argue, 'in a regime of weak capability for policy implementation – that is, weak capability . . . to enforce rules – the actual practice is "deals", and there are ubiquitous and widespread deviations of actual practice from "rules", that create winners and losers' (2012: 39). Rules, if they are properly implemented, are impersonal, while the term 'deal' refers to actions that are the result of the characteristics or the actions of specific individuals, and that are 'one-off'. They have no implications for future transactions between other individuals. Deals may be 'open' or 'closed'. In the latter case the possibility of a deal depends upon the identities of those concerned; in the former they depend only upon the actions of the agents involved. And deals may be 'ordered' – they will be honoured once negotiated – or 'disordered', when there is no certainty that the arrangement will be delivered upon. We may surmise that a movement from disordered to ordered deals is likely to be conducive to growth – investors will be more likely, for example, to invest in the capital equipment that is crucial for growth but that involves a large sunk cost; and that a shift from closed to open deals may be conducive to sustained growth, because it implies movement away from cronyism and increased competition. But there is no necessary, linear movement from closed, disordered deals to open and ordered ones. It will depend upon the settlements made between economic and political elites.

Kar and Sen (2016) have elaborated upon these arguments, in an analysis of the political economy of India's growth episodes. The two authors also refer to the significance of the differences between various economic agents, distinguishing between 'rentiers', those who operate in export-oriented industries from which they can secure high rents (for instance, from having monopolistic control over a particular natural resource); 'power-brokers', those who also operate in sectors (like real estate, construction, utilities and telecommunications) in which high rents can be secured, but who serve domestic markets; 'workhorses', who operate in competitive industries (including smallholder agriculture, and informal manufacturing and services) supplying domestic markets; and 'magicians', who work in competitive but export-oriented sectors such as the garments industry, or the supply of IT services. Kar and Sen argue that the interactions of these actors, their relations with political elites, and the sorts of deals in which they are engaged have exercised a very important influence on trends in growth in India.

2.2 India's History of Economic Growth

Joshi's broad overview (2017: ch. 2) of the history of economic development of independent India, showing that it falls into two halves, with the break coming around 1980 (see table 2.1), reflects a common understanding – though some think that the break came a little earlier, in the late 1970s. Kotwal et al. (2011) confirm that between 1951 and 1979, average growth rates remained below 4 per cent, and they say that the departure from the trend line after 1980 is both clearly visible in the data, and demonstrated in econometric testing. If an adjustment is made, however, for the sharp decline in GDP that took place in 1979–80, then the break is seen to have occurred in 1975–76. What is also noteworthy is that the variance in the growth rate declined sharply: from 15.8 in the 1970s, to 4.6 in the 1980s, and to 1.5 in the 1990s.

Bosworth and Collins (2015) have calculated a set of growth accounts for India, based on data from the Indian national accounts, in order to assess the contributions to growth of changes in inputs of labour and capital, and of TFP. They estimate (see table 2.2) that over the twenty-year period from 1960 to 1980 output increased, on average, by 3.4 per cent per year; output per worker increased by 1.3 per cent; and the contribution of TFP was a negligible 0.2 per cent. But then, over the thirty years 1980–2010, output increased by 6.2 per cent per annum; output per worker by 4.7 per cent; and the contribution of TFP was 2.5 per cent. Their data also show (table 2.2) a marked step up in rates of growth of output, output per worker and in TFP in the decade of the 1980s by comparison with the previous two decades; a small increase in output growth per year but also a drop in the growth of TFP in the decade of the 1990s; and then a very marked increase in all three variables in the 2000s.

What seems to have underlain the improvement in TFP from the 1980s onwards – taking place especially in services (see Bosworth and Collins 2015, table 1) – was a sharp increase in private investment in equipment. This, in turn, appears to have been made possible by increases in the savings rate in the 1970s, driven especially by household savings, and thought to have

Table 2.2 Sources of Growth in the Indian Economy, 1960–2012 (annual % rate of change)

Period	Output	Employment	Output per worker	Physical capital	Land	Education	Factor productivity
				Contribution of:			
1960–80	3.4	2.2	1.3	1.0	−0.2	0.2	0.2
1980–2010	6.2	1.5	4.7	1.7	0.0	0.4	2.5
1980–90	5.4	2.0	3.4	1.0	−0.1	0.3	2.1
1990–2000	5.7	2.2	3.4	1.3	−0.1	0.4	1.8
2000–10	7.7	0.3	7.4	2.9	0.1	0.6	3.7
2010–12[a]	5.6	0.8	4.8	2.3	0.1	0.4	1.9

SOURCE: Bosworth and Collins (2015, table 1) (these authors' estimates, as described in their text)

[a] Average change of 2011–12 and 2012–13

been the outcome of the bank nationalization that took place in 1969, and of increasing numbers of bank branches, the result of the policy enforced by the Reserve Bank of India for banks to open up branches in areas previously poorly served by them. The increase in the savings rate was closely matched by increased investment rates; and Sen (2007) has shown that the increase in capital formation from the mid-1970s involved a rise in investment in equipment, as opposed to investment in construction, that had predominated hitherto. Cross-country research has shown this to be the form of investment that matters most for growth, and Sen argues, 'the increase in private investment in equipment had a strong positive effect on growth, working its way through both capital accumulation and aggregate productivity growth' (Kar and Sen 2016: 31, citing Sen 2007). He thinks that the new trend followed both from the financial deepening that had taken place, and from the decline in the relative price of machinery that had resulted from relaxation of import controls. The analysis still leaves open, however, the important question as to why private investment increased in the way it did in the 1980s – it doesn't automatically follow from an increase in the savings rate. We return to this question below.

If the broad picture of India's history of economic growth is that it falls into two halves – with growth having been erratic in the first period, and then becoming steadier in the later one, pulling up the average – there is now some consensus around the view that it is possible to distinguish three or perhaps four distinct growth episodes, and over the possibility that India entered into a new episode after about 2010, with – the growth figures touted by the Modi government after 2014 notwithstanding – lower rates of growth, and big question marks over the maintenance of high growth rates. There were serious concerns about economic growth early in 2019, in the run-up to the national elections, confirmed by data that came in shortly after Narendra Modi's resumption of power. Shortly after this event, data were published showing that the growth of GDP in the first quarter of 2019 had slowed to the lowest level (5.8 per cent) for five years (Kazmin 2019b). This was the fourth quarter running when GDP growth had slowed. The growth rate plunged even lower later in 2019 (as reported in *The Hindu*, 29 November 2019).

The identification of growth episodes is not a simple matter, and it is possible to justify different arguments about the determinants of growth by the selection of different break points. To give an example, in table 2.3 we reproduce calculations of India's economic growth over different periods, according, on the one hand, to Atul Kohli (2006a, 2006b) – and see comparable calculations by Rodrik and Subramanian (2005) – and, on the other, to Arvind Panagariya (2008). The conclusion that Kohli drew from his periodization was that growth took off in the 1980s, probably because of a shift in the attitudes of political elites. Kohli suggests that the shift to a more business-friendly environment may have been more significant than the 'market-friendly' reforms initiated in 1991. Panagariya sets out to downplay the scale of the growth upturn that Rodrik and Subramanian, and then Kohli, describe for India in the 1980s, in developing his own argument about the success of liberalizing economic reforms in India in the 1990s.

There is a strong case for a more systematic approach to the distinguishing of growth episodes in India, one not driven by a particular hypothesis. Such an approach requires both ensuring that the structural breaks identified are statistically significant and that each of the episodes distinguished has 'a single underlying medium-term growth rate', over a substantial period (so as to distinguish them from business cycle fluctuations and short-term shocks). This is the analytical procedure that Kar and Sen have followed (2016: 5), and it leads them to identify three distinct episodes: 1950–92, 1993–2001 and 2002–10, with a possible fourth after 2010. They do recognize, however, a 'nascent recovery' in the 1980s – the period of the distinct break in India's history of growth that we and Joshi and many others have identified – and though the acceleration in that period was not sufficient to satisfy their conditions for a structural break, Sen (2014) detected a shift from the trend line of growth

Table 2.3 Two Analyses of Four Phases of India's Economic Growth (total GDP growth % per annum)

Panagariya:		Kohli:	
1951–65	4.1	1950–64	3.7
1965–81	3.2	1965–79	2.9
1981–88	4.8	1980–90	5.8
1988–2006	6.3	1991–2004	5.6

Sources: Panagariya (2008); Kohli (2006a, 2006b)

in the late 1970s. There is also the view – expressed, for instance, by Joshi (2017), in line with Kar and Sen's analysis – that there was a distinct period of particularly high growth in the 2000s, from 2002–3 to the end of the decade, with a fall thereafter. There appear to be substantial grounds, therefore, for thinking in terms of the three growth episodes, with the possible fourth after 2010, that Kar and Sen distinguish, or even of five episodes, if we pick out as distinct the period from around 1980 to 1992. We now consider each of these episodes, in turn, arguments about what was going on in each of them, the settlements between political and economic elites that they reflect, and their implications for changes in those settlements.

2.3 Economic Growth 1950–1992: A Story of Failure?

India won independence in 1947, just as the specialist field of development economics was taking off, and the approach that was taken to economic development in the new country reflected the orthodox views of the time, about market failure or absence, about the importance of economic diversification and industrialization, and about the need for strong and enlightened state actions. India had to industrialize as quickly as possible, and it seemed to make sense that this would mean protecting new domestic industries from international competition. 'Import substitution industrialization' was the framework to be adopted. Most imports were made subject to discretionary licensing; and on the other side of the trade regime what has been called 'export pessimism' seemed reasonable. There was very general agreement, even among Indian capitalists, that the state had to play a leading role in raising the finance that was required. It was generally accepted – in a context in which Soviet planning was seen as having been remarkably successful in bringing about rapid industrialization – that the state should plan development. A key instrument in the policy framework was the Industries (Development and Regulation) Act of 1951, setting up a system of licensing, controlling entry into industry and governing most aspects of firm behaviour. Licensing, of industries and of imports, together meant that competition, both domestic and foreign, was restricted, and this in turn – it came to be recognized – led to inefficiency (Bhagwati and Desai 1970 – the first sustained intellectual critique of planned industrialization – and Bhagwati and Srinivasan 1975 are definitive sources on the arguments involved). Indian entrepreneurs found themselves tied up in red tape or mired in rent-seeking activities, given the revenues that could be obtained by securing a licence with an actual or a near monopoly in a particular industry. Inefficiency was not at all incompatible with profitability. The era of what came later to be pilloried as the 'licence-permit raj' was once described by a leading industrialist to one of us as that of the 'handkerchief-on-seat' culture – meaning that customers just had to wait their turn, whether for the supply of vital equipment or for consumer goods such as motor-cycles or cars.

The story of India's economic growth in the long period of the political dominance of the Congress Party, from the foundations of the republic through to 1989 – only briefly interrupted, by the Janata government that ruled from April 1977 to the beginning of 1980, following Mrs Gandhi's Emergency of 1975–77, when democracy was suspended – is, therefore, often represented as one of failure. According to Kar and Sen, 'For most of this period, the Indian economy experienced a prolonged stagnation in growth right up to the 1970s, with a nascent recovery in the growth rate in the late 1980s' (2016: 29). Their analysis, however, like that of many others, shows clear differences from decade to decade (see their fig. 1.2, giving decadal averages of growth of output per capita): there were higher levels of growth per capita in the 1950s (at about 2 per cent per annum) than in the 1960s (1.49 per cent), and the 1960s were better than the 1970s (0.84 per cent), which was the time of the so-called 'Hindu rate of growth', when the rate of economic growth hardly kept pace with that of the population. Then there was 'recovery' in the 1980s (3.19 per cent), even if the acceleration was not sufficient statistically to count as a structural break.

There is another way of understanding the history of the period, however. According to this view, state planning of the economy, in a framework of import substitution industrialization, was really quite a success story, at least to begin with. Thanks especially to the Second Five Year Plan, designed by P. C. Mahalanobis, the country achieved a remarkable transformation of its industrial base over a very short period of time. The industrial growth rate was above 5.5 per cent per annum in the 1950s, and about 6 percent in the 1960s (Kar and Sen 2016: fig. 3.2), and investments in that time in heavy engineering and infrastructure can be shown to have delivered significant benefits for long-run growth. Unlike other countries that pursued import substitution industrialization strategies, India succeeded in developing the capacity to make machines (a point made notably by Griffin 1999).

But in spite of its relative success in the 1950s and early 1960s (the period of the first three five-year plans), state planning entered into crisis in the mid-1960s. An important book from the time had the title *The Crisis of Indian Planning* (Streeten and Lipton 1968). A range of factors were involved, including the failure to address the problems of the low productivity of Indian agriculture, and the persistent poverty of the mass of the rural population – which also had the effect of constraining the demand side of economic growth. But the increasing inability of the state to raise the necessary resources to maintain the rate of public investment was especially important (Hanson 1966). From the mid-1960s, the rate of economic growth declined quite sharply (as the calculations of both Panagariya and Kohli, reproduced in table 2.3, clearly show). In the view of liberal economists, especially, the situation was exacerbated by policies enacted under governments headed by Mrs Gandhi after 1969 that were decidedly anti-business. Leading banks were nationalized (in 1969); the passage of the Monopolies and Restrictive Trade Practices (MRTP) Act 1970 was aimed at increased regulation of big business houses; and the Foreign Exchange Regulation Act (FERA) in 1973 struck at inflows of foreign investment and technology (see Panagariya 2008: ch. 3).

The conclusion reached by Kar and Sen, 'that the policy framework played an important role in contributing to the economic stagnation of the 1960s and 1970s' is well-founded, no doubt. And policy distortions helped to shape a manufacturing sector that used too little labour and too much capital (Kochhar et al. 2006: 17). We think that it is also important, however, to acknowledge both that the late 1960s and 1970s were difficult times in many developing countries – not least in the wake of the oil price rises of 1973–74 and a global economic downturn – and that capabilities were built in India at this time that stood the country in very good stead in later years. We think, for example, of the investments in human capital through the technology, management and research institutes that were established, as well as of the investments in heavy engineering and in infrastructure.

We do not believe, therefore, that the first thirty years of independent India should be written off simply as a time of economic failure, while recognizing that there is no doubt of the accumulation of problems making increasingly for stagnation. The relationships in this time, between the economic elite and the Congress political elite, were uneasy, with mistrust on both sides – not an environment at all conducive to crucial investments involving large initial sunk costs. The Congress political elite was divided: a minority, but one to which Nehru was at least sympathetic, influenced in part by a positive reading of the Soviet experience, sought to move India in a socialist direction; but most were inclined to be supportive of private business even if they thought that the public sector had to be the key driver of growth. The result was that, as Vivek Chibber showed, in an important study of the state and late industrialization in India, 'the Indian state managers' agenda was frustrated by a well-organized offensive launched by domestic capitalists' (2003: 9). India did not build, at this time, a developmental state of the kind established, for example, in South Korea, in which the state was able 'to harness capitalists to its project' (Chibber 2003: 9). Their influence in the leading political bloc meant that the prominent business groups were able effectively to scupper the disciplinary part of state-planning. The Planning Commission lacked the capacity to discipline either ministries or firms. At the same time, as Chibber also explains, the Congress government was very effective in weakening the labour movement that might have supported disciplinary planning.

While successfully resisting disciplining by state managers, capitalist firms benefitted from the subsidies and protection offered them under the import substitution industrial strategy. Bureaucrats were able to exercise a great deal of discretion in the allocation of licences, permits and quotas, and big Indian companies devoted a huge amount of effort to lobbying, so as to secure them, as well as to making demands on government to modify regulatory policy. As Bhagwati puts it, 'the industrial-cum-licensing system . . . degenerated into a series of arbitrary decisions . . . because the administrators were so empowered' (1993, cited by Kar and Sen 2016: 39). In terms of the analytical framework that Kar and Sen set out, there was a disordered deals environment, not at all conducive to growth. It was inclined to be closed as well. South Indian industrialists whom John Harriss interviewed (in 2000), for instance, spoke about their having been excluded from a lot of deals-making in Delhi.

Accelerating Growth in the 1980s

As we have argued, the 1980s saw an acceleration in the rate of economic growth over the trend line of the previous three decades (see table 2.1), even if it was only a 'nascent recovery' according to Kar and Sen. We referred earlier to the proximate factors that brought about capital accumulation and the improvements in TFP that are clearly observed in data on the 1980s. But what happened to bring about the changes that took place in patterns of investment, pushing up levels of private investment, and encouraging more investment in machinery?

The nature of state–business relationships began to change when Mrs Gandhi was returned to power in the general election of January 1980, after the collapse of the short-lived Janata regime. Several leading scholars argue that government attitudes changed at this time from being anti- to pro-business (De Long 2003; Rodrik and Subramanian 2005; and Kohli 2006a, 2006b). Kohli says, 'just after coming to power in January 1980 . . . Indira Gandhi let it be known that improving production was now her top priority. In meeting after meeting with private industrialists, she clarified that what the government was most interested in was production' (2012: 30–1). Rodrik and Subramanian, in their joint work, argued that a change in the attitudes of the Congress political elite towards business had a big impact. A much more pro-business orientation on the part of political leaders made for significantly higher growth rates, because India had, until that time, performed so poorly in relation to the quality of its economic institutions – which meant small changes brought about big shifts. The change of attitude may have been a matter of political calculation on Mrs Gandhi's part – promising to strengthen her hand against the threat still posed by the opposition – but it started to establish a more collaborative relationship between state and business: 'the Indian state clearly signaled to domestic capitalists its intention to credibly commit to an environment where private enterprise would be supported and growth-enhancing policies followed' (Kar and Sen 2016: 41).

This trend was further accentuated under the government headed by Rajiv

Gandhi, who came to power at the end of 1984, in the general election that followed the assassination of his mother in October that year. Gandhi was interested in new technologies, and sought to encourage new industries, bringing in entrants to the business elite. Non-traditional business groups began to emerge, especially in western India and in the south. And, though they were modest ('half-hearted', as one of us put it at the time: Harriss 1987), Rajiv Gandhi's government did introduce some reforms of industrial and trade policy, opening them up, even if only a little. We noted earlier the implications of the softening of import restrictions for the price of capital equipment for Indian investors. The consequence of changing political attitudes, of the advent of new business elites, and of the reforms that were implemented, was that by the late 1980s the deals environment had become both more ordered and more open, and this is seen by Kar and Sen as having been 'the crucial enabling factor behind the increase in private investment in equipment' (2016: 41).

These arguments are not universally accepted. Arvind Panagariya, whose analysis of phases of growth we referred to earlier (see table 2.3) argued that only in the three years from 1988–89 to 1990–91 was there a distinctively higher growth rate, and that this was the fruit of the modest, piecemeal reforms that had been pursued to that time. The real break in the growth trend came only with more thorough-going market-friendly reforms that were launched in 1991 (Panagariya 2008). Panagariya, and others too, also thought that the growth of the 1980s depended upon unsustainable fiscal expansion. Large fiscal deficits were run up, government debt expanded hugely through the decade, exerting a big stimulus to demand – but in a way that was held to be unsustainable. Kotwal et al. (2011), from their review of these arguments and the evidence for them, reach the judicious conclusion that all of the factors that are referred to may have played a part. None of the other explanations, however, addresses the crucial question of how the settlement between business and political elites changed. The more ordered deals environment that Kar and Sen discern in the 1980s was then extended in the 1990s.

2.4 India's 'Economic Reforms' and Growth in 1993–2001

In 1991 Indian economic policy took a new direction, in which the aim has been to promote economic growth through support for private enterprise. Under a minority Congress government headed by P. V. Narasimha Rao (whose own role in the change that took place has often been underestimated), the Finance Minister, Dr Manmohan Singh, embarked on far-reaching policy reforms that took India away at last from the state-led, closed framework established in the early years after independence. The measures that were initiated by Dr Singh, known generally as India's 'economic reforms', and that have been continued with greater or lesser determination under succeeding governments, have been directed at reform of India's investment regime, its trade policy regime, its tax system and its financial sector – broadly in line with the arguments long advanced by economists such as, notably, the Columbia professor Jagdish Bhagwati and the Yale professor T. N. Srinivasan, following from their criticisms of the licence-permit-quota regime. Their advocacy of liberalizing reform for long had little purchase among policy makers, but at last it took over the mainstream of official thinking on economic policy. Ideas matter. But it is hard to change official mind-sets, and it took a particular moment, even for ideas that had been expressed with vigour over a good many years, finally to shift official thinking (Mukherji 2013).

The particular moment that made for a tipping point was that of the economic crisis that confronted the Rao government as it came into office. The immediate cause of the crisis was an abrupt fall in remittances, and oil price increases that were brought about by the Gulf War of 1990–91, but it was underlain by the deficit that followed from the expansionary fiscal policies that had been pursued by Rajiv Gandhi's government, a widening current account deficit, and mounting external indebtedness. By the early summer of 1991, India had sufficient reserves to pay for only two weeks' worth of imports. There certainly was a liquidity crisis, but it might have been tackled without embarking on structural reform. That it was 'the harbinger of a significant structural adjustment-cum-liberalization reform' (Kar and Sen 2016: 46), was the result of the persuasion of the international financial institutions and of the economic liberals in the Indian establishment, in a wider context in which neo-liberalism had become intellectually dominant (Harvey 2005). By 1991, it was widely thought by economists that the Indian economy was in urgent need of further and more radical reform. Even Rodrik and Subramanian (2005), though they thought that the growth surge that revived the Indian economy after 1991–92 was powered very substantially by the productivity growth and manufacturing base put in place in the 1980s, recognized that further reforms were necessary.

In July 1991 a new Industrial Policy Statement abolished licensing except for 16 industries. The numbers of industries reserved for the public sector were reduced; automatic permission for foreign equity participation up to 51 per cent was granted for a number of high-tech, high-investment priority industries; there was significant trade liberalization in regard to capital and intermediate goods (though little change at this stage so far as consumer goods were concerned); there were financial reforms; and macroeconomic stabilization was achieved with devaluation of the exchange rate and reduction of the fiscal deficit.

Kar and Sen put it that 'The increase in economic growth that was witnessed in the 1980s was consolidated in the growth episode of 1993–2001 when the growth of GDP per capita accelerated from 1.86 per cent per annum in 1950–1992 to 4.15 per capita per annum in 1993–2001' (2016: 45). Their choice of the verb 'consolidated' is appropriate given that the rates of growth of GDP per annum, and of GDP per capita per annum, increased only very modestly in 1993–2001 over those attained in the 1980s. Private investment responded positively through the 1990s, following the reforms, and there was notably strong growth in private corporate investment. There was strong growth in the private sector, involving especially those whom Kar and Sen describe as 'magicians' (working in competitive export-oriented sectors) and 'workhorses' (supplying competitive domestic markets). The sectors that saw the strongest growth were communications (at an average of 15.7 per cent per annum through the period); banking and business services (averaging 7.4 per cent per annum, though within this sector IT grew at 15 per cent per annum); and the 'traditional' services – trade, hotels and restaurants (6.5 per cent per annum). The growth of manufacturing, too, was solid (an average of 4.9 per cent per annum) – with pharmaceuticals doing particularly well – and manufacturing contributed more to exports than hitherto.

In the political sphere, the long era of Congress dominance had come to an end, and India experienced a series of minority governments (from the 1989 general election, until that of 2014 when the BJP won an absolute majority). Politics became increasingly competitive, with the BJP coming to rival the Congress Party nationally, and taking over at the head of a governing coalition in 1998, while significant regional parties held the balance of power. But the Congress and the BJP subscribed to more or less the same ideas about economic policy – those that had taken over the mainstream in 1991 – so that changes of government had little impact. State–business relations became more inclusive with the entry both of new political actors and of new business elites, in industries such as pharmaceuticals and telecommunications, and often from traditionally non-business communities especially from the south and the west (Damodaran 2008). Atul Kohli writes at length about the 'pro-business tilt' on the part of government, from the 1980s, and argues, 'While business groups in India are not quite "hegemonic" in the Marxist sense of that word, India is by now very much a capitalist market economy in which Indian capital exercises enormous indirect and direct power' (2012: 42). Pranab Bardhan had argued, influentially, in a book on *The Political Economy of Development in India*, first published in 1984, that there were in India three 'dominant proprietary classes' as he called them – the big bourgeoisie, big farmers, and a white-collar class of bureaucrats and professionals. He showed how the compromise of power between the three classes meant a whole lot of trade-offs that substantially accounted for the frittering away of public resources in subsidies, transfers and rents. What Kohli argues is that there has been a very significant shift in the power relations of the Indian state, and that 'the commitment to growth via the private sector . . . has strengthened the position of business groups in Indian politics' (2012: 59). Certainly, the dismantling of the licensing regime from 1991 meant that the discretionary powers of bureaucrats (an important fraction of Bardhan's third proprietary class) were substantially reduced, so removing a major source of disorder in the deals environment. At the same time, the relaxation of import controls meant that the deals environment became more open. The further shift towards more ordered and more open deals underlay the rise of private sector investment, an increasing share of it in equipment (there was almost a doubling of private corporate investment in machines over the decade).

Kar and Sen enter a qualification into their account of this period, noting that, 'the Indian state's collusive relationship with certain sections of the business elite in the pre-reform period remained, and it may have been accentuated by the rise of increasingly powerful regional business groups that were closely connected with regional political elites' (2016: 53). So, they say, 'closed deals existed side by side with open deals', and many traditional industries were still dominated by entrenched business elites (2016: 54). For all that there was a significant opening up of big business to new entrants in the 1990s, and although some of the old business groups lost out, others of them – the Tata group most prominently – consolidated their positions.

2.5 'Superfast' Growth, Slowdown and Questionable Recovery: 2002–2015

For all India's relative success in stabilizing and raising rates of economic growth in the last years of the twentieth century, the international financial press remained cautious and even pessimistic about the country's prospects, and it was still the case in 2003 that 'the Indian elephant' was compared unfavourably with 'the Chinese dragon'. On the occasion of the Indian prime minister Atal Behari Vajpayee's visit to Beijing in June 2003, the liberal newspaper *The Economist*, for instance, pointed out that 'In the ten years from 1992, India's GDP per head grew at 4.3 per cent per year, China's twice as fast', and it argued that 'In the BJP India is saddled at the moment with an irresponsible government that is better at pandering to religious zealotry than pressing for economic reform' (*The Economist*, 2003). Less than a year later, however (21 February 2004), the paper had changed its tune, saying that with growth that might reach 8 per cent in 2003–04, 'the signs of economic good sense in India are increasingly robust', and speaking of 'a moment of shining opportunity', in line with the election slogan that the BJP government had adopted. Now *The Economist* seemed to rate the Vajpayee government much more positively.

The shift in the way in which the progress of the Indian economy was being reported internationally by 2004 is one marker of the recognition of the possibility that growth was accelerating again. Indeed, this did happen, from 2002 according to Kar and Sen's analysis – they calculate the average rate of growth of per capita income in 2002–10 as 6.42 per cent. According to Joshi (2017, table 2.2) the growth rate of GDP per annum accelerated to 8.5 per cent over the period 2003–04 to 2010–11, or in other words attaining to 'superfast growth', while World Bank researchers report a growth rate of 8.8 per cent in 2004–08 (Ahmad et al. 2018). Joshi attributes the acceleration to the cumulative effects of reforms, reflected in the rise in corporate savings and investment, and in overall productivity. These arguments draw on the work of Bosworth and Collins (partially reported in table 2.2 above), showing the strong upward shift in the rates of growth of output, TFP and physical capital in 2000–10, by comparison with the preceding decade. These authors, too, see the acceleration as being consistent with the lagged effects of the reforms; and they also report on increasing savings and investment rates in the 2000s – the savings rate peaked at 37 per cent in 2007, before falling back, as both household and public savings declined. The World Bank researchers, however, refer to excessive credit growth in the period, and it is for this reason that they describe the growth that was experienced as 'unsustainable'. The former Governor of the Reserve Bank of India, Raghuram Rajan (Governor in 2013–16), in a note to a parliamentary committee in 2018, referred to the large number of bad loans that were made through the banking system in 2006–08, leading to the banks being weighed down with Non-Performing Assets in subsequent years (Rajan 2018).

The sectors of the economy that had driven growth in the 1990s – communications; finance, insurance, real estate and business services (including IT); trade, hotels and restaurants; and registered manufacturing – all continued to contribute strongly to growth acceleration, and were joined by the construction and transport industries. But there was also a shift within manufacturing towards natural resource-using sectors, especially refined petroleum products. Kar and Sen enter significant qualifications to the story of superfast growth, pointing out that there may even have been regression in regard to the structural transformation of the economy. This transformation can be understood as being reflected in moves by firms to more complex products, which is what had happened in India in the 1990s. But the weighting of such more complex products fell during 2002–10, a shift reflected most clearly in the sharp increase in the share of exports coming from what the authors describe as rentier sectors (such as petroleum products). Overall, Kar and Sen's analysis shows that growth depended more than before on rentier capital (operating in export-oriented industries from which high rents can be secured), and on the capital of those they refer to as 'powerbrokers' (operating in sectors such as real estate, construction, utilities and telecommunications in which high rents can be obtained, but serving domestic markets), though the contribution of the 'magicians' remained strong. An analysis by Gandhi and Walton (2012) of the sources of the wealth of Indian dollar billionaires, however, shows a marked increase in the significance of 'rent-thick' sectors from 2003, and that these sources of wealth outweighed others through to 2012.

These trends involved a further change in the deals environment, in which there was reversion towards more closed deals (Kar and Sen 2016: 53–5). *The Economist* (2018a) commented on this period, 'Industries such as power generation, mining, telecoms and infrastructure require large chunks of capital and lots of interaction with government. That attracted plenty of entrepreneurs whose core competence was using their connections with officials, in order both to win necessary permits and to secure financing from state-owned lenders'. There were crony-capitalist deals in high rent natural resource sectors such as the mining of bauxite, coal, iron ore, manganese ore and natural gas (in a period in which there were price increases for many minerals). The Commission headed by Justice M. B. Shah that reported to government in 2012 showed up the extent of illegal mining, underpayment of mining royalties and over-extraction, involving closed deals depending on collusion between ruling politicians and mining companies (Shah 2012). The preferential allocation of licences for coal mining, together with the scam in telecommunications, over the allocation of 2G spectrum licences to mobile phone operators, were widely regarded as evidence of the way in which the Congress-led government (which came to office first in 2004, when voters rejected the BJP claim that India was 'shining', and won office again in 2009) had become mired in corruption. The 2G affair, which involved ministers from the Tamil party, the DMK, an important coalition party in central government, exemplifies a point made by Kar and Sen. They say, 'Given the veto power exerted by numerically small but powerful groups of politicians in regional parties [e.g. the DMK] that comprised ruling coalitions in the 2000s, the deals that economic elites have had to strike with political elites increasingly accommodated the interests of these parties, with implications for both the "ordered" nature of these deals as well as their "open-ness"' (2016: 65). Rent extraction by regional parties in the fractured politics of this period, and the increasing costs of election campaigns (which help to account for the increasing criminalization of politics – on which see Vaishnav 2017), were key factors underlying the surge of closed deals in rent-thick sectors that contributed considerably to super-fast growth, until 2010–11.

These arguments are borne out by the recognition, subsequently, of the problems caused by the way in which banks became saddled in these years with Non-Performing Assets. As Raghuram Rajan argued, in the note referred to above, 'it is hard to tell banker exuberance, incompetence and corruption apart'. But, he went on, 'Finally, too many loans were made to well-connected promoters who have a history of defaulting on their loans'. There were too many crony-capitalist deals, in other words (Rajan 2018; and see also Kapur 2018).

After 2010–11, the growth rate slipped, right back to 5.4 per cent per annum in the period 2011–12 to 2014–15 according to Joshi's figures (2017: table 2.2). The picture of what has happened in these years is complicated, however, by a controversial change in the methodology used by India's Central Statistical Office (CSO) for calculating GDP, announced in January 2015, not long after Narendra Modi took up office as prime minister, following the victory of the BJP in the general election of 2014. The *Wall Street Journal* reported (30 January 2015), 'India surprised economists Friday evening by ratcheting up its official economic-expansion figure for the previous fiscal year, marking it as a year of sharp recovery rather than continuing stagnation, and putting India's growth rate much closer to China's'. According to the former method of calculating GDP, growth in 2013–14 was 4.7 per cent; according to the new method it was 6.9 per cent (and 7.4 per cent in 2014–15 as compared with 5.5 per cent, according to the old way of calculating GDP).

There was fierce debate amongst Indian economists about the new method, with influential voices on both sides (for discussion, see Kar and Sen 2016: box 6.1). Somewhat later, the respected journal, the *Economic and Political Weekly*, published an editorial under the title 'Lies, Damned Lies, and Statistics' (11 June 2016), noting 'glaring anomalies in the GDP data', and pointing out, for example, that the old series of growth numbers for manufacturing showed 1.1% growth in 2012–13, while the new method reported 6.2%. But if we follow the advice of Kar and Sen, who suggest that it is prudent to refer to both data series, we find that there is no question that the per capita growth rate has fallen by comparison with the 2002–10 period: it stood at an average of around 6.4 per cent per annum in 2002–10, 3.94 per cent over 2011–14 according to the old definition and 4.91 per cent over 2012–16 according to the new definition (Kar and Sen 2016: fig. 6.1). Then, in June 2019, embarrassingly for the new government that had taken up office only a few weeks earlier, the former Chief Economic Adviser to the Government of India (2015–18), Arvind Subramanian, published a paper with the Centre for International Development at Harvard University, that called into question all the estimates of GDP growth for the period from 2011. As we explain below, Subramanian's work suggested that actual growth over the period from 2011 to 2017 may well have averaged only about 4.5 per cent per year (A. Subramanian 2019).

There is no doubt, then, about the slowdown after 2010–11, and there are question marks over whether or not there really has been recovery since 2014. It is not just that there is such a gap according to the different ways of calculating GDP, but also that there is no consistency between different approaches to the assessment of the performance of the economy. In particular, there are indications that manufacturing industry is not doing at all well. India is perhaps 'deindustrializing' according to the Harvard economist Rodrik (2015; and see Amirapu and Subramanian 2014). The proximate cause of the slowdown after 2010–11 was the relative decline in corporate investment, and this had still not recovered by the end of 2019 (Seth 2019). The underlying factors, for Joshi, as for other economists, and the media, had to do with a souring of the investment climate because of the failures of the Congress-led United Progressive Alliance (UPA) government of 2009–14 – the scandals in which it was involved, and the policy paralysis which resulted from their exposure. A further factor was the deteriorating macro-economic position, reflected in rising inflation and widening deficits (Joshi 2017: 27). Data on Gross Capital Formation (investment in plant and machinery) show, however, an average of 31.8 per cent of GDP in 2014–18, the years of the Modi government, as compared with an average of 39 per cent in 2004–13, under the UPA, and of 33 percent in the decade before this (Ghatak and Mukherjee 2019).

Probing these arguments, Kar and Sen (2016: 85–8) suggest that the loss of investor confidence – on which there is evidence from international surveys

may be understood as the outcome of negative political feedback from the closed deals environment that had developed after 2002, and the evidence of crony capitalism. Discontent over corruption, for which the government was held responsible, not the private sector, was focused in 2011 by the campaign of the India Against Corruption movement, of which the Gandhian social worker Ana Hazare was the figurehead. The legitimacy of the state was seriously eroded. These developments further encouraged the mobilization of non-elites, for example, over land acquisition for industrial projects, and helped to bring together the official accountability institutions – the office of the Comptroller and Auditor General (CAG), the Central Bureau of Investigation (CBI) and the judiciary. The kinds of closed deals that had obtained could no longer be made, and there was a sharp fall in the growth rates of the rent-thick sectors of the economy.

The loss of credibility of the Congress Party and the UPA on the one hand, and the extraordinary campaign performance of Narendra Modi, as the prime ministerial candidate of the BJP, on the other, brought the BJP into office in 2014, with an absolute majority in the Lok Sabha, the lower house of the Indian parliament. This was the first time that a single party had won a majority for thirty years. Hopes ran high, among India's capitalists, that Modi would re-establish the legitimacy of the state, and restore business confidence. There were concerns, however, about his close relationships with particular businessmen, from his long period in office as chief minister of Gujarat, when some business groups had been favoured – for example, over land acquisition (Jaffrelot 2018). These concerns did not go away, for in spite of well-publicized actions against some big businessmen, under a reformed bankruptcy code introduced by the Modi government (*The Economist* 2018a), it was still thought that some businessmen gained from close relationships with the prime minister and the ruling party. An important case in point had to do with the way in which India's richest man, Mukesh Ambani, built up his telecoms company Reliance Jio, thanks, it was thought, to exceptionally favourable political and regulatory decisions (Stacey and Mundy 2018).

On the face of it, the Modi government was successful initially in restoring economic growth. In 2015, amid much fanfare, it was declared that India's rate of economic growth had at last overtaken that of China, and that the country now was the fastest growing of all the major economies. It was a great moment for those political leaders and bureaucrats for whom this had long been the target – though regarded with scepticism by those who were not persuaded by the new method for calculating India's GDP. Controversy over the methodology for computing growth rates was further fuelled in 2018, when the Central Statistical Office announced a downgrading of the official annual growth rates for 2005–2012, when the Congress-led UPA government was in office, from 7.75 per cent per annum to 6.82 per cent, while it showed the growth achieved under the Modi government in its first four years in office as 7.35 per cent per year. It was widely thought that the downgrading of the growth rate of the earlier period was unconvincing, given the boom of 2004–08 (Mundy 2018). The credibility of Indian growth statistics was called even further into question early in 2019 with the effective collapse of the National Statistics Commission – an autonomous body, set up in 2005 to raise the standards of official data – following the resignations both of its acting chairman and of its last independent member, who complained of having been sidelined by the government (Kazmin 2019a).

Controversy over the validity of India's official economic data reached a new moment of drama with the publication in June 2019 of the paper by former Chief Economic Adviser Arvind Subramanian, referred to earlier. Essentially, in the research reported in the paper, Subramanian compared data on 17 standard 'real' indicators that are usually strongly correlated with GDP growth – indicators such as electricity consumption, two-wheeler sales and commercial vehicle sales – with the GDP data. His emphatic conclusion was that 'A variety of evidence suggests that the methodology changes introduced for the post-2011 GDP estimates led to an over-estimation of GDP growth' (2019: 26), and, as we noted, he reckoned that growth in 2011–17 may well have been only about 4.5 per cent per year. This matters a lot, he argued, not only for reputational reasons, but more for policy-making: 'The Indian policy automobile has been navigated with a faulty or even broken speedometer' (2019: 27).

Still, in 2017, three years after he had come into office, Narendra Modi was complimented by *The Economist*, in an editorial (24 June 2017), for having 'pushed through reforms that had stalled for years, including an overhaul of the bankruptcy law and the adoption of a nationwide sales tax (GST) to replace a confusing array of local and national levies. Foreign investment has soared, albeit from a low base'. The paper went on, however, 'Alas, these appearances are deceiving' – describing Modi as at best a cautious reformer, and as having failed, in particular, to tackle the serious problems of the financial system. At that point, state-owned banks still accounted for 70 per cent of all loans, but were in great difficulty because of having extended credit to big industrial groups for financing projects that failed to come off. They were shackled, as we noted earlier, by the volume of their Non-Performing Assets. The rate of increase of bank loans to industry had fallen steadily after 2010, from 30 per cent to zero by early 2016, and these loans then declined in absolute terms. The question marks over the sustainability of high rates of growth were pointed up in the Government of India's *Economic Survey* for 2016–17. The *Survey* drew attention, in particular, to the 'twin balance sheet problem', referring to the coincidence of a highly leveraged (that is, heavily indebted) corporate sector with a banking sector that is encumbered with bad loans (*Economic Survey 2016–17*: ch. 4) – as a result, it is reasonable to suppose, of the extensive crony capitalism of the previous period of super-fast growth.

To these rather fundamental problems of the Indian economy there were added further difficulties as a result of what was called 'demonetization' (or, popularly, in India, as 'notebandi'), when on 8 November 2016, the prime minister suddenly announced that all Rs 500 and Rs 1000 notes were to be withdrawn from circulation, from midnight that day, with the objective – it was said at the time – of benefiting the poor by flushing out black money held by wealthy people. In the event, virtually all the notes that were demonetized in November 2016 were returned to banks, as the Reserve Bank of India reported in 2017, and it remained to be seen how many of the large number of cases that were then being brought by the income tax authorities against suspected holdings of black money that had been deposited, would be brought to a successful conclusion. In 2017 government ministers argued that demonetization hadn't been about black money at all. It was, they said, directed at bringing about behaviour change and encouraging the move from cash to digital transactions. Or about cutting the flow of money to terrorists. Different justifications were offered on different occasions. What seemed certain, however, was that the move had caused more than a passing difficulty for the very large numbers of businesses that depended upon cash in their transactions (*The Economist*, 2017), and that this contributed significantly to the slowdown in the economy, shown up in data released in September 2017, on growth in the first quarter of that year – down to 5.7 per cent, the lowest for three years (or 3.7 per cent or less according to the old method of calculating GDP). This was the fifth consecutive quarter in which growth had contracted. The growth rate had gone back to what it was when the Modi government came into office.

The fragility of the recovery of the economy after 2015 was exposed, there-fore, by late 2017, and reflected in mounting criticism in the press, directed especially at the finance minister, rather than at the prime minister. In part, this was a response to the unhappiness of the small businessmen who had historically constituted the support base of the BJP, and in earlier times of its predecessor, the Jan Sangh. Such business people were among those who had suffered most as a result of notebandi (see Mahaprashasta 2017). Subsequently, however, in 2018, as we noted at the beginning of this chapter, it seemed that the rate of economic growth returned to higher levels – though still adrift of 'superfast' growth – in spite of the persisting problem of the Non-Performing Assets held by the banks and consequent problems of the availability of credit, for which the Modi government encountered increasing criticism (Kazmin 2018b). The government's wish that the Reserve Bank of India (RBI) should encourage more bank lending was among the factors that led to tension between government and Bank later in 2018 (Kazmin 2018c), which eventually resulted in the resignation of the then Governor of the RBI, Urjit Patel, amid widespread expressions of concern about the undermining of the independence of the Bank (Editorial Board 2019).

2.6 Conclusion

For the first three decades following independence in 1947, India experienced highly variable economic growth rates, but averaging less than 4 per cent per annum. This period of the 'licence-permit-quota raj' saw bureaucrats holding important discretionary powers, and these helped to give rise to what Kar and Sen describe as a disordered deals environment, not conducive to growth. Though sometimes written off, this period was not wholly unsuccessful. The industrial structure of the country was transformed in a remarkably short period of time, and skills were built up that have served the Indian economy very well in more recent years. Yet decisions taken in this period, or decisions not taken, or failures of policy implementation have had highly significant consequences over the longer run. Governments failed to tackle the problem of improving the productivity of Indian agriculture (on which, see chapter 4), except by means of a regime of subsidies that have tended to benefit larger farmers only in certain parts of the country – Punjab, Haryana, western UP and coastal Andhra Pradesh in particular. The country became set on a path of industrial development that was *not* based on labour-intensive manufacturing of products for export; and set, too, on a path that protected manufacturing of many products in small-scale units, with the result that there are relatively very few middle-sized establishments in Indian industry. There is a 'missing middle'.

Economic growth picked up significantly from the early 1980s – or the later 1970s according to Sen – partly because of a more positive attitude towards private business on the part of the political elite. This evidently helped to stimulate private investment in the 1980s, especially in equipment, drawing on improvement in the savings rate in the 1970s with the financial deepening that took place in those years. Then in 1991, in the context of a liquidity crisis, a tipping point was reached, and the long-standing advice of liberal economists at last was accepted by policy makers. India undertook what were described as 'economic reforms' and started on a path of deregulation and liberalization that brought the 'licence-permit-quota raj' to an end. The discretionary powers of bureaucrats were reduced, if not eliminated – collusive relations remained, between some big business groups and political and bureaucratic elites. But as Kar and Sen describe it, the deals environment became both more open, and more ordered, with a positive impact on rates of growth, which now became much less variable.

Then, at last, India attained more or less 'superfast' growth for about five years from 2003–04. The cumulative effects of the economic reforms were reflected in the rise of corporate savings and investment in this time, and in marked improvement in productivity. Yet, according to the analysis by Kar and Sen, broadly supported by Joshi, this period of exceptionally high growth saw the establishment of more closed deals, involving particularly companies operating in high rent sectors – and it was the political backlash against this, later in the period in office of the second Congress-headed United Progressive Alliance government, that soured the investment climate. It also became clear, subsequently, that the banking system had encouraged excessive credit growth in the boom years, a lot of it involving crony-capitalist deals. The weight of Non-Performing Assets held by banks became a constraint on growth, and as corporate savings and investment declined, so economic growth faltered. Indications of recovery after 2014 were disputed at the time, and prime minister Modi's later claims that India's economy had grown faster during his tenure than at any other time were called into question because of doubts about the validity of new official statistics.

Worries about the economy played very little part in the general election of 2019, however, as prime minister Modi succeeded in focusing attention on matters of national security and of nationalism. Big business seems generally to have given him and his party the benefit of the doubt, while looking – as reported in the financial press (Kazmin 2019b) – for urgent action regarding access to land and capital, and labour market flexibility. These hopes were certainly not realized in the first months after the election, when, as we noted earlier, evidence of the slowing of GDP growth was published (Kazmin 2019c). The sharp fall in the sales of cars was seen as 'the most alarming symptom of broader economic slowdown' (Parkin 2019a). Then the first budget of the new government, put before parliament in July 2019, promised to increase tax revenues and imposed a tax surcharge on the 'super-rich', measures that were seen as threatening by business people – though the government shortly afterwards sought to allay business fears by cutting corporate tax rates to their lowest levels in the history of independent India. The publication of data for April–June 2019 showed the slowest rate of growth of the economy for six years, highlighting 'the depth of malaise that has gripped a country that not long ago reveled in its status as the world's fastest growing economy' (Kazmin 2019d; see also Kazmin 2019e), and the growth rate dipped even lower, to 4.5 per cent in the third quarter (*The Hindu*, 29 November 2019). The short- and medium-term prospects for the Indian economy did not appear to be at all positive.

3

How 'Inclusive' is India's Economic Growth?

3.1 Introduction: Economic Growth and 'Development'

Economic growth is not synonymous with 'development' – if, by the latter, we understand the improvement of well-being throughout society. We follow the great Indian economist, Amartya Sen, in believing that development should be understood as being about expanding the real freedoms of people to lead lives that they have reason to value (Sen 1999). This means, in Sen's terms, thinking about development in terms of 'capabilities' – people's abilities to do things, and to live lives that they value – rather than in terms of 'commodities'. This does not mean that commodities – both goods and services – are of no account at all. Clearly not, for if people have insufficient means to secure adequate nutrition, clothing, shelter and the services that they need in order to lead a worthwhile life, then the objectives of development cannot be achieved. Material poverty matters hugely, and economic growth – which involves expanding the supply of commodities – does matter. A critical question, however, is that of whether, or how far, growth serves to reduce material poverty, and to increase opportunities for people to realize the end of leading lives that they have reason to value. In this chapter we are concerned with the question of how well India is doing in regard to these objectives. We are especially concerned with the extent to which continuing low levels of education and health – human capital, in economists' language – have limited opportunities for a majority of India's people.

The way in which growth is achieved matters a great deal. Clearly, if the benefits of growth accrue mostly to a small fraction of the population, then development objectives may not be realized for the majority. An important question is that of how far increasing material inequality is consistent with the realization of development goals. Former British prime minister, Tony Blair, once argued that increasing inequality in the country didn't matter, because it was like a rising tide, with increasing wealth 'lifting all boats'. But increasing inequality may mean that opportunities for lifting their boats (to extend the metaphor) are denied to some, or that they lift their boats much less than they might have been able to. Do people benefit from growth because they are active participants in the growth process, or do they benefit only by 'trickle down' from the wealth of the few? Does the growth process increase opportunities for people to lead lives they have reason to value?

Recognizing the importance of these questions, Governments of India have made commitments to the goal of 'inclusive growth'. This was the theme of India's Eleventh Five Year Plan, for the period 2007–12, and the title of the first main volume of the Plan document. It was said that:

> The central vision of the Eleventh Plan is to build on our strengths to trigger a development process which ensures broad-based improvement in the quality of life of the people, especially the poor, SCs/STs, other backward castes (OBCs), minorities and women' (Planning Commission 2008: 2)

The list of those whose quality of life is to be improved, according to this statement – and a comparable one in the Twelfth Five Year Plan, which repeated the objective of bringing about inclusive growth (Planning Commission 2013: vi) – is a long one, accounting for all but a fairly small minority of the population of the country. According to the Census of 2011, the Scheduled Castes (SCs) accounted for 16.6 per cent of the population, and the Scheduled Tribes (STs) for a further 8.6 per cent. Add to this quarter of the population the numbers of those officially designated as members of the 'Other Backward Classes' (OBCs – according to the official definition, 'backward classes', not 'castes'), who are estimated to make up around 40 per cent of the population (according to National Sample Survey estimates, reported in *Times of India*, 1 September 2007), and we have two-thirds of the population of India. To this should be added, in the light of accumulating evidence about their disadvantage in many spheres of life, most of the Muslims (the most significant 'minority') who made up 14.2 per cent of the population in 2011. Even if we take no separate account of women, the Plan document clearly refers to a large majority of the people in the country.

In this chapter we take up the question of how far the 'vision' of improving the quality of life of the majority has been realized. First, having considered the problems that surround the construction and measurement of poverty, we present evidence showing that while progress has been made in regard to the alleviation of poverty – variously understood – in the aggregate, the rate at which it has been reduced has probably been lower than might have been expected, or in comparison with other South Asian countries (notably Bangladesh), at least in part because of increasing inequality. But for us, the most telling criticism of India's performance, in regard to the well-being of Indians, is that it remains the case that a very large proportion of the population is still vulnerable to falling into poverty, even after years of high rates of economic growth. We also show that the relative exclusion of the groups referred to specifically in the Plan documents has continued. In practice the benefits of growth in India continue to be very unequally distributed, and social divisions, of gender, caste and religion have in many ways become more profound. We reflect upon these trends, and the evidence from rich empirical studies of the severe constraints upon social and economic mobility in India. We go on, in the next chapter, to discuss what limits the achievement of development goals in India today.

3.2 Constructions and Measurements of Poverty

In 2011 the question of how poverty is defined and measured became the subject of intense political debate in India, following the submission of an affidavit from the Planning Commission to the Supreme Court, setting out the official poverty lines of Rs 26 per person per day in rural India, and Rs 32 in urban centres. In one intervention in the debate, the Deputy Chairman of the Planning Commission was challenged to live in Delhi on Rs 32 per day. These measures of poverty were derived from work done originally in the early 1970s, in which the poverty line was set at the average monthly consumption expenditure of households whose members were able to consume 2,400 calories per person per day in rural India, or 2,100 in urban India (these intakes of dietary energy being reckoned to be what was required in India for sustaining life and necessary activity). Consumption expenditure data comes from regular sample surveys conducted by the National Sample Survey Office (NSSO); and the poverty line has been regularly updated, using consumer price indices – though the numbers, increasingly, have had little to do with actual calorie consumption. An economist who has devoted his professional work to poverty measurement, S. Subramanian, comments that 'officially "price corrected" poverty lines progressively fall short of calorific norms on the basis of which they were initially rationalised' (2016). Still, the methodology, and the measures, are roughly equivalent to the World Bank's procedures, which established the well-known poverty line of $1 per person per day (later $1.25 per day and since October 2015, $1.90 per day) at purchasing power parity (PPP) exchange rates, that has been widely referred to in assessments of the extent of poverty across the world (critiqued by Reddy and Pogge 2009). The measures, both of the World Bank and of the Government of India, are distinctly niggardly, allowing for not much more than the maintenance of life. Vijay Joshi suggests that they can be described as reflecting 'extreme poverty' (2017: 29).

In India the basic methodology has been revisited and rejigged on a number of occasions, by expert groups of economists, most recently by a committee chaired by Suresh Tendulkar, which reported in 2009 – and whose estimates became the stuff of controversy in 2011, so leading to the constitution of an another expert group, in 2012, chaired by C. Rangararan, which reported in 2014 (and raised the poverty line, so that by 2011–12, according to this committee's methodology, there were 96 million more poor people in India than according to the Tendulkar-based count: see Joshi 2017, table 2.4). Subsequently, following the replacement by the BJP government in 2015 of the Planning Commission with the NITI Aayog ('National Institution for Transforming India'), yet another committee has in turn reviewed the recommendations of these expert groups – with what outcome is unknown at the time of writing (in March 2019, by which time no official estimates of poverty levels had been published since 2011–12). The upshot has been the proliferation of quite wildly divergent estimates of the extent of poverty in India, produced by different official bodies. The Tendulkar Committee produced an estimate of 37.2 per cent of the population in 2004–05 (407 million people), when the (old) official estimate for that year stood at 27.5 per cent (302 million people). These are 'headcount poverty ratios' – referring to the proportion of the population unable to meet the minimum consumption requirements set out in the methodology described earlier. At about the same time, and with reference to the same date, another committee, chaired by N. C. Saxena, argued that for practical purposes – of providing for the welfare of the people – the estimate of the incidence of poverty should be increased to 50 per cent; while the National Commission on Enterprises in the Unorganised Sector, chaired by Arjun Sengupta, estimated that 77 per cent should be considered poor. The World Bank estimate of the incidence of poverty in India in 2005 was 40 per cent; that of the Asian Development Bank, about 50 per cent. S. Subramanian has commented that 'the official methodology has thrown the door open to complete anarchy' (2016). And this remark is with reference to the preferred conventional procedures for measuring poverty levels, based on NSSO data on household consumption expenditure. Another whole dimension of debate arises from the fact that observations of mean consumption reported in India's National Accounts are significantly (and increasingly) above those provided by the survey data – though the survey data are generally preferred, because they measure living standards directly.

That there should be so many different estimates points to the considerable technical difficulties associated with defining and measuring poverty – which involves a whole series of judgement calls. A respected Indian economist, A. Vaidyanathan, who has devoted much of his long professional life to these matters, has written that 'it is not possible to arrive at a definitive estimate of poverty incidence that can be used as a reasonably robust benchmark' (Vaidyanathan 2013: 41. See also Krishnaji 2012 for a similar argument by another senior economist). He was referring here especially to the problem of identifying 'the poor' for the purpose of allocating welfare benefits supplied by government. An important instance of this is that of access to foodgrains and other basic consumer goods at controlled, low prices, through India's Public Distribution System (PDS). This has been targeted, in principle, since 1997, to those defined as being 'Below the Poverty Line' (BPL). But how are the 'BPL' to be identified? The main reason why the poverty line calculations offered by the Planning Commission in 2011 became the subject of so much controversy was that it was suggested that the poverty estimates to which they gave rise would be used for targeting purposes – though the Tendulkar Committee had expressly advised against this. The absurdity of the procedure was pointed up in a cartoon in the English language newspaper *The Hindu* (22 September 2011), which showed an obviously poor man crossing the road to join his family, living on the pavement, and saying to a passing motorist who was offering him some coins, 'No thanks. I've earned Rs. 25 today. I don't want to lose my BPL status'.

   This is not to say that the attempt to measure the incidence of poverty in a country, to track trends over time, and to make comparisons across regions, is worthless. These certainly are important data for any responsible government, and in a democracy should be expected to play a part in its evaluation by the electorate (so governments have an incentive to set the poverty line low, in order to enhance the chances of producing a favourable impression). It is for this reason that we go on to review evidence on poverty trends in India, and on the extent of poverty among different social groups, as these are given by the conventional monetary measures. But we should remind ourselves that the poverty line is a construction, not a truth (and, in India, a construction that might be significantly improved – see Subramanian 2014). An aggregated measure does not, of course, take account of differences between individuals, between, for instance, those who are disabled in some way and others, or between people living in different localities with very different needs in terms of clothing and shelter. And the monetary measure of poverty may not take account of important differences that have to do with public services, such as the availability or not of clean water, which exercises such an important influence on nutrition and health. So, as Vaidyanathan has also argued

> Strategies to address the myriad and varied disabilities of the poor cannot be decided on the basis of the overall incidence of income poverty. They need to be based on assessments of the deficiencies of access and realization relative to accepted minimum desirable levels of specific components of living standards such as food intake, unemployment and underemployment, housing, connectivity and indicators of health and education status' (Vaidyanathan 2013: 41).

Latterly, several different attempts have been made to come up with multidimensional assessments of the incidence of poverty, taking account of direct measures of nutrition and health, and of other indicators of living standards, of which the best known is that of the Oxford Poverty and Human Development Initiative (www.ophi.org.uk). The Multidimensional Poverty Index (MPI), published since 2010 by the United Nations Development Programme (UNDP), is based on the work of the Oxford Group. We consider this, too, in what follows, where we discuss the findings of the mainstream of poverty research relating to India.

3.3 Poverty Trends in India

Economists associated with the World Bank, Gaurav Datt, Rinku Murgai and Martin Ravallion, point out that among developing countries, India has the longest series of national household surveys suitable for tracking living conditions, and they have reported on their findings from these data for the 60 years from 1957 to 2012 (Datt et al. 2016a, 2016b). Their analysis refers to the definition of the poverty line established by the Planning Commission in the 1970s (the one anchored in the nutritional norms of 2,400/2,100 calories per person per day), updated in the conventional way, using urban and rural price indices. They find that there has been a definite downward trend in poverty since the early 1970s, according to the standard measures, with acceleration after 1991 – when India embarked upon the economic reforms described in chapter 2 – despite increasing inequality. Poverty reduction since 1991 has been more responsive to growth than it was before – there has been a higher growth elasticity of poverty incidence reduction. Still, as Ravallion has shown elsewhere, the growth elasticity of poverty in China, historically, has been about twice that of India, probably because of more favourable initial conditions. With relatively low inequality in access to land and human capital, the poor in China have gained more from growth (though over time these favourable conditions have been eroded with increasing inequality in incomes and in education and health), while opportunities for the poor in India have been restricted by low levels of education and health (Ravallion 2012).

The strong suggestion in this analysis that India's policy shift at the beginning of the 1990s, and the higher and more consistent economic growth that the country has seen since then, has had positive outcomes in terms of poverty reduction, is apparently confirmed in other analyses that focus more on the trends of the last two decades. Himanshu and Kunal Sen, whose analysis refers to the Tendulkar measure of the poverty line, present evidence that leads them to the 'inescapable conclusion that poverty has declined faster [over the period 2004–05 to 2009–10, when India was experiencing 'superfast' growth] than in the previous period [1993–94 to 2004–05]' (2014: 78). They estimate that the rate of poverty decline in the more recent period was 1.12 per cent per annum (even though their figures are lower, for reasons that they explain, than those of the Planning Commission), compared with 0.74 per cent per annum over the previous decade. One measure of the intensity of poverty, the poverty gap, shows marginally better improvement in the later period than the earlier one; but according to a second measure, the squared poverty gap, performance in the later period was worse. This suggests the possibility that the poverty decline was associated with an increasing share in the population of those who are vulnerable to falling into poverty (see also Dang and Lanjouw 2015). And Himanshu and Sen find slower improvements in consumption expenditure among the most vulnerable people – those employed as agricultural labourers in the rural economy, and as casual daily paid wage labour in the towns – by comparison with all households (Himanshu and Sen 2014: 81–3).

This, ultimately mixed picture of recent trends, is borne out also in research by the World Bank economists Amber Narayan and Rinku Murgai (2016). They too refer to Tendulkar-based poverty estimates, and report that the pace of poverty reduction accelerated after 2004–05 – and then increased even further in the two years after 2009–10. This accelerated rate has been found surprising, however, given the deceleration of the economy in this period (as discussed in chapter 2), and it has also been pointed out that 2009–10 was a year of particularly severe drought – so we should probably not build too much upon the apparently sharp increase in the rate of poverty reduction after 2010 (see 'Editorial' 2013). Prosperity has been rising, Narayan and Murgai find, but the share of the bottom 40 per cent of the population in total consumption has fallen, with the rate of growth in this bottom group lagging behind the rate of growth of consumption for the population as a whole (in line with Himanshu and Sen's observations regarding agricultural and casual labourers). The authors comment that poverty reduction would have been greater had consumption growth in the lower half of the population matched or exceeded average gains for the population. This finding recalls those of Petia Topolova for the period from 1993–94 to 2004–05, when there was also a shift in the distribution of income against the officially poor (in contrast to what had happened in the 1980s). Topolova concluded that 'Distribution neutral growth would have generated a poverty decline in rural India that was 22 per cent higher; in urban areas, the decline in poverty would have been 76 per cent higher' (2008: 8). Increasing inequality does matter, in relation to poverty reduction.

Even more significantly, Narayan and Murgai also report a lot of churning, with a fairly high rate of downward as well as upward mobility (as Dang and Lanjouw 2015 also show), and they find that though the 'middle class', who are neither poor nor vulnerable to poverty, has increased as a share of the population (from 23 to 34 per cent), it is still the case that 'Those who are in the vulnerable group struggle to rise into the middle class, despite the opportunities afforded by rapid economic growth' (2016: 7). The point here is pithily put by a former civil servant, now professor of public policy, Anirudh Krishna, who writes:

> Official statistics tend to depict a rosy-picture of fast declining poverty [exactly as the studies we have reviewed seem, at first, to show], suggesting

a situation in which people are only moving up – and out of poverty. But India has one of the highest rates of poverty creation internationally. Between three and five per cent of the country's population falls into poverty each year, adding to the large number of people already poor ... Vulnerability to shocks is pervasive. Many who have moved out of poverty continue feeling its gravitational attraction (2017: 22).

Krishna points out that, according to the findings of a fairly large body of micro-studies, large numbers of people experience big fluctuations in their economic circumstances, moving into and out of poverty. Research undertaken in different parts of India has shown between 55 and 88 per cent of all households as having experienced poverty for the entire year or for shorter periods (Krishna 2017: 99). Krishna provides a summary of data from studies of movement into and out of poverty in four states, and from three all-India studies. The most recent of these (for the period 1993–2005) shows 4 per cent more households moved *into* than out of poverty (2017, table 4.1, p. 102). And data from Krishna's own studies in four states and two cities showed that more than 80 per cent of households that had succeeded in 'escaping' from poverty remained stuck within 'the zone of poverty'. The pathway out of poverty most commonly followed – migration to the city – has inbuilt limitations because secure, formal jobs are very rarely open to poorly educated, low-skilled migrants from rural areas. The activities in which employment has been growing include, especially, construction, in which there are very few 'good jobs'. Also, the numbers of those employed in transport, as drivers, have been growing relatively fast, as have the numbers employed in retail sales, in catering, as maids, and in personal services. Very few of these jobs will offer either much security or more than a rather basic income. In line with Krishna's findings, Narayan and Murgai, and Dang and Lanjouw, find that higher levels of education, urban residence, being engaged in wage work, and belonging to social groups *other than* Dalit, adivasi or OBC, are positively associated with higher-than-average chances of upward mobility – suggesting that the objectives of 'inclusive growth' have been at least somewhat disappointed. We say more about this later.

Krishna makes the very important point that 'The repeated observation of pervasive poverty creation suggests that something is deeply wrong with a policy that has a lot to say about raising people above the poverty line but contains nothing at all about preventing future poverty' (2017: 103). His own extensive research into poverty dynamics in India has shown that though no single type of event, or particular household characteristic, is responsible for pushing people into poverty, ill-health has been found everywhere to be significant. He reports, 'Between 3.5 per cent and 6.6 per cent of households in rural areas, and between 2.5 per cent and 5 per cent of urban households, averaging 5 per cent of the entire population, fall below the poverty line each year on account of poor health and the high cost of qualified medical care' (2017: 105). So fixing health care, making it more accessible to poor people, and more effective, is the critically important preventive measure that will save people from being pitched into poverty. Yet public expenditure on health in India remains very low, at about 1 per cent of GDP, comparing very unfavourably with comparator countries – not that more funding alone will solve the problems of the health care system. Krishna, again, comments, 'In Bangladesh, Vietnam and Thailand, countries whose recent growth record is no better than India's, people spend less, incurring fewer debts, for obtaining medical treatment' (2017: 115). It is to be hoped that a massive new health insurance scheme – known as Ayushman Bharat – announced by the Finance Minister in the Budget of 2018 will serve to correct India's very poor record in regard to the provision of health care.

Given Krishna's well-reasoned arguments, the picture of health in India that comes from recent official studies is quite depressing. A massive report, entitled *India: Health of the Nation's States*, was published by the Government of India in November 2017, accompanied by paper published in the medical journal *The Lancet* (2017), based on studies of a very large number of disease conditions and injuries and risk factors over a 26-year period (Bhuyan 2017). Health is a state responsibility in India, and though some funding, as well as policy and legislation, is provided by central government, states have wide scope in implementation. The largest proportion of health spending comes from the states' budgets. Over time, each of the states has developed its own health story, and there are very large inequalities. Nine states – Assam, Bihar, Chhattisgarh, Jharkhand, Madhya Pradesh, Odisha, Rajasthan, Uttarakhand and Uttar Pradesh – have been classified as 'high focus', implying that they need special attention. Together they account for disproportionate shares of infant, child and maternal deaths, even while failing to spend the funds that they have allocated for healthcare. In some cases, even when these states have increased spending, outcomes have not improved by as much as might have been expected, because of inadequacies in the existing health infrastructure and personnel (Rao 2017).

The disparities between states in regard to health care, which belie the stated intentions of planners and policy makers to achieve 'inclusive growth', are reproduced in comparisons of poverty reduction. Both Himanshu and Sen, and Narayan and Murgai find higher rates of poverty decline in initially richer states, so that there is increasing divergence between all the major states. There is an increased concentration of those who are most vulnerable to poverty in the states that are classified as 'low income' (Assam, Bihar, Chhattisgarh, Jharkhand, Madhya Pradesh, Odisha, Rajasthan and Uttar Pradesh). Given their large populations and their poverty rates, UP, Bihar and MP together account now for 44.2 per cent of all India's poor people (Narayan and Murgai 2016: fig. 11a). Except in the case of Odisha, poorer states (notably Assam, Bihar, Chhattisgarh and Jharkhand) have shown only marginal decline, or even some increase in the incidence of poverty (Himanshu and Sen 2014: 80). And simplistic arguments about the positive relationship between economic growth and poverty reduction are belied by the observation that the states that have seen the highest rates of growth of net state domestic product, since 2004–05 – states such as Bihar, UP, Chhattisgarh and Odisha – have not generally (the exception is Odisha) seen high rates of poverty reduction. Indeed, poverty actually increased in Chhattisgarh between 2004–05 and 2009–10 (Himanshu and Sen 2014: 86). Work by Radhakrishna (2015), using somewhat different measures, reaches the same conclusions for the period since India initiated economic reforms: growth has been pro-rich and urban-biased; welfare improvements would have been better if inequality had not increased; inter-state inequalities increased, and the slowest reduction in poverty has been witnessed in the states with the highest initial incidence of poverty. Growth has certainly not made for 'inclusive growth' by reducing the disparities in levels of well-being across the major states.

The question then arises as to how far the trends that are shown up using conventional poverty measures are qualified when account is taken of a range of direct indicators of well-being. Some of these measures radically qualify the suggestion that deprivation is being very significantly reduced in India, as a result of high rates of economic growth. India's infant mortality rate in 2012 was 47 per 1,000 births, three times the rates in China, Brazil and Russia, and about 20 per cent higher than the international trend predicts for a country with India's GDP per capita (Coffey and Spears 2017: 5). According to data from the National Family Health Survey (NFHS) of 2005–06, after twenty years of high rates of economic growth, 48 per cent of Indian children under the age of five were stunted (low height for age), and 43 per cent were underweight. These figures had come down by 2015–16, according to NFHS-4, but there were still more than a third of Indian children who were abnormally short and skinny. The numbers of those who were found to be stunted stood at 38 per cent, and 36 per cent were underweight, while the share of children who were wasted (low weight for height) actually increased from 19.8 to 21 per cent. More than one-third of India's children were at risk of permanent physical and/or mental impairment as a result of poor nutrition. Indian children are shorter, on average, than children in Sub-Saharan Africa who are poorer; and 'height is steeply associated with cognitive achievement in a developing country such as India', as Coffey and Spears explain (2017: 136). These authors point out that while differences in height reflect both genetic differences and differences in the health and nutrition of young children, 'genetic differences would not cause height and cognitive achievement to be correlated; the correlation is a product of children's environments' (2017: 136).

Much depends upon whether or not children grow up in a healthy environment, and in India this is profoundly influenced, negatively, by the persistence of open defecation. According to NFHS-4 (2015–16), more than 56 per cent of all households did not have access to improved sanitation (though this was down from 70 per cent in 2005–06); and 52 per cent of all Indian households defecated in the open (63 per cent of rural households). And many of those who do have access to 'improved sanitation' continue to defecate in the open (though the Government of India's *Economic Survey* for 2017–18 presents data showing that 91 per cent of those with toilets actually use them, suggesting that the Swachh Bharat Mission [SBM] – launched by prime minister Modi in 2015, with the objective of eliminating open defecation by 2 October 2019, the 150th anniversary of Gandhi's birth – has had some success; and see Joshi 2018 for an upbeat account of the success of the SBM). We will return to the significance of these observations in chapter 4.

How, then, does the Multidimensional Poverty Index (MPI) reflect upon trends in the reduction of poverty and on improved well-being in India? This is calculated from the combination of ten indicators, each per household: (i) education: years of schooling; school attendance; (ii) health: under-5 mortality; nutrition; (iii) living standards: access to electricity; to improved sanitation; to piped water; housing quality; cooking fuel used; assets owned. Sabina Alkire and Suman Seth have calculated the MPI for India, and across Indian states, for the period 1999–2006 (Alkire and Seth 2015). Although they report that income poverty – or monetary deprivation – does not generally proxy accurately for other deprivations, their calculations of the reduction in the MPI over this period, across Indian states, do not suggest a very different picture from that based on the conventional poverty measures. They find a statistically significant decline in the MPI nationally – overall, India reduced the proportion of multidimensionally poor (a headcount ratio) by 8.3 per cent over the period, or by 1.2 percentage points per annum – a higher rate, in fact, than that of the reduction in monetary poverty over the period they have studied. In 2006 the headcount MPI for the country as a whole stood at 48.5 per cent. But neither West Bengal nor any of what used to be referred to as the BIMARU states (Bihar, Madhya Pradesh, Rajasthan and Uttar Pradesh) had reduced poverty by very much, whereas the four south Indian states, and Maharashtra, had all experienced very significant reductions. Across the various subgroups Alkire and Seth considered, too, poverty had fallen fastest among the *least* poor, so that disparities had increased between the groups. The Scheduled Tribes had experienced the slowest reduction in poverty. What is also striking, in the analyses of trends in the MPI, is India's relatively poor performance by comparison especially with Bangladesh. India's eastern neighbour has succeeded in reducing the MPI about twice as fast, though with a similar rate of growth of national income (Alkire and Seth 2015).

The picture that we take from the work of Himanshu and Sen, and that of Narayan and Murgai, on recent trends in poverty reduction, relating principally to the period of 'superfast growth' from around 2003, complemented by the observations of Krishna from empirical research on poverty dynamics, is a distinctly mixed one – an historically fast rate of decline of poverty in the aggregate (according to the conventional measures), but offset by increasing inequality and the persisting vulnerability of a large share of the population to downward movements into poverty. As Krishna says, 'Policymakers in India have vested their hopes in the idea that economic growth will eventually eradicate poverty, and until then, palliatives like subsidized food or make-work programmes [on which see chapter 8 in this book] will be sufficient. These formulations have not been efficacious. A large share of India's population – more than half by any reasonable measure – continues to live in the shadow of poverty, and many more remain vulnerable to becoming poor in future' (2017: 113). The focus has been wrong. Vast intellectual and practical effort has gone into poverty measurement, and into bringing the aggregate numbers down by means of a myriad of programmes intended to alleviate poverty. This perhaps makes for good press for governments. Far too little attention has been given to the prevention of poverty through accessible and effective health care, or to improving people's chances of taking advantage of opportunities in a growing economy through much better education and training. A disproportionately large share of Indians, historically, have had little or no education, while on the other hand a disproportionately large number have had tertiary education. Relatively few of them have had secondary education. The pattern and performance of education in India has restricted the chances for very many people of moving into more productive and better paid employment (see chapter 13).

3.4 Durable Inequalities in Indian Society, Mobility and the Missing Middle Class

We drew attention earlier to the findings from recent research that higher levels of education, urban residence, being engaged in wage work, and belonging to social groups *other than* Dalit, adivasi or OBC are positively associated with higher-than-average chances of upward mobility. These observations point to the significance in India of what the social historian Charles Tilly (1998) refers to as 'durable inequalities' – inequalities, that is, across groups of people defined by relatively rigid social discriminators. This is the case, without question, of distinctions relating to caste, tribe and religion.

   The economist K. P. Kannan was a member of the National Commission on Enterprises in the Unorganised Sector (NCEUS), appointed by the Congress-led United Progressive Alliance government, in 2004, to examine problems faced by the unorganized, or informal sector of the economy, and by the 92 per cent of Indian workers who are informally employed. The Commission distinguished different groups in regard to poverty: (a) the 'poor and marginally poor', comparable with those distinguished by the $1.25 per capita per day

Table 3.1 Percentage Distribution of Population by Poverty Status and Social Groups, 2004–05 and 2009–10

			Population		
	Total	Adivasi/Dalit	Muslim	OBC	Others
Poverty status 2004–05					
1. Poor & marginally poor	40.8	54.8	49.7	40.6	19.6
2. Poor & vulnerable (incl. 1)	76.7	87.8	84.5	79.9	54.8
3. Middle & high income	23.3	12.2	15.5	20.2	45.2
All	100.0	100.0	100.0	100.0	100.0
Poverty status 2009–10					
1. Poor & marginally poor	32.1	45.2	39.6	30.8	13.8
2. Poor & vulnerable (incl. 1)	69.0	81.9	78.9	70.8	44.5
3. Middle & high income	31.0	18.1	20.1	29.2	55.5
All	100.0	100.0	100.0	100.0	100.0

SOURCES: NCEUS (2007) for 2004–05; computed from unit level data from National Sample Survey 61st Round. Reproduced from Kannan 2018, table 2.1

international poverty line of the World Bank; (b) the 'poor and vulnerable', comparable with the international poverty line of $2 per capita per day; and (c) those who are not poor, classified as 'middle and high income'. Kannan (2018) presents data on the incidence of poverty in terms of these three groups, and across social categories, showing that in every poverty group the highest incidence of poverty is among Dalits and adivasis, followed by Muslims, then OBCs, and finally Others (see table 3.1).

Evidence presented by other scholars shows up big differences also between Dalits and adivasis. Radhakrishna (2015) offers the data presented in table 3.2.

The slower rate of decline among Scheduled Tribes (ST) by comparison with others, shown in Radhakrishna's data, is to be matched with Alkire and Seth's finding, referred to above, that the MPI declined least among STs between 1999 and 2006. Kannan's calculations (2018: 35–8) of the rate of reduction

Table 3.2 Incidence of Poverty and the Rate of Decline During 1993–94 to 2010–11, Rural and Urban, All-India

Group	1993–94	2010–11	Decline % per annum
Scheduled Tribe	62.6	43.0	−1.7
Scheduled Caste	60.1	29.4	−2.8
OBC	39.0	20.7	−2.6
Others	39.0	12.5	−3.8
All	45.1	21.9	−2.9

SOURCE: Radhakrishna (2015)

of poverty across groups shows that between 1999–2000 and 2004–05 it was lowest among Dalits/adivasis and Muslims. In the 'poor and marginal' category, they did somewhat better than 'others' in the period 2004–05 to 2009–10, and about the same as the OBCs; but they did less well again in the 'poor and vulnerable' category, in comparison with OBCs and 'others', over this second period. Among Dalits and adivasis, 82 per cent were still 'poor and vulnerable in 2009–10, after those years of 'superfast growth'. 'Inclusive growth' really hasn't happened.

Kannan's conclusion, 'It is clear that the burden of poverty is concentrated among the socially disadvantaged groups – Dalits/Adivasis and Muslims – to a very significant degree' (2018: 35), is unquestionably correct, and reflects 'durable inequalities'. These are illuminated by the ethnographic research, in five sites, spread across India, reported by Alpa Shah, Jens Lerche and their co-workers in the book *Ground Down by Growth: Tribe, Caste and Inequality in Twenty-First Century India* (2018). The anthropologists found that the casual labour supplied especially by Dalits and adivasis, some of it by Dalits and adivasis from eastern India who have travelled across the country for work, is a significant factor in the processes of accumulation that are going on. Shah and Lerche argue that 'the entrenchment of social difference in the expansion of capitalism takes place through at least three inter-related processes: *inherited inequalities of power; super-exploitation based on casual migrant labour; and conjugated oppression* (that is the intertwined multiple oppressions based on caste, tribe, class, gender, and region)' (Shah and Lerche 2018: 2, emphasis in the original). Here they are referring to inequalities of power between people that are inherited from local caste hierarchies and from historic class differences related to landholding and occupations in the rural economy; to the kind of exploitation of migrant casual labour that is richly documented in their ethnographies, and that sees employers using a range of tactics to ensure that labour remains insecure and dependent; and to the ways in which ideologies of caste and patriarchy intersect with class exploitation to produce oppression. These three processes produce durable inequality (and see chapter 11).

The significance of these enduring inequalities, grounded in rigid social discrimination – that is to be equated with racism – is shown up, as well, in research on social and economic mobility in India. Between 2009 and 2012, Anirudh Krishna and a team of researchers interviewed more than 2,000 people who had gained admission to one of five engineering colleges, or eight business schools, or to one of three different classes of government employees. He was interested in the social backgrounds of those who are able to gain admission to the kinds of institutions from which it is possible to enter into the most sought-after careers. One conclusion was outstanding: people brought up in rural areas are at severe disadvantage in gaining entry. The chances of gaining admission for individuals who are poor, rural, Scheduled Caste or Scheduled Tribe (75 per cent of whom in the case of SCs and more than 90 per cent in the case of STs are rural, according to any definition), and who are women, are virtually zero (although women from relatively privileged urban backgrounds are now doing quite well). Very few SCs and STs are able to gain entry, and the numbers of Muslims are less than half, in proportion to their share in the population of India. The parents of new entrants to these prestigious institutions tend to be highly educated themselves, and in professional positions. More than 90 per cent had fathers with college degrees and mothers with at least high school education – when, in 2005 (according to data from the India Human Development Survey), in only 7 per cent of rural and 15 per cent of urban households did both fathers and mothers have at least high school education. In all societies, elites tend to reproduce themselves, but the tendency is particularly marked in India, and the odds of entry to the top-ranked educational institutions are stacked very heavily against those from social groups that have historically been discriminated against.

More generally, research in India shows a high level of intergenerational continuity in occupation type and income category. Drawing on data from the Indian Human Development Survey of 2011–12, Iversen et al. (2017) find the probability of any large inter-generational ascents to be very low, and there is no clear evidence of improving mobility over time. India also compares unfavourably with China, these researchers find, as regards mobility. There is a higher degree of social mobility among urban residents, and there are especially high risks of downward mobility among people living in rural areas. There is notably low mobility among Scheduled Castes and Tribes, and a particular risk of downward mobility for the sons of SC and ST professionals. Studies both of the difficulties of access for Dalits into good jobs, and of the particular constraints on Dalit entrepreneurship, very clearly show up the significance of the durable inequalities from which they suffer (Harriss-White et al. 2014; Thorat and Newman 2010).

Krishna's studies, with others, of both poverty dynamics and the severe limits on socio-economic mobility in contemporary India, draw attention to the significance of the failure of the Indian economy, in spite of high rates of growth, to create very many employment opportunities. This is a problem that was very clearly recognized by Narendra Modi in the course of his campaign for election as prime minister in 2014, and his promises to create more opportunities accounted for at least some of the support that he garnered among younger people. Modi promised to create 250 million jobs in a decade – but the first year of his tenure, 2015, saw the fewest jobs created since 2008. It is a salutary fact, on which we will comment further in the next chapter, that the economy, during Modi's term as prime minister in 2014–19, signally failed to generate more productive employment. But the constraints on mobility also have to do with failures on what Krishna refers to as 'the preparation side' – especially the problem of unequal and low-quality education, shown up in the strong evidence from the Annual Status of Education Reports (ASER) of the NGO, Pratham, of declining standards of basic literacy and numeracy from already low levels, over the years since the passage of the Right to Education Act in 2009 (Harriss 2017). The quality of technical training, too, in India, is poor – the World Economic Forum's *Global Competitiveness Report* has commented on India's 'miserable performance', in regard to 'technology-readiness, higher education, training and skill development' (and see chapter 13).

Krishna's studies of the few exceptions, of young people from poor rural backgrounds who have made it into an elite college, also show up the significance of information, of role models and of enabling facilities (such as libraries or counselling), usually provided by an outsider in such cases. These elements, in addition to basic education, seem to be required if even very bright and capable young people from poor rural backgrounds are to develop what Appadurai (2004) has referred to as a 'capacity to aspire'. Another of Krishna's surveys, of the career achievements of village people, canvassed in 105 villages, showed that the highest positions that had been achieved were usually only those of village schoolteacher, *jawan* (ordinary soldier), or police constable, and that very few people indeed could think of achieving any position beyond these.

The relative lack of socio-economic mobility in India is reflected in what *The Economist* (2018b) has referred to as 'the missing middle class'. As the journal says, there have been, and there remain, great expectations on the parts of many large international companies about the potential of the Indian market – supposedly there are 300 to 400 million Indians who are now joining the global middle class. But there is mounting evidence that the market in India for the sorts of products and services that are associated with the global middle class – drinking coffee in Starbucks, for instance – is actually quite limited. It is reported that in India Starbucks has opened about one new shop a month over two years, while new Starbucks outlets have opened in China every 15 hours. Though this observation makes for good journalism, it may not be a good indicator because it is probable that consumer tastes over much of India, not just income, limit the demand for Starbucks' products. And what defines the middle class? This is always, and everywhere, a difficult question. India's National Council of Applied Economic Research (NCAER) has proposed a cut-off of Rs 250,000 annual income, which is about $10 a day, at market rates. Calculations by Chancel and Piketty (2017) lead to the conclusion that only 78 million Indians (6 per cent or so) had that sort of income, and for many of them the price of the latest iPhone, costing $1,400 in India at the time of which *The Economist* was writing, would have accounted for around 40 per cent of their annual income.

The definition of 'middle class' in these calculations seems unduly restrictive, however. Data from a Consumer Economy survey conducted in 2016, for instance, suggest that by that time 11 per cent of Indian households owned a car, and that 36 per cent owned a two-wheeler (Bhattacharya 2016). A study of the middle class by the sociologist Aslany (2019) aims to take account of the different conceptualizations of the middle class by Marx, Weber and Bourdieu, and develops a composite index taking account not only of income and possession of consumer goods, but also of skills and credentials, housing, and social networks. Drawing on data from the Indian Human Development Survey of 2011–12, Aslany reaches the conclusion that around 28 per cent of the population can be considered middle class, though rather more than half of them are 'lower middle class', and would not be described as middle class according to the reasoning of *The Economist*.

Debate about the definition and size of the Indian middle class will go on. India has, without doubt, a very large market for consumer goods – expected, for example, until the sharp downturn in demand for all motor vehicles in 2019, to become the third largest market in the world for automobiles. And how much the middle-class market will grow – as so many of the big corporates have expected it will – is influenced, negatively, by the way in which the top 1 per cent of earners in India, those who were making more than $20,000 per annum, have been squeezing the rest. The top 1 per cent earn 22 per cent of all income, according to Chancel and Piketty's calculations (compared with 14 per cent in China) – and they are succeeding in capturing an increasing share of all national growth. Given this, and the failure of the economy to generate productive employment, the vast majority of Indians will still struggle to make it into the ranks of Aslany's 'lower middle class'.

3.5 Conclusion

We have argued that economic growth is not of value for its own sake, but only in so far as it improves the well-being of the people, and their chances of leading lives that they have reason to value; and we have addressed the question of how far India's historically high rates of economic growth have been successful in making it possible for Indians to realize these objectives. Our conclusion is that the country has been much less successful in translating economic growth into 'development' than was hoped for by the policy makers who laid out the objective of achieving 'inclusive growth'. Though material poverty – deprivation in regard to the most basic necessities of a decent life – has been reduced, in the aggregate, according to conventional measures, and increasingly so as India's rate of economic growth has increased, it remains the case that a majority of Indians are still vulnerable to falling into poverty. Moreover, a study by S. Subramanian (2019) of data from a survey of consumer expenditure in 2017–18 – the results of which the government had sought to withhold from the public – suggests that income poverty nationally had increased again after 2011–12. Public provisioning of health care, which is the most important protection that poor people have against falling into poverty, is poor, and it compares very unfavourably with neighbouring countries. Direct indicators of well-being, such as the infant mortality rate and measures of nutrition among children, show that India is doing much less well than it should be in relation to the level of GDP per capita.

It also remains the case that the burden of poverty is borne disproportionately by those in the social groups that have historically been most discriminated against – Dalits, adivasis and, increasingly, Muslims – who are subjected to oppression (akin to racism) as well as to exploitation. The rate at which economic growth reduces material poverty has been less than in comparator countries – and notably less than in China – and it has been held back by increasing inequality. Social and economic mobility is very restricted, opportunities are very limited for the great majority of Indians, and one of the reflections of this is that the middle class is less numerous than has been supposed. Why hasn't India done much better than this? This is the question we take up in the next chapter.

4

Why Isn't India Doing Better at Realizing 'Inclusive Growth'?

4.1 Introduction: The Pattern of India's Economic Growth

In the last chapter we showed that even though the rate of decline of poverty – as it has been measured conventionally – has increased, as economic growth has accelerated, India has still made only very modest progress towards improving the well-being of the mass of the people. In spite of the intentions of policy makers, growth has not been 'inclusive', and as we said, social divisions, of gender, caste and religion, have in many ways become more profound. In this chapter we develop our explanation for this state of affairs. We begin with the problem of the particular pattern of India's economic growth and what has been called the 'lop-sided' or 'stunted' transformation, to which we referred briefly in chapter 2. This leads us into discussing, first, the problems of agriculture and of the rural economy more widely, and then the challenges of 'jobless growth'. By 2019 India was seen as experiencing an 'employment crisis', in spite of the efforts of some economists to support claims of the success of the Modi government in creating jobs. We conclude with some discussion of the ways in which social relations have hindered the achievement of capability-enhancing growth.

Economic growth is certainly necessary if there is to be improvement in the quality of life of the people of a historically poor country such as India, but the particular pattern of economic development substantially determines how effectively growth brings about such improvement. The Twelfth Five Year Plan document clearly recognized this, saying 'one can easily imagine a growth process which may not be sufficiently inclusive to ensure the spread of benefits to the mass of the population. For example, any growth process which ignores agriculture will miss out on opportunities to improve incomes for a large part of the population' (Planning Commission 2013: xi). The text continues:

> The proportion of the population depending mainly on agriculture has been falling, but it is still too large, given the shrinking contribution of agriculture as a percentage of GDP. We must therefore plan for a substantial percentage of those currently engaged in agriculture to shift to higher productivity non-agricultural occupations ... To be truly inclusive

the growth process must be job creating . . . (and) . . . growth from highly
capital intensive sectors . . . or one that is dependent on high end skills
. . . cannot provide a sufficient expansion in employment to the large
numbers of the labour force with mid level skills . . . This calls for robust
growth in the manufacturing sector, including especially in small and
medium enterprises. The Twelfth Plan therefore seeks to achieve a faster
growth in manufacturing, with particular emphasis on the medium,
small and micro enterprises, which provide the best scope for absorbing
labour currently employed in low productivity occupations (Planning
Commission 2013: xi).

Implicitly, the planners were referring to the extent to which the structural
transformation of the Indian economy has been, in the words of one author,
'stunted' (Binswanger-Mkhize 2013). Others describe India's transformation as
'tortuous' (Bardhan 2009), 'lopsided' (Government of India 2009), or 'thwarted'
(Government of India 2018). The idea of structural transformation describes
the historical pattern of development of the now most 'advanced' economies: the share of agriculture in both GDP and employment declined steeply
with the rise of industry and services; and rural–urban migration brought
about increased urbanization (Timmer 2009). Agriculture supplied food and
raw materials, labour and savings for the processes of industrialization and
urbanization. A dynamic agricultural sector increased labour productivity,
and pushed up wages, but the relative importance of agriculture in the whole
economy declined as the industrial and service sectors grew more rapidly.

This is what happened in China, too. In the 1970s China still had an
agrarian economy. When reforms began in 1978, the initial focus was on
productivity growth in agriculture, and as farm incomes rose, demand for
non-farm services and locally-produced goods increased, creating non-farm
jobs. In 1978–84, total factor productivity in agriculture increased at over 5
per cent per annum; agricultural output grew at 47 per cent; and the share of
the labour force in agriculture declined from 69 to 50 per cent (Kotwal 2017).
The process of structural transformation had been set on the way. An important question about the process has to do with the relative rates at which the
shares of agriculture in GDP and in employment decline, and the relationship
between the two shares depends, as Timmer (2009) explains, on the pace of
change outside agriculture, and on the labour intensity of those activities.

In India a large gap has opened up between the decline in the share of
agriculture in GDP, and its share in the labour force. In 1950–51 agriculture accounted for 61 per cent of GDP and for 76 per cent of employment
(Chandrasekhar 2007), while it now contributes less than 20 per cent of GDP
(around 16 per cent in 2017 – see table 4.3), but still employed more than 50
per cent of the labour force as recently as 2009–10, according to data from the
National Sample Survey (NSS) (see table 4.1). Only after 2005 did the absolute
numbers of those employed in agriculture start to decline. And rural–urban

migration has been relatively limited: India's population remains almost 70 per cent rural, and the contribution of natural increase to urban population growth still stood at 44 per cent between 2001 and 2011 (Binswanger-Mkhize 2013: 12, note 1). Kotwal et al. showed that the fastest growing sectors of the Indian economy have been capital- and skilled labour-intensive, and that up to 2004–05 'increases in demand for unskilled labour by nonfarm sectors has still not matched the increases in labour force' (2011: 1184).

There has been no real change in regard to these characteristics of the Indian economy since 2004–05, as shown in the *India Employment Report 2016* (Ghose 2016), and the Government of India's *Economic Survey 2017–18* (Government of India 2018: volume I, chapter 5). The most rapidly growing and most productive activities in the economy have not been employment intensive, so that labour has remained locked in agriculture and in less productive activities, especially trade, transport and construction (which has made up an increasing share of the category of 'other industry' employment, shown in table 4.1 – the category that has grown most significantly). The information technology sector, on the other hand, which has been the most dynamic sector of the economy, and has contributed substantially to India's exports – it has 'facilitated continuing growth by generating foreign exchange' – contributes 'only a small part of GDP and a negligible part of the total employment' (Kotwal et al. 2011: 1179). Whether or not the IT sector will continue to play such a role

Table 4.1 India: Employment by Sectors (% of total)

Sector/years	1993–94	1999–2000	2004–05	2009–10	2011–12	2015–16	2017–18[b]	Net increase 2004–05 to 2017–18 (millions)
Agriculture	63.3	60.4	57.2	52.1	47.8	45.8	44.8	−43.8
Manufacturing	10.2	10.5	11.5	10.8	12.3	9.8	8.9	−9.0
Other industry[a]	4.1	5.0	6.3	10.3	11.4	12.4	12.9	+34.6
Services	20.4	22.0	22.8	24.7	26.3	28.6	29.9	+40.9
Unemployed	1.9	2.2	2.3	2.0	2.2	3.4	4.4	+11.1
NEET (15–29 years age group) (millions)			70.3		83.9	103.3	115.6	

[a] 'Other industry' includes construction, mining, and the production of electricity, gas and water. Construction has become the most important component.
[b] Estimates for the year 2017–18 are projected figures under the assumption that all else remains unchanged.
NEET = Not in Education, Employment or Training

Sources: Authors' calculations from Mehrotra et al. (2014, table 1); and Mehrotra (2019, table 1). Both report National Sample Survey data; and the second also data from Annual Survey 2015–16, Labour Bureau.

is in doubt, as we write in 2019, given advances in technology that have, for example, automated jobs such as data entry.

Growth has not, therefore, been at all like the pattern suggested as desirable in the Twelfth Five Year Plan. The pattern of India's economic growth is distinctive. India – substantially because of the legacy of capital-intensive industrialization that was encouraged under the first three five-year plans, ignoring the country's comparative advantage – has largely failed to develop internationally competitive employment-intensive manufacturing industry. Growth has been led by services, which now account for almost 50 per cent of GDP, but for barely 30 per cent of employment (tables 4.1 and 4.3). The history of growth in India contrasts very sharply with that of China, where labour-intensive manufacturing was the driver (see table 4.2 which shows the very stark contrast between India and China, in the distribution of employment across sectors); and it is argued that India's overall growth rate, over a long period, has been lower than that of China mainly because of the poor performance of the manufacturing sector (Kotwal et al. 2011: 1169).

In India the share of manufacturing in GDP has remained stuck at 15–16 per cent since the 1980s (Binswanger-Mkhize 2013: 6), while in China the share stands at twice this level (see table 4.3). Over the years from 2006–07 to

Table 4.2 Sectoral Employment in India and China (%)

	Agriculture		Industry		Services	
	Male	Female	Male	Female	Male	Female
India						
2005	49.3	70.9	21.0	14.4	29.8	14.7
2010	46.1	65.3	24.0	17.8	29.9	17.0
2012	49.3	59.7	26.1	20.9	31.0	19.4
China						
2007	3.6	3.5	47.0	40.5	46.2	52.6

SOURCE: World Bank, *World Development Indicators*

Table 4.3 India and China: Sectoral Shares of Value Added (% GDP)

	India					China	
Year/Sector	2000	2005	2010	2014	2017	2005	2017
Agriculture	21.9	17.8	17.5	16.8	15.5	11.6	7.9
Industry	28.4	30.7	30.1	27.7	26.3	47.0	40.5
(Manufacturing)	16.5	16.6	16.2	15.1	15.1	32.1	29.3
Services	41.3	42.9	45.2	47.8	48.7	41.3	51.6

SOURCE: World Bank, *World Development Indicators*

2013–14, the average growth of manufacturing was lower than the rate of GDP growth. The share of manufacturing in employment in India – it remained for long at 11–12 per cent (table 4.1) – has increased very little. In the period from 1993–94 up to 2004–05, there was even a decline in the numbers employed in organized-sector manufacturing, though overall employment in manufacturing was maintained because of the growth in the unorganized sector. According to data presented by the National Commission on Enterprises in the Unorganised Sector, the absolute numbers of all protected 'formal sector' jobs *declined* marginally from 33.7 million to 33.4 million between 1999–2000 and 2005–5 – though for some time subsequently, they increased again (Himanshu 2011: 56). After the middle of the second decade of the twenty-first century, according to Mehrotra's data (see table 4.1), employment in manufacturing (organized and unorganized) declined in absolute terms.

Following the argument of the Twelfth Five Year Plan about the pattern of development that is desirable for achieving 'inclusive growth', we will examine, first, the state of agriculture, where roughly half of the labour force is still employed, and that of the rural economy more widely, concluding with some observations on the Mahatma Gandhi National Rural Employment Guarantee Scheme. We then consider the recent history of employment patterns, outside agriculture, examining the argument that India has been experiencing 'jobless growth', or what some scholars believe amounts to the 'exclusion' of labour (Sanyal and Bhattacharyya 2009). We comment on the 'Make in India' campaign announced in 2014, that was intended to address the employment problem – but seemed, five years later, to have been ineffectual in arresting the negative trends in employment in India. And we conclude with comment on the controversy over the employment crisis in 2019, in the run-up to the general election.

4.2 Has the Growth Process Ignored Indian Agriculture?

The fact that there has been such little movement out of agricultural employment – and an absolute movement out only after 2005 (amongst men only after 2009–10) – even as the share of agriculture in GDP has steeply declined, means that the majority of the people of India have continued to depend, directly and indirectly, on agriculture for their livelihoods. So, if the agricultural economy has not been doing well – if productivity has not been increasing – then it follows that it is likely that most of the people haven't been doing very well either. The work of Gaurav Datt and Martin Ravallion has shown that historically in India the reduction of poverty – as conventionally defined – depended substantially on agricultural growth, and even though these authors' more recent work has shown the increased significance of urban growth for rural poverty reduction, the performance of the agricultural economy still matters (Datt and Ravallion 1998; Datt et al. 2016a, 2016b). As the *Economic Survey* for 2017–18 put it, 'Though the share of agriculture . . . in gross value added (GVA) is on the decline, in the quest for inclusive development in India, agriculture sector will remain an engine of broad-based growth which will reduce inequalities and provide food security' (Government of India 2018, volume 2: 119).

Agricultural growth rates have lagged behind those of the non-agricultural economy, and disproportionality – the gap, that is, between the growth rates of agriculture and of non-agriculture – increased sharply from about 2 per cent in the 1970s to just under 4 per cent in the 1990s, and to more than 5 per cent between 2000–01 and 2003–04. Pranab Bardhan, writing of the period up to 2004–05, argued forcefully that 'the agriculture sector is in bad shape' (2009: 31), after a decade of low growth rates (only 0.5 per cent per annum over the period 1992–93 to 2002–03, according to Ramakumar's (2014) calculations – though 2.3 per cent per year over the period 1994–95 to 2004–05, according to Chand and Parappurathu [2012]; see table 4.4). But growth rates improved significantly after 2005, to 3.37 per cent per annum according to Chand and Parappurathu (2012), the highest level since independence, and to 3.8 per cent per annum according to the Government of India (2016: 75). So, even if there remained a significant gap in terms of growth between agriculture and non-

Table 4.4 Agricultural Growth Rates

(a) Bhalla and Singh (2009)
Annual compound growth rate (%) of value of output

1980–83/1962–65	1990–93/1980–83	2003–06/1990–93	2003–06/1962–65
2.24	3.37	1.74	2.36

SOURCE: Calculated from Ministry of Agriculture data

(b) Chand and Parappurathu (2012)
Trend growth rates (% per year) in agricultural GDP (including crops and livestock)

1960–61 to 1968–69	1968–69 to 1975–76	1975–76 to 1988–89	1988–89 to 1995–96	1995–96 to 2004–05	2004–05 to 2010–11
0.70	1.93	2.71	3.21	2.30	3.37

SOURCE: National Accounts Statistics

(c) Ramakumar (2014)
Annual growth rates (%) of agricultural production

1949–50 to 1964–65	1967–68 to 1980–81	1981–82 to 1991–92	1992–93 to 2010–11	1992–93 to 2002–03
3.10	2.30	3.40	1.59	(0.5)

SOURCE: Calculated from Ministry of Agriculture data

agriculture, it had been narrowed. Chand et al. also showed that the disparity in the productivity of urban and rural workers narrowed after 1999–2000, though by 2011–12 an urban worker was still producing 2.8 times the output of the rural worker (2017: 65). Is the growth process now embracing Indian agriculture as it has not before? Is it possible, indeed, that – with the movement of labour out of agriculture – the moment of structural change has been reached?

India's 'Agrarian Question': A Brief History

The idea of 'the agrarian question' refers to the role of agriculture in economic development, and we have argued that successful structural transformation requires increased productivity in agriculture (as happened in China, especially after 1978). The first industrializing economies saw the development of agricultural capitalism, together with what has been described as the 'differentiation of the peasantry' (see Harriss 1982b), and it seemed to some observers in the 1970s that such a process was taking place in India. In the twenty-first century, however, the Indian agricultural economy is still characterized by extensive small-scale, household-based production. Decline in the average size both of owned and of operated holdings, resulting from rural population and labour force growth, has been a long-term trend (Basole and Basu 2011). The average farm size is now 1.15 ha, and it continues declining steadily, according to the *Economic Survey* of the Government of India for 2016–17. The distribution of both ownership and of operational holdings is distinctly pear-shaped, and what are described as 'marginal' operated holdings (of one hectare, or less, in extent) now account for more than 70 per cent of the total – and findings of the Foundation for Agrarian Studies from village surveys in Andhra Pradesh, Uttar Pradesh and Maharashtra show that it was virtually impossible in 2005–06 for households with operational holdings of even *two* hectares of land (who account for all but a very small share of all the cultivators in the country), to earn an income sufficient for family survival. The net annual incomes from crop production of very many households were found to be negative (Ramachandran and Rawal 2010). The great majority of holdings, therefore, are unlikely to be capable of providing the main source of livelihood for the household; and findings from the Human Development Survey, conducted in 2004 by the National Council for Applied Economic Research with the University of Maryland, showed that almost half of the income of the average rural household by that time came from non-farm employment – and that this was true also of agricultural households. Chand and his co-authors found that by 2004–05 the share of agriculture in rural incomes had been reduced to 39 per cent (Chand et al. 2017: 71). There is definitely a trend towards part-time farming (Himanshu et al. 2011). A key question is whether this trend is indicative of a shift towards a 'productive and modern model of part-time farming', as Binswanger-Mkhize hopes (2013: 10), and is an indication that India has at last reached the moment of structural change. The problem with this argument is that the growth of GVA in agriculture remains subject to considerable fluctuation from year to year, and it seems possible that the decline of employment in agriculture is at least partly due to negative scale effects, rather than being the outcome of long-term structural transformation (Abraham 2017: 15).

Estimations by Vikas Rawal (2008), using data from the 59th round of the National Sample Survey (NSS) for 2003–04 showed that fully 80 per cent of rural households owned either no land, or only up to one hectare, and that they accounted altogether for only 22 per cent of all the land owned, while the 2.1 per cent of households with five hectares and more owned altogether 27 per cent of the land. Even after the extensive sub-division of landholdings that has taken place, therefore, inequality in land ownership remains high. The absolute numbers, and the relative share in the rural population of households without land – which have for long been considerable – have been increasing. The data from 2003–04 are not strictly comparable with those from an earlier round of the NSS, for 1992, but Rawal suggests that they showed an increase of as much as six percentage points in landlessness, while inequality in land ownership also increased. Still, over most of the country, landlordism, where small producers depend for access to land and other assets upon the owners of large estates, has declined. The share of leased-in land in the total operated area, according to the NSS, declined from 10.7 per cent in 1960–61 to just 6.5 per cent in the *kharif* (summer) season of 2002–03 – though it increased again subsequently, back to a little over 10 per cent (Murali and Vijay 2017). Traces of classic 'landlordism' remain, however (see Ramachandran et al. 2012), and inequality in land ownership still gives considerable power locally – economic, social and political – to the small numbers of the larger landowners (now mostly capitalist farmers).

That there is still evidence of landlordism in rural India in the twenty-first century is an indication of the fact that Indian governments failed adequately to implement the redistributive land reforms to which they were ostensibly committed in the 1950s. Many scholars believe that such agrarian reforms, had they been carried through in the way that they were in China, in Taiwan and in South Korea, would have created a much more dynamic agricultural economy in India, raising productivity and rural incomes (Lipton 1974). As it was, the response of Indian governments to the failures of agricultural growth in the 1960s was to resort to the new technology of the green revolution, involving a 'package' of new inputs – modern, higher-yielding varieties of wheat and rice, cultivated with substantial amounts of chemical fertilizers, and usually with assured irrigation. Successful though this was in raising growth rates by the 1980s – by which time the green revolution technology was widely disseminated (see table 4.4) – and in making India self-sufficient in foodgrains, the strategy required substantial state intervention, including investment in research and infrastructure, and the provision of extensive subsidies, both for key inputs (fertilizers, electricity and water supplied through public irrigation schemes) and for underpinning the prices that farmers receive for their products – mainly to the benefit of bigger farmers in the states of Punjab, Haryana, western Uttar Pradesh and Andhra Pradesh. Agriculture also benefitted from legislation requiring major banks to open rural branches and to meet certain targets for the supply of credit to agriculture. In the context of India's economic reforms, all these subsidies have been reduced (even if not by nearly as much as liberal economists wish), and at the same time domestic agriculture has been progressively opened up to the world market, exposing some cultivators to much greater price volatility (see Vakulabharanam 2005 for an account of liberalization measures in agriculture).

Trends in the Agricultural Economy

One tragic but powerful marker of the fact that many cultivators have not been doing at all well in recent times is the high rate of suicides amongst them, that began to be reported in the late 1990s. A systematic study of this phenomenon by Nagaraj et al. (2014), based on an analysis of the data on 'Accidental Deaths and Suicides in India' published by the National Crime Records Bureau, for suicides amongst those described as 'self-employed in farming/agriculture' over the period 1997–2012, presents evidence suggesting that the rate of suicides amongst farmers is high by comparison with that for the general population. More significantly, these authors find that farm suicides were concentrated in a contiguous region, semi-arid and poor, within the states of Maharashtra, Andhra Pradesh, Telengana, Karnataka and Chhattisgarh. In this area farm suicides increased at a faster rate than both farm suicides across the country as a whole and other suicides in the region itself. It is a region, the authors suggest, in which agro-ecological conditions make for high levels of vulnerability, where, under the impact of policies of economic liberalization, agriculture has been particularly badly affected by the withdrawal of state services, and where there is a lack of alternative livelihood opportunities.

As Ramachandran and Rawal (2010) pointed out, government expenditure in the rural economy declined in relative terms following the inception of India's economic reforms. Investment in agriculture as a proportion of GDP fell from 1.92 per cent in 1990 to 1.31 per cent in 2003, and gross capital formation in agriculture, again as a percentage of GDP, declined from 3.8 per cent in 1980–81 to 1.7 per cent during 2004–05. The same authors explain how financial liberalization meant that the expansion of public sector rural banking was brought to an end, and many rural branches of commercial banks were shut down; the credit–deposit ratios of rural commercial banks fell sharply;

advances to small farmers, to Dalits and to *adivasis* declined – while the share of informal credit in the principal borrowed by rural households increased. Agricultural research and extension languished. There was some reversal of these trends under the United Progressive Alliance government after 2004. At the same time, however, the costs of inputs increased sharply, because of the decline in administrative price support, while the minimum support prices offered by government to ensure remunerative prices for farmers' output did not compensate 'the actual costs of production per unit of output for most crops in a majority of states' (Ramachandran and Rawal 2010: 74) – so farmers were subjected to a severe costs–prices squeeze. Until 2007–08 the prices of most agricultural commodities in world markets witnessed a downward trend, though not without fluctuations. Price volatility increased the vulnerability of many cultivators. Altogether, policy changes inspired by a liberal approach in economic policy – particularly the slowing down of public investment – had an adverse impact upon agriculture, certainly in the short term.

Government was compelled, however, in the new millennium – according to Chand and Parappurathu – to return the share of public investment going to agriculture to 1980s levels, because 'deceleration in the growth of total factor productivity in the North Western region, especially in wheat and rice growing areas, (had) put pressure on production of major staples and forced government to take measures to reverse such trends' (2012: 61). As public investment had dipped down from the mid-1980s, so had private investment; and with increased public investment, private investment, too, began to grow again after about 2005. Increased investment in agriculture, according to Chand and Parappurathu, together with expansion of credit (though see Ramakumar and Chavan 2014 for evidence that qualifies this claim, because of the share of the credit extended that has been going to agri-business), improved supply of quality seeds, and the movement of terms of trade in favour of agriculture, brought about recovery in the period of the Eleventh Five Year Plan (2007–12). Their argument is confirmed by Deokar and Shetty, who argue that 'The year 2004–05 was a turning point' (2014: 101), note policy initiatives that increased public and private investment in agriculture, and report both 'a quantum leap in farm productivity since around 2004–05' (2014: 103) and diversification in favour of higher value horticultural crops.

After 2012, however, there were several poor monsoons and the agricultural growth rate dropped again. The Government of India *Economic Survey 2015–16* shows that growth in agriculture over the whole period since 1992–93 had seen at best only a marginal upward trend, accompanied by high volatility from year to year. The *Survey* comments:

> The shortfall in growth in agriculture is explained by the fact that 60 per cent of agriculture in India is rainfall dependent and there have been

two consecutive drought years in 2013–14 and 2014–15. Moreover, there are issues of expansion in irrigation and its efficiency, growth of capital formation in the sector has been declining and there is volatility in the markets, especially of prices, altering and distorting cropping patterns of some crops. This suggests that for the agriculture sector to achieve a target of 4 per cent, a significantly different approach has to be followed (Government of India 2016: 99).

Subsequent *Economic Surveys*, for 2016–17 and 2017–18, present similar arguments. That for 2017–18 states that 'The government is keen to double the income of the farmers, by 2022' (Government of India 2018, volume 2: 114), reflecting promises made on a number of occasions by the prime minister, and the mounting protests of farmers, in most states, some of them on a scale not seen for a long time. The disappointments of farmers in parts of Gujarat with the performance of the Modi government at the centre, helped to account for the fall in the support for the BJP in the state elections of 2017. It was not surprising, therefore, that the government promised to increase the minimum support prices offered to farmers in the budget of 2018, and then, in the run-up to the 2019 elections, provision for income support to farmers cultivating less than two hectares (Kazmin 2019b; and see our discussion of farmers' agitations in chapter 9).

Unfortunately, therefore, the performance of the agricultural economy over the period since the inception of the economic reforms means that 'opportunities to improve incomes for a large part of the population' have not been realized. Neither liberalization policies, nor the earlier mode of state intervention in agriculture, effectively addresses the fundamental problems of inefficient and often wasteful use of agricultural resources – including the failure to use irrigation water efficiently, partly because of neglect of the maintenance of irrigation structures and limitations of their design; the 'mining' of groundwater, so that it is not replenished; excessive use of chemical fertilizers; and degradation of soils. There is a long history of poor use of key agricultural resources in India, by comparison with China and elsewhere in East Asia. This was a theme developed years ago by Myrdal in his monumental *Asian Drama* (1968). In the early 1950s, Myrdal showed, the overall productivity of agriculture (in relation to land) was roughly twice as high in China as in India – and it remains so still. In 1999–2000 yields of rice per hectare in China stood at 4.1 tonnes, while in India they were just under 2 tonnes (and still only 2.4 tonnes in 2015–16, according to the *Economic Survey* for 2016–17). Efforts to bring about a new green revolution, and to raise the productivity of rice agriculture through the cultivation of new hybrid varieties, are facing problems comparable with those that were encountered earlier, when higher yielding varieties were introduced. The great majority of cultivators, the small farmers, find hybrids unsuited to their strategies for reducing risk (Taylor 2018).

The problems of agricultural productivity are connected with institutional weaknesses, as in irrigation management – which is also generally much more efficient in East Asia – and in credit and marketing organization, that are in turn compounded, argues Vaidyanathan, 'by government policies for pricing of water, electricity, fertilizers and credit [all still subsidized] which induce demand growth far in excess of available supplies . . . and encourage inefficient use of scarce agricultural resources' (Vaidyanathan 2006: 4013; and for detailed corroboration Harriss-White and Janakarajan 2004). Tackling such problems calls for more than just increasing public investment (see also Vaidyanathan 2010: chs 4 and 5).

Trends in the Lives and Livelihoods of India's Rural People

Given the erratic and generally disappointing performance of Indian agriculture, what has happened to rural livelihoods? The observation of high rates of suicide among farmers was the most dramatic reflection of agrarian distress early in the new millennium. The Indian labour force as a whole had grown only very slowly in the period from 1993–94 to 1999–2000, when liberalizing economic reforms were starting to take effect, substantially because of the very low growth of rural employment, at only 0.66 per cent per annum. Employment then grew more rapidly in the period up to 2004–05 (at about 2 per cent per annum according to Abraham 2017: 13), including in agriculture, but it is likely that this was a reflection of distress. Real wages for most groups of workers actually declined in this time, and a large share of the increase in employment was accounted for by self-employment, much of it amongst women. There are strong reasons for thinking that employment growth in this period was distress-driven. As Himanshu notes, 'female work force participation rates tend to increase in times of distress, either natural ones such as drought, or manmade, such as the deceleration in the growth rates of agricultural output and wages during 1999–2000 and 2004–05' (2011: 47). The subsequent decline in agricultural employment was observed first amongst women, and it seems that many of the women who had moved into the workforce 'moved back into their homes as soon as the situation improved because of higher agricultural productivity . . . aided by increased incomes due to programmes such as National Rural Employment Guarantee Scheme and the consequent increase in wage rates' (Editorial 2010: 7). The growth rate of real agricultural wages, having declined from the early 1980s through to the middle of the first decade of the twenty-first century, increased quite rapidly thereafter, as a result, it seems, of a combination of factors including: the higher rate of growth of agriculture; higher agricultural prices; increased public expenditure in rural areas, a part of it for the Employment Guarantee Scheme; and rural non-farm employment growth (Binswanger-Mkhize 2013: 12, note 3).

Early in the twenty-first century the rural non-farm sector has become the most important source of new jobs in the Indian economy (Binswanger-Mkhize 2013: 8). The growth of rural non-farm employment has come about mainly in services, transport, and especially in construction, which accounted for almost 19 per cent of non-farm jobs by 2004–5. Subsequently, J. J. Thomas calculated, construction was by far the most important source of all non-agricultural employment, and he concluded that 'For rural males it accounted for 70 per cent of the net increase in non-agricultural employment in 2004–2012' (2014: 17). After that time, however, according to the data analysed by Abraham, there was an absolute decline in construction sector employment, especially in urban areas (2017: 16), contributing to the overall decline in employment, on which we comment below. Throughout this period, members of the scheduled castes and tribes are found to have been 'markedly more likely to be employed as agricultural labourers than in non-farm activities, even controlling for education and land' (Binswanger-Mkhize 2013: 9). The conclusion is clear: the generally lower paid agricultural labour force is becoming increasingly 'dalitized'. Though agricultural wage rates have increased in recent years, evidence from the National Council of Applied Economic Research shows 'a significant differential between average farm and rural non-farm wages of 47 per cent, and the premium has been stable since 1999' (Binswanger-Mkhize 2013: 9).

The growth in non-farm employment is often associated with increased migration, both rural–rural and rural–urban, much of it circular (when people move to and fro between village homes and distant work sites). Estimates of the numbers involved vary, and Krishna, drawing on the available literature, gives the range of 80–150 million people, so that – he thinks – 40 per cent or more of the labour force is now a floating population (2017: 64). What we know of the conditions of life and work of this mobile labour force shows that though workers may earn more than in agriculture, their livelihoods are characterized by high levels of vulnerability, and that they may be subject to conditions of employment that are described as 'neo-bondage'. This term has come to be used to describe employment relations from which the dimension of patronage is missing, but in which workers, by accepting advances of wages, effectively sacrifice their freedoms, and may subject themselves to atrocious treatment at the hands of employers, or of the intermediaries – 'jobbers' – who have recruited them (Breman 2008; Breman et al. 2009; Shah et al. 2018).

In this context there is, unsurprisingly, a very large demand for employment under the Mahatma Gandhi National Rural Employment Guarantee Scheme (MGNREGS). The Act setting up the Scheme, which was passed by Parliament in September 2005, and extended to all districts in the country in April 2008, created a justiciable 'right to work' for all households in rural India (though who bears the legal responsibility for conferring the right is hazy: see Mathur 2016: 76–9). All rural households whose members are willing to do unskilled manual work at a minimum wage notified for the programme are entitled to 100 days of work per year. They are supposed to be given work within 15 days of making an application for it, and if they are not, then they should receive an unemployment allowance. The scheme is characterized, therefore, by self-targeting and the expectation is that people will no longer come for work if better employment opportunities are available. It is a clear reflection of the employment problem of rural India that a study based on responses given to questions in a round of the National Sample Survey in 2009–10 should have shown that across the country as a whole 45 per cent of rural households wanted employment under the Scheme. Of these only 56 per cent actually got work. The 'rationing rate' – meaning the share of households that wanted work but did not get it – was, therefore, 44 per cent at the all-India level, and in only three states (Rajasthan, Tamil Nadu and Himachal Pradesh) was it less than 20 per cent. As the authors of the study concluded, there is 'clearly a large excess demand for work' (Dutta et al. 2012: 57) – and it may well be argued that MGNREGS does not in fact guarantee employment. The research showed that there is a higher demand for work in the poorer states, as might be expected – in line with the self-targeting mechanism – but the poorer states also have a greater unmet demand. Still, the findings of this study and of many others do show that the Scheme – for all the many problems in its implementation (Mathur 2016 provides a scathing account) – is reaching the rural poor, members of the Scheduled Castes and Tribes, and the OBCs, and drawing women into the labour force (see Drèze and Khera 2009; Khera 2011). Dutta and her co-authors found that the participation rate of women was twice that in the casual labour market. Some observers claim, too, that the Scheme has tightened rural labour markets and driven up wages for other work (e.g. Ghosh 2014).

There can be no doubt about the importance of the employment scheme, or of the contribution that it is making to the livelihoods of many rural people. It was feared by a number of economists, including some who had not been uncritical of the scheme, that it might be phased out by the BJP government, after it had come into office in 2014 (letter in *Economic and Political Weekly*, 18 October 2014). This did not happen, though there were increasing concerns about the implementation of the programme (Aggarwal 2016). It is also an indictment of India's pattern of economic growth that there should be so much demand for work under the programme. It supplies only poor-quality work, after all, and that there should be so much demand for it shows how few 'good jobs' are available. It is an indication of the failure of 'inclusive growth' that so many people should depend on what is largely a welfare programme.

4.3 'Jobless Growth', 'Excluded Labour' and 'Make in India'

The argument that India was experiencing 'jobless growth' was first advanced when it was observed that National Sample Survey data showed that the rate of growth of the workforce as a whole, in the late 1990s, following the passage of India's liberalizing economic reforms, fell below the rate of population growth, and well below its rate of growth in the 1980s and early 1990s (see Dev 2008: ch. 7; Himanshu 2007; and Unni and Raveendran 2007, all of whom estimate the total growth of the workforce between 1993–94 and 1999–2000 at less than 1 per cent per annum). The higher rate of growth of employment over the following five years – when the annual rate of employment growth in the rural economy stood at 1.97 per cent and that in the urban economy at 3.22 per cent (Chandrasekhar 2007) – was regarded by some as evidence of the success of the economy in creating jobs. But we have referred above to the indications that much of the growth in employment in this period was driven by distress. It was significant that the average daily wages of regular workers had declined by 2004–05, in comparison with 1999–2000 (particularly for women), indicating the growth of poorly remunerated jobs in urban areas in regular salaried employment. Subsequently the estimates contained in the report on the 64th round of the NSS for 2007–08 confirmed the misgivings of scholars who were sceptical of the idea that the economy had seen the creation of a lot of 'good quality employment' (Editorial 2010). Total employment increased at a rate of only 0.17 per cent per year between 2004–05 and 2007–08 – the lowest rate of employment generation in three decades. It was later calculated that over the period between 2004–05 and 2009–10 – in the time of 'superfast growth' (see chapter 2) – employment growth had declined to 0.7 per cent per annum, and then 'further slowed to around 0.4 per cent per annum between 2009–10 and 2011–12' (Abraham 2017: 13). The same author's analysis of data sources for what had happened after 2011–12 showed a further deceleration of employment growth during the period 2013–14 to 2015–16, when it seems that for the first time in independent India 'we have an absolute decline in employment' – more widespread in the urban areas, but in rural areas limited to women (Abraham 2017: 14).

Jobs in construction accounted for half of the total increase of 48 million non-agricultural jobs between 2004–05 and 2011–12 (see table 4.1), and as J. J. Thomas says 'These construction jobs, which were overwhelmingly in the rural areas, were likely to be of poor quality' (2014: 17). More than half of the remaining 24 million jobs were in 'traditional' services activities. Manufacturing added just 5.1 million jobs (and since 2011–12, according to the data reproduced in table 4.1, it seems that there has been an absolute decline in employment in manufacturing); and the relatively high productivity sector of finance, insurance, real estate and business services added 5.8 million jobs. For rural men, jobs in construction, as we noted, accounted for 70 per cent of the net increase in non-agricultural employment. The share of women in all the incremental employment of the period from 2004 to 2012 was small, and J. J. Thomas's argument that 'The low rate of female labour force participation is a severe obstacle to India's social and economic

Table 4.5 The Composition of the Indian Labour Force, 2011–12

Sector	Worker type	Wage index	% distribution across types	Growth rate 2000–12	Average education level (years)	Incidence of poverty (%)
Organized	Regular, formal	100	8.4	3.2	12.4	3.2
Organized	Regular, informal	36.9	5.8	9.5	9.3	8.7
Organized	Casual	23.9	3.1	6.5	4.4	29.9
Unorganized	Regular, informal	26.3	7.2	0.9	7.6	16.2
Unorganized	Casual	20.0	27.1	−0.2	3.8	37.6
Unorganized	Self-employed		18.1	1.5	6.1	23.6

SOURCE: Indian Employment Report 2016 (Ghose 2016, tables 2.2–2.5)

KEY: 'Sector' distinguishes 'organized' as referring to units with ten employees and more; 'worker type' distinguishes between workers in terms of the regularity of their employment, and the extent to which they benefit from legal protection. (Note the significant number of workers who are *informally* employed in organized sector units, and who benefit from few, or perhaps none, of the provisions in employment legislation.)

development' (2014: 17) is well taken (see also Ghose 2016: 7–10; Chand et al. 2017).

The overwhelming majority of Indian workers, therefore, have not been able to find what we might label as 'good jobs' in the organized or formal sector, and the most dynamic and productive sectors of the economy, and they take up activities in the unorganized or informal economy, outside the purview of most employment legislation, and which are often not very productive (see table 4.5).

As table 4.5 shows, the small fraction of the labour force in regular, formal employment in the organized sector is privileged, with wages more than twice those of workers in any other group. Other workers in the organized sector, who don't have contractual benefits, also earn very much less. Latterly there has been a sharp increase in the numbers of workers employed under informal contracts in organized sector companies, as firms, facing increasing competition, have sought to cut costs by sub-contracting and employing contract labour. In the organized sector as a whole, the share of informally employed workers rose from 32 per cent in 1999–2000 to 54 per cent in 2004–05, to 67 per cent in 2011–12 (Mehrotra et al. 2014: 52). As Dougherty observed 'a dichotomy has emerged, with net increases in employment occurring almost exclusively in the least productive, unorganized and often informal part of the economy' (cited by Kotwal et al. 2011: 1176).

Workers who are informally employed have no protection – against the loss of their jobs, or in the event of illness – and receive no benefits from employers. Not only are they usually low-paid, but their work and their incomes are commonly irregular, though they may also work very long hours and in hazardous workplaces. It is reliably estimated that more than half of India's GDP comes from such unregistered, informal activity, and that it accounts for more than 90 per cent of livelihoods – almost half of them being generated from self-employment (see Lerche 2010 for discussion of the informal economy and classes of labour). The NSS provides no data on the earnings of the self-employed, but it is highly likely that, in aggregate, this is one of the poorest classes.

The evidence analysed by Abraham, showing an absolute decline in employment from about 2012, including in the unorganized sector, led him to conclude that the decline:

> is a widespread phenomenon, affecting most labour-absorbing sectors ... (and) ... The fact that the productive non-agricultural sectors of the economy, such as manufacturing, have shown negative growth in employment does not fit the structural change argument. The absolute fall in employment in sectors such as construction, which acted as an employer of last resort for the ones displaced from agriculture, implies the dismal state of employment creation in India (2017: 16).

The two sectors with the highest employment elasticities in 1999–2000 to 2009–10, construction, and the real estate, finance and business services sector, subsequently saw a sharp fall in their growth (given by GVA) as well as in employment creation. 'Business services' include information technology and back office processing, which made such an important contribution to the Indian growth story, and it seems likely that their decline had knock-on effects on the construction sector (Abraham 2017: 17).

These are the reasons why it has been argued, by Sanyal and Bhattacharyya (2009), that in India now a large share of the labour force as a whole is best described as 'excluded', being unnecessary for the growth of the economy as a whole, and surviving in a wide range of activities that are of only marginal significance for the dynamic, corporate sector. Of course, there are informal activities that are integrated within the circuit of capital, as they may be through sub-contracting and outsourcing, but a great deal of informal activity, which involves extensive self-employment, constitutes – Sanyal and Bhattacharyya argue – a non-capitalist production space. This is the economy of surplus or 'excluded' labour, that does not contribute to capital accumulation. Labour has not only been 'ground down' by the ways in which the Indian economy has been growing – as Shah et al. argue (2018) – but also 'ground out'.

As Bardhan has pointed out, the problem with this argument is that Sanyal and Bhattacharyya suggest that the non-capitalist space accounts for the great majority of informal workers, when the evidence on the point is scanty. This is a fair criticism though Bardhan's own further arguments certainly provide no convincing rebuttal of the idea that there is an extensive force of excluded labour. He refers to data showing that 'the all-India average market value of fixed assets owned per enterprise was Rs 58,000 in 2005–06 [$1200+] in the informal manufacturing sector' – but the conclusion that he draws when he says 'so the average informal enterprise is not run by destitute people' (2009: 34) is misleading (see, however, Bardhan's later reflections, 2018). The great majority of informal enterprises, after all, are *not* in the manufacturing sector. The further question, of course – posed by Sanyal and Bhattacharyya – is just how much informal activity really can be considered to be the site of capital accumulation.

We have no means of mapping the distribution of informal economic activity and employment between that which is firmly within circuits of capital accumulation and that which is outside, and the notion of exclusion is, to say the least, tendentious when we do know that garbage pickers, say, are linked ultimately to circuits of capital (as when they supply scrap metal for industry). Rather than referring to a large share of the labour force as being outside the sphere of capital accumulation, therefore, it is more sensible to think in terms of its being 'excluded' from the dynamic sectors of the economy, and engaged in activities of such low productivity as barely to allow for survival. There is no question that India's transition is indeed 'tortuous'; and there remains a 'marginal mass' of labour which barely survives without welfare provisioning on the part of the state, now especially through the National Rural Employment Guarantee Scheme and enhanced support for food security through the Food Security Act passed in 2013.

The crucial failure to develop employment-intensive manufacturing industry in India has been recognized, however, and the promise of creating better employment opportunities for the youthful population – supposed to give India a 'demographic dividend' (because of the numbers of new entrants to the labour force outweighing the increase in numbers of dependents: see chapter 13) – played an important part in bringing Narendra Modi into power, as prime minister, in 2014. Shortly after he took up office as prime minister, Modi initiated, on 25 September 2014, a 'Make in India' campaign, intended to make of India a second China. As he said, 'We launched the Make in India campaign to create employment and self-employment opportunities for our youth ... we want the share of manufacturing in our GDP to go up to 25 per cent in the near future' (speech of 13 February 2016). Such a step-up in manufacturing was expected to generate 100 million new jobs. The question of whether or not these objectives can be attained is one of the crucial issues of Indian development. Mr Modi made much of the so-called 'Gujarat model' of development, referring to the success of economic growth in his home state during the period in which he was chief minister there. But this did not augur well for the country, given that Gujarat's growth has not been employment intensive. Though, clearly, the 'Make in India' campaign could not be expected to give rise to immediate results in terms of job creation, the evidence on employment trends from 2014, reported above, is not at all encouraging. The employment scene was indeed 'dismal', as Abraham put it, three years after the launch of 'Make in India'.

Now, despite low wages, the threat of labour-displacing technologies is real in India. Robots have entered into use fairly widely in the automotive industry, for instance. The prospect, therefore, 'of the organized sector expanding rapidly and absorbing labour at a brisk rate seems a bit remote', and Indian policy makers must look to improving productivity in the unorganized sector, starting with agriculture (Kotwal 2017). For this to happen, much will depend upon improving basic education and skill levels, infrastructural development, and much better access to insurance, credit and banking services for the self-employed and other workers in the vast unorganized or informal sector.

It seemed altogether likely, in 2018–19 (at the time of our writing), that what has been described as 'jobless growth' – contrary to 'inclusive growth' – would continue, and in the few months before the 2019 general election there was widespread talk of an 'employment crisis', affecting especially those young people from whose labour India was supposed to benefit through the 'demographic dividend' (see chapter 13). The scale of the problem is indicated in the data shown in table 4.1, regarding those whom Mehrotra describes as 'NEETS' – people in the age group 15–29 who are not in education, employment or training. There were by about the time of the 2019 election more than 100 million young people who were in such circumstances, according to Mehrotra's calculations (2019; and see also Jeffrey 2019). Presenting relevant data, Mehrotra commented, 'The more educated you are, the more likely you will be unemployed'. He was responding to the widely discredited attempts by another economist, Surjit Bhalla, to show impressive increases in employment after 2014 (in addition to Mehrotra's article, see also The Wire Staff 2018). Kannan and Raveendran (2019) have gone so far as to describe the period as one of 'job-*loss* growth' (emphasis added), referring to the periodic Labour Force Survey conducted by the NSSO in 2017–18. This shows not only an unprecedented increase in the rate of unemployment, but also a fall in the absolute numbers of workers since 2011–12.

Arvind Subramanian, Chief Economic Adviser (2014–18) to the government led by Narendra Modi, included India among the lower income countries that he described as 'late convergers' (late in catching up, that is, with richer countries). Such countries, he argued, 'face three challenges that largely spared their predecessors in east Asia [the 'early convergers'] in the previous four decades: the backlash against globalization, climate change and automation'. The mounting political hostility to globalization means that late convergers face a much more hostile trading environment – 'large countries such as India cannot hope to export their way to growth without risking a protectionist backlash'; climate change 'threatens to keep agriculture vulnerable and locked in low productivity', when the productivity of agriculture is already a big problem in India; while 'automation and robotics will demand better skills that the late convergers cannot dream of providing'. What Subramanian foresees is the continuing migration of labour from low productivity agriculture to 'not-so-high productivity services' – from rural informality to urban informality, or in other words, locational change, not structural transformation (Subramanian 2018).

4.4 Conclusion: Binding Economic and Social Constraints

The ways in which the Indian economy has developed since independence have militated against the achievement of the wider development goals that would have delivered more for the great majority of the people. As we showed in chapter 3, there is no doubt that India's economic growth has been effective in reducing poverty and improving well-being – but by much less than might have been expected or than had been hoped for. The characteristics of India's growth path go a long way towards explaining this. Critical factors are:

- the failure to implement agrarian reforms in the early years after independence, given the political power of the richer landholders, and the subsequent failure to improve the productivity of agriculture over much of the country – in spite of, and to an extent, because of extensive subsidies;
- the pattern of industrial development, which saw the rise of inefficient, capital-intensive units in both public and private sectors, in the era of regulation but with high levels of protection, when domestic demand was also weak (partly as a result of the failure to address the agrarian problem);
- the consequent failure to develop labour-intensive, export-oriented manufacturing industry – a path of development which it is now too late for India to pursue;
- all of which has translated into the failure of structural transformation in the Indian economy; a very distinctive pattern of service sector-led growth; a 'jobless' growth path that has opened up very little opportunity except for a thin layer of well-educated people, mainly from the higher castes; and the enormous extent of informal employment which leaves very many people vulnerable to poverty.

These economic problems are compounded by factors that have to do with aspects of Indian society. We referred in chapter 3 to the ways in which the exploitation of labour under capitalism in India intersects with social discrimination, especially against Dalits (those designated by the state as Scheduled Castes), tribal people, or adivasis (designated as Scheduled Tribes), and increasingly against Muslims, in a way that greatly limits their opportunities for improving their life-chances. Many of the Dalits were slaves until well into the nineteenth century (Viswanath 2014), and the residues of slavery remain to this day – as they do in the very different context of the United States. In contemporary India the poorest jobs, notably as agricultural labourers, are held increasingly by Dalits, who are still often excluded from even slightly better paying jobs.

We have also referred (and will do so again in chapter 13) to the failures of basic education in India, which contribute powerfully to the weaknesses also of skill development that are now recognized as constraining India's economic development. In spite of the commitment made in the Constitution of India to the establishment, within ten years of its promulgation in 1950, of universal basic education, it is only in the very recent past that this goal has come near to being realized, following the passage of the Right to Education Act in 2009. Investments in tertiary education in the early years of the Indian republic, on the other hand, were significant, and have underlain India's success in IT and other knowledge-based industries – but this has been very largely to the individual benefit mainly of higher caste people (as Anirudh Krishna's research, discussed in chapter 3, has brought out). There has rarely been much commitment on the part of politicians and senior officials to basic education, and it has been persuasively argued that this reflects an upper caste mindset that has resisted the extension of education to those who have historically been subject to caste discrimination (Weiner 1991). Even in the twenty-first century there is evidence of discrimination against Dalits and adivasis in schools (Vasavi 2015) – and no doubt, as well, of their comparable disadvantage in access to other public services. All of this militates against the hopes for 'inclusive growth'.

Caste, and in particular the practices associated with untouchability, also contribute to India's relative failure in regard to the improvement of well-being, because of their implications in regard to sanitation. We referred to evidence, in chapter 3, showing India's modest performance, in relation to the country's GDP per capita, with regard to such indicators as infant mortality or the nutrition of children, and how this may be explained in part, at least, by the continuing prevalence of open defecation. Recognition of this problem led prime minister Modi to institute his Swachh Bharat Mission, directed at eliminating the practice, principally by a massive crash programme of construction of latrines. The research of Coffey and Spears (2017), however, shows that the provision of latrines – even if the construction is correctly done, which often is not the case – is insufficient as an answer to the problem. This is because latrines are commonly left unused by some members, at least, of the households to which they belong. Coffey and Spears provide evidence and reasoning which casts doubt on whether the recent figures presented by the Government of India about toilet usage accurately reflect the practices of very many people (2017: 26–65). Their criticisms were refuted by Yugal Joshi, Director of the Swachh Bharat Mission (Joshi 2018), but the subsequent publication by Coffey and Spears and co-authors of their findings from re-surveys of rural sanitation behaviour in late 2018, in the four states of Bihar, Madhya Pradesh, Rajasthan and UP, show that while rural latrine ownership had increased considerably from 2014, open defecation remained very common. Among the most important reasons for this, and for the preference on the parts of many rural people for open defecation, is concern both about their proximity to a latrine pit, and the problem of how to empty it. This is a task associated in people's minds, with caste-defined duties, not of all Dalits, but of people from particular Dalit communities who were responsible, historically, for manual scavenging – clearing away the faeces of others, one of the most ritually defiling tasks of all. Very few people indeed, even among other Dalit communities, are willing to dig out a latrine, because of its connotations in regard to deeply held values regarding (symbolic) purity and pollution. And those Dalits who were manual scavengers very often now resist having anything to do with their hereditary, stigmatizing occupation. So those who have, or who are offered latrines, who are commonly misinformed about how slowly properly constructed pits fill up, and about the sterility of decomposed human waste, which renders it safe to handle from the point of view of hygiene, worry about how they will have a pit cleaned out. For many, better to have nothing to do with one. Thus it is that whole communities of people are exposed to the serious collective health hazard which is caused by open defecation, and which reduces the chances of the survival of infants and children, and increases the risks of debilitating illness at all stages of life.

In sum, oppressive social practices associated with caste discrimination compound the problems that are associated with India's particular history of economic development, and they together mean that the country is doing much less well than it might, in bringing about 'inclusive growth' and realizing greater well-being for people.

5

Can India's Economic Growth Be Reconciled with Sustainability and Environmental Justice?

5.1 Introduction: The Costs of Environmental Degradation

In November 2017 television news programmes across the world reported on the smog that was then affecting India's capital city, Delhi. Film footage showed cars trying to make their way on the city's roads in conditions of almost zero visibility. A public health emergency was declared, and some of the Delhi-ites interviewed for the news reports spoke of feeling that they were living in a gas chamber. The concentration of harmful *pm2.5* (micro-particulate matter, produced by combustion, including that from motor vehicles) that gives rise to life-threatening heart and lung conditions, rose to levels almost thirty times above the safe limits defined by the World Health Organization (WHO) – reaching above 700 micrograms per cubic metre (and immediately before this book went into production in November 2019 the concentration of *pm2.5* reached as high as 1,000 micrograms per cubic metre of air). By comparison, the highest reading in London – not the cleanest city in the world – in November 2017 was 69 (*Daily Telegraph* [London], 9 November 2017). In the WHO database of 2018, India had the doubtful distinction of having ten cities placed in the top eleven most polluted in the world (as given by *pm2.5* concentration). Delhi was then ranked sixth worst.

The very poor air quality in India's cities is one outstanding marker of the failures of environmental protection in the country, which are having negative effects on the health of very many people. Early in 2018 the Environmental Performance Index (EPI), the tenth to have been produced, biennially, by a team from Yale and Columbia Universities, was published (available at www.epi.envirocenter.yale.edu). Air quality was described in the report as being the leading environmental threat globally to public health. The EPI ranked 180 countries on twenty-four indicators across ten issue categories (air quality; water and sanitation; heavy metals; biodiversity and habitat; forests; fisheries; climate and energy; air pollution; water resources; and agriculture). India was ranked 177th overall, just behind Nepal, and two places above Bangladesh – but was placed 180th in regard to environmental health (assessed by the measures for air quality, water and sanitation, and heavy metals [lead exposure]). China, commonly believed to have more severe environmental problems than India, was ranked 120th, and India scored worse than other countries at comparable income levels. Given the findings that we have referred to in chapter 3 about the significance of ill-health in making many Indians vulnerable to poverty, the country's very poor standards of environmental health are extremely worrying. The EPI report stated that investment in safe drinking water and modern sanitation had been found to translate relatively quickly into improved environmental health. We have referred in chapters 3 and 4 to the big problem of open defecation in India, and it is unsurprising that India's record in regard to water quality is about as bad, or perhaps even worse than that on air quality (Greenstone and Hanna 2014). There has been less action, however, on the part of civil society in regard to water quality, than there has been over air pollution – perhaps because the wealthier people who are the most vocal are able to take private action to ensure the quality of their own water supplies. But the harm caused to society by both air and water pollution is not properly costed (those who cause the damage don't pay for it, or pay for it adequately) and regulations are not enforced (Joshi 2017: 124).

There is little question about India's poor performance in regard to environmental protection. To the stories of air and water, we might add those of the damage caused to the environment and to livelihoods by shrimp aquaculture on the coasts of Tamil Nadu and Andhra Pradesh (the social and economic *costs* of which have been calculated to be 3.5 times the earnings), by mining, by the degradation of forests, by the huge increase in the use of plastics, and latterly by India's emergence as a large importer of hazardous and toxic wastes from the major industrial countries, ostensibly for recycling (on these and other areas of concern, see Shrivastava and Kothari 2012: ch. 4). There is abundant evidence that India is suffering from massive environmental degradation. A report by the Global Footprint Network and the Confederation of Indian Industry (CII – India's most influential business association), published in 2008, found that Indians use almost twice what the country's natural resources can sustain, and in a foreword to the report, a leading industrialist – not an environmentalist – said, 'India is depleting its ecological assets in support of its current economic boom and the growth of its population' (Shrivastava and Kothari 2012: 139).

Given present trends, it is calculated that the national demand for water may be 50 per cent higher than the available supply by 2030 (Joshi 2017: 126); and according to the Composite Water Index report published by the Niti Aayog in 2018, 21 major cities (including Delhi) were expected to reach zero groundwater levels by 2020, affecting access for 100 million people (Matto 2019). The reality of the pressure on India's water resources was brought home to residents of Chennai in the hot summer of 2019, when water levels in the city's reservoirs dropped below 10 per cent, and 50-wagon trains were used to carry water in from outlying districts. Farmers' wells were reported as being drained dry. According to a noted agricultural economist, Ashok Gulati, 'The civil strife in this country will start from water, not from religion. Over the next 10 to 20 years, the situation is going to worsen because it requires massive investment and I don't think we prioritise water' (Findlay 2019). There is a rich literature on urban water supply systems and the politics and social relationships that are involved in securing access to water, based on research in both Mumbai and Delhi. This shows – qualifying the statement with which we began this paragraph – how 'water scarcities that already structure our present are effects of distributive practices and not production (or supply)' (Anand 2017: 229; see also Bjorkman 2015; Truelove 2019). This literature shows just how doubtful is the idea that there are either straightforward technological or market solutions to the huge problem of supplying water to India's burgeoning city populations.

At about the same time that the citizens of Chennai confronted an especially severe shortage of water, it was reported that the India Meteorological Department was about to lower its baseline of what is held to be a 'normal' monsoon, by 1–2 cm. Greater variability in rainfall was expected, too. 'India is in the middle of a multi-decadal epoch of low rainfall', according to the head of research with the department (Shrikanth 2019). This implies increased difficulties, especially for the very many Indian farmers whose cultivation is dependent on the rains. About 80 per cent of water use is for agriculture, and it is known to be massively wasteful (see chapter 4). It was in this context that prime minister Modi, in one of his first major policy statements following his re-election in 2019, announced the creation of a new Jal Shakti ('Water Power') Ministry and called for major initiatives in regard to water conservation, while also promising piped water for all households by 2024 (only 17 per cent of village households in India had connections in 2017–18: see *Times of India*, 16 June 2019).

A World Bank study makes a systematic attempt at measuring the costs of environmental degradation in India, with reference to different types of pollution: (i) urban air pollution (from particulate matter and lead); (ii) inadequate water supply and poor sanitation; (iii) indoor air pollution (for example, from burning of dung or wood for cooking); and to three types of resource damage: (iv) damage to cropland from salinization, water logging and soil erosion; (v) degradation of pasture; and (vi) deforestation (Mani 2014). In each case the study takes a benchmark referring to what is considered to be the normal state of the environmental resource in question (for instance, the level of *pm2.5* that is believed to be the state of the air, before pollution resulting from urbanization and industrialization; or a measure of the productivity of cropland without salinization, water logging or soil erosion). The study refers to data regarding the current situation (as of 2009), averaging across India, and calculates the opportunity cost to society of the physical damage that has thus been established. Clearly many assumptions are involved and the estimates arrived at are subject to high levels of uncertainty. The study presents, therefore, a range of estimates. The midpoint of the estimates of the sum of the costs of all six types of environmental damage is equivalent to 5.7 per cent of GDP as of 2009 (the lowest estimate being 2.6 per cent and the highest 8.8 per cent), with contributions from the six categories of damage as follows:

- urban air pollution: 29%
- indoor air pollution: 23%
- cropland degradation: 19%
- water supply, sanitation: 14%
- pasture degradation: 11%
- forest degradation: 4%

As well as measuring the costs of environmental damage, the World Bank study also estimates the value to society of the contribution of natural capital in the form of ecosystem services – such as the contribution of forests to recreation and ecotourism, water recharge, the prevention of soil erosion, and to carbon sequestration. There are very good reasons, indeed, for arguing that natural capital should be included in accounting for economic growth (Dasgupta 2013). GDP, as conventionally measured, may grow and the Human Development Index improve, but at the expense of the 'mining' of natural capital – as we have seen very clearly in villages we know in India, where the growth of the agricultural economy over the last forty years has been at the expense of the decline of the water table, and of the availability of groundwater, which is not being recharged. The Nobel laureate Kenneth Arrow, with the Cambridge economist Partha Dasgupta and others, have argued that in order to assess whether economic growth is compatible with sustaining well-being over time, the focus should be on wealth rather than income (and see Bennett Institute 2019). Thinking in terms of wealth per capita rather than GDP is a way of capturing intergenerational well-being, or as Arrow and his co-authors put it: 'Sustainability is demonstrated by showing that a properly defined, comprehensive measure of wealth is maintained through time' (2012: 317). Such a measure for India over the period 1995–2000, which they present, shows growth of wealth per capita to have been less than 0.2 per cent per annum, suggesting a radically different picture of the economy from that provided by GDP figures. Dasgupta headed an Expert Group on Green National Accounting that reported to the Government of India in 2013, advocating the inclusion of both natural and human capital in the national accounts, though so far without effect on government practice (Pande 2013).

But it is not only accounting for the changing value of natural capital that matters – and we will have more to say in this chapter about the limitations of an economistic approach to the conflicts that inevitably arise over access to and the use of natural resources. It has been found, in a study of the economics of ecosystems and biodiversity conducted for the European Commission that, 'the most significant beneficiaries of forest biodiversity and ecosystem services are the poor, and the predominant impact of a loss or denial of these inputs is to the economic security and well-being of the poor' (TEEB Foundation 2008). While it is difficult to quantify the effects of environmental damage on different groups of people, there can be little doubt that those most affected are those who are most vulnerable by virtue of their age, gender, class and social status. A significant part of the health burden, for instance, is borne by children up to the age of 5. It is calculated that 12.6 per cent of mortality among the under 5s is due to water pollution and poor sanitation, and another 9.8 per cent due to indoor air pollution (Mani 2014: 19). Given the dependence of so many of the poorer people of India on agriculture, it is they who suffer disproportionately from the degradation of cropland and pasture, while forest dwellers, very many of them adivasis, suffer disproportionately from the degradation of the forests. Often, among these poorer groups it is women who suffer most – given their responsibility, for instance, for the collection of fuel, fodder and water, access to which commonly becomes more difficult, so requiring more of their time and energy. As Bina Agarwal wrote in an oft-cited article, 'In so far as there is a gender and class (caste/race)-based division of labour and distribution of property and power, gender and class (caste/race) structure people's interactions with nature and so structure the effects of environmental change on people and their responses to it' (1992: 126). Poverty is both cause and consequence of environmental degradation. The productivity of degraded land is lower, so poorer people may be compelled, in effect, to mine their resources, and a downward spiral of impoverishment and environmental degradation sets in.

Poorer people, too, may also bear a disproportionate share of the costs of measures taken to tackle environmental damage. For instance, an earlier attempt at dealing with the problem of air pollution in Delhi – following civic activism and using the legal instrument of public interest litigation – led to a court order in July 1998 that required the relocation of many small industries, held to be polluting, away from the centre of the city, and the conversion of all buses, lorries and auto-rickshaws from diesel and petrol to cleaner compressed natural gas (CNG). Though these seem progressive measures, based on a recognition of the social right to a clean environment, the costs fell disproportionately on the poor, because of the loss of jobs, and the costs to auto-rickshaw drivers of the conversion of their vehicles to CNG (Veron 2006). Concerns about the environmental sustainability of economic growth are intimately linked with questions of environmental justice – which requires the fair distribution of environmental benefits and burdens (Martinez-Alier 2016).

In sum, the costs of the environmental degradation associated with India's economic growth are very large, and they are borne disproportionately by poorer people, indicating the extent of environmental injustice that growth has produced. In this chapter we consider, first, the questions at issue in the debate in India over environment and development, and in particular concerns over environmental injustice, which must not be regarded as just an 'add-on' to concerns about environmental sustainability. We go on to discuss the drivers of environmental conflicts, and responses to them, before we consider environmental policy and regulation. The country has an impressive legal framework for environmental regulation, and an extensive set of organizations that are dedicated to its implementation. Yet there is strong evidence that regulation as it has been practised, whether directly by state agencies or through market mechanisms or local organizations, has been profoundly unsatisfactory. There are critical and unresolved issues over the respective roles of the judiciary and the administration, and of technocrats on the one hand and of citizens and local communities on the other. The present set-up is inadequate in regard to environmental protection, while being seen – with justification – as slow and obstructive for economic development. Studies such as that by the World Bank (Mani 2014), as well as by official Indian bodies, such as the Planning Commission's Expert Group on Low-Carbon Strategies (Planning Commission 2014), suggest that 'greening' India's development need not require very great sacrifices in regard to growth. Yet the possibilities of the adoption of appropriate policies are compromised by the ways in which the environment debate has been politicized.

5.2 The Environment and Development Debate: Must Growth Come First?

The Constitution of India now includes clauses that refer to the responsibility of environmental protection. Article 48A makes it a responsibility of the state to 'endeavour to protect and improve the environment', while Article 51A(g) makes environmental protection a fundamental duty of every citizen. But these articles were only introduced into the Constitution with the 42nd Amendment, passed in 1976. As originally drafted, the Constitution made no explicit mention of the environment, though Article 47, for instance, concerning the duties of the state in regard to the health of the people, carries implications in regard to environmental protection. The state has to be concerned, in this connection obviously, with pollution of air and water, which has such an important bearing on health.

But the focus of government policy has invariably been on economic growth. The First Five Year Plan has a chapter on 'Forests and Soil Conservation', which reflects an understanding of the services that nature supplies, but the emphasis in that Plan, as in its successors, was on harnessing natural resources in the service of economic growth – initially there was particular emphasis on water, to be harnessed through big dam projects. The country then saw the emergence of significant environmental movements in the 1970s, and in the following decade environmental protection became established as a policy concern. The Environmental Protection Act was passed in 1986; in 1992 a National Conservation Strategy was published, and there were Policy Statements on Environment and Development and on Control of Pollution – all taken up in the Ninth Five Year Plan (1997–2002); in 2006 the National Environment Policy was published; and the last of the Five Year Plans, the Twelfth (for 2012–17), in line with the international policy discourse, includes a chapter on sustainable development. Yet there can be no doubt about the absolute priority accorded through all these years to economic growth, and never more so than in the period since the inception of economic reforms in 1991 – as the economist Kanchan Chopra, who has been intimately involved with environmental policymaking through these years, has said (see Chopra 2017: 63). Latterly, the objectives of achieving 'double digit growth' and of overtaking China's rate of economic growth have generally been emphasized, and in this, as in optimistic predictions of India's future growth, no account is taken of environmental costs.

India's approach to the problem of climate change most clearly reflects official thinking on the relationships of environment and development – and refers back to a statement made by Indira Gandhi, as prime minister of India, at the UN Conference on the Environment held in Stockholm in 1972. Mrs Gandhi argued then that, 'The environment cannot be improved in conditions of poverty . . . The environmental problems of developing countries . . . reflect the inadequacy of development'. And, she said, 'Ecological crises should not add to the burdens of the weaker nations'. It was in this vein that the environmentalists Agrawal and Narain, in a publication entitled *Global Warming in an Unequal World* (1991), argued that the idea that a country such as India should share part of the blame for warming was tantamount to what they called 'environmental colonialism'. This was India's underlying position in climate change negotiations – referred to in an analysis of climate thinking in India as 'the Third World discourse' (Isaksen and Stokke 2014) – at least until the conference in Cancun in 2010. The Indian position was – and it remains an influential argument – that India is still a poor country, and needs economic growth to reduce poverty, with the consequence that her emissions of greenhouse gases must necessarily increase. The Indian concern was, therefore, to protect the space for growth, and the country was for long wary of accepting limitations targets. Only after the publication of the Fourth Assessment Report of the Inter-Governmental Panel on Climate Change in 2007, and thanks to the role played in it by Indian climate scientists, did India's position start to change. It has been recognized that India faces serious problems as a result of global heating, and the climate crisis is now seen, contrary to how it was seen before, as a shared international challenge and responsibility. That it has to be taken into account in the development strategy of the country is reflected in the full title of the Ministry of Environment, Forests and Climate Change. Narendra Modi, as prime minister, has aimed to make India the world leader in renewable energy, and climate policies have come to be seen as a potential opportunity for economic growth – in what Isaksen and Stokke (2014) refer to as a 'Win-Win' discourse.

The dominant view has been, however, that India is 'too poor to be green'. The country needs to be richer before it can start cleaning up the environment (Temper and Martinez-Alier 2007). This is a view – held by some on the left as well as by right-wingers – that wins support from the idea of the 'Environmental Kuznets Curve' (EKC), first developed in the early 1990s and popularized through the World Bank's *World Development Report 1992*. Named after the 'inverted U' curve described by the economist Simon Kuznets, showing how income inequality first increases but then decreases after a certain point as economic development proceeds, the EKC hypothesizes, similarly, that in the early stages of economic growth, degradation and pollution will increase, but then, beyond some level of income per capita, they will decline (see, for example, *The Economist* 2019b, making an argument of this kind with regard to air quality). The idea is that after a certain level of income is reached citizens begin to demand environmental goods, and use resources to clean up pollution and reverse degradation. Indeed, wealthier societies, such as those of Germany and Britain, have been able to an extent to 'dematerialize' their economies – using less energy and materials per unit of GDP.

Unfortunately for the proponents of 'growth first', who have found support for their views in the theory of the EKC, the statistical evidence on which it is based is not robust (Stern 2004). Mani, in the World Bank study referred to earlier, says quite bluntly, 'devastating for the proponents of the environmental Kuznets curve are findings from recent statistical analyses showing that the early estimates on which optimism was based were spurious' (Mani 2014: 5). It is also hard to envisage how India will be able to clean up much of the present damage to the environment at some point in the future when the supposed peak of the EKC is reached.

The conflict between economic growth and the environment also raises the profound ethical questions to which the idea of environmental justice draws attention. How far should the interests of society as a whole – or 'national interests' – outweigh the needs and interests of local communities? The big dams that Nehru once described as the temples of the new, modern India, and other big development projects, have displaced very large numbers of people – the exact figure is debated. It may have been 'only' 20 million people, or perhaps as many as 60 million, or even more (see chapter 9). It is known that a disproportionate share of them were adivasis. For a long time, almost no attention was paid by governments to their resettlement and rehabilitation. They were, effectively, sacrificed in the cause of national economic growth. They are among those fairly large numbers of people in the country who are described by Gadgil and Guha in their study of *Ecology and Equity* (1995) as 'ecological refugees', displaced people who live on the margins of India's islands of prosperity (perhaps as much as a third of the population, Gadgil and Guha reckon). They come from among those called by the same authors, 'ecosystem people' – the majority of the population, still depending on the natural environments of their own localities to meet most of their needs – and both groups are very clearly distinguished from the 'omnivores', those who are the beneficiaries of India's development, able to enjoy the produce of the entire biosphere, and yet who make up only a rather small minority of the population. Does not environmental justice require not only that there should be a fair distribution of the environmental costs and benefits of economic development, so that the 'ecosystem people' don't lose out, but also that there should be what we may call participatory parity? Shouldn't 'ecosystem people' have as much right to participate in decision making as the 'omnivores'? Questions of recognition are as important as distribution, and call for 'respect for alternative life-styles and non-exploitative relationships to the land' (Mawdsley and Williams 2006: 661).

These questions arise in a particularly acute form in parts of India that are especially well endowed with key resources, such as Odisha. This historically poor state has about one-third of India's iron ore reserves, a quarter of the country's coal, half of its bauxite, and more than 90 per cent of its nickel and chrome. Bauxite processing is highly energy intensive, and Odisha has been calculated to account for as much as 1 per cent of global carbon emissions. Since 1980–81, the value of mining and quarrying in the state has grown by more than 10 per cent every year, and Odisha has attracted large numbers of big investment projects, according to some estimates coming second only to the industrialized state of Gujarat in terms of the value of FDI that it brought in (in 2009) (Martinez-Alier et al. 2014). It has been said that the state is the object of a kind of latter-day 'gold rush'. But this has brought many confrontations with the adivasis, the tribal peoples who make up more than 20 per cent of the population of the state, and who include thirteen tribes that are considered to be 'Particularly Vulnerable Tribal Groups'. It is the tribal people and other marginalized groups who have borne most of the costs of mineral extraction, and of the infrastructural projects and processing industries associated with it, as their ways of life have come under threat. But the big corporations involved have encountered stiff resistance. There have been many deaths in encounters between the companies and local people. Some corporations have been led to withdraw their projects; others have been held back by legal action, undertaken by organizations committed to environmental justice (Padel and Das 2010; Kumar 2014).

A former Environment Minister in the Government of India, Jairam Ramesh, has argued that the opposition between environment and development can be bridged by implementing regulatory norms, and by proper economic valuation – such as that proposed by an expert committee chaired by the economist Kanchan Chopra, which reported in 2006. Ramesh has said, 'What we cannot measure, we cannot monitor, and what we cannot monitor, we cannot manage' (quoted by Temper and Martinez-Alier 2013: 79). Certainly there are environmental services that can be valued in monetary terms – and exercises to establish such valuations may be useful. But there are 'services' that defy this sort of valuation, as Chopra argued, explicitly, in the report on valuation of the environment. Biodiversity hotspots and protected areas are 'priceless', the report said, and 'it is also difficult to capture cultural values through economic tools, other than those directly related to ecotourism' (quoted by Temper and Martinez-Alier 2013: 83). What price can be set on the destruction of a people's culture and way of life? What price can be set on biodiversity? A monetized regime of environmental management may only enable the rich and powerful to buy rights that lead to the destruction of what is, in fact, irreplaceable. In the following discussion, as we consider environmental conflicts in more detail, we will explain further why the 'proper valuation' of natural resources is an inadequate answer to the opposition between environment and development.

5.3 Environmental Conflicts: Capital, State, Civil Society and People

A case that illustrates the relationships between business, state, civil society and people, in conflicts over natural resources (explained in detail by Temper and Martinez-Alier 2013), is that involving the UK-based company, Vedanta, which signed a Memorandum of Understanding (MoU) with the Government of Odisha in 2003, for the construction of an alumina refinery and a coal thermal plant, and also proposed to extract bauxite from an area adjacent to the refinery in the Niyamgiri Hills in Kalahandi and Rayagad Districts of the state. This brought the company and the Government of Odisha into conflict with the rights of the tribal peoples who inhabit the hills, and for whom the hills are sacred. Niyamgiri mountain is forested with valuable *sal* trees, and provides a habitat for diverse plant and animal species, as well as the means of livelihood for two Kondh tribes, both notified by the Government of Odisha as Primitive Tribal Groups, eligible for special protection. The story of how the conflict evolved shows up the problems that follow from the involvement of so many different agencies – and the significance of the fragmentation of 'the state', which is not at all a unitary actor. Different state institutions took different positions in regard to the interests of capital and of local people on different occasions, and the central government and the state government were not always on the same side, so that what we may refer to in the abstract as 'the state' was not always supportive of the big business interests involved, the structural power of capital notwithstanding. The case also reflects the general argument that Chopra has put forward in her work on development and environmental policy, 'Environmental justice movements, to have an impact on policy, have to associate themselves with institutions of the judiciary, the executive or the legislature' (2017: 43).

Following the agreement between Vedanta and the Government of Odisha, in September 2004 the Ministry of Environment and Forests (MoEF) of the Government of India gave the project environmental clearance, having been assured by the company that it would not require the diversion of forest land. This formal clearance was then challenged in the courts by three environmentalists who charged the company with having provided incorrect information about not requiring forest land. These proceedings led the Central Empowered Committee (CEC – set up by the Supreme Court in 2002 to advise it on forest matters) to undertake an investigation. The CEC noted the lack of in-depth study of the impacts of the proposed mine; that the company had not disclosed the requirement for forest lands; and that, given that the area comes under Schedule V of the Constitution of India, which sets up special governance mechanisms for areas of central India that have been 'scheduled' as tribal zones, there should be no question of the transfer of tribal land to non-tribal outsiders. The CEC argued, therefore, for the revocation of the permission that had been given to Vedanta, but referred the case back to the MoEF, which then set up a further investigation of the environmental implications.

While all this was going on, Vedanta continued with the construction of the refinery, displacing more than 100 tribal families as it did so. At this point the company denied that the mining plan was part of the same project as the refinery, in order that the construction of the refinery should not be declared illegal; but it later reversed this plea, arguing that without access to the bauxite in the hills, the company would incur heavy losses. In 2007 the Supreme Court reached a judgment on the case, in which it ignored the recommendations of the CEC report, and came down on the side of Vedanta, finding a loophole to enable a Vedanta subsidiary – a company called Sterlite – to apply to go ahead with mining, 'if sufficient payment was forthcoming to offset negative environmental effects, in the name of the national interest' (Temper and Martinez-Alier 2013: 84). The judgment was framed as one involving 'a delicate balance between conservation and development', but in the end the Court asserted the 'public interest' in the development of the area. The judge specifically stated that 'tribal people have no place in this case', and declined to give petitioners permission to speak on their behalf.

Subsequently, in 2009, the MoEF granted environmental clearance even while the matter of forest conversion was still pending, and protest by tribal people, and on their behalf by civil society activists, continued. The MoEF was constrained in July 2010 to appoint a special committee, headed by a former senior civil servant, N. C. Saxena, to report on the case, which it duly did about a month later. The Committee's report, as well as providing rich documentation of the biodiversity of the Niyamgiri Massif, and of its importance for the well-being of the tribal Kondhs who inhabit it, offers damning criticism of the failures of the Government of Odisha to comply with the legal requirements of the Forest Rights Act that had been passed in 2006. It states finally that 'The MoEF is advised not to believe the Orissa (Odisha) government's contentions without independent verification' (Saxena et al. 2010: 6). Vedanta was declared to be in illegal occupation of forest lands, described as 'an act of total contempt for the law on the part of the company and [involving] an appalling degree of collusion on the part of the concerned officials' (Saxena et al. 2010: 7). The Committee went on to point out that the amount of bauxite that could be mined would last for only about four years in meeting the increased requirement of an expanded refinery, and it concluded:

> This Committee is of the firm view that allowing mining in the proposed mining lease area by depriving two Primitive Tribal Groups of their rights over the proposed mining site in order to benefit a private company would shake the faith of tribal people in the laws of the land, which may have serious consequences for the security and well-being of the entire country (Saxena et al. 2010: 9).

The case made by the Saxena Committee, which led the Minister of Environment to withdraw the environmental clearance that had previously been given, and to refer the case to the National Green Tribunal (a specialized body, set up in 2010), was on legal and procedural grounds. The mining project was declared illegal, without any consideration being given to the sacred values that were involved, or to issues of biodiversity or people's livelihoods. Later, in 2013, the mining proposal was rejected by the *gram sabhas* (the village assemblies) in the Niyamgiri Hills; and in May 2016 the Supreme Court rejected a petition by the Odisha Mining Corporation for the reconvening of the *gram sabhas* to consider a further mining proposal (*The Hindu*, 18 May 2016). In this case, the views of local people were allowed to have weight, but there can be no guarantees that the same space for participation in decision making will always be opened up.

We have described this case at some length, not only because it shows up the cumbersome nature of India's environmental regulation, with so many institutions being involved, but rather because it shows how, even though it is supported by the local state – to the extent that the state flouts the law – big business does not always get its way, and civil society activism can be successful in supporting the interests of people who have little possibility of exercising voice for themselves; it shows how a central government ministry may be pitted against a state government over an environmental problem; it shows how far the Supreme Court has become involved, and how the Court can take different positions in regard to the differing interests of capital and people, even rejecting the advice of a special committee that it has itself set up; and it shows how the Court and the executive may be pitted against each other. It also shows, as Temper and Martinez-Alier emphasize, the severe limitations of economic evaluation as an approach to the resolution of environmental conflicts.

As a result of a number of cases over forest use that were brought before it in the late 1990s (the Godavarman case, as it has become known, was especially important), the Supreme Court came to assume the roles of policy maker, law maker and administrator in regard to India's forests (Rosencranz and Lele 2008). Large tracts were brought under centralized control, under the Court, and made accessible to market forces, and it was in this context that the Court, in 2005, appointed the expert committee headed by Professor Kanchan Chopra to advise on the valuation of ecological services, by means of the calculation of their net present value (NPV). The intention was that those benefiting from the diversion of forest lands should pay compensation in advance for the loss of ecosystem goods and services that would otherwise flow from the forest tract concerned over a period of time – reflected in the calculation of NPV. The intention may have been reasonable enough, but the practice has been hugely problematic. First, the Central Empowered Committee that the Supreme Court had appointed was selective in its adoption of the recommendations of the Chopra Committee, in particular giving a much heavier weighting to 'flagship species' (so-called 'charismatic' species such as tigers and elephants) for which tourists, with their high purchasing power, are willing to pay, than to the needs of local people with little purchasing power (for example, for firewood). 'National interests' were to be prioritized over those of local communities, with no space for democratic participation in decision making. Standard rates were set for each of the officially defined classes of forest, disregarding local particularities, and so treating the environment as a standard consumable commodity. Chopra's injunctions about the 'pricelessness' of biodiversity and of cultural values were ignored. There were differences of view over the appropriate discount rate. The case showed up, as Temper and Martinez-Alier say, that 'outcomes to forest conflicts depend on imbalances of power regarding both the ability to impose a decision . . . and the ability to impose the procedures to reach that decision' (2013: 81). The result has been, as the judgment of 2007 of the Supreme Court in the Vedanta case showed, that the environment has been opened up for purchase. Sunita Narain, Director of the Centre for Science and Environment in Delhi, perhaps India's leading environmental organization, puts it, 'If you can pay, you can cut the forest, destroy the wildlife. No forest is so precious it cannot be had. Not by the poor, but by the rich' (cited by Temper and Martinez-Alier 2013: 86).

But is this a harsh judgement, specific to forestry concerns, given India's wider environmental policies? We turn to consider these.

5.4 Environmental Policy and the Practice of Regulation

Just as the Vedanta affair was taking off, in 2006, the Cabinet of the Government of India approved the *National Environment Policy* (NEP), and this continues – in principle, according to its website – to guide the work of the MoEF. The document sets out the philosophy on which it is said to be based, in terms of three foundational aspirations (NEP 2006: 2):

- human beings should be able to enjoy a decent quality of life
- humanity should become capable of respecting the finiteness of the biosphere
- neither the aspiration for the good life, nor recognition of biophysical limits should preclude the search for greater justice in the world.

These are certainly laudable aspirations, and they reflect the fact that the policy, its title notwithstanding, is a statement about sustainable development. All the many challenges that India faces are said to 'coalesce in the dominant imperative of mass poverty' (NEP 2006: 1), and the focus of the document is clearly on reconciling environmental concerns with the overriding aim of realizing economic development. It has been roundly criticized by environmentalists because of this, and it is held to be anthropocentric and utilitarian, and insufficiently sensitive to the need for protection of biodiversity (Geevan 2004). Ashish Kothari, one of India's best-known environmentalists, commented that while the policy provides a fair diagnosis of the environmental challenges that India confronts, it 'falls seriously short of pointing to the fundamental changes needed in development and economic planning, and governance or decision making regarding natural resources, that would put India onto a path of sensitive, sustainable development' (2004: 4723).

Kothari and others were critical of the failure to question the mainstream model of development, prioritizing economic growth, and of the economistic thinking reflected in a statement such as, 'the polluter should, in principle, bear the cost of pollution, with due regard to the public interest and *without distorting international trade and investment*' (NEP 2006: 12, emphasis added). It was felt that the document stressed the importance of speeding up the environmental clearance of projects (said, by an official committee to be 'the largest source of delays') rather than the stringent application of environmental standards, stating as it does that, 'The objective is to reduce delays and levels of decision making, realize decentralization of environmental functions, and ensure greater transparency and accountability' (NEP 2006: 17). The emphasis on decentralization of authority was seen as double-edged. In so far as the idea of decentralization implies that more authority over decision making should be devolved to the states, then, given the competition between them for investment, there must be a considerable danger of them seeking to relax or evade environmental standards (as was shown by the behaviour of the Government of Odisha in the Vedanta case). At the same time, it was argued, the Policy paid insufficient attention to the importance of vesting more powers in communities (given their dependence upon their local natural resources).

Similar criticisms were levelled against another statement on environmental policy, made eight years later, in the report of a High Level Committee, appointed in 2014 by the new government headed by Narendra Modi, and chaired by T. S. R. Subramanian, a former Cabinet Secretary (see Menon and Kohli 2014; Banerjee 2015). The Committee's proposals aimed, sensibly enough, at simplifying clearance procedures and making them more transparent. But they were seen as further weakening environmental regulation – through more devolution of authority to the states, and through the idea of developing a special 'fast-track' mechanism for clearing what were described as 'linear projects' such as transmission lines and irrigation channels, as well as 'power and mining sectors and strategic border projects'. The Committee aimed to 'insulate technical project decision making from both corruption and popular pressure' – to increase the role of technocrats, in other words, and to sideline public participation – and it proposed the setting up of new institutions that would be charged with collecting data, appraising standards, monitoring compliance and enforcing penalties. Yet it failed, critics argued, adequately to recognize the problem of the lack of institutional capability in India – to which the NEP made at least a passing reference, when noting that Environmental Impact Assessment (EIA) would continue to be the principal methodology used in environmental regulation (NEP 2006: 18).

The procedure, which was made mandatory by the Environment Protection Act of 1986, requiring preparation of EIA reports, also requires engagement with project-affected communities through public hearings, and appraisal of project documents by experts. The quality of EIA reports has been such, however, as to give rise to many court cases. The administration and judiciary are pitted against one another, and the public hearings have been reduced, it is said, to a farce. A fundamental problem is that the EIA process generally begins too late, after land has been acquired and contracts entered into, meaning that, later on, delays do occur and accusations of obstruction are raised – whereas elsewhere in the world, steps have been taken to ensure that assessments take place while industrial and infrastructure projects are being planned (on these and other points, see Menon and Kohli 2015). These are problems that the Subramanian Committee was intended to address.

The Committee sought to increase the authority of technocrats. But does India have adequate technical capacity? Banerjee points out that most of the State Pollution Control Boards (SPCBs), the country's largest environmental regulators, lack manpower, infrastructure and competence, as well as being riddled with corruption. Many positions are left vacant in SPCBs, and the salaries that are offered by them are inadequate. The Odisha SPCB, to cite one example, is said to have seen the demands made upon it increase three- or fourfold over the decade 1997–2007, while the staff was increased by only about 50 per cent. 'No SPCB has a position for an economist or a biologist or an ecologist or a statistician' (Banerjee 2015: 36), and the situation was said to be only a little better in the Central Pollution Control Board. The six regional offices of the MoEF are expected to monitor thousands of projects a year, but hardly monitor a hundred. Compliance is based on self-reporting, but this is rarely verified, and offenders are rarely penalized. Yet the High Level Committee proposed that business should be granted the privilege of 'utmost good faith' – promoters being expected to provide all the relevant information, not just that directly asked for. In view of the actions of Vedanta in Odisha, we may wonder whether this is a justifiable proceeding.

In the event, the recommendations of the High Level Committee were rejected in parliament in 2015, and the problems of reconciling environmental and social justice with the demands of economic growth remain fraught. Sunita Narain's concern that no resources are so precious that they cannot be bought – by the rich – remains significant; the assessment of environmental impacts of development activities remains subject to enormous difficulties; the problems caused by the involvement of so many different agencies in clearances – setting up the possibility of the playing off of different agencies against one other – also remain.

5.5 Conclusion

It is generally recognized that the course of economic development that India has been pursuing is *not* environmentally sustainable, and that dangers arising from environmental pollution and degradation threaten both the present and future generations. These problems will only be compounded by the impacts of global heating on the country, such as the increasing frequency of extreme climatic events, in a context of the likely decline in rainfall across much of the country. The way in which economic growth is being pursued increasingly offends against the criteria of environmental justice, as big business penetrates further into frontier areas in pursuit of valuable natural resources. Then capital and the state justify their actions with reference to the backwardness of these areas and to the need for their 'inclusion' in national economic progress. As the Government of Odisha said, for instance, in its representations in the Supreme Court over the Vedanta case:

> It is easy for nonresident urban environmentalists and advocacy NGOs to romanticize tribal way of life and culture in the sylvan backdrop of forest

and biodiversity. However, a reality check would reveal a life of abject poverty and deprivation bordering on dehumanizing conditions (cited by Temper and Martinez Alier 2013: 85).

The voice of the Kondhs concerned was sought to be silenced (as it was, quite literally, in Court hearings on the case). And there is little sign that those whose communities and ways of life are disrupted by industrial and infrastructure projects will benefit from them, any more now than was the case in the past.

Attempts to value natural capital and ecosystem services are undoubtedly useful, but such economic analysis provides at best only partial answers in conflicts of interest like those involved in the Vedanta case – and as that case shows, the economic approach is liable to favour the interests of the rich. Such a technocratic approach is not insulated against the influence of power.

The challenges of sustainable development – addressed globally in the 2030 Agenda for Sustainable Development, adopted by the United Nations in 2015, that aims to 'balance prosperity and protecting the planet' – were taken up in India's National Environment Policy, adopted nine years earlier. But it remains the case that the pressures of realizing high rates of economic growth usually take precedence. This was shown up by events in late 2017 and the early months of the following year. In March 2018, prime minister Modi hosted India's biggest diplomatic summit in years, to launch the International Solar Alliance, a new international body aimed at helping fund solar projects in poor countries. But it was ironic that evidence was mounting, at exactly the same time, that the spectacular growth in the Indian market for solar energy – that had followed from the government's setting, early in 2015, of ambitious targets for renewable power – was coming to a halt (Kazmin 2018a). Part of the reason for this was that the solar power industry was facing increased costs as the result of the imposition of high 'emergency' tariffs on solar parts made in China and other countries – in a bid to protect the few Indian manufacturers of solar panels. It was reported that 'Indian manufacturers . . . have welcomed the plans, arguing that they would boost Mr Modi's hopes to boost domestic manufacturing, under a scheme he calls "Make in India"'. The same report mentions, 'The duty was called for by some of India's biggest panel makers, led by the Adani Group, which is controlled by the billionaire businessman, Gautam Adani' (Stacey 2018). The involvement of this businessman, in particular, is noteworthy, because he is known to be very close to the prime minister (Jaffrelot 2018). The episode seems to bring out very well the persisting tensions between sustainability and the demands of economic growth, and the possibility that the shorter-term interests of capital will prevail. Prime minister Modi's appearance in the role of an environmentalist in a television show in 2019 (Parkin 2019b) offered, at best, a slender hope of a reversal of priorities.

PART TWO

POLITICS

6

Has India Become the Hindu Rashtra?

6.1 Introduction: 'God Man' to Government

On 19 March 2017 a young monk, Yogi Adityanath, was sworn in as the chief minister of the most populous of India's states, Uttar Pradesh (UP). This followed a remarkable victory in the elections to the state Legislative Assembly, when the Bharatiya Janata Party (BJP) succeeded in defying the expectations even of the party's own high command, never mind those of India's leading political pundits, in winning 312 of 403 seats. Adityanath was reported to have been the unanimous choice for chief minister of the new BJP legislators – though it was widely believed that the appointment reflected the wishes of the prime minister, Narendra Modi, and of his principal lieutenant Amit Shah, president of the BJP. Adityanath was at the time serving his fifth consecutive term as MP for the constituency of Gorakhpur, in north eastern Uttar Pradesh, where he had been appointed as the Mahant, or head priest, of the Gorakhnath Mutt (monastery) in September 2014. In combining a political role with that of heading the Mutt, Adityanath continued a tradition extending back for a half a century – both his predecessors having been MPs for Gorakhpur (initially representing the Hindu Mahasabha – on which, see below), as well as Mahants (Jaffrelot 2014). But the appointment of the head of a religious institution as a state chief minister was unprecedented, and reflected – or so it appeared – the institutionalizing of the relationship between the Hindu religion and the state under the government of the BJP, following its triumph in the national elections of 2014. The party, as we noted in chapter 1, had then won an absolute majority in the Lok Sabha – the lower house of the Indian parliament – the first time this had been achieved for thirty years.

Adityanath's appointment shocked Indian liberals, not just because of the ascent of a Hindu religious leader to a very important political position (perhaps second only to that of the prime minister, given the centrality of UP in Indian politics) in a country that proclaims secularism in its Constitution, but more because he is held to stand on the extreme fringe of a movement – the Vishwa Hindu Parishad (the VHP, the 'World Hindu Council'), an organization of Hindu religious leaders – that is itself seen as extreme. He started a youth organization, the Hindu Yuva Vahini, shortly after he was first elected (then as the youngest MP) to the Lok Sabha, and the Vahini was soon implicated, as was Adityanath himself, in communal violence in Gorakhpur and neighbouring districts. He has been described as 'akin to a feudal lord who maintains his grip on his people and his writ runs over his territory through a mixture of religion, terror and personal loyalty' – in a poor, violent and crime-ridden part of the country (Katju 2017). A film clip of a meeting shows Adityanath sitting impassively on a platform from which a member of the Vahini urged the Hindu audience to dig up the graves of Muslim women and rape the corpses. He made the idea of the 'love jihad' – a supposed Islamist conspiracy to seduce Hindu women and to convert them to Islam – a rallying cry, and he exhorted Hindus to convert a hundred Muslim women to Hinduism for every one Hindu woman converted to Islam. In 2005 he had led a 'purification drive' to convert Christians to Hinduism, and he was reported as having said 'I will not stop until I turn the UP and India into a Hindu rashtra [Hindu state]'.

Adityanath became a passionate advocate of the *ghar wapsi* ('homecoming') campaign, driven by the VHP, that sought the conversion, or in its own terms, the 'reconversion' of Muslims and Christians to Hinduism, and that gained in strength following the BJP victory of 2014. The *shuddhi* (purification) movement had been started in the 1920s, and was advocated by the Hindu nationalist leaders Veer Savarkar and M. S. Golwalkar (Noorani 2015). But early in the twenty-first century it was taken up again in earnest by the Rashtrya Swayamsevak Sangh (RSS), the core organization of the Sangh Parivar – the family of organizations dedicated to Hindu nationalism – with the formation of a specialized outfit called the Dharm Jagram Manch (DJM). Donations were sought for funding conversions (more for Muslims than for Christians) and the DJM was reported to be receiving funding from the United States and Europe. The objective of the organization, according to the leader of the DJM, in a press report of December 2014, was to ensure that there would be no Muslims or Christians left in India by the end of 2021. He explained that this didn't mean that they would all be sent out of the country but rather that 'they have to understand that they were originally Hindus and, keeping this in mind, adhere to Hindu values and way of life'. In practice, this would mean that Christians and Muslims could not expect equal citizenship of India unless they became Hindu (Ramakrishnan 2015a).

Yogi Adityanath's elevation to the chief ministership of the most populous state marked a distinct shift in the stance of the BJP. Hitherto the BJP, in office at the centre, had tended towards moderation, downplaying key issues for Hindu nationalists in the interests of maintaining broad political support, and often provoking criticism from the RSS, and the ire of the VHP (see Muralidharan 2003; Venkatesan 2003). Now, it seemed, the gloves were off. Narendra Modi, both in his electoral campaign in 2014, and in the earlier part of his prime ministership, had always emphasized his commitment to *vikaas*, to development, rather than to the objectives of Hindu nationalism.

But now the objectives of *vikaas* and of the achievement of the Hindu rashtra – the Hindu state – were being brought together. *Time* magazine asked in an article whether Modi was 'really a reformer focused on generating the jobs the country needs, or is the language of development, propagated via an unremitting stream of slogans, speeches and tweets by the prime minister and his top officials, actually a cover for *Hindutva*, an ideology that sees India as a Hindu nation?' In fact, as Kanchan Chandran argued, citing the *Time* article, 'Modi has always been both a reformer and a Hindu nationalist, and this two-dimensional package is the essence of his appeal' (Chandra 2017).

God is Back is the title of a book by two writers for *The Economist* (Micklethwait and Wooldridge 2009) who document the resurgence of religion very widely across the contemporary world, and its implications. These include its impact in political life, and this resurgence has seen, early in the twenty-first century, the rise of political leaders in a number of countries who draw explicitly upon religion. An example from Europe is Viktor Orban, the prime minister of Hungary (in office 1998–2002 and then from 2010 onwards), who heads a political party, Fidesz, that proclaims four fundamental values: 'God, your homeland, your nation, freedom and family'. Orban became notorious in Western Europe for introducing constitutional changes in Hungary that restricted civil liberties and the freedom of speech, and weakened the judiciary, and for his proclamation of what he described as 'illiberal democracy'. Subsequently, following his opposition to the entry of refugees into his country in 2015, Orban became identified with the defence of a Europe supposed to be under siege by outsiders from different cultural and religious backgrounds. He himself began to speak of his regime as exemplifying 'Christian Democracy', and 'Christian values, or a particular interpretation of them, have become the centerpiece of Hungarian government messaging' (Walker 2019). This won the enthusiastic approbation of US President Donald Trump, who is himself – remarkably, perhaps, given his widely known moral transgressions – much loved by evangelical Christians in the United States (McCarthy 2019).

In 2018 Viktor Orban claimed a mandate 'to build a new era', defining an era as 'a special and characteristic cultural reality . . . a spiritual order, a kind of prevailing mood . . . determined by cultural trends, collective beliefs and social customs'. He aimed, he said, to embed the political system in the 'new era' – defined by Christian values (Hopkins 2019). These words might well apply to the political project of Narendra Modi and the Hindu nationalist organizations, effectively rejecting secular, liberal values and emphasizing the primacy of the community of Hindus. In this chapter we outline the history of Hindu nationalism, and the steady spread of what we refer to as 'banal *Hindutva*' – or everyday forms of Hindu nationalism – and its links with communal conflict (or what is more generally known as ethnic violence, here between religious communities). Such conflict is an instrument, as well as a reflection of the rise of Hindu nationalism. We return, finally, to an account of how the move towards the Hindu rashtra accelerated under the BJP government after 2014, and compare this specifically Indian experience with manifestations of authoritarian populism in other parts of the world (including Orban's Hungary).

6.2 The RSS, the BJP and the Struggle for *Hindutva*

Hindu nationalism began to develop alongside and even before 'secular' Indian nationalism. It has its origins in movements for religious revival and reform in the nineteenth century that responded to colonialism and to Christianity in a way that was both oppositional and emulative. They sought to create the community of Hindus without, initially, invoking hostility to those of other faiths – though such 'othering' followed soon after. John Zavos, in his study of this early history (2000), argues that in the late nineteenth century there came together with religion a recognition of the need for 'organization' as an essential facet of modernity – Indians had to be better organized if they were to contend with colonial power. This is still emphasized by the Rashtriya Swayamsevak Sangh (RSS), the core organization of Hindu nationalism, which states on its English language website that 'Strength . . . comes only through organization [and it] is therefore the duty of every Hindu to do his best to con-solidate the Hindu society'. An early manifestation of this impulse was in the formation of Hindu 'sabhas' – distinctly modern organizations of Hindus – in different parts of the country, and the establishment in 1915 of the All India Hindu Sabha as a representative body for them. It was this body that became active as the Hindu Mahasabha in the 1920s, when Vinayak Damodar Savarkar became one of its leaders.

It was Savarkar who formulated the idea of *Hindutva* in a book with this title, written in English and so clearly intended for a middle-class readership, first published in 1923. Both orthodox and reformist Brahmin intellectuals had by that time sought to find 'an internal principle of unity' in religion, but Savarkar tailored this 'to emphasise territorial origin and broad cultural commonalities' (Khilnani 1997: 159–60). He effectively translated upper caste ideology into a decidedly modern conception of ethnic nationalism. *Hindutva* is taken to mean 'Hindu-ness', but it is said, emphatically, not to be equated with Hinduism. It is an idea, rather, of a political community united by geo-graphical origin, racial connection and a shared culture based on Sanskritic languages and 'common laws and rites' (Khilnani 1997: 161). Savarkar writes:

> A Hindu then is he who feels attachment to the land . . . of his forefathers
> – as his Fatherland; who inherits the blood of the great race whose first
> and discernable source could be traced from the Himalayan altitudes . . .
> and who . . . has inherited and claims as his own the Hindu Sanskriti, the
> Hindu civilization (Savarkar 2003 [1923]: 100).

Hindutva is, as the BJP now argues on its website – though without referring explicitly to Savarkar – 'a nationalist and not a religious or theocratic concept', and it describes the idea as one of 'cultural nationalism'. Savarkar evidently intended to emphasize the unity of Hindus, irrespective of caste and other distinctions (which had cut across the endeavours of the early Hindu nationalists), while at the same explicitly 'othering' Muslims and Christians, who 'cannot be recognized as Hindus; as since their adoption of the new cult they had ceased to own Hindu civilization as a whole' (2003 [1923]: 100–1). Savarkar's primary concern may have been with the organization of Hindus, but hostility to Islam and to Christianity was the inevitable corollary. Hindu nationalists, including leaders of the BJP, though they have claimed to adhere to religious pluralism, have subsequently clearly expressed anti-Muslim or anti-Christian sentiments in other statements.

The Constitution of India defines the state as 'secular', but the conception of secularism adopted by the authors of the Constitution, as we explained in chapter 1, took it as meaning equality of treatment of different faiths by the state, rather than clear separation between the affairs of the state and religion. The Government of India, however, subsequently allowed both Muslims and Christians to follow the personal and family laws that are intrinsic to their religious traditions – as implied by the freedom of religion laid down in Articles 25–28 – but undertook reform of the civil code affecting Hindus, in line with liberal principles. This has exposed the state to vigorous charges from Hindu nationalists, of being only 'pseudo-secular'. Some, notably those associated with the publishing house Voice of India, who accuse even the RSS of being 'soft', contrast the 'intolerance' of the monotheistic religions with the 'tolerance' of Hinduism. They then find in this reason for wishing to suppress these other religions and to propagate what is in effect a theology of hatred – without perceiving in the least the bitter irony in this (Nanda 2009: 160–8).

Hindutva ideas have animated the Rashtriya Swayamsevak Sangh from its foundation by Dr Keshav Baliram Hedgewar in 1925. Since that time the *Sangh* has always sought to bring about a kind of a social revolution from below, not by taking over state power, but through the establishment of a highly disciplined organization, and the disciplining (through exercise) of the bodies of young men in the daily meetings of its local cells, or *shakhas* – of what has been called 'the brotherhood in saffron' – capable of spreading and inculcating into people the *Hindutva* idea of the nation. The organization depends upon the activities of full-time activists and propagandists – *pracharaks* – of whom prime minister Narendra Modi was once one. The RSS has recognized the importance of basic education – in remarkable contrast with the egregious failures of the Indian state in this regard. The Indian state, rather strangely by comparison with many others, has not sought to promote Indian nationalism through basic education nearly as much as it might have done, had education been made more of a priority (though as Bénéï has explained, there certainly is a lot of attention given to 'nation building' for those who do go to school; Bénéï 2001, 2008). The RSS, however, because it has played a significant part in the shaping of modern Hindi, has ensured that 'moralising within a (Hindu) revivalist world view became entrenched in school text-books' (Kumar 1993: 544). There are as many as 70,000 schools across the country that are under its management (Panikkar 2001), and ethnographic research by Peggy Froerer has shown how successful these can be in inculcating the ideas and values of *Hindutva* specifically in rural, *adivasi* areas, and in opposition to the work of Christian missions and their schools (Froerer 2007).

To further its aims, the RSS has also built up its 'family' of organizations, the *Sangh parivar*, within which the BJP is the formal party political member. The party has its origins in the Jana Sangh, established in 1951 by S. P. Mookerji, a former President of the Hindu Mahasabha, and which maintained both a close but never straightforward relationship with the RSS, and a significant though minor role in north Indian politics until it joined the ruling Janata coalition in government in 1977–80. Following the unravelling and defeat of that coalition, members of the Jana Sangh and of the RSS regrouped, in 1980, as the Bharatiya Janata Party. After winning only two seats in the Lok Sabha elections of 1984, the BJP made rapid electoral advances thereafter, and by the 1990s rivalled the Indian National Congress as the most significant national – rather than only regional – political party. As well as the BJP, the *Sangh parivar* includes most notably the Vishwa Hindu Parishad (VHP) – founded in 1964 specifically to confront the perceived threat from Christianity – and the Bajrang Dal, a youth movement set up by the VHP in 1984, and that has sometimes supplied its 'shock troops' for attacks on minorities. It includes as well organizations for students, for women, for education and social service and for cultural activities.

Since the late 1980s there is no doubt that there has been a significant shift in India's political culture, such that *Hindutva* has claimed the imaginations of an important share of both elites and the masses – except, so far at least, in the south Indian states of Kerala, Tamil Nadu and Andhra Pradesh (see chapter 1, table 1.5; and Palshikar 2015). For all the considerable strengths of the *Sangh parivar*, however, the success that it has had in bringing about this shift has been due largely to the failures of the Congress Party. In spite of its electoral strength in the early 1980s, the Congress lost direction, especially in the time of Rajiv Gandhi's prime ministership (1984–89), leaving a vacuum in Indian politics and creating a space for the rise of Hindu nationalist politics, articulated by the BJP but with the vigorous support of other members of the *parivar*. This culminated, at last, in 1998, in the electoral success of the BJP (Corbridge and Harriss 2000: ch. 5). A critical event in this history was the destruction of the old mosque, the Babri Masjid, at Ayodha in December 1992, subtly orchestrated by leaders of the BJP (as the official commission of enquiry, the Liberhan Committee, finally reported to parliament in 2009 – and see also Vachani 2017), which marked the high point of Hindu nationalist agitation, and tested the Indian polity as never before. As the anthropologist Thomas Blom Hansen wrote on the occasion of the 25th anniversary of the demolition of the mosque, the event itself, and the riots that followed, changed India:

> In the triumphalist narratives of the Rashtriya Swayamsevak Sangh (RSS) and Shiv Sena, December 6 was the beginning of a new era where a righteously angry Hindu majority began to shape public discourse and political life in the country, For everybody else, December 6 marks the beginning of an era of unbridled majoritarianism that has polarized and divided Indian society more deeply than ever (Hansen 2017).

But by this time, too, the weaknesses of the Congress Party organization and of the governments of India from the mid-1980s had led a good many senior ex-officials and servicemen, and members of the upper middle classes more generally, to look to the BJP as capable of supplying stronger, less corrupt government, that would enable India to attain the more significant place in the world to which many of them believed their country was entitled by virtue of its size and history. The message of *Hindutva*, mediated by the BJP, seemed to promise that India would take its 'rightful' place amongst the nations of the world only if Indians were truly 'themselves' – that is 'Hindu' – rather than trying to emulate the West (Hansen 1996a). The widespread euphoria in India over the testing of a nuclear bomb in 1998, shortly after the BJP took over leadership of the government of India for the first time, clearly reflected these sentiments.

In the 1996 general election the BJP had won most seats in an inconclusive election, in spite of securing a much smaller share of the vote than the Congress (see tables 1.3 and 1.4). Atal Behari Vajpayee, the leader of the BJP, was invited by the President to form a government, but this lasted only 13 days before being defeated in a vote of confidence. This experience led the party to recognize the compulsions of power, the need to build an electoral coalition with other parties, and that for this to be possible it had to be ready to soften its stance on some issues that are seen as central to the project of Hindu nationalism – the critical matters having to do with building a temple for Lord Ram on the site of the Babri Masjid at Ayodhya, with the civil code (those matters of personal law over which the *Sangh parivar* has claimed that the Hindu majority is disadvantaged by comparison with the religious minority communities), and with the question of Article 370 of the Constitution concerning the special status of Kashmir (opposed by Hindu nationalists, who accused it of encouraging separatist sentiments). Further elections in February 1998 finally brought the BJP into office, in a coalition government, but it was brought down by the defection of a coalition partner after only a little more than one year. At last, in September–October 1999, the party, at the head of a coalition (the National Democratic Alliance [NDA]) with 13 other partners, won a majority that enabled it to govern for a full term.

The BJP-led government, constrained as it was by the demands of coalition partners, largely disappointed the hopes and aspirations of the RSS and of the VHP for the advance of the *Hindutva* project, as we noted earlier (and see Jaffrelot 2010). But it presided over a period of increasingly successful economic growth, and in January 2004 the party seemed to be riding high. The BJP leader and prime minister, Vajpayee, confidently called an early general election for April–May 2004. The party set out to fight those elections on the strength of Mr Vajpayee's own credibility as a proven, respected prime minister, and on the platform of 'India Shining' – the idea of India as a now successful country taking its rightful place as one of the leaders amongst the nations of the world.

The hubris of Indian Shining was soon to be exposed. In the general election of 2004, the BJP lost to a Congress-led coalition that came to call itself the United Progressive Alliance (UPA), as a result not of any great shift in national politics but rather because of the outcomes of the different contests in the various major states. Still, the BJP's share of the vote declined again nationally (see tables 1.3 and 1.4), from the peak of more than 25 per cent of the electorate as a whole that it had achieved in 1998; and the party's vote share declined even further in the next general election of 2009, to less than 19 per cent. In these elections, to the surprise of many, the Congress succeeded in increasing its number of seats quite dramatically, even if not its share of the popular vote, and in securing a strong position for the United Progressive Alliance in the new parliament. The remarkable rise of the BJP appeared to have been checked.

But this did not mean that the rise of Hindu nationalism had been halted, given the many ways in which India has become, remarkably perhaps, 'more Hindu'. As one writer put it, in the title of a book, 'globalization is making India more Hindu' (Nanda 2009). Hindu religiosity has become more and more publicly apparent, through temple construction and renovation – some of it involving non-resident Indians, mostly from North America; through the renewal and the invention of ritual; and through the actions and the followings of new religious leaders or 'gurus'. Any semblance of separation between religion and the state has long gone, and there is now – Nanda suggests – a 'state-temple-corporate complex' that has rendered Hindu nationalism banal: 'The banal, everyday Hindu religiosity is simultaneously breeding a banal, everyday kind of Hindu nationalism' (Nanda 2009: 140). Veronique Bénéï, some years before Nanda, wrote of the 'banal nationalism . . . peculiarly tainted with religion' that she observed being inculcated in schools in Maharashtra (2001: 212). This is the kind of banal nationalism that, for instance, leads mostly young men to attack other young people who want to celebrate Valentine's Day – something that has taken off in India substantially because of the huge success of a leading manufacturer of greetings cards in selling Valentine cards – or to try to stop young middle-class women from behaving in ways that the young Hindu men consider 'un-Hindu'.

It was not only everyday Hindu nationalism that flourished in spite of the political defeats of the BJP. There is also often a violent edge to Hindu nationalism that shows no sign of decline. These trends go some way to accounting for the resurgence of the BJP in the general elections of 2014. Even as late as mid-2013, in spite of the evident failings of the UPA government in its second term, mired as it was in major corruption scandals that seemed to immobilize it, most commentators believed that the BJP was in almost as bad a shape as the Congress Party. At that time, the claim made by Sumantra Bose that 'Coalition governments in New Delhi are a certainty for the foreseeable future' (Bose 2013: 109) appeared unexceptional. How was it, then, that the BJP was able to secure an absolute majority in the Lok Sabha in 2014? It came about, very largely, because of the personality of the man chosen by the BJP in September 2013 as its candidate for the position of prime minister, Narendra Modi, and the remarkable election campaign that he fought. Modi did not need to rely much himself on Hindu nationalist rhetoric, given the extent of banal *Hindutva* – while his record as chief minister of Gujarat at a moment when the most devastating outbreak of communal violence in independent India took place in the state, in 2002, meant that his credentials, for ardent Hindu nationalists, were unquestionable.

On 27 February 2002, one of the carriages of a train carrying *kar sevaks* (volunteers) from Ayodhya was set on fire by a mob, reportedly of Muslims, in the railway station of the town of Godhra, killing 59 people. In the immediate aftermath there was an orgy of violence against Muslims across the northern and central parts of Gujarat (the geography of violence is significant, as we will explain) with the evident connivance and even encouragement of the forces of the state. The events were described as a pogrom. Muslim businesses as well as homes were quite systematically destroyed and reports showed that members of the middle and upper classes of Gujarati society, as well as lumpen elements, were involved in their looting. The attacks were not confined to the towns and cities and *adivasis* in particular joined in attacks in rural areas – reflecting in part the success of the educational work carried on among them by the RSS. Hindu spiritual leaders of Gujarat remained silent. Not only were politicians and the state involved in the perpetration of violence, but the government of Gujarat was quite blatantly partisan in its subsequent response, in the provision of relief to victims and in blocking efforts to secure justice for them (Chandhoke 2009a; Chandhoke et al. 2007; Yagnik and Sheth 2005: ch. 11).

It might have been thought that these horrific events, condemned by the BJP leaders at the centre, albeit with riders about the responsibility of Muslims themselves for what had happened, would have given rise to revulsion against the politicians who had been implicated in them and have reinforced the voice of the secular opponents of communalism. In the state elections that followed not long afterwards, however, in December 2002, the BJP – led by Narendra Modi, who conducted a vicious campaign, making many stridently anti-Muslim statements – swept to a third consecutive victory (then almost unprecedented in the see-saw world of Indian state politics). The National Executive of the party claimed that 'The people of Gujarat endorsed our commitment to cultural nationalism and voted us back for a third time in a row'. But what was so striking about the election results was that the BJP 'won 52 of the 65 violence-affected Assembly constituencies on the basis of a twelve percentage point swing . . . (while) . . . elsewhere in the State, where the impact of violence was muted or weak, the contest was more normal and the BJP suffered setbacks' (Editorial 2002). The constituencies in which the BJP was particularly successful were also those that had previously been held by Congress – so the victories seem clearly to have signalled 'that *Hindutva* mobilization through communal riots was successful' (Yagnik and Seth 2005: 285). Gujarat was described by the BJP as 'the laboratory for *Hindutva*', and as the verdict of the 2002 elections showed – repeated in subsequent elections – the state has become the bastion of Hindu nationalism. This record, and the success that Modi was able to claim for the Gujarat 'Model for Development', given the state's growth performance, were the platform for his successful general election campaign in 2013–14, when the BJP secured an absolute majority in the lower house of parliament.

6.3 Temples, Gods and Gurus: Banal Hinduism, Banal *Hindutva*

God is Back, the title of the book by Micklethwait and Wooldridge (2009) to which we referred earlier, was also the title of the cover feature of the Indian news magazine *Outlook* in its issue for 21 August 2000; and it was a striking finding of the State of the Nation Survey conducted by the Delhi-based Centre for Study of Developing Societies in 2007, that urban, educated Indians are more religious than their rural and illiterate counterparts (though one might question how well a survey can take account of different meanings associated with religion). The conviction of modernization theorists that economic development and industrialization must inevitably bring about secularization, both in the sense that individuals no longer experience the need for belief in the supernatural, and in that of the separation of state and religion – which becomes restricted to the private sphere – is clearly confounded by contemporary changes, in India as elsewhere in the world (Nanda 2009: ch. 5). Indeed, it is doubtful whether 'modern' societies have ever been as 'disenchanted' with religious experience as classical sociologists thought would be the case.

Research on the religious beliefs and practices of owners and managers of big companies in the south Indian city of Chennai provides some insights into the processes of modernization in Indian society. The anthropologist Milton Singer published in 1972 an influential book, entitled *When a Great Tradition Modernizes*, and its 'capstone' (as one reviewer put it) was a long essay about 'industrial leaders' based mainly on interviews conducted in Madras (as the city was then called) in 1964. Singer was especially interested in big business people because he thought that they were those who must be at the cutting edge of modernization, so that it would be through them that he could best study Indian modernity. For similar reasons, John Harriss chose to study people of the same social class but in the context of globalization, in a study that substantially replicated Singer's, carried out nearly four decades later (Harriss 2003a).

Singer found that, contrary to what he believed that Weber had argued in his comparative research on different religious traditions, there is in Hinduism a set of beliefs quite comparable with those that Weber (in *The Protestant Ethic and the Spirit of Capitalism*) had identified in Calvinism and thought conducive to the development of capitalism. The interpretations of the scriptural text the *Bhagavad Gita* that were current amongst business people in the 1960s – and are still – offer striking parallels with Calvinism (as well as tying in closely with a burgeoning self-improvement literature in contemporary India). There was, Singer argued, an 'industrial theodicy', representing the 'modernization' of Hinduism without secularization. For the industrial leaders of Madras:

> 'the essentials of Hinduism' consist more in a set of beliefs and a code of ethical conduct than in a set of ritual observances. In this sense, the effect of industry is to change the traditional conception of the essentials of Hinduism from an emphasis on the correct ritual observances and family disciplines to an emphasis on philosophical principles, devotional faith, and right conduct (Singer 1972: 342).

Harriss observed, however, in his later study of big business people in Chennai, that – though one or two amongst them expressed themselves as being uninterested in religion – most showed a great deal of interest in and involvement with temple-going and public worship, following 'god-men' and gurus, and in the miraculous and ecstatic religion, as well as in the philosophical principles of what is called (by some of them) 'the Vedic Heritage'. Several of the big business houses of the city supported the work of a particular religious teacher, or guru, Swami Dayananda Saraswathi (1930–2015), who operated both in the United States and in India, who taught in English in Chennai to packed middle-class audiences, who was active in the VHP, and was a guru to Narendra Modi. Modi tweeted after Saraswathi's death that his demise 'is a personal loss'. The foundation that was associated with him, funded by some of the business houses, produced a 'Vedic Heritage' teaching

kit directed at the education of middle-class children in India and in North
America (Fuller and Harriss 2005).

Others of the 'industrial leaders' of Chennai who were active followers of
more traditional religious teachers – as were some of their predecessors in the
1960s – spoke freely of their experiences of the miraculous. The dusty Chennai
suburb of Nanganallur, where some IT companies are located, had seen a
wave of construction of new temples – one of them the site of a massive idol
of Hanuman, the monkey god of the *Ramayana*, who had become is increasingly the object of middle-class devotion – and it was the home of a 'god-man'
followed by some of the IT entrepreneurs, and with whom, too, miracles were
associated. The notion of the clear separation of religion and business affairs,
which Singer referred to as 'compartmentalization' – an idea familiar to at
least one of the businessmen who had read Singer's work – was flatly rejected
by Chennai's contemporary industrial leaders.

Religious activities of these kinds, and the frank religiosity that was shown
by many big businessmen in Chennai, are shared very widely among members
of India's 'new middle class', and across the country as a whole – as they are
much more generally. Jean Comaroff presents evidence showing how, in recent
decades, in different parts of the world, the hegemony of rationalist ideology
has been disturbed (2008: 2). In India temple building and restoration, the
popularity of the invented tradition of what are actually new religious rituals,
and the large followings of gurus and religious teachers who appeal to middle-
class professionals, some of them by claiming that modern science has only
rediscovered ideas and principles that are to be found in ancient Sanskrit texts,
are widespread (as Meera Nanda's 2009 account shows). In Chennai, at least,
all of this may not be quite as new as the comparison of Harriss's account with
Singer's might suggest, for Singer's fieldwork notes (found in an archive in the
Regenstein Library of the University of Chicago) show that he too encountered
ideas and practices in 1964 not unlike those that were found commonly in 2000.
That he set these observations aside in his published work and rather emphasized the 'industrial theodicy' was probably a reflection, at least in part, of the
concern of the businessmen themselves in 1964 to project an image of being
'modern' citizens of the secular Nehruvian state. Their successors, however, no
longer felt any such inhibitions, and some of them quite clearly expressed the
idea, dear to the *Sangh parivar*, that in order to be strong, India must be 'Hindu'.

The regular appearance of political leaders and politicians and of senior
civil servants at temple functions contributes to the impression that the
state really is identified, in practice, with Hinduism. And in these days of
public–private partnership, it is wholly unsurprising that there should be
collaboration between the state and the corporate sector in the support of
religion – in 'the state-temple-corporate complex'. Some of the most senior
Indian businessmen appear alongside the politicians at temple functions.
Actions of this kind, and the way in which, as Bénéï has shown in an ethno-

graphic study, Hindu symbols and ideas are woven into the everyday routines of physical exercise and recitation in schools, immediately directed at building national consciousness, actually inculcate 'banal Hinduism' – that is, familiar, unquestioned, everyday religious practice. Bénéï found that teachers who were not at all sympathetic to militant Hindu nationalism saw nothing wrong 'with Hinduism being taught in school as part of "Hindu culture"', just as, these days, there is nothing at all questionable for most people about the association of politicians and of the state with religious observance. As Bénéï goes on to say 'many people – even those not belonging to the Hindu fold – conceive of Indian culture and the Indian nation as essentially Hindu, without this conception *necessarily* being accompanied by any communalist claim or politically militant Hindu identity. Such is the ambiguity of Hinduism as both culture *and* religion. It is on this very ambiguity that militant religious nationalists play' (2001: 212, emphasis in the original).

There is a certain ambiguity, too, in the teachings of some of the gurus to whom middle-class Indians are attracted. Swami Dayananda Saraswathi argued that Hinduism is not *a* religion, but simply 'religion', and that it encompasses diversity. It actually embraces all the ideas that are found in Islam or in Christianity in a way that is much more cogent than are these 'founder religions'. But at the same time Saraswathi wittily belittled these other religious traditions, asserting the greatness of Hinduism, and decrying religious conversions as a kind of violence. His arguments may not have been intended to justify religious violence in response, but they could be taken as having that implication. He ended one of his sermons with the words 'Strength is being what you are. You are a nobody if you don't know that. It is in this sense that Hindus must be strong'. Everyday religiosity, 'banal Hinduism', which has been increasing in contemporary India, can easily slip into acceptance of Hindu nationalist ideas. They too become familiar, accepted, everyday – 'banal *Hindutva*'. This is the way in which the 'saffronization' of state and society that Christophe Jaffrelot detected is taking place, whether the BJP is in power, or not; or as the political analyst Suhas Palshikar has put it, public opinion generally has been tilted towards *Hindutva*. The BJP has increasingly taken over the centre ground of Indian politics, while at the same time the centre ground has become increasingly majoritarian (Palshikar 2015).

6.4 Banal *Hindutva*, Communal Violence and the State

Michael Billig, who invented the idea of 'banal nationalism', associates it with 'the flag hanging unnoticed on a public building' (cited by Nanda 2009: 140). Hindu nationalist ideas have penetrated the public discourse in India in such a way that they too are almost unnoticed for much of the time. But flags are sometimes waved with passion, as Billig also says, and so too is *Hindutva* associated with popular passion, as was seen so strikingly in the destruction of the Babri Masjid in 1992 and in the many riots around the national *yatras* (processions across the country), carried on by BJP leaders, that preceded it. Though Hindu nationalism has become part of the everyday common-sense of many Indians, therefore, it is not always 'banal'. The state, as we have said, has become identified, increasingly, with Hinduism, and it plays a significant role in regard to the communal conflict – incidents of violence between people from different religious communities – that has become both reflection and driver of the rise of Hindu nationalism.

Steven Wilkinson observes that though there were serious communal riots in the 1960s and 1970s, there was no sense then that the integrity of the nation was under any threat from religious polarization and violence. This changed in the succeeding decades, substantially if not entirely because of Hindu nationalist agitation (Wilkinson 2005: 1–3), as was brought out in Asghar Ali Engineer's documentation and analysis of riots from the early 1980s (Engineer 1984). And Paul Brass concludes from his detailed studies of the city over many years that 'though many communal riots in Aligarh and elsewhere in India have involved persons and parties not part of the *Sangh parivar*, militant Hindus have played a central role in every large-scale riot in Aligarh at least since 1961, however electorally weak or strong they were' (2003a). Brass's analysis of the way in which religious violence is produced in that city, and elsewhere, shows the presence of 'a network of actors, groups and connections . . . whose effect is to keep a town or city in a permanent state of awareness of Hindu–Muslim relationships'. What he calls the 'institutionalized riot systems' that are created by these networks produce violence (there is an explicit imagery of theatre here; Brass 1997: 284).

It is hard to say, however, whether such systems exist generally, and other ethnographies suggest the likely importance of particular contingent and conjunctural factors. Philippa Williams, for example, was doing research in Varanasi (Benares) in North India, at the time of a terrorist attack in March 2006, when bombs were exploded at the Sankat Mocha temple, killing 21 people, and two more people were killed a little later in further blasts at a railway station. The city had not previously been immune from communal clashes and it was feared that tensions would erupt in violence again as a result of the bombs. That they did not has understandably quite complex and very particular causes, according to Williams' analysis (2007). She highlights the agency of particular individuals, and it appears from her account that the determination of the chief priest (Mahant) of the Sankat Mocha temple that radical Hindu politics must be kept out of the religious space of the temple, played an especially important part. The Mahant successfully foiled attempts by a BJP leader to exploit the attack for political ends.

Of course each individual case of the outbreak of ethnic violence has its own particular explanation. But Brass's argument, and even more that of

Wilkinson in his attempt to develop a general explanation for communal violence, emphasizes the over-arching importance of the response of the state. Brass says 'where the policy of a state government is decisively opposed to communal riots ... riots will be either prevented or contained' (2003b), while Wilkinson states, as forcefully, 'state-level patterns of law enforcement dominate local factors – state law enforcement can prevent violence even in so-called riot-prone towns and facilitate it even in towns with no previous history of riots' (2004: 17). There are many local reasons for the occurrence of inter-community tensions that can give rise to violence but whether they do or not depends heavily upon how governments act.

The question then arises of what factors account for differences in governments' responses. Wilkinson's answer, based on careful statistical and historical analysis of rioting in different Indian states and in several other countries, is that much depends on the extent and nature of electoral competition. His key finding is that politicians in highly fractionalized political systems have incentives to provide security to minorities 'in order to retain their electoral support today and the option of forming coalitions with minority supported parties tomorrow' (2004: 237). In these circumstances even anti-minority politicians may be constrained to prevent ethnic violence – as happened in some Indian states in 2002 after the Godhra incident. At that time BJP politicians in Gujarat, a state with a low level of party competition and one in which they did not have to depend on any support from the Muslim minority, accurately calculated that they could reap political dividends from the violence. Meanwhile other state governments, in more competitive electoral environments, or those in which the ruling party depended on Muslim support, prevented riots (Wilkinson 2004: 154–60). Political competition, then, forces compromises – of the kind that the BJP was constrained to make in order to win and to retain power in central government in 1998–2004. The culpability of militant Hindu nationalists, however, for many incidents of communal violence, in circumstances in which they are not subject to such political constraints, is quite plain.

Amrita Basu, in an analysis of the circumstances of the intermittent violence of Hindu nationalists against minorities, persuasively advances two theses. First, that Hindu nationalist anti-minority violence has been more likely when the BJP, with close ties with the RSS and VHP, has achieved power in one of India's states, and the national government has effectively condoned their actions. Second, that Hindu nationalist forces have been more militant where upper castes/classes are strong and fully support the BJP, and lower caste/class parties and movements weak. These factors came together in Gujarat in 2002 in a 'perfect storm' – an unprecedented convergence of forces – as Basu shows in detail (Basu 2015).

If Basu's argument is broadly correct, and Jaffrelot's parallel one about the moderating effect of the constraints of coalition politics on the BJP, or Wilkinson's on the way in which political competition can make for compromise, then we are led to ask what the consolidation of the majority of the BJP at the centre and in many of the states portends. Having reduced the hitherto major national party, the Congress, in the 2014 elections, to only 44 seats in the Lok Sabha (so that, not commanding 10 per cent of the seats in the house, it could not even be recognized as the official opposition party), and won an absolute majority; with its crushing victory in the crucial legislative assembly elections in UP in 2017; and by that time holding power in 13 of the 29 states, the BJP established itself as unquestionably the dominant national party. Suhas Palshikar confirmed this view, in an article entitled 'India's second dominant party system' (harking back to the way in which political scientists referred to the dominance of the Congress Party in the 1950s), writing:

> In 2014, Modi's handsome victory inaugurated a new framework of party competition. The BJP emerged as the dominant party not in mere numeric terms, but more substantively. It stretched to a large number of states, received support from a cross-section of society, placed the leadership factor at the centre of competitive politics and above all, set the tone for political debates (2017: 14).

This analysis was amply confirmed by the remarkable victory that the BJP won in the national elections of 2019. As we pointed out in chapter 1, the BJP won 50 per cent or more of the vote in twelve of the major states – and in sixteen of all twenty-nine states. Only in Tamil Nadu, Kerala and Andhra Pradesh in the south, and in Punjab in the northwest was the juggernaut of the *Hindutva* party halted. Data from the pre- and post-poll surveys conducted by Lokniti also showed that the party did indeed receive support from a broad cross-section of society, but from *Hindu* society. Among Hindus, nationally, the BJP won support from 44 per cent, and from more than this (52 per cent) among upper caste Hindus, but much less than this (34 per cent) among Hindu Dalits (though it won support from 44 per cent of 'Hindu' adivasis). At the same time, the Hindu–Muslim divide saw an unprecedented consolidation (Sardesai and Attri 2019). The central importance of the factor of Narendra Modi's leadership was shown up in the fact that almost one-third of those who voted for the BJP in the election said they would not have done so had Modi not been the prime ministerial candidate (Shastri 2019).

The question is: has this dominance, and the BJP's control over the state, been translated into the assertion of the *Hindutva* agenda? Has India become, indeed, the Hindu rashtra?

6.5 *Hindutva* Rising

To begin with, certainly, the new BJP government in 2014, its majority notwithstanding, seemed not to emphasize the *Hindutva* agenda (Palshikar 2015).

This was in line with Modi's campaign in the election, which had been focused on development. The prime minister himself assured religious minorities of protection, and he distanced himself from some of the more extreme statements made by BJP politicians. But the government effectively created a space, nonetheless, in which it became possible increasingly for Hindu majoritarian sentiments to be expressed – as in the rhetoric of 'love jihad' and in the campaigning over *ghar wapsi* (to 'reconvert' Muslims and Christians to Hinduism) that we described at the beginning of this chapter – and for there to be more or less open attacks on minorities. The language of BJP politicians, as well as of the leaders of the RSS and the VHP, became increasingly blatant in support of such actions (as Palshikar 2015 documents). By 2017, when the BJP successfully fought the legislative assembly elections in UP without appointing a single Muslim candidate – in a state in which Muslims make up 20 per cent of the population – there was no doubt that, as the senior journalist Siddharth Varadarajan put it, 'Muslims in UP and elsewhere in India are already marginalized economically and politically, and their apprehension is that things are going to get worse from here on' (in *The Wire*, 12 March 2017). Even before the UP elections, in a public forum in Kerala in January 2017, the civil society leader Harsh Mander commented on the lack of outrage in the country 'at the way Muslims have been made second class citizens over the last two years'.

A particular focus for the mobilization of Hindu majoritarian sentiment was over the issue of cow protection – the animal being sacred for Hindus. Cow protection has a long history, and it was central to the formation of Hindu nationalism even in the late nineteenth century (Zavos 2000: 81–7). In the 1920s Gandhi tried to reason with Hindu nationalists that, as a Hindu himself, he too felt strongly about the protection of cows, but that this principle should not be served by attacking Muslims. The Constitution of India, at Article 48, among the (non-justiciable) Directive Principles, committed the state only to 'take steps' towards prohibiting the slaughter of cattle – a response to the Hindu sentiment that predominated in the Constituent Assembly. Article 21, however, among the Fundamental Rights, that are justiciable, and which guarantees 'personal liberty', has been interpreted as embracing the right to privacy, and thus the right of the individual to eat what he or she chooses. And in practice, though it has been regulated, the slaughter of cattle has always been permitted in India. But state governments led by the BJP in Maharashtra and Haryana in 2014–15 passed laws banning cow slaughter, and in April 2017 the chief of the RSS, Mohan Bhagwat, called for a national ban on cow slaughter – though he did admit that it would take time to implement such legislation, given the diversity within the country (reported in *Indian Express*, 10 April 2017).

These official moves and pronouncements both encouraged and responded to the mobilization of cow protection vigilantism. In a particularly notorious incident, on 28 September 2015, a Muslim, Mohammed Akhlaq, was lynched in the village of Bisara in the Dadri region of Western Uttar Pradesh, following the broadcasting of messages by a local temple claiming that he and his family had engaged in cow slaughter, and were storing and consuming beef. Meat was found in Akhlaq's refrigerator – which later tests showed, however, to be mutton. But by that time Akhlaq was dead, and his name was entering the vocabulary of north India – in the verbal form, 'to be akhlaqed'. A Union Minister said that the incident was an accident; both a Member of Parliament from the BJP and a leader of the VHP said that all those who 'indulged' in cow slaughter would meet with Akhlaq's fate. The prime minister took public notice of the event only on 8 October. Even then he did not openly condemn the killing, but said only that Hindus and Muslims should not be fighting each other but getting together to fight poverty (see Ramakrishnan 2015b). Subsequently, some of those responsible for Akhlaq's murder, far from being punished, were actually rewarded by being given jobs, following the intervention of the local BJP MLA (The Wire Staff 2017).

The murder of Akhlaq was not the only case involving accusations of cow slaughter. 'Across India', it was reported in the British press, 'there have been increasing reports of violence involving *gau raksha* gangs – whose members (*gau rakshaks*) number in thousands – that patrol highways and country roads at night, hunting for cattle being smuggled to Bangladesh, or the few Indian states where slaughtering the animals is allowed' (Safi 2016). In 2015, officials in Uttar Pradesh reported around 100 major and minor cases of assault in which the accusation of cow slaughter was said to have been the cause (Ramakrishnan 2015b). In August 2016, an attack on another Muslim family in a village in Haryana, involving murder and rape, was carried out by cow protection volunteers. The incident was trivialized by the BJP chief minister. Along the highway in the state, Muslim stallholders were subjected to inspections – by uniformed police rather than by *gau rakshaks* – to check whether the meat they were selling was cow or buffalo, even though the Haryana Cow Protection Department had no laboratory facilities for testing the meat. Stallholders chose to close down, rather than run the risk of being 'aklaqed' (personal communication from Harsh Mander). It has not been only Muslims who have been subjected to violence. In July 2016, four Dalit boys in the village of Una in Gujarat were stripped and thrashed by *gau rakshaks*, though they had only been skinning a dead cow. This last incident, in the prime minister's state, led to widespread condemnation, the development of a protest movement amongst Dalits, and concerns in the BJP about the upsetting of its stratagems for winning Dalit support (see reports in *Frontline*, 19 August and 2 September 2016).

In April 2017, a Muslim dairy farmer died following an attack by *gau rakshaks* in Rajasthan (*Indian Express*, 5 April 2017). The event was initially denied by BJP politicians, though it led the RSS chief, even as he called for a national ban on cow slaughter, to condemn violence. But the significance of the issue of cow slaughter for the advance of *Hindutva* is plain. The events surrounding *gau raksha* illustrate, too, 'a pattern in which the structured *Hindutva* right – the RSS and the BJP – interfaces with loose society-based outfits' – in this case an organization such as the Bhartiya Gau Raksha Dal (website: www.bgrd. in) (Venu 2017) – who have become as it were, the stormtroopers of Hindu nationalism. It was unsurprising that amongst the first actions of the new government of Yogi Adityanath in UP was the closing down of so-called illegal slaughterhouses – mainly public municipal slaughterhouses that had been allowed to sink into poor condition – to the detriment of the livelihoods of many, and not only Muslims (Ramdas 2017).

The actions of BJP-run states in regard to cow protection, and *gau raksha* vigilantism – more or less sanctioned by the pronouncements of political and religious leaders – were particularly dramatic ways in which the *Hindutva* agenda was advanced, at the expense of liberal freedoms that are laid down in the Constitution of India. And hate speech became more common. Rewards were offered, for instance, at different times for the beheading of the communist chief minister of Kerala, and of Mamata Banerjee of the Trinamul Congress, chief minister of West Bengal. A statement such as that by a BJP MLA from UP – to the applause of his audience – that 'I promise I will break the hands and legs of any person who doesn't consider the cow to be mother, or kills a cow, is unwilling to say 'Vande Mataram' or isn't proud to utter nationalistic slogans', became almost commonplace (reported in *Times of India*, 27 March 2017). The freedom of religion is certainly at risk.

But cow protection activism was not the only way in which constitutional liberties were attacked in the name of 'the nation', as defined by majoritarian Hindu nationalists. By 2017 the accusation of 'anti-national' behaviour was used to justify attacks on the freedoms of expression and of association, focusing particularly though not exclusively on Jawaharlal Nehru University (JNU) in Delhi – which has the reputation of being both one of India's best universities and a bastion of liberal and left thinking. Early in 2016, the President of the Students' Union at JNU was arrested on the charge of sedition – for having uttered 'anti-national' slogans – and subsequently beaten up as he was being taken to court. The row began with a meeting organized by students of which the main purpose was to articulate the grievances of Kashmiris, and which was opposed by students from the Akhil Bharatiya Vidyarthi Parishad (ABVP), the student organization affiliated with the RSS (Internet Desk 2016). A year later, ABVP supporters forcibly prevented – as 'anti-national' again – the holding of a conference at Ramjas College in Delhi, to which speakers connected with the JNU events had been invited, amidst a lot of violence (there is a chilling interview with an ABVP supporter, who was involved. See Lather 2017).

The remarkable victory of the BJP in the Uttar Pradesh legislative assembly election early in 2017, and the elevation of Yogi Adityanath – with which we began this chapter – marked the ascendance of majoritarian Hindu nationalism over secular, plural, liberal conceptions of Indian nationhood, certainly in the Hindi heartland of north and central India. The hopes that liberals may have had about the resilience of their values were crushed in the general election in 2019 when Sadvi (an honorific denoting a religious ascetic) Pragya Singh Thakur, was selected by the BJP in Bhopal to fight against the former Congress chief minister of Madhya Pradesh, Digvijay Singh. This was a controversial selection because Thakur was still under charge in a case of terrorism, that of the bomb blast near a mosque in Malegaon, Maharashtra, in September 2008, when six people were killed and many others injured. Thakur was named as one of the 'principal conspirators' behind an action that was intended to harm Muslims. Her selection as a parliamentary candidate by the BJP was the first time that a mainstream political party had ever fielded a candidate implicated in a terror case and it is easy to imagine the abuse that would have been piled upon it had the opposition Congress selected such a candidate. Then Thakur compounded controversy by making a statement in which she described Nathuram Godse, the man who killed Mahatma Gandhi, as a 'patriot'. In the uproar that followed, Narendra Modi said he could never forgive her for this remark. The BJP issued a show cause notice (a reprimand). But Thakur remained unscathed and went on to win her election with a substantial majority (and later, in November 2019, to repeat her description of Godse).

It had become increasingly plain, well before the 2019 election, that Hindu nationalism was pitted as much against those described as India's secular, liberal or left elites – of whom Digvijay Singh can well be seen as a representative – as against minorities. Ram Madhav, a general secretary of the BJP claimed, 'The mob, humble people of the country are behind Modi . . . they are enjoying it' (cited by Varshney 2017). Hindu nationalism is both a response to and a protest against liberal elites, and it has little time for the liberal freedoms of religion, expression and association. The Hindu rashtra is coming to be. A constitutional republic had effectively become a majoritarian state by mid-2019. Many members of the minority communities know this because of the environment in which they live, in fear of being subject to violence. Following the 2019 general election there were a number of incidents in which members of minority communities were forced to repeat the Hindu chant 'Jai Shri Ram'. A video that went viral on social media showed a 24-year-old Muslim, Tabrez Ansari, tied to a pole, blood and tears streaming down his face, pleading for his life and being made repeatedly by his attackers to utter the chant. He was subsequently handed over to the police and locked up. He died four days later from his injuries (*BBC World News*, 16 July 2019). Prime minister Modi's response to the death of Tabrez Ansari, speaking in the Lok Sabha, was to say that the incident was 'sad', but that the state of Jharkhand should not be blamed for it – which was hardly the point.

Incidents of this kind led a group of forty-nine eminent Indians – scholars, writers, film-makers, actors – to write a letter (on 23 July 2019) to Narendra Modi, as prime minister, calling upon him to take action over the lynching of Muslims, Dalits and other minorities: 'Regrettably, "Jai Shri Ram" has become a provocative war cry today … many lynchings take place in its name'. And, they said, 'You have criticized such lynchings in Parliament Mr Prime Minister, but that is not enough! What action has actually been taken against the perpetrators?' (quotes from the letter, published by NDTV, 24 July 2019). The government's response was to appoint Amit Shah, Modi's principal lieutenant, and by then Home Minister of India, to head a Group of Ministers, first appointed to address the problem of mob violence a year earlier, but which had signally failed to take action.

Shortly afterwards, the government announced that there was a serious threat of terrorist violence in Kashmir, and tourists, Indian and international, as well as Hindu pilgrims on their way to an important holy site, the cave at Amarnath, were required to leave the state while the security forces were reinforced. This was followed, on 5 August 2019, by the dramatic announcement in parliament, by Amit Shah, that the government had abrogated both Article 370 of the Constitution of India, which had given the state of Jammu and Kashmir – the only one with a Muslim majority – a special status, and Article 35A, which had provided special rights and privileges to 'permanent residents' of the state, including the restriction of the right to acquisition of property in the state to them. Shah also announced that the state was to be bifurcated into two Union Territories, Jammu and Kashmir, with its own legislature – though as a Union Territory, subject to greater control by the central government – and Ladakh (without a legislature and so under the direct rule of the central government). These moves were accompanied by the clamping down on civil liberties in the state, the detention of political leaders and of many others, and the closing of access to the state for opposition politicians as well as to Delhi-based foreign journalists – restrictions that were still in place for months after the abrogation of the articles of the Constitution. Still, the change in the status of Jammu and Kashmir was supported by most of the opposition parties, and greeted with wild rejoicing by many Indians, though it was highly controversial and its legality was questionable. It represented, in the way it was done, a serious challenge to the constitutional principles of federalism in India (Tillin 2019; and see chapter 7). It was defended by Amit Shah, and later by Modi, as being necessary for the development of the state and for the well-being of Kashmiris – who were said now to enjoy the same rights as all other Indians – as well as being essential for the defeat of terrorism. But whatever else the move was intended to achieve, it marked the realization of one of the critical objectives of Hindu nationalists, who had always opposed the implicit separatism in the special status accorded to Kashmir. It was a marker of the authority of the Modi government and of the establishment of the Hindu rashtra (Taylor 2019).

The abrogation of Article 370 was followed in November 2019 by the realization of another of the long-standing core objectives of Hindu nationalists. On 9 November the eagerly awaited judgment of the Supreme Court concerning the legal status of the land that had been occupied by the Babri Masjid in Ayodhya, and the construction of a Hindu temple on the site, was delivered. The Court's decision, applauded by many Hindus, was that the land should be handed over to a trust to build the temple, even while it found the destruction of the mosque to have been illegal. The verdict was, inevitably, very controversial, seeming as it did to reward those who had broken the law – but the long-standing ambition of Hindu nationalists to build a temple on the site sacred to them as the birthplace of Lord Ram was close to being achieved.

Further, by late 2019 it seemed likely that the Hindu rashtra would become inscribed within the very concept of Indian citizenship. This was not an entirely new development – the secular status of Indian citizenship has long been contested by sections of the Hindu right. While the Indian Constitution and the Citizenship Act of 1955 established that Indian citizenship would be based on place of birth, this had been challenged by social and political responses to migration from other South Asian countries. In the east and northeast, there have been demands to exclude from citizenship the children of illegal migrants from Bangladesh, even if born in India, while in the west, there have been agitations to give special access to citizenship to migrants of certain faiths (particularly Hindus and Sikhs) born in Pakistan (Jayal 2014). Already in 2004, amendments to the Citizenship Act introduced a religion-based exception to the principle of citizenship by birth, and in 2016, the BJP Government appeared to endorse a reformulation of the principles of citizenship by introducing the Citizenship Amendment Bill (CAB). The CAB would render individuals from specific minority religious communities in Afghanistan, Bangladesh and Pakistan – including Hindus, Sikhs, Buddhists, Parsis and Christians, but not minority Muslim communities such as Ahmadis or Sufis – to be eligible for Indian citizenship if they are facing persecution. To all appearances, this would be in violation of Article 14 of the Constitution, which grants all persons – irrespective of citizenship – equality before the law. It would, effectively, deny Muslim non-citizens from neighbouring countries equal rights to protection from persecution (Gauba and Singh 2017). The Bill would push further open the door to a profound shift in India's conception of citizenship: from one based on place of birth to one derived from religious and ethnic identity (Jayal 2019).

Despite encountering significant opposition to the CAB since introducing it in 2016, the BJP Government persisted in its efforts to pass it into legislation in the years that followed. This determination was partly due to the politics emerging from the unexpected outcome of the National Register of Citizens (NRC) in Assam, where the immigration of people from Bangladesh has long been a problem. A National Register of Citizens was first completed in Assam in 1951, but it then remained dormant until it was revived in 2005, and its renewal was ordered by the Supreme Court in 2013. The NRC is intended to determine the citizenship status of residents of the state of Assam, in order to fulfil the requirements of the Assam Accord of 1985 – which had mandated that those who migrated to Assam after 24 March 1971 be regarded as illegal immigrants. The NRC required documentary evidence of having been Indian, or of one's ancestors having lived in India prior to 1971, in order to be eligible for citizenship – a difficult process in India, where many lack access to such documentation. While some Hindu nationalists had publicly supported the NRC, with the view that it would lead to the deportation of illegal Muslim immigrants from Bangladesh (described at one point by Amit Shah as 'termites'), the Register ultimately found many Hindus and members of tribal communities among the 2 million residents of Assam declared ineligible for citizenship, and under threat of being placed in detention centres. In response, BJP politicians in Assam were forced to assuage fears that Hindus would be deported or rendered stateless as a consequence of the NRC's findings, arguing that the CAB would allow Hindus without the relevant documentation to apply for their citizenship – so adding a strong and urgent impetus to the CAB's legislation (Jayal 2019). The politics driving the CAB could not be clearer: an intention to bolster the state's capacity to discriminate in matters of citizenship on the basis of religious identity, thereby entrenching the notion of India as a Hindu, rather than secular, nation. The threat that the NRC, with its associated detention centres, would be extended nationwide (*India Today*, 2019) seemed to show that the citizenship of all Muslims might be called into question.

6.6 Authoritarian Populism and the Indian Case

Ram Madhav's remark, referring to the 'humble people of the country', implicitly pits them against 'elites' – a classically populist line of argument, according to which politics is a struggle between the 'people' and, on the other side, unfairly advantaged and probably corrupt 'others', who may also be defined as racially 'other'. There are both politically left and right variants of populism. In India, Mrs Indira Gandhi, as prime minister, justified the suspension of India's democracy through her declaration of Emergency Rule in 1975 with the argument that she was taking control in the face of opposition from a corrupt elite, in order to deliver a broadly socialist agenda for the benefit of the masses. In 2014, Narendra Modi campaigned in India's general election on a platform that included the claim that he was an outsider to the corrupt, Congress-dominated political elite, and that he would deliver the people from it. Later, in office, he argued that his action in November 2016 in ordering the withdrawal of all Rs 500 and Rs 1000 notes from circulation – what was called demonetization, or *notebandi* (see chapter 2) – was directed at undoing a corrupt elite, for the benefit of the people. This line of moral claims-making clearly convinced many of 'the people', even those who suffered considerably from demonetization. At the same time, he showed himself increasingly to be ready to use his electoral majority, implicitly if not explicitly, to condone attacks on minorities, as we have explained above, and to justify attacks on the courts and on the independence of the press (see Varshney 2017). Modi seemed to represent one instance of a much wider trend towards authoritarian populism (originally conceptualized by Stuart Hall 1985), generally tied to a nationalist narrative.

The context for this, in India as elsewhere, is a world in which the modern promise of progress has been disappointed for many people. The bottom 40 per cent of the population of the United States, for example, has seen no improvement in living standards for forty years. Very many Indians face limited prospects for much improvement in their lives, even while they are probably increasingly aware of the wealth of some others, not least through images that they see on their mobile phones (see chapter 3). Americans and Indians alike, in common with people elsewhere in the world, experience precariousness and a lack of agency – and feel resentments, which may be directed against elites or against 'others'. Political life is increasingly taken over by feeling in place of reasoned debate (Davies 2018). Then appeals to nationalism may become very persuasive. Political leaders who offer a simple narrative – reflected in such slogans as 'Take back control' in the United Kingdom, with an implicit appeal to an idea of a former national greatness, or 'Make America Great Again!' – win wide support. Such politicians, who present themselves as 'strong men' – or 'authoritarian truth tellers', as Comaroff describes them (2008: 2) – have proven to have electoral appeal. Examples include Shinzo Abe in Japan, Recep Erdoğan in Turkey, Donald Trump in the United States, Vladimir Putin in Russia, and Viktor Orban in Hungary – and Modi in India (who even went so far as to vaunt his chest measurements whilst campaigning in the 2014 election). Such leaders, who are more or less charismatic, and who encourage personality cults around themselves, are common, even if not essential features of authoritarian populism. As Ian Scoones and his fellow authors have put it:

> [Authoritarian populism] justifies interventions in the name of 'taking back control' in favour of 'the people', returning the nation to 'greatness' or 'health' after real or imagined degeneration attributed to 'others' [old elites, whether they are 'insiders' or 'outsiders'] . . . [and it] . . . frequently circumvents, eviscerates or captures democratic institutions, even as it uses them to legitimate its dominance, centralise power and crush or severely limit dissent (Scoones et al. 2018: 3).

In the Indian case, appeals to sectarian religious forces, identified with 'the nation' (which is held to be Hindu), play a further significant, and very dangerous part in the mix.

Modi's representation of himself as the strongman, capable of protecting Indians, played very well in the 2019 election, and fairly certainly accounted for his crushing majority. His government did not appear to be in a strong position at all at the beginning of the year, having lost control of three important state governments – those of Rajasthan, Madhya Pradesh and Chhattisgarh – late in 2018, and confronting criticism for its failure to deliver on its promises in regard to economic growth, employment and agriculture. Shrewd observers of Indian politics reckoned that, though the BJP would probably win more seats than any other party, there was a strong likelihood that the coming election would result in a hung parliament. But then, in February, an attack by a suicide bomber on a convoy of vehicles carrying security personnel at Pulwama in Jammu and Kashmir, resulting in the deaths of forty men, blamed on Pakistan, made it possible for Modi to play the part of the strong defender of the nation. A retaliatory raid into Pakistan, though it may actually have been botched, won an enthusiastic reception in India. Matters of security and national pride then overwhelmed concerns that voters may have had about agrarian distress or the employment crisis. It was Modi's 'strength' that won voters' support, not the performance or the platform of the BJP government (see Jenkins 2019 for an assessment of the 2019 elections).

6.7 Conclusion

We have explained the long history of Hindu nationalism, and the rise of its party political wing to a position of dominance in Indian politics. We cannot predict the future, and we acknowledge that it is perfectly possible that the BJP will lose its majority in the future. 'Anti-incumbency' remains a significant factor in Indian elections, even if there are now several states in which one party has remained in office over several elections (the BJP, for example, in Gujarat, Madhya Pradesh and Chhattisgarh, or the Biju Janata Dal in Odisha). The BJP has yet to win strong backing in most of the south of the country, and both nationally and even in a state such as Uttar Pradesh in 2017, it is far from winning a majority of the popular vote (in UP in 2017 the party secured 75 per cent of the seats on the strength of only 40 per cent of the vote). But what we have shown is that Hindu nationalist ideas have by now become commonplace – what we refer to as 'banal *Hindutva*' is firmly part of the everyday common-sense of Indian politics. The BJP may lose elections in future but the party – with its partners of the *Sangh parivar* – has very successfully brought about the conflation of nationalism and *Hindutva* (so that now to be 'anti-BJP' is to run the risk of being thought to be 'anti-national': Palshikar 2017). Alternative ideas of the nation and secular liberalism are definitely in retreat, before the advance of the specifically Indian form of authoritarian populism. At the same time, the BJP, thanks largely to Modi's inspiration, has very effectively projected the idea of a 'new India' that is a land of hope and opportunity, rather than one in which the life chances of most people depend upon welfare provided by the state. The combination of these sets of ideas is very powerful, to the point of being hegemonic, and it underpins the Hindu rashtra.

7

Is India's Democracy at Risk?

7.1 Introduction

When enacted in 1950, the Constitution of India declared the new nation as a sovereign, democratic republic. Building on Western democratic traditions, the Constitution specified the structures, procedures and duties of government, including the separation of powers between the different branches of government – the legislature, executive and judiciary. It defined the 'fundamental rights' of all citizens, including personal liberty, equality before the law, freedoms of speech and association, and freedom of religion; and it provided protection for the rights of minorities. Since its independence, India has been largely successful in upholding the promise of democracy contained within the Constitution – in contrast to many other countries – hosting regular, relatively free and fair elections. Since 1990, governments have introduced reforms to make Indian democracy more participatory and transparent, notably through the 73rd Amendment to the Constitution, passed in 1992, which decentralized government and provided mechanisms for greater local-level representation and accountability. At the same time, marginalized communities' struggles for recognition have ensured a greater diversity of voices are now heard within the public sphere (e.g. Gorringe 2016b, 2017).

Yet trends over the last decade suggest India may be witnessing a reversal in its democratic status. This has been especially evident since the election and growing power of the Modi government in 2014, which has shown only wavering commitment to democratic norms. Autocratic styles of governance, enhanced efforts to silence critical voices in the media and civil society, and the arbitrary detention of political opponents have raised concerns that India's democracy is at risk. This has been reflected in the reports of several independent international monitors. Among them was the 2019 Varieties of Democracy (V-Dem) Report, which aggregates the assessments of expert observers of countries' performances on a wide variety of democratic indicators (V-Dem 2019). The V-Dem Report saw India fall on most democratic indicators between 2008 and 2018, when it was ranked 85th out of 179 countries as a liberal democracy, and in 88th place as an electoral democracy. India showed a precipitous decline on indicators for the deliberative aspect of democracy, with clear signs of a decrease in reasoned, public justification for political decisions. For these reasons, the Report placed India on red alert as one of twenty-four countries in the world passing through a wave of 'autocratization'.

To evaluate the state of democracy in India, we make a distinction between formal and substantive democracy. We understand formal democracy in terms of the observance of the relevant procedures required to ensure all citizens have a voice and are capable of holding governments to account, including the conduct of regular, fair elections, universal suffrage and legal protections for free expression and association. Substantive democracy we define in terms of broad-based participation, inclusive social policy, and a positive feeling of involvement in politics among the masses. Historically, India has been relatively successful as a formal democracy yet has had more limited success as a substantive democracy. We contend that substantive democratization is particularly at risk in India today.

7.2 India as a Formal Democracy

It is commonly held that for a country to negotiate a transition to democracy, specific conditions must exist (Lipset 1994: 6; see also Linz and Stepan 1996; Przeworski et al. 1996). Democracy requires a culture of equality, high levels of public education, strong well-organized political parties, and a vibrant civil society. Linz and Stepan (1996) add to this list of prerequisites a need for a strong bureaucracy, a political society that is independent of dominant groups, and an 'institutionalized economic society': norms, institutions and regulations that mediate between the state and market.

Political scientists also argue that democracy tends only to thrive in countries that are capitalist, wealthy and growing economically (Lipset 1994; Przeworski et al. 1996). For example, Przeworski et al. (1996: 50) draw on comparative survey data to suggest that a country must maintain an annual economic growth rate of at least 5 per cent in order to consolidate itself as a democracy. A robust capitalist economy discourages distributional conflict. It also reduces the importance of the state as an economic resource and therefore discourages power holders from trying to monopolize government positions. In addition, a sound economy decreases the possibility that those in power will illegally retain office when voted out by an electorate. Capitalist growth may lead to the emergence of an organized working class as well as a middle class, which can demand an expansion of rights and democratic freedoms and organize to hold elites to account (Rueschemeyer et al. 1992; Lipset 1994: 3).

In 1947, India lacked most of the presumed prerequisites for democratic transition and consolidation: it was a poor, mainly agricultural country. As Barrington Moore (1966) observed, the bourgeoisie – historically the drivers of democratization – were weak and fragmented, while landlords, who had anti-democratic interests in retaining access to unfree labour, remained economically and politically influential. The economic growth rate was well below 5 per cent throughout the 1950s and 1960s. There was only a very limited organized working class – the class that Rueschemeyer et al. (1992) regard as essential to the consolidation of democracy. In the social and political realm, India did not possess the culture of equality and inclusive civil society held to be necessary for democracy. The colonial power had made no effort to educate the mass of the population in India, and colonialists systematically reinforced caste and class inequalities (Dirks 2001).

But India possessed some features that would facilitate democratic deepening. The nationalist movement in India had fostered some sense of 'unity in diversity' and a commitment to adult franchise (Sarkar 2001). The role of the Indian National Congress in the anti-colonial struggle in India bestowed upon the Congress Party popularity and legitimacy. Adeney and Wyatt (2004) argue that the existence of a political party enjoying widespread popular support largely explains the different political trajectories of India and Pakistan. The Muslim League, which was the dominant political party in Pakistan in 1947, was not as integrated into wider society as was the Congress Party. Moreover, the Congress Party was fairly socially heterogeneous in terms of region, language and caste, as compared to Pakistan, where there was tension between a Punjabi-dominated army and administration, on the one hand, and a majority population of Bengalis, on the other. Good leadership is also often identified as a major precondition for democratic consolidation (Linz and Stepan 1996). Nehru was revered in many circles, and he believed that democracy was the only viable political system.

The British also helped in some ways to prepare the ground for democratic consolidation. While neglecting to prepare the mass of the population for democracy, the British bequeathed a system of representative government on India that emphasized legal equality, civil rights and a judiciary independent of the executive (see Washbrook 1988; Sarkar 1996). Washbrook (1997: 37–9) argues that the British also established a regime of colonial governance that served as a foundation for the strengthening of formal democracy. The British placed power in the hands of a small coterie of rich leaders at the centre while buying off local bigwigs. In this system, elected 'native' boards, comprised mainly of powerful sections of society, were responsible for multiple aspects of governance. Local elites, notably rich peasants in the countryside, became key intermediaries in patronage networks extending down to the local level.

This patronage system assumed a new form under the Congress Party, which ruled India unchallenged from independence to 1967. During the 1950s and 1960s, members of the dominant castes at the local level, usually upper or middle castes, acted as brokers or bosses for the Congress Party. They transferred money up through the organization to politicians and cultivated clients at the village level through the offer of posts, contracts and access to public resources (Bailey 1957; 1963; Brass 1965; see Corbridge and Harriss 2000: 49ff.). This patronage system effectively suppressed popular dissent. Relatively untroubled by threats to its power, the Congress was able to concentrate on consolidating formal democracy.

Linz and Stepan (1996) emphasize the deleterious effects on democratic consolidation associated with elite dominance of political institutions. In India's case, however, a fairly benign and committed leadership used an elite-led patronage system to strengthen democratic institutions. Among Nehru's key achievements in the arena of democracy were his ability to see through the enactment of the Constitution, establish a civil service on the foundations of the British model (Potter 1986), and ensure that elections were held regularly and to a large extent fairly during his term in office. Shani (2018) has shown what a remarkable achievement the organization of the first national elections under a universal franchise, in 1952, was, and how much it contributed to the establishment of a sense of democratic citizenship.

The success of India's formal democracy since independence is reflected in the consolidation of the country's principal democratic institutions. India's new Indian Administrative Service (IAS), which was constructed along British lines, contributed to effective government and political stability during much of the post-colonial period (Potter 1986). India's Supreme Court also played a constructive role. It guaranteed people's right to basic needs, encouraged public interest litigation, and assisted victims of state lawlessness (Rudolph and Rudolph 2001; Mooij 2014). It remains an active institution in advancing both the fundamental rights and directive principles embedded in the Constitution, as evidenced, for example, in its role in establishing India's new rights agenda, discussed in chapter 8. It must be acknowledged, however, that the Supreme Court has sometimes assumed responsibility for matters outside its remit, such as the setting of school fees, and there is rightly concern over such abrogation of power (Mehta 2007). But this should not detract from the part that the Supreme Court has played in democratic consolidation. The Election Commission in India has been another guarantor of India's democratic strength, especially in the 1990s, when election commissioner T. N. Seshan significantly tightened oversight of elections.

Clouding this picture of democratic institutional strength is the problem of intra-party democracy. Political dynasties have become prevalent within major parties (Chandra 2016), and the procedures through which individuals are promoted within parties, appointed to vacant seats, and chosen as candidates for elections are mired in corruption, secrecy and cronyism (see Sridharan 1999). Parties are also increasingly opting to field candidates with criminal records, both because they may bring in substantial funds and because of the belief that the public associates criminality with a determination to overcome obstacles to achieve results (Vaishnav 2017). The dominance of entrenched interests prevents newly mobilized groups and dissenting voices from acquiring power within parties. Notwithstanding these pressing issues, India's main democratic institutions have remained reasonably resilient.

A further blemish on Indian democracy is its mixed record with respect to human rights. The Indian state's ability to uphold human rights has come under considerable strain (e.g. Drèze and Sen 2013). A major problem is that of Hindu majoritarianism. At the national level, and in several states, Hindu right-wing political parties and organizations have been able to usurp people's citizenship rights by seizing the reins of power and justifying unconstitutional action on the ground that they act on behalf of 'the people' (Gupta 2007). The anti-Muslim pogrom in Gujarat in 2002 is one of the most obvious instances of aggression, and this and other incidents have created widespread minority anxiety and resistance.

The Indian state's capacity to sanction the abuse of human rights takes other forms, too. In its efforts to suppress secessionist movements, especially in Kashmir and the north-east, the Indian government has resorted to draconian legislation, justified in the name of national security. The Armed Forces (Special Powers) Act, first legislated in 1958, provides the military with exceptional powers to maintain public order in areas deemed 'disturbed', and has been applied to parts of the north-east since 1958, Punjab during the Khalistan insurgency of the 1980s and 1990s, and in Kashmir since 1990. The United Nations and international NGOs have repeatedly raised concerns that the Act has resulted in human rights abuses in these regions. A strong-arm approach has also been apparent in state operations in other parts of India, as evident in the enactment of the Prevention of Terrorism Act (POTA) in March 2002. This law permitted detention of a suspect for up to 180 days without the filing of charges in court. It also allowed law enforcement agencies to withhold the identities of witnesses and to treat confessions made to the police, which are commonly made under duress, as an admission of guilt. Other worrying dimensions of the Indian state's abuse of citizenship rights are the government's tendency to deploy paramilitary units to control the public, extra-judicial police assassinations of suspected criminals (see Jalal 1995), and the militarization of India's borders (Jones 2009).

Commentators' concern about human rights abuses in India have risen since the assumption of power by prime minister Modi in 2014. As outlined at length in the previous chapter, interpreters of India's political scene have pointed to the emboldening of extremist groups such as cow vigilantes (*gau rakshaks*) under Modi and see the government's reluctance to intervene to protect minorities from communal violence as a clear sign of a declining commitment to human rights. The government's legislative agenda has also undermined human rights and aspects of due process. For example, the Unlawful Activities (Prevention) Act (UAPA) of 2019 allows the union government to designate any organization or individual as a terrorist without having to follow any procedure (though there is some scope for a post-decision review

Table 7.1 Voter Turnout in Lok Sabha Elections, 1967–2019

Election Year	Male (%)	Female (%)	Total (%)
1967	n/a	n/a	61.04
1977	65.63	54.91	60.49
1989	66.13	57.32	61.95
1999	63.97	55.64	59.99
2004	62.15	53.64	58.07
2009	60.24	55.82	58.21
2014	67.00	65.54	66.44
2019	n/a	n/a	67.22

Source: Electoral Commission of India statistical reports

process). This is of particular concern to the Muslim community, who have already been marginalized by global discourses emerging from the 'war on terror'.

But against such observations of the state's abuse of human rights and associated limits on some key basic freedoms must be placed other evidence. Even in instances of government-imposed restraints on democracy, Indian citizens have mobilized to guarantee their rights. In 1975, Indira Gandhi imposed Emergency Rule, elections were suspended, political and civil organizations were disbanded, and the media was gagged. This move generated widespread popular resentment, which, in turn, contributed to Indira Gandhi's losing national elections in 1977. Also indicative of Indian public intolerance of state coercion was popular opposition to POTA, which the government was forced to repeal in 2004. Rights-based public activism has also become marked over the past two decades – as we discuss in chapter 8.

Popular involvement in democratic politics is also evident in the sphere of elections. Table 7.1 points to consistently high voter participation in central government (Lok Sabha) elections between 1967 and 2019, with a notable rise since 2014. State-level data typically point in similar directions (see Yadav 1999; Yadav and Palshikar 2009).

There is also evidence that elections have become fairer (Robinson 1988; Singh 1992; Wilkinson 2007). In a study of the period between 1952 and 1977 in a village in rural Andhra Pradesh, Marguerite Robinson (1988) found that a former system of elite-controlled 'vote bank' politics collapsed in the 1970s. Jagpal Singh (1992) and Jan Breman (1993) note similar declines in vote bank politics in western UP and Gujarat, respectively. In a rather different vein, Steven Wilkinson (2007: 35) argues that the central government in India became increasingly unwilling to rig elections in politically-sensitive regions during the 1990s and early 2000s.

It is not only that people participate in elections, but that they invest powerful meanings in the act of voting. This point comes across in the comparative nationwide research project led by Banerjee on the 2009 elections in India (Banerjee 2014). Banerjee and her team collected stories about how people vote, what they feel about the act of casting their ballot, and what elections mean to them more broadly. Their research uncovered people's deep attachment to the practice of voting in widely varying parts of India. From poor women in central India to male landless labourers in the south to frustrated youth in the sensitive north-eastern areas, there was a consensus that voting was a citizenship 'right', and constitutive of one's individuality and humanity.

There have also been moves in the past thirty years to extend the reach of representative government in local areas. In 1992 the passing of the 73rd Amendment Act increased both the power and representativeness of local government in India. The Act implemented a three-tier system of local government in all states of India with populations of over 2 million people. Under this new system, *panchayat* councils would play a central role in the provision of public services, the creation and maintenance of public goods, and the planning and implementation of development activities (for discussion, see Manor 2010c). The Act stipulated that *panchayat* elections should be held every five years and provided a periodic 33 per cent reservation of *panchayat* seats for STs and SCs. In 2009, the union government mandated that 50 per cent of *panchayat* seats be reserved for women. Summarizing studies over the 1990s, Drèze and Sen (2002) argued that *panchayat* elections have elicited keen public interest, and voter turnout has been high.

The increasing fairness of elections, people's investment in the act of voting, and the decentralization of representative government are dynamics intimately linked to a further key strength of India's democracy: the emergence since the 1960s of a genuinely competitive multi-party system. As we outlined in chapter 1, between 1950 and 1967 the Congress Party dominated Indian politics, comfortably winning the national elections of 1952, 1957 and 1962. By contrast, the period from 1967 to 1989 was associated with the rise of political parties expressing regional demands, left parties such as the Communist Party of India (Marxist), and organizations, parties and movements representing specific sectional interests, for example those led by prosperous farmers in Uttar Pradesh (UP). The Congress Party continued to be mostly successful in central government elections – with the exception of the period from 1977 to 1980 – but faced important challenges from other parties.

In 1989 a National Front coalition won the Lok Sabha elections, and this led to a period marked by much higher levels of electoral competition, associated with the rise of low-caste political parties and Hindu nationalist political organizations. The parties most successful in challenging the Congress in the 1970s and 1980s tended to be ones that represented middling sections of Indian society rather than those at the base of caste and class hierarchies. But in the early 1990s, in India a more profound democratization of electoral politics occurred, what Yadav (1996) terms a 'second democratic upsurge' (to distinguish it from the first upsurge beginning in the 1960s). In the late 1970s the ruling Janata Party had investigated strategies for extending positive discrimination to 'Other Backward Classes' (OBCs): castes above the SCs and STs in the Hindu caste hierarchy but nevertheless suffering from social and economic deprivation. The resulting Mandal Commission Report, published in 1980, outlined a programme for reserving seats in educational institutions and government bureaucracies for OBCs. In August 1990, prime minister VP Singh found it expedient to act on the Mandal Commission's recommendations. The move had the effect of reorganizing political coalitions; strong and assertive regional blocs of OBC voters emerged.

The rise of OBC politics was intertwined with two other notable forms of democratic expression that emerged in the early 1990s. First, there was an upsurge of politics among Dalits. The rise of Dalits was especially obvious in India's most politically influential state of UP, where the pro-Dalit Bahujan Samaj Party (BSP) formed coalition governments in 1993, 1995, 1997 and 2002, and won a landslide victory in the state elections in 2007. Mayawati, a Dalit woman and former school teacher, has led the BSP since 1995. The rise of low-caste political parties was fundamentally related to the Election Commission's successful effort to reduce the illegal 'capture' of electoral booths and a former tendency of higher caste voters to intimidate low-caste voters or 'weaker sections of society' more broadly (Robinson 1988; Vaishnav 2017).

A second and more reactionary form of democratic expression, relating in complicated ways to both the rise of OBC and Dalit politics, was the emergence of the BJP and associated social and political mobilization among organizations representing the Hindu Right. The forces of *Hindutva* sponsored a series of high-profile political campaigns in the late 1980s and 1990s, and the BJP held power at the centre between 1998 and 2004. The BJP again won power in 2014, achieving an outright majority for the first time. The BJP's further victory in the 2019 elections, with an increased majority, suggests that Indian democracy has now entered a new phase, wherein a dominant Hindu nationalist party occupies the type of overwhelming power that was wielded by Congress in the 1950s and 1960s (Palshikar 2017). In the 2019 election, the BJP won 37.36 per cent of the national vote, which secured them 303 of the 543 seats up for election, an increase of 21 seats over the party's already strong victory in 2014. The BJP's allies in the National Democratic Alliance secured a further 50 seats in 2019. The BJP's strong performance extended even to one of the southern states, where they had historically performed poorly. In Karnataka, the BJP achieved their best ever result, securing 25 of the 28 seats available in the Lok Sabha. There were, however, states that bucked the trend – notably Punjab, Kerala, Tamil Nadu and Andhra Pradesh, which voted strongly against the BJP and its allies. It is also noteworthy that, although in state government elections late in 2018 the BJP lost control of the legislatures of Madhya Pradesh, Chhattisgarh and Rajasthan, these results did not have a strong bearing on the elections for the Lok Sabha just a few months later. In Rajasthan, for example, where Congress had won convincingly in the 2018 state government elections, the BJP took all 25 available seats in the Lok Sabha elections in 2019.

In sum, India's consolidation as a democracy has occurred in four spheres: via formal institutions such as the Election Commission, by means of increased public action in the sphere of rights, through the electoral process, and by way of increased participation of low-caste groups in competitive politics. In each sphere, there are reasons to enter qualifications and caveats. It is important to highlight human rights abuses in Kashmir and against minorities, the problem of intra-party democracy, and the unconstitutional role now being played by the Supreme Court in some aspects of governance. There are understandable concerns about human rights abuses during Modi's tenure in power, which we discuss in greater detail in section 7.4. But India's achievements to date remain impressive.

Formal democracy has had positive implications for the Indian population. Five key points stand out. First, democracy has played a role in guaranteeing the territorial integrity of the Indian nation. India's competitive democratic system has enabled regional forces to press demands while allowing the centre to remain in its position of overall authority. That several regions have been able to campaign successfully for status as separate States within the Indian federation is indicative of this point.

Second, formal democracy has had a positive effect on people's freedom from organized violence. Steven Wilkinson (2004) has argued that political competition, especially the intensification of competition in India since the early 1990s, acts on the whole to discourage political parties from alienating minorities. More broadly, previous governments' commitments to secularism and human rights have militated against widespread overt state oppression of the type that has occurred in Pakistan and Sri Lanka. Yet, as discussed in chapter 6, the recent decline in electoral competition and the Modi government's weaker commitment to the norms of secularism and human rights has reduced the extent to which Indian democracy offers citizens – particularly minorities – protection from violence.

Third, democracy has precipitated a vibrant, noisy and diverse media. Until recently, the state has had limited influence over the media in India, and the opening up of formal democracy has intersected with the growth of new forms of democratic expression. In a notable study, Manuel (1993) discussed how the increasing availability of the portable cassette player enhanced opportunities for political dissent in India in the 1970s. More recently, Doron (2010) has traced how the success of the BSP in UP was closely related to activists' use of mobile phones. Dia Da Costa (2010) has examined increasing democratization through the lens of political theatre in eastern India. Mazumdar (2007) offers a parallel account of cinema, discussing the representation and production of democratic practice in Bollywood films.

Fourth, formal democracy has generated multiple forms of social mobilization and organization, from campaigns against corruption (Jenkins and Goetz 1999), to environmental movements around big dams (Baviskar and Sundar 2008), to movements against child and bonded labour (Weiner 1991). A number of scholars are now focusing on the growing role played by NGOs in India – grassroots non-profit organizations and international organizations – in processes of social development (e.g. Kamat 2002; Mehta 2007; Lerche 2008). For Mehta (2007), these organizations represent a type of 'post-democracy', since they are unaccountable to the people they serve. NGOs, especially proselytizing organizations, may be divisive or else depoliticize society (see Lerche 2008). But there is also good evidence that some NGOs, collaborating in particular ways with state agencies, can foster inclusive social development (Appadurai 2002; Manor 2010a; see also discussion in chapters 8 and 10).

Fifth, democracy may have been important in preventing famine in India. In authoritarian China a series of famines killed between 23 and 30 million people in 1958–61. Drèze and Sen (1991) argue that the famines could not have occurred in India because the Indian government would have been compelled to answer questions from opposition parties, the media and the public at large. Drèze and Sen also argue that many of the coercive measures introduced by the Chinese government since the early 1960s, including the One Child Policy, would not have been tolerated in democratic India. Whatever the flaws in India's democracy, there are important reasons for stressing the value of formal democracy over authoritarian rule.

7.3 India as Substantive Democracy 1947–2014

1947–1990

The extent to which India is a 'substantive democracy' is much more open to question, however. For a country to be a 'substantive democracy', it must meet three criteria (cf. Huber et al. 1997). First, individuals should be able to participate in political life in a meaningful way, for example by being able to play fulfilling roles on local government councils or to petition authorities for help through reference to their rights. Where they feel aggrieved, citizens should be able to complain and see their complaints heeded. Second, a country is a substantive democracy where social inequalities that impede political participation are addressed and where social policy is broadly inclusive and progressive. If people lack food, shelter and education, or depend on powerful brokers for basic needs, effective political participation is unlikely. Third, a positive feeling of involvement in democratic and political life is a prerequisite of substantive democracy.

It is useful to begin by considering the success of the Indian government in promoting substantive democratization with reference to two periods: 1947–90 and the early 1990s to 2014. In the first period, the state's record in generating participatory, inclusive democracy is unimpressive. During the 1950s and 1960s, the Congress Party enhanced the power of the already dominant middle and upper castes in local arenas. Elites were able to control the votes of the poor (Shukla 1992; Singh 1992; Lerche 1995, 1999). Dominant castes could also manipulate policy directives to prevent the implementation of radical measures, such as land reform and agricultural taxation.

The Congress system of 'patronage democracy' also limited opportunities for the poor to complain about government services or become involved in politics at the local level. Anthony Carter's (1974) account of elite politics in Maharashtra showed that locally dominant intermediaries often blocked lines of communication between senior political figures and the masses in the 1950s and 1960s. The lowest tier of government, the local, village-level councils (*panchayats*) also tended to be controlled by Congress bigwigs. The poor had strong reasons to avoid becoming involved in democratic politics. The patron-client system was systemically corrupt and crime-ridden. Those attempting to reform it at the local level would face censure and reprisals. Moreover, even those who entered the fray would have required money to acquire posts. A certain level of 'corruption' was a prerequisite for obtaining local power.

These problems of democratic participation were exacerbated by ordinary people's illiteracy and, perhaps also, their lack of basic understanding about democracy and citizenship. According to Sudipta Kaviraj (1991), most Indians in 1947 did not understand the principles of impersonal government enshrined in the Constitution because they believed primarily in other ideas of authority, for example based around family and caste (as had been shown by ethnographic studies, e.g. Epstein 1973). Kaviraj's (1991) writing suggests that the poor lacked not only the institutional strength required to influence government practice but also the sense of citizenship rights that is a necessary foundation for democratic protest (see also Chatterjee 2004 and chapter 10).

The decline of the Congress Party dominance in the late 1960s created some new opportunities for upper sections of the OBCs and middle castes to participate in politics (see Robinson 1988; Breman 1993; Corbridge and Harriss 2000). There is considerable evidence that this first democratic upsurge generated a novel sense of entitlement (cf. Kaviraj 1991), and maybe in some areas of India a new belief in the capacity of democracy to deliver on its promises. There was some relaxation in patron-client relations in many areas as a result of social measures introduced by Indira Gandhi alongside a broader improvement in off-farm employment opportunities for labourers (see Robinson 1988; Breman

1993; Lerche 1999). In addition, Indira Gandhi's populist rhetoric served to politicize the issue of poverty, putting the question of economic inequality onto the agenda (Kohli 2001).

But Indira Gandhi's shift to dismantle the Congress Party and opt for populist messages was also associated with costs from the point of view of grassroots democratization. Her decision to delink Lok Sabha elections and Assembly elections and the general increase in electoral volatility encouraged a type of narrow gamesmanship among political leaders (Rudolph and Rudolph 1987). A system took root – Rudolph and Rudolph (1987) call it 'demand politics' – in which parties made promises to selected sections of the electorate in return for votes. The political scientist Kanchan Chandra (2004) has analysed this process in considerable depth. She makes the persuasive argument that both political leaders and people on the ground lack the ability to identify specific class or sectional interests. In general, politicians in India do not appeal to 'the middle classes', as they do in the United States, or 'working classes', as was common in some parts of Europe, because these social categories have little meaning on the ground. Instead, political parties use caste, ethnicity and other bounded identities as a type of signal for mobilizing votes (see also Banerjee and Pande 2009). For example, villagers voting for a Jat politician would expect the elected official subsequently to enact pro-Jat policies and channel resources to the Jats and castes of a similar standing.

From the perspective of politicking at the regional and local levels, the 1970s and 1980s were associated with the further criminalization and debasement of democratic practice in most parts of India. One type of corrupt politics – organized patronage systems orchestrated by the Congress Party – was replaced by another variation of this system wherein politicians lavished support on key voters which they then recouped after victory through tapping state bureaucracies and black markets for funds. Elections are expensive in India. Politicians need to recover the money they spend getting elected, and they do so through pressing top officials in different government bureaucracies to collect illegal 'side incomes'. These senior state functionaries make money by exerting pressure, in turn, on subordinates within government bureaucracies, who accumulate money through a range of corrupt dealings, for example by charging the public for services that are officially free. This system exists not only for many public bureaucracies, such as irrigation (see Wade 1985, 1988), but also within the police. Police acquire illegal incomes through bribes, extortion and pay-offs. Some of this they keep themselves and the rest is passed on upwards through the police system and onwards to senior politicians (see Jeffrey 2000, 2001; Jauregui 2014). Such corruption has doubly negative implications for the poor, compelling them to pay for services that should be free and increasing their exposure to theft and violence.

Vaishnav (2017) provides insight into this problem in his account of the relationship between the development of demand politics in India and the 'criminalization of politics'. After the 2014 elections, a third of serving MPs in the Lok Sabha faced criminal charges and a fifth of all MPs faced charges in relation to serious infractions such as causing grievous bodily harm or in relation to murder. After the 2019 elections, the number with criminal charges was higher than 40 per cent. Vaishnav traces the rise of these criminal politicians to the decline of Congress power in the 1980s, which gathered pace in the 1990s and 2000s. Deprived of contacts within a dominant party, criminals sought to avoid prosecution and punishment by entering politics themselves. Criminals are commonly able to use their largesse and reputation for 'getting things done' within a patronage-based system. Indeed, their reputation as 'doers' and their actual capacity to provide some benefits to the populations they serve often overtrumps public concern about their criminal past, and Vaishnav makes the point that criminal politicians are more likely to be re-elected. Nevertheless, and as Vaishnav also points out, the rise of criminal politicians, by creating a culture and appearance of impunity for known criminals, erodes the rule of law. It also diminishes citizens' trust in government and governance more broadly.

Alongside growing bureaucratic corruption, police malfeasance and the criminalization of politics, routine access to justice became increasingly difficult for ordinary people in India in the 1970s and 1980s. During this period, India's federal judicial system developed a huge backlog of cases. Thousands of prisoners were left in limbo awaiting trial, and the average time it took to get a judgment increased dramatically. Drèze and Sen (2002) note 250,000 prisoners were awaiting trial in 2000. In the early 1990s, Atul Kohli (1990) warned that intensified political competition in India and attendant forms of corruption and state inefficiency had created a 'crisis of governability' in many states (see also Bonner 1990).

India did not experience rapid substantive democratization in the period between 1947 and 1990, if we define substantive democracy in terms of broad-based participation in everyday local politics, ordinary citizens' capacity to complain to local bureaucracies, and the democratic distribution of resources. There was a complex geography to this general picture, since the nature of people's participation in politics varied to some extent between States (see Kohli 1990; Harriss 2003b). Reflecting its distinctive history, the State of Kerala, in particular, bucked the national trend (Heller 2009). In Kerala the struggle against British rule took the form of a broad-based lower-class movement. In the post-colonial period, the communist state government built on this legacy, mobilizing against upper castes (Heller 2000). The degree and scope of public legality, integration of subordinate groups into public politics, effective mobilization, and large networks of cooperative societies all marked Kerala out from other States of India in the period between 1947 and 1990, throwing India's general 'crisis of governability' into stark relief.

1990–2014

The period between 1990 and 2014 might be regarded as the 'high water mark' of Indian democracy. As noted in our discussion of formal democracy, the 1990s witnessed the development of a more competitive electoral climate, which in some ways rendered Indian democracy more inclusive. It provided entry points for emergent low-caste political parties, which claimed to represent those who had limited opportunities to participate in the upper-caste dominated 'patronage democracy' of decades past. Yet, the extent to which these changes led to more substantive democratization remains open to debate and there were significant regional variations. In what follows, we analyse the impacts of Dalit politics in different States of India during this period, to understand whether they provided a basis for more meaningful democratic participation amongst marginalized communities.

Between 1990 and 2007, the rise of low-caste politics was dramatic across India, including in Uttar Pradesh. Under Mayawati, the BSP tried to raise the political, economic and social standing of Dalits in UP, especially members of the Chamar caste. The BSP transferred Dalits into key positions within government and improved Dalits' access to reserved positions in government training and professional courses (Duncan 1997, 1999; Frøystad 2005: 230). Mayawati also tried to create a 'climate of fear' among government bureaucrats through implementing a measure that made discrimination against Dalits punishable with imprisonment (Jaffrelot 2003). She extended efforts to target development resources towards villages with large Dalit populations, especially via an 'Ambedkar Village Scheme' (see Pai 2002). In addition, Mayawati embarked on an ambitious symbolic programme, establishing parks, statues and libraries dedicated to Dr. Bhimrao Ambedkar and other Dalit heroes.

The BSP improved Dalits' access to development schemes, at least during the 1990s (Pai 2002). It has also raised the confidence of Dalits in UP (Pai 2002; Jeffrey et al. 2008; Jaoul 2007, 2015). Sudha Pai (2002) notes the rise in the 1990s and early 2000s of a new generation of educated Dalit young men who questioned established relationships of dominance in rural western UP, especially through celebrating Dalit pride and the possibility of social improvement via education. Pai also emphasizes the practical importance of these men, who represented Dalit interests within local government *panchayats*, acted as intermediaries between their community and the state, and organized social mobilization (see also Jaoul 2009).

The rise of the BSP – and of its competitor, the Samajwadi Party which represents OBCs in UP – was also accompanied by an influx into the formal electoral realm of new beliefs not shaped by the high ideology of Western-style liberal democracy (see Alam 2004; Michelutti 2007). For example, Lucia Michelutti (2007) describes how Yadav leaders within the Samajwadi Party portrayed democracy as a distinctively 'Yadav' achievement – an 'ancient quality' passed down to the Yadav community from their ancestor-god Krishna. Such examples amount to what Michelutti terms the 'vernacularization of democracy'.

But substantive democratization in UP in the 1990s and early 2000s was partial at best. The BSP failed to address more significant barriers to democratic participation for Dalits and other marginalized groups. There remained widespread problems of bureaucratic inefficiency, corruption and maladministration that generated numerous difficulties for ordinary people, especially the poor, women, low castes and Muslims. Local government *panchayats* remained ineffective as instruments of mobilization and complaint and were often not inclusive, with men dominating women (Ciotti 2010), and higher castes exploiting lower castes and Muslims (Lieten 1996; Lerche 1999). The judicial system in UP remained inefficient and mired in personal favouritism (Madsen 1998). Moreover, the criminalization of politics deepened in the context of the rise of the BSP because of a general inflation in the competitiveness of politics and a continued increase in the financial rewards attached to office (see Brass 2011). The inability of the BSP to address the concerns of marginalized people in UP became still more evident after its victory in 2007. Mayawati placed less emphasis on Dalit empowerment, directing energies instead into cultivating a support base among upper castes and glorifying her own power. This shift in tactics, coming as it did on top of the BSP's already variable record in terms of ensuring broad-based participation and addressing social inequalities, led to disquiet among Dalits. Thus, the BSP's success in the 1990s and early 2000s, though notable for unsettling the caste composition of government and public office, ultimately did not lead to widespread Dalit political participation beyond the ballot box, and apathy took hold (Jeffrey and Young 2012).

Noting the common failure of the democratic upsurge in the 1990s and early 2000s to seed widespread, substantive democratization in north India, Gail Omvedt (2003) advised commentators to 'look south', especially to Tamil Nadu. At first blush, Tamil Nadu appears to have been more successful in linking formal to substantive democratization during this critical phase of Indian politics. Tamil Nadu had a recent history of local Dalit mobilization. It also possessed a party with an ideological commitment to addressing caste-based social injustices. But Dalits in Tamil Nadu continue to face widespread discrimination and limited opportunities for mobility. They remain somewhat dependent on higher castes in many parts of the State (e.g. Anandhi et al. 2002; Harriss et al. 2010; Gorringe 2017).

Consideration of a Dalit political movement, the Dalit Panther Iyakkam (DPI), in Tamil Nadu provides a further basis for thinking about the gap between formal and substantive democracy. Gorringe (2017) notes the importance of the DPI in demanding rights, resources and power for Dalits in the 1990s. By mobilizing outside mainstream institutions and applying pressure on existing political parties, the DPI, as well as other Dalit movements, challenged higher caste hegemony and spread new ideologies of equality and practical democracy. But Gorringe also notes the failure of the DPI and other Dalit social movements to press for better working conditions, fairer access to key services, or comprehensive social support for the very poor. He also observes that many Dalits in Chidambaram district of Tamil Nadu lack access to food, secure dwellings and effective police assistance. In this context, many of the poor in the areas where Gorringe has worked argue that they have 'no democracy' (Gorringe 2017).

The entry of the Dalit panthers into electoral politics created further contradictions between formal and substantive democratization in Tamil Nadu. The DPI's avatar as a political party – the Viduthalai Ciruthaigal Katchi (VCK) (Liberation Panther Party) – contested a series of Lok Sabha and Tamil Nadu State Assembly elections, beginning in 1999. But it has had limited success in terms of electoral seats won or its capacity to shape a transformative Dalit agenda for the State as a political party in power. Gorringe (2017) argues that the VCK was forced to 'adjust' in the context of electoral politics, moderating former expectations, retreating from a radical agenda, and watering down key policy stances and messages. Moreover, numerous allegations quickly began to circulate regarding corruption and profiteering within the VCK. Dalit activists at the local level felt betrayed, and some turned to other parties (Gorringe 2017). Moreover, the Dalit movement in Tamil Nadu remains divided by caste: Paraiyars, Pallars and Chakkilivans often mobilize along distinct lines.

There are important differences between politics in Tamil Nadu and UP. The Dalit panthers in Tamil Nadu, to a greater extent than the BSP in UP, had a strong party and movement-based organizational structure that could act as a check on political leaders. On the other hand, the VCK – and other parties in Tamil Nadu representing low castes – was not as electorally strong as its north Indian counterpart. There were also similarities between UP and Tamil Nadu, however, in terms of political dynamics in the 1990s and early 2000s. In both States, as in many regions of India (Mosse 2010), the 'second democratic upsurge' of Dalits within electoral politics de-radicalized low-caste assertion and failed to generate sustained inclusive social policies. Dalits were drawn into alliances with higher castes that did not share their ideological drive. These coalitions then prove too feeble and fissiparous to address issues such as land redistribution or minimum wages. Low-caste party political leaders often responded by playing up questions of personality as a cover for a lack of action on issues that affect their largely poor constituents (Currie 1998; see also Mosse 2010). Moreover, internal party organization was often weak or non-democratic; the BJP is probably a more disciplined party than either the BSP or VCK, and the Hindu Right has arguably been better at coordinating between its electoral and movement-based wings. In addition, low-caste political parties tended to represent only particular castes (jatis) among Dalits, and they enrolled richer male Dalits to a greater extent than others – which in some instances had the effect of further marginalizing the voices of poorer Dalits and Dalit women (Anandhi 2017). It is important to note that low-caste political parties have rarely found common cause with Muslims.

A rather different possibility for formal democracy to trigger substantive democratization in the 1990s and early 2000s emerged from Madhya Pradesh, where it was the Congress Party that was most active in trying to foster poor people's empowerment. In Madhya Pradesh in the 1970s and 1980s the Congress tried to integrate the concerns of poor people, including Dalits, into its policies and functioning (Manor 2010b; Pai 2010). A further drive towards substantive democracy occurred with Digvijay Singh's assumption of the chief ministership in 1993. Singh increased funding to local level *panchayats*, reformed how his party and the bureaucracy functioned, and introduced a successful Education Guarantee Scheme in 1997 (Manor 2010b). He also strengthened the accountability of government, through holding discussions with key civil servants about governance issues and by reaching out to downtrodden sections of society. This reform programme culminated in the 'Bhopal Conference' of January 2002, which focused on 'transforming India through a Dalit paradigm' and involved 250 academics, professionals and activists. The Conference led, in turn, to a 'Bhopal Declaration' which outlined a programme for enhancing Dalits' control over economic and political processes.

James Manor (2010b) argues that this visible success of the Congress Party in Madhya Pradesh in the period between 1993 and 2003 helped pave the way for the Congress Party's resurgence at the national level between 2004 and 2009 and thus for more progressive social policies at the centre (discussed in greater detail in chapter 8). The Congress at the centre tapped into the frustrations of the poor and lower middle class regarding the social distribution of the benefits of India's economic reforms, and its success in the 2004 Lok Sabha election campaign owed something to this fact. In 2009, the Congress was again victorious. It mobilized lower classes fairly effectively (see Yadav and Palshikar 2009), and implemented some potentially far-reaching welfare policies between 2004 and 2014 – notably the National Rural Employment Guarantee Scheme (NREGS). It also introduced the Right to Information (RTI) Act in 2005. This Act not only emphasized freedom of expression and addressed official censorship in the US right-to-information tradition, it was also geared to improving government transparency and changing how bureaucracies work. RTI has been effective in curbing corruption within various government schemes in some parts of India (Jha 2010). The Congress should not take too much credit for these initiatives, which emerged out of prolonged public campaigns. But the success of the Congress provides some indication of a scaling up of Madhya Pradesh's 1990s experience of democratization to the national level. Indeed, the success of these progressive policies is further reflected in the fact that the BJP has continued most of them since its election at the Centre in 2014 and attempted to rebrand them and claim them as its own.

The extent to which Digvijay Singh and his Congress Party were able to foster grassroots democratization in Madhya Pradesh is open to question, however. Pai (2010) praises the Congress Party for recognizing a need to engage with Dalits and tribals in the state. But she claims that the Congress Party was only partly successful in empowering Dalits. Pai focuses on two of the major programmes that emerged out of the Dalit Agenda produced as part of the Bhopal Conference: a land distribution initiative and a project designed to ensure that companies source key services from Dalits, a scheme termed 'supplier diversity'. The land distribution for Dalits encountered strong resistance from local elites, who would lose out as a result of the reforms. Supplier diversity was more successful. But even this initiative was undermined by poor infrastructure, caste-based discrimination and corruption. While careful to acknowledge the increasing confidence of the poor in Madhya Pradesh, Pai concludes that the actual benefits to Dalits and tribals of Digvijay Singh's reforms were rather limited. Paralleling the situation in UP and Tamil Nadu, dominant castes in Madhya Pradesh continued to obtain privileged access to the State at the local level, because they were better able to navigate corrupt networks, had superior access to channels of complaint, and could make more effective use of the disciplinary and judicial arms of the state. In Pai's view, Digvijay Singh's reforms lacked traction because he did not politicize marginalized communities or anticipate ground-level resistance. For example, the Bhopal Declaration was largely formulated by intellectuals from outside the State, showed a lack of understanding of the basic struggles in which Dalits are engaged, and offered nothing to dominant castes, who were always likely to oppose measures that trespassed on their privileges.

Madhya Pradesh therefore complements the UP and Tamil Nadu cases. In the 1990s and early 2000s, UP and Tamil Nadu had powerful currents of grassroots mobilization. But the social movements that resulted in the formation of the BSP and VCK do not appear to have created parties capable of strong leadership on key issues affecting the poor. Madhya Pradesh had strong leadership. But it lacked a corresponding grassroots movement able to see through radical changes introduced by the government. In neither the instance of bottom-up assertion (UP, Tamil Nadu) nor top-down transformation (Madhya Pradesh) has formal political change been greatly effective in improving people's everyday capacity to participate equitably in politics and obtain vital resources.

In some respects, the period between 1990 and 2014 appeared as a relatively propitious moment for low-caste and broader minority political expression in India. In this period, politics was especially plural, and regional and minority parties had relative success. But even when parties with a commitment to representing marginalized communities have been in power at the State level, this has not translated into improvements in those communities' access to power and resources. Electoral representation was not sufficient to bring about a transformation in democratic participation; problems of patronage, corruption, poor quality services and entrenched social hierarchies all prevented widespread substantive democratization for Dalits and other minorities during this period.

7.4 Substantive Democratization Since 2014

Many commentators argue that the growing power of Modi's BJP government since 2014 has further threatened substantive democratization. This comes in part as a result of the weakening of India's formal democracy – including its key democratic institutions – over the same period. When the BJP won an absolute majority of seats in the Lok Sabha in 2014, it ended the period of coalition governments and high levels of electoral competition that had characterized India since 1989. It was also the first time that a party overtly critical of key tenets of liberal democracy had held an outright majority. The BJP had, of course, risen to power via democratic means, but Hansen (1999: 6) argues that discourses espoused by the broader Hindu nationalist movement suggest 'only a skin-deep commitment to democratic procedures'. The Hindu Right's understanding of democracy can be framed as majoritarian, rather than liberal, with a disinterest in representing minority concerns. Moreover, the authoritarian structure of Sangh Parivar organizations such as the RSS suggest a degree of hostility towards dissent. Ambivalence towards normal democratic procedures has been evident in some actions of the Modi government and this, when combined with other actions of the broader Hindu nationalist movement, has undermined aspects of Indian democracy.

The BJP is not the only party to have relied on non-democratic tactics when in government. At various times in India's history, both central and state governments have done so in order to achieve their objectives. For example, the UPA governments of 2004–14 – which were notable for having introduced legislation to enhance spaces of democratic participation – at times adopted highly coercive, non-democratic means of handling dissent from social movements, especially those opposing development projects and land acquisition (Walker 2008; Levien 2011; Chacko 2018). This kind of coercion, however, was rarely perceived as legitimate by the general public – it was often met with furious opposition from civil society. Chacko (2018) argues that the Modi government has been able to take non-democratic modes of governance to new levels through appeal to populist discourses. When the Modi government has suppressed critical voices in civil society, for example, it has attempted to justify this by claiming its critics are anti-national liberal 'elites' – thereby positioning itself as the virtuous defender of the national interest and of 'the people' (also identified with the majority community).

Anti-democratic trajectories were evident from the first year of the Modi government. Ruparelia (2015: 758) argues that the newly elected government effected a significant 'restructuring of power in contemporary Indian democracy, narrowing the space for deliberation and contestation'. Ruparelia identifies four key instances of this restructuring. First, the government centralized decision making around the executive – in particular, around Modi and a small inner circle of advisors. Executive ordinances were used to pass legislation and the Prime Minister's Office wielded disciplinary power over the everyday workings of government, limiting the autonomy of ministries. Second, there was a significant curtailing of normal procedures of parliamentary scrutiny. Parliament sat infrequently, bills were passed with minimal deliberation, and the government refused to recognize any official leader of the opposition. Third, information coming out of the government was tightly controlled. In particular, interactions between the prime minister and senior ministers with mainstream media were kept to a minimum. Fourth, the government enacted legislation that diminished forms of democratic oversight that previous governments had introduced.

There have been claims that India's fundamental democratic institutions have been undermined since 2014. For example, numerous allegations were made that the Indian Election Commission failed to act impartially during the 2019 elections (e.g. Sharma 2019). Some have also questioned whether the separation of powers between the government and judiciary has been compromised. In January 2018, four senior justices of the Supreme Court held a remarkable press conference, alleging the Chief Justice of the Supreme Court, Deepak Misra, who had been appointed by the Modi government in August 2017, had undermined the Court's impartiality. Justice Misra, they claimed, had interfered in the allocation of judges to politically sensitive cases, including an investigation into the death of B. H. Loya, the judge overseeing a case involving allegations of murder committed by the Government of India's Home Minister, Amit Shah (Safi 2018). This weakening of formal democratic institutions has resulted in a decline in substantive democratization since 2014.

The decline in formal democracy, intersecting with other dynamics, is making it more difficult for some citizens to participate in public life and hold governments to account. Partly, this is a result of public policy. Policies of previous governments that had procedures for public consultation and participation built into their design – such as the Land Acquisition and Resettlement Act (2013) and the Forest Rights Act (2006) – have been rolled back, while the Modi government's flagship initiatives such as the 'Smart Cities Mission' adopt a technocratic approach that provide minimal scope for democratic participation (Ruparelia 2015). The Modi governments' changes to the Right to Information Act also served to offset previous gains in substantive democratization. The Act had provided an avenue for citizens to hold politicians and administrators to account, by allowing them to access information about their entitlements and the activities of public officials. Amendments to the Act made in August 2019, however, significantly weakened the initial legislation by allowing the union government to determine the salaries, tenure and terms and conditions of Information Commissioners, who handle requests from the public for information under the RTI. Critics noted that the statement of objectives and reasons attached to the Amendment Bill did not provide adequate justification of the need for this significant curtailment of the Information Commission's autonomy (Kumar 2019).

These restrictions on citizens' capacity to partake in the democratic process have been more pronounced for citizens from minority communities, as evident in relation to Kashmir. As we discussed in chapter 6, on 5 August 2019, Home Minister Amit Shah announced the abrogation of Article 370 of the Constitution of India, which had granted the state of Jammu and Kashmir a special status, including the right to have its own constitution and a constituent assembly with a degree of autonomy to create its own laws. It was also announced that the state would be bifurcated into two Union Territories – Ladakh on the one hand, and Jammu and Kashmir on the other. Although the new Union Territory of Jammu and Kashmir would continue to have a legislature, its degree of autonomy would be curtailed compared to both the prior arrangement under Article 370 and that prevailing in other states of India – the central government would have control over matters pertaining to law and order, for example. Although prime minister Modi insisted Jammu and Kashmir would only temporarily have Union Territory status, the move raised major concerns about the future of democracy in India's only Muslim-majority state.

It is worth remembering that the democratic status of Kashmir's accession to India was always questionable. Occurring under the duress of an invasion by tribal groups from Pakistan and accompanied by a (still undelivered) promise of a plebiscite on the matter of an independent Kashmiri nation state, governments since the time of Nehru have been mindful of the need to win the consent of the people of Kashmir for their inclusion in the Indian Union. Article 370 of the Constitution was largely intended to provide Kashmir with the autonomy needed to win that consent. The manner of its repeal by the BJP showed total disregard for the voices of those in the region. The Constitution had stated that the removal of Article 370 should only occur with the support of the state legislature of Jammu and Kashmir – yet, this was not obtained, given that the state legislature had been suspended. Indeed, there was a lack of any genuine attempt to build consent for the change – the central government's decision was imposed unilaterally. In the immediate wake of the decision, political leaders in Kashmir were arbitrarily detained, public assembly was banned, and both the internet and phone services were shut down, all for an extended period. The ability of citizens lawfully to express dissent was denied. At the time of writing in August 2019, it was unclear whether the decision to revoke Article 370 would be challenged in the Supreme Court. Whatever the final outcome, the moves seemed an ominous sign of the Modi government's intention to deny minority citizens the right to substantive participation in the democratic process.

The erosion of India's substantive democratization since 2014 is especially evident in relation to freedom of expression. This has three dimensions. First, there has been an assault on the freedom of the press. Although India remains formally committed to press freedoms, in practice, journalists – particularly those critical of the ruling party and its ideology – are finding it increasingly difficult to report freely as a result of concerted campaigns of harassment and intimidation by Hindu nationalists. In 2019, India ranked 140th out of 180 countries in the World Press Freedom Index, compiled by Reporters without Borders (2019b), and its ranking had declined consistently since 2017. Reporters without Borders cite smear campaigns against journalists led by online *Hindutva* activists, Hindu nationalist attempts to purge views deemed 'anti-national' from public debate, and the fact that six journalists were murdered in 2018 in connection with their reporting as reasons for India's declining press freedom ranking. They noted an intensification of attacks on the press in the lead up to the 2019 general election. Perhaps the most prominent journalist to have been murdered since 2014 was Gauri Lankesh, editor of a local newspaper and long-term critic of Hindu nationalism, who was shot in her home in Bangalore by three men in 2017. Those charged with her murder were involved in Hindu extremist groups. The incident incited fear in many journalists critical of the ruling party – particularly women (Romig 2019).

Modi's own relationship with the press has been strained since his time as chief minister of Gujarat. In the lead up to the 2014 elections, he dodged journalistic inquiry into his role in the 2002 anti-Muslim pogrom in Ahmedabad, through populist appeals to common people's capacity to separate 'the truth' of what happened from the 'lies' of political commentators – whom the Modi team positioned as part of a secular elite (Ohm 2015). During the 2014 election and since that time, Modi has shown a strong preference for online platforms such as Twitter for conveying his political messages, rather than facing journalistic scrutiny in the form of television interviews or press conferences (Pal et al. 2016). Some commentators have suggested that the government has pursued actions – such as the raiding of offices of NDTV News in June 2017 for alleged financial irregularities – intended to intimidate and demonize reporters critical of the BJP government. Since 2014, many media outlets have stepped back from their mandate to hold the government to account, which may reflect the biases of their owners. Reporters without Borders (2019a) finds remarkable concentration of ownership in India's newspaper landscape, where just four outlets capture more than three-quarters of all readers – and that many of these outlets have political ties (especially to the BJP) and economic investments that pose significant conflicts of interest. Against this background, dissent is increasingly corralled into a small number of publications, such as *The Wire* and *Economic and Political Weekly*.

A second component of the attack on the freedom of expression relates to academic freedoms. Bans on scholarly works whose analysis is deemed 'offensive' to Hindu nationalist sentiments began prior to the Modi government's assumption of power but have been associated with the broader rise of the Hindu nationalist movement. In a noteworthy example, Wendy Doniger's book *The Hindus: An Alternative History* was withdrawn from India by its publisher, Penguin, in 2014, after four years of legal proceedings. Complaints about the book were levelled by *Hindutva* activist Dinanath Batra, who alleged that the book was an offense against Hindu sentiments and part of an international conspiracy to denigrate Hindus. Taylor (2014) argues that such acts of censorship should not be seen in isolation and are part of a long campaign to rid India of material deemed offensive to Hindus. Such efforts have been successful, Taylor suggests, both because of their use of section 295A of the Penal Code – which prohibits insulting the religious sentiments of any community – and, more importantly, because of the ever-present risk of mob violence against alleged offenders. Such attempts at censorship are not limited to Hindu nationalists. As Lal (2014) notes, there have been prominent attempts by Dalit politicians to press criminal proceedings against those who cause offense to the sentiments of the lower castes. Moreover, in 1988, India was the first country in the world to ban Salman Rushdie's *The Satanic Verses*, for alleged offence caused to Muslims. Nonetheless, Hindu nationalist censorship campaigns remain especially concerning, given that they are supported by the ruling party of the country.

The erosion of academic freedom extends to campus politics. There has been a concerted effort on the part of the state to limit and neutralize academic freedom on university campuses (see also chapters 6 and 13). This has included crude attempts to brand dissenting voices as 'anti-national', the close policing of speakers and curricula on campuses, and a low-level assault on the social sciences and humanities. These dynamics have discouraged the research and commentary on caste, class, gender and other inequalities required for effective critique. Again, the politicization of universities, curricula and research should not be regarded as 'new' in India, having been recognized as a significant barrier to good governance in higher education for several decades (Saxena 1990), but the extent of the politicization since 2014 appears to have increased.

The third sense in which the freedom of expression has been undermined relates to the right to dissent. In some instances, critics of the government and of the dominant ideology have faced criminal prosecution. The most noteworthy case of this to date has been the 'Bhima Koregaon case', which has seen several activists and lawyers imprisoned in what is widely regarded as a miscarriage of justice. On 1 January 2018, Dalit activists gathered in the town of Bhima Koregaon to commemorate the 200th anniversary of the Battle of Koregaon, in which low-caste Mahars joined forces with the British to defeat the Brahmin Peshwas. The event has been held annually since 1928 and is regarded as an important day to celebrate a Dalit victory over Brahminism and to acknowledge the bravery of the Dalit soldiers who were grossly out-numbered (Thakur and Moharana 2018). Yet the bicentennial attracted a counter-demonstration by organized *Hindutva* forces, which resulted in violent clashes in which a 16-year-old Dalit boy was killed and Christian and Muslim shops were torched. There were claims that police deliberately failed to con-tain the violence. After months of waiting for the instigators of the violence to be brought to justice, in June 2018, the Pune police made surprise arrests of a group of five human rights activists and lawyers, whom they claimed were responsible for the violence. A further six activists and lawyers were arrested in relation to the incident in the months that followed, including the Dalit intellectual and activist Anand Teltumbde – who was later released after a court deemed his arrest illegal. The arrests were surprising, given that several of the accused had no known links to the Bhima Koregaon event. The accused, who were labelled 'urban Naxals', were also alleged to have been involved in spreading Maoist ideology and plotting to murder the prime minister. At the time of writing in August 2019, the accused faced the indefinite delay of their bail hearings and still – more than a year after their arrest – had not received access to the evidence of their alleged crimes, and hence were unable to defend themselves (Shantha 2019). Commentators noted the significance of the arrests – and the failure to take any action against *Hindutva* agitators – in branding both the Dalit movement and leftist critics of the regime as both anti-national and anti-state (EPW 2018). At the very least, the event under-mines confidence in the capacity of the state to act impartially and permit critique of the ruling government in contemporary India.

While the freedom of expression of those opposed to the government is being undermined, the government is tacitly allowing – or even encouraging – forms of 'free expression' that undermine the safety and rights of minori-ties. The Modi government has emboldened ultra-nationalist elements of the Sangh Parivar such that they have been able to dominate political discussion in many parts of India and prevent minority voices from being heard, further undermining substantive democratization. For example, in UP colleges and universities, Hindu Yuwa Vahini (HYV) organizations have spread rapidly. Yogi Adityanath established HYV as a militant youth body. In UP today, participants often act as a type of shadow state, policing aspects of everyday social and religious behaviour, including interfaith relationships and the consumption of meat (Jaffrelot 2017). The rise of such organizations has had the effect of crowding out more moderate political organizations or those representing minorities. They also spread a type of masculinist religious chauvinism and

intimidation that discourages open debate and the type of free-spirited political participation associated with the notion of a substantive democracy. There
has also been an upsurge in outright violence and a decline in the rule of
law in recent years across India. This has included lynchings, mob violence,
the destruction of property and everyday harassment (see chapter 6). The
constraints this places on the carriage of justice are noteworthy: witnesses
routinely withdraw evidence in criminal cases against *Hindutva* activists for
fear of violent reprisals (Chatterjee 2017; *The Economist*, 2019a).

These multiple threats to substantive democracy under Modi's leadership
have reached such a level as to invite comparisons between the current BJP
regime and India's Political Emergency of 1975–9. Yet, the Emergency, by its
very nature, was regarded as temporary and exceptional – and not a more
enduring curtailment of democratic freedoms, as now appears to be occurring. Moreover, a key difference between the late 1970s and the present is the
existence now of a large-scale human infrastructure through which the ruling
BJP can promulgate its views, including the RSS as well as HYV and similar
organizations. This human infrastructure acts as a bulwark against the type
of rapid public critique of democratic deficiencies that occurred in the 1970s.

7.5 Conclusions

The question of whether the Modi government's actions place India's
democracy at risk must be set against the backdrop of the long arc of India's
democratization. Competitive elections have been and remain an integral
part of Indian social and political life. Voter turnouts in elections are high and
have increased steadily since independence. At least until 2014, the overall
trend has been towards increasingly competitive elections. Since the passage
of the 73rd Amendment of the Constitution in 1993, processes of democratic
decision making have been decentralized and made more participatory, with
panchayats becoming more representative and having a greater say on how
resources are allocated, locally. The Right to Information Act has made governments more transparent (though this may have been undermined since the
Amendment of 2019) and the rise of Dalit politics since the early 1990s has
provided a degree of political voice to those historically excluded from the
political process. Together, these factors suggest India has been and remains
relatively successful as a formal democracy.

Where India's democracy is quite seriously at risk is in its status as a substantive democracy. The majoritarian and autocratic tendencies of the Modi
government have undermined the freedom of expression and the rights of all
citizens – particularly minorities – to participate in the democratic process on
equal terms. Freedoms of religion and of association have been compromised.
Increases in political violence and a culture of intimidation have undermined

the partial gains in substantive democracy that India had witnessed since 1989. It is increasingly difficult for marginalized communities such as Muslims and Dalits to mobilize to protect their rights and gain greater representation. Thus, while India is likely to remain a formal democracy for the foreseeable future, it may be one in which large sections of the population lack the means of democratic participation outside the ballot box.

It is possible that the work of Linz and Stepan (1996) on democratic theory, while a poor guide to India's experience in the first sixty years after independence, may be becoming more relevant in contemporary India. The absence of a strong education system, rising inequality and the absence of a political society independent of dominant groups is much more evident in India in 2019 as compared to India in 2009 or 1999. This may be leading to a rapid democratic decline of the type being witnessed in other major countries around the world.

It is important to add that neither Modi nor the broader Hindu nationalist movement can be regarded as exclusively responsible for India's declining status as a substantive democracy. Aspects of the Indian polity that long predate the rise of Hindu nationalism have placed constraints on substantive democratization, including bureaucratic corruption, police harassment, an ineffective local and regional judiciary, the criminalization of politics, and elite capture of local government councils. Some of the factors that allowed India to consolidate itself as a formal democracy – an expansive network of patronage founded on caste and class inequalities – are precisely those that impede substantive democratization. The result in most parts of contemporary India is a mismatch between the rising aspirations of citizens and real possibilities for transformation.

8

Why Hasn't Democracy Made Indian Governments More Responsive?

8.1 Introduction: Economic and Social Rights and the Indian Constitution

The idea of 'rights-based development' is by now well established, having been given considerable impetus by the influential work of Amartya Sen. Development for Sen, as we discussed in chapter 3, is understood in terms of people's abilities to plan for and to lead full human lives. People possess sets of capabilities which they are able to realize, or not, according to the circumstances of their lives. In this, freedoms, both negative ('freedom from . . .') and positive ('freedom to . . .') are clearly indispensable – and freedom is both a condition for and an outcome of development. Those who are subject to arbitrary arrest or who are denied political freedom or who lack freedoms of expression and association – who do not enjoy, in other words, civil and political rights, and who are prevented thereby from planning their own lives – are unable to realize their capabilities as human beings. But those who, say, through malnutrition in childhood (the lot of so many children in India), suffer neurological damage, are also prevented from 'life-planning' and leading full human lives. There is a strong case, therefore, for the argument that economic and social rights – such as rights to adequate nutrition and to health and to livelihood – are also essential for, even constitutive of, development, though there are scholars who do not agree with this position. This is at least partly because many states seem to lack the capacity to satisfy these rights (e.g. Little 2003: ch. 5), and there are those in India now who argue that governments simply cannot supply food security, or wages in MGNREGS (see chapter 4), at the level that is demanded by activists. The then-prime minister, Manmohan Singh, argued this in an interaction with journalists in 2010 (Varadarajan 2010).

Rights-based thinking in public policy internationally was both reflected in and furthered by the Universal Declaration on Human Rights of 1948, to which India was a signatory. Even at that time, however, a good deal of largely independent thinking was going on in the country, in the deliberations of the Constituent Assembly that was responsible for drawing up the Constitution of India, promulgated at last in 1950. Once described as 'a baroque legal promissory note' (Khilnani 1997: 35), the Constitution offers an extraordinarily ambitious political design, promising what is in effect social democracy, aiming to reconcile private property and a capitalist economy with the claims of social justice. The original document began, in The Preamble, with the fine words:

> WE, THE PEOPLE OF INDIA, [have] solemnly resolved to constitute India into a SOVEREIGN DEMOCRATIC REPUBLIC and to secure all citizens:
> JUSTICE, social, economic and political;
> LIBERTY of thought, expression, belief, faith or worship;
> EQUALITY of status and opportunity;
> And to promote them all;
> FRATERNITY assuring the dignity of the individual and the unity of the nation . . .

But in the end, in the Constitution, a distinction was drawn between Fundamental Rights (in Part III), which established both LIBERTY, and EQUALITY of the status of citizens, and what are called Directive Principles (the subject of Part IV of the Constitution), which are concerned with social and economic JUSTICE, and with EQUALITY of opportunity. This substantially reflects the distinction between civil and political rights on the one hand, and economic and social rights on the other. In earlier deliberations, the Indian National Congress intended to establish economic and social rights, as well as civil and political rights (as both Jayal 2013 and Chandhoke 2016 explain, in their accounts of the Draft Constitution for India drawn up in 1928 by a committee headed by Jawaharlal Nehru's father, Motilal). In the event, however, the members of the Constituent Assembly effectively 'demoted' (Chandhoke's word) economic and social rights. The Fundamental Rights, which are justiciable, include the Right to Equality (here there is, amongst others, an article [No. 17] on Abolition of Untouchability); and the Right to Freedom, including – of particular significance in the present context – Article 21 on the right to protection of life and liberty; as well as rights against exploitation, but also the right to property, as well as to freedom of religion and cultural and educational rights.

The Directive Principles, however, are said (in Article 37) not to be 'enforceable in any court (though) the principles therein laid down are nonetheless fundamental in the governance of the country and it shall be the duty of the state to apply these principles in making laws'. They include among others, the 'right to work, to education and to public assistance in certain cases' (Article 41); 'living wage etc for workers' (Article 43); and (Article 47) 'duty of the State to raise the level of nutrition and the standard of living and to improve public health'. The drafting history of the Constitution shows that 'the non-enforceable nature of the Directive Principles was intended to be temporary and modifiable when the country became ready to enforce them' (Birchfield and Corsi 2010: 711). And, indeed, the distinction between the

Fundamental Rights and the Directive Principles has been whittled away by orders of the Supreme Court, even though, as yet, only the right to education has been formally established as a Fundamental Right.

What has happened has been that judgments of the Supreme Court, extending back over many years – some of its most progressive rulings were made in the early to mid-1980s – have in effect rendered non-enforceable Directive Principles justiciable in a court, and upgraded the status of social welfare to that of a fundamental right (Birchfield and Corsi 2010: 713; Chandhoke 2016). A judgment of 1970, for instance, argued, 'The mandate of the Constitution is to build a welfare society in which justice, social, economic and political, shall inform all institutions of our national life. The hopes and aspirations aroused by the Constitution will be belied if the minimum needs of the lowest of our citizens are not met' (referred to by Birchfield and Corsi 2010: 711). Since then it has been interpretations of Article 21 of the Constitution, on the 'right to protection of life and liberty', that have been especially significant. Those who drafted this Article may have had in mind protection against arbitrary arrest and detention, but the judges have interpreted it to mean the right to life with dignity and to embrace both the right to education and the right to food.

So India has seen, early in the twenty-first century, some remarkable policy innovations, intended to deliver economic and social rights – what has been described as a 'new rights agenda'. In this chapter we will discuss the history of this agenda, and briefly review how far Indian governments have succeeded in implementing it. We consider evidence that since 2014, the BJP governments, headed by Narendra Modi, have gradually whittled away at the rights agenda, and in spite of early policy pronouncements, resorted to a frankly welfarist agenda (in which the state delivers benefits, but not as a right) – that has, however, served them well politically. Finally, we address the question of why Indian voters have not held their governments to account over the delivery of social services.

8.2 The 'New Rights Agenda'

The 'new rights agenda' came about largely as a result of pressures from within civil society, often articulated by particular individuals who may be described as policy entrepreneurs (Jenkins 2013: 609), and generally in interaction with judicial activism (Ruparelia 2013). The best-known of these policy innovations is the National Rural Employment Guarantee Scheme (NREGS) – now called the Mahatma Gandhi National Rural Employment Guarantee Scheme – legislated for in 2005, that we described briefly in chapter 4. The world's largest rights-based safety net programme, MGNREGS gives all rural households the right to up to 100 days of guaranteed wage employment per year, at an agreed minimum wage. In 2005, as well, the Right to Information

Act (RTI) was passed, making it mandatory for government agencies to release information about their activities to individual citizens upon request. The Right to Information is foundational to the whole rights agenda, because as stated on its website by the Mazdur Kisan Shakti Sangathan (MKSS), which initiated the struggle for this right, 'transparency and accountability of systems of governance are basic to access any right (and) access to relevant information [in official documents] is a fundamental tool for ensuring transparency and accountability of government'.

A year after the passage of NREGS and the RTI, *The Scheduled Tribes and Other Traditional Forest Dwellers (Recognition of Forest Rights) Act 2006* gave tribal communities and other forest dwellers rights in the forests that had been denied to them before. Then *The Right of Children to Free and Compulsory Education Act 2009*, made the enrolment, attendance and completion of schooling of every child up to the age of 14 the obligation of the state. *The National Food Security Act*, which is designed to guarantee that people will not go hungry by providing foodgrains at low and regulated prices to about two-thirds of the population, was passed in 2013. The government also sought to address the problems and the needs of the huge numbers of unorganized workers in the country, first through the appointment in 2004 of the National Commission for Enterprises in the Unorganised Sector (NCEUS), and then in the passage of the Unorganised Workers Social Security Act of 2008, which marks a step towards the formalization of such work, and the protection of workers, even if the legislation falls far short of what the NCEUS had advocated.

The initial drivers of the new rights agenda were not politicians and political parties – though the UPA government of 2004–14 created an important space for policy innovation, beneath the umbrella of the National Advisory Council (NAC). This was set up by the Congress Party President, Mrs Sonia Gandhi, to oversee the implementation of the Common Minimum Programme (CMP) that the Congress, heading the Alliance, agreed with its coalition partners and with the left parties (on the outside), and which promised 'growth with a human face'. Neither was the new welfare architecture that was created the outcome of extensive popular mobilization. It was rather the result of lobbying by civil society activists (whose actions are also discussed in chapter 10), and of judicial intervention – the two having tended to work together. The origins of MGNREGS (in a context, in India, of a long history of public works programmes) are shared with those of the more recent, much more fiercely contested right to food, finally established with the Food Security Act of 2013. A Supreme Court judgment of November 2001, in a case brought by the Peoples Union for Civil Liberties (PUCL) against the Government of India, through the instrument of public interest litigation – in a context in which there was famine in parts of Rajasthan at a time when it was very well known that the Food Corporation of India held massive stocks of foodgrains – explicitly established a constitutional right to food.

[The Court] not only held that specific government food schemes constituted legal entitlements . . . setting out in detail minimum allocation levels of foodgrains and supplemental nutrients for India's poor, but also outlined how those government schemes [including the Targeted Public Distribution System, the Midday Meals Scheme for schools, and the Integrated Child Development Services programme, amongst others that are less well known] were to be implemented (Birchfield and Corsi 2010: 695).

Essentially the Court's judgment rested on the view that the right to life under Article 21 includes the right to food. Subsequently the relationships between the judicial system, the Right to Food campaign – a loose coalition of civil society groups, the establishment of which was stimulated by the action of the PUCL in bringing its case – and the Commissioners whom the Court required to be appointed to oversee the implementation of its orders, worked quite effectively, and in such a way as to act at least as a check upon actions of the government intended to deregulate and liberalize the economy, where these moves conflicted with food security (see Birchfield and Corsi 2010: 732–51). The struggle that went on over the Food Security Act for several years showed up, however, how strong the opposition was from many in government to the objectives of the Right to Food campaigners, because of what was believed to be the cost of food security, and because of the evidence of high levels of leakage from the Public Distribution System. The implementation of the Act has continued to be a site of contestation, as we explain below.

The same civil society activists who demanded the Right to Food were then influential in the decision of Congress leaders to include the idea of the employment guarantee in the Party's manifesto for the 2004 election, and subsequently in the Common Minimum Programme. Key activists with the Right to Food campaign – Aruna Roy, a former officer in the elite Indian Administrative Service, and a driving force in the MKSS, which launched the campaign for the Right to Information (also invoking a ruling of the Supreme Court), and the economist Jean Drèze – were also members of the National Advisory Council, and the two of them presented a draft bill at its first meeting. There was subsequently considerable conflict between different government departments over the bill, with both the Ministry of Finance and the Planning Commission questioning the financial feasibility of a national employment guarantee. The Act that was finally passed, however, after a struggle on the part of the activists, included most of the provisions of the original proposals. The story shows, as Chopra argues in her analysis of the making of NREGS, the significance of (1) the creation of a new forum and network, outside regular political institutions – the NAC; (2) powerful and sympathetic state actors and networks – notably Mrs Sonia Gandhi and some high-ranking officials; (3) civil society actors (including individual policy entrepreneurs, as they may be described, such as Aruna Roy and Jean Drèze) and their networks; and (4) political compulsions – the importance of left support, from the outside, for the UPA (Chopra 2011: 102). Only in regard to the last of these did conventional party politics enter in. The significance of the support of the left parties must not be ignored, however, and the later weakness of the left in parliament was one factor accounting for blocks to the passage of a meaningful National Food Security Act.

The story of the passage of the Right to Education Act (RtE) includes a similar set of factors, the Act having been 'forged outside the realm of electoral politics . . . laws were enacted with little input from political leadership, and were eventually passed by the Indian Parliament with virtually no debate' (Mangla 2015: Abstract). Successive governments of India for long failed to allocate sufficient resources or attention to honour the mandate upon the state of Article 45 of the Constitution – among the Directive Principles – that government should 'endeavour' to provide free and compulsory education to all children up to the age of 14 within a period of ten years (i.e. by 1960). Education in India has always been significantly under-funded. A succession of committees and reports – most recently, the Subramanian Committee Report of 2016, which was intended to contribute to the formulation of a new education policy for the country, and the Draft of the National Education Policy submitted to government at the end of May 2019 by the committee entrusted with its design (see chapter 13) – have advocated that resources equivalent to at least 6 per cent of GDP should be spent on education. But education expenditure as a share of GDP has rarely reached 4 per cent, and the *Economic Survey* of the Government of India for 2015–16 records that over the period from 2008–09 to 2014–15 it 'hovered around [only] three per cent'. This is way below the international average, and below the levels of expenditure in countries that compare most closely with India (Panagariya et al. 2014: 259). The Subramanian Committee Report noted the low status of education in the bureaucracy and said, 'While no formal studies appear to be available, it can generally be postulated that the overall "quality" of education is a function of the (limited) political attention that the sector has received' (MoHRD 2016: 5, 37).

There was a great deal of critical discussion and debate over RtE among activists outside parliament, and amongst bureaucrats, but not actually among elected politicians in the House. It was a judgment of the Supreme Court in 1993, depending on the argument that the right to life implies a right to a basic education, that stimulated civil society activism, crystallizing around the formation of the National Alliance for the Fundamental Right to Education (a network of a large number of civil society organizations) in 1998. Subsequently, in 2002, the 86th Amendment to the Constitution of India introduced Article 21A, which declares that 'The State shall provide free and compulsory education to all children of the age of six to fourteen years, in such manner as the State may, by law, determine'. This underlies the Right to Education Act which was passed as much as seven years later, the lengthy delay being partly due to contestation over the inclusion, or not, of pre-school education, and of post-elementary education – both, in the end, excluded from the Act (though they will be included in future, if the recommendations in the New Education Policy put before government in 2019 are accepted).

The history of the Forest Rights Act was a little different. In this case more than 200 grassroots organizations and people's movements from across ten states came together in 2003, in a loose network known as the Campaign for Survival and Dignity, to carry forward 'protest or campaign' politics on behalf of the rights of forest peoples (Kumar and Kerr 2012). But in this case, too, the role of an individual policy entrepreneur – B. D. Sharma, a former Commissioner for Scheduled Tribes and Scheduled Castes – was significant (Bose 2010).

Not only did the new legislation promise social rights, but it also embraced governance reform. As Ruparelia noted, 'A distinctive feature of India's new welfare paradigm ... concerns its efforts to promote greater political transparency, responsiveness and accountability' (2013: 571) – by means of institutional mechanisms whereby ordinary people and their associations can demand accountability (though the transparency demands of NREGS have a double-edged outcome, and have contributed to making the scheme, certainly in its early days and in a remote district of Uttarakhand, more or less impossible to implement. See Mathur 2016). This is the significance of the Right to Information Act in the context of the new rights framework, and there are transparency clauses in other parts of the rights legislation, encouraging the mobilization of people to hold the state to account, and to claim their rights as citizens. Section 17 of The National Rural Employment Guarantee Act 2005, for example, states that 'The Gram Sabha [the village meeting that is the basic institution of the *panchayati raj* system of local government] shall conduct regular social audits of all the projects under the Scheme taken up [in the local area]'. By 'social audit' is meant a public process of reviewing official records and of establishing whether or not there is a correspondence between what is reported and what has actually happened. The Food Security Act, too, legislates for social audits of the functioning of ration shops. Such auditing was pioneered in Rajasthan by the MKSS, using the instrument of a *jan sunwai* (public hearing). In the course of events of this kind, detailed accounts, derived from official expenditure records and other supporting documentation, were read aloud to assembled villagers, as Jenkins and Goetz explained (1999). The fact that in Rajasthan the conduct of these events should have been vigorously resisted by local officials is a testament to how powerful a vehicle of accountability they can be (Subrahmaniam 2009). The resistance has, however, been successful in blocking social auditing of MGNREGS in Rajasthan, and only in Andhra Pradesh have social audits been at all regularly conducted. But the principal of citizen participation is an important one, and it is reflected, for instance, in the provisions that were made in the new Land Acquisition Act (The Right to Fair Compensation and Transparency in Land Acquisition, Rehabilitation and Resettlement Act, 2013) for involving and securing the consent of those affected (Jenkins 2013).

The 'new rights agenda' involved remarkable developments. In the context of the evidence and argument that we reviewed in chapter 4 concerning the effective *exclusion* – rather than inclusion – of a large share of the labour force in India, the legislation that was passed and the programmes that were introduced bear out Chatterjee's contention that 'under conditions of electoral democracy [it is now] unacceptable for the government to leave these marginalized populations without the means of labour to fend for themselves'. He goes on to say 'That [leaving them to fend for themselves] carries the risk of turning them into the "dangerous classes"' (Chatterjee 2008: 62). The validity of this last point is perhaps shown in the Maoist insurgency that has won such strength in those parts of India with the most marginalized populations (see chapter 9). But it is also important to note that the new welfare programmes that have been implemented in India, as they have been elsewhere in Asia, in response to worsening socio-economic inequalities (*The Economist* 2012), complement the labour market flexibility that seems to be required for tackling the competitive pressures of the neoliberal global economy. M. Vijayabaskar argued this in a study of labour in the south Indian city of Tiruppur, a major centre of the knitwear and garments industry:

> Though the emerging social regime in Tamil Nadu appears to go against the tenets of neoliberal reforms that mandate cut-backs in public provisioning of social services, the state has been able to shift the question of labour welfare away from the workplace to the lived spaces, from the domain of capital to the domain of government of dispossessed populations. This shift partly ensures that capital accumulation can now proceed unencumbered by the burden of protecting workers' livelihoods (Vijayabaskar 2011: 45).

We should note, too, that labour rights, far from featuring in the new rights agenda, have been defended with some difficulty by the trade unions.

These broad dynamics help to explain why it is that in India policy has been focused on the provision of a 'safety net' largely funded from enhanced tax revenues. This is certainly very important for the livelihoods of very many Indians, but as Anirudh Krishna argues (in work that we cited in chapter 3), social protection is insufficient to eliminate poverty. If people are to move out of the shadow of poverty then they must have access to education of reasonable quality, and to affordable health care. Education certainly doesn't guarantee social mobility (see Jeffrey et al. 2008), but without it, people's prospects are generally severely limited. The importance of access to health care is shown in research that demonstrates the significance of episodes of ill-health in pushing people into poverty. So sustainable improvement in well-being in

India requires more investment and more attention to education and health. Yet neither has figured at all prominently on the agendas of politicians, as we noted above in regard to education. And a striking feature of the rights activism in contemporary India is that there has been little progress with regard to public provisioning of health care. As the Government of India's *Economic Survey 2015–16* concedes, Indians are very heavily reliant on private health care, and the country has done very poorly in regard to Universal Health Coverage (an index developed by the World Bank to measure progress in health sectors), in relation to comparator countries (GoI 2016, volume 2: 202–9). We will return to the question of why, even in the context of the rights agenda, there has been such little focus on the sectors that are of so much importance for the development of people's capabilities.

8.3 From Rights Legislation to Implementation

There have been serious problems of implementation of the new rights agenda, no doubt. The MGNREGS has been the object of a great deal of criticism, as being an 'expensive gravy train', supposedly subject to enormous leakages – among other ways, from the over-reporting of person-days worked. There certainly is extensive corruption – though it has been significantly reduced by effective use of information technology (Jenkins and Manor 2017; but see also Marcesse 2018) – and we also referred in chapter 4 to studies showing that there is a large unmet demand for work under the scheme, especially in the poorer states. At the same time many states experience difficulties in expending the budget for the scheme. A report of the Comptroller and Auditor General of India (the CAG) noted, for instance, that over the period from April 2007 to March 2012, 'in fourteen states and one Union Territory, only 30 per cent of the annual plan budget was utilized' (Mathur 2016: 19). It surely is a problem that, for example in 2017–18, the government spent Rs 12,312 under MGNREGS on every poor person in Kerala, as against a paltry Rs 918 in Bihar, or Rs 943 in UP. There may be a case for the earmarking of funds for states, on the basis of poverty, when at present poorer states are effectively punished because they are unable to compete with better governed states in attracting funds from the central government (N. C. Saxena, personal communication). Yet there is also good evidence that the programme has reached the rural poor, members of the Scheduled Castes and Scheduled Tribes, and that it has drawn women into the labour force (Drèze and Khera 2017). Bardhan argues that the leakages are small compared with the costs of the subsidies paid by government that benefit only the rich (2015: 227).

The realization of the objectives of the National Food Security Act depends upon the Public Distribution System (PDS), involving large numbers of ration shops across the country, and this has been subject to even more criticism than has NREGS. The temptations for those running these shops to sell on the grain, and other commodities, at market prices, that they should be releasing to citizens with ration cards at regulated low prices, are considerable. In 2004–05, according to data from the National Sample Survey, 54 per cent of the foodgrains in the PDS 'leaked' away, and though this figure had been reduced quite significantly, to 42 per cent by 2011–12, it is still a high figure and lends weight to those who call for the abandonment of the food security scheme (Paul 2016; and for discussion, Drèze and Khera 2017). There is also a lot of evidence showing that the PDS is subject to serious errors both of 'inclusion' (when those who do not need a ration receive it nonetheless) and of 'exclusion' (referring to those in need who do not receive food) – partly because effective targeting to those 'Below the Poverty Line' (BPL) is hugely problematic. Detailed studies show that there are many ration card holders who are not among the intended beneficiaries, and many who should be ben-efiting who do not hold ration cards (Ghatak 2016). But there is a great deal of variation between states, both in terms of the coverage of public distribution and its efficiency, and there is strong evidence that it can be run – to the great benefit of poor people – with very modest losses, as it is in Tamil Nadu and in Chhattisgarh (Himanshu and Sen 2011; Drèze et al. 2016). Drèze and Khera (2017) provide estimates of the impact of the PDS on poverty reduction in eight states, that range downwards from 61 per cent in Tamil Nadu, with an 'India' average of 18 per cent. On the basis of a study carried out in six of the poorest states after the passage of the NFSA, Drèze and co-authors have argued that 'India's PDS has come a long way . . . It has turned from a morass of leaky and poorly targeted transfers to a critical form of support for a vast majority of poor households' (Drèze et al. 2019: 36).

With the rights to employment and to food that have been established, India has in place at least the elements of a working system of social security, as Drèze and Khera (2017) have argued. These elements are:

- *School meals*, providing an important supplement to the nutrition of school-going children, and reaching 81 per cent of those in government schools by 2011–12, and 50 per cent of all children.
- *Integrated Child Development Services* (ICDS), providing nutritional and health support for pregnant and lactating mothers and children up to the age of six, reaching more than 50 per cent of mothers and children by 2011–12
- *MGNREGS*, the rural employment guarantee scheme (discussed above and in chapter 4)
- *The Public Distribution System* (discussed above)
- *Social security pensions*, for widows, the elderly and disabled people, reaching about 20 per cent of those who were eligible by 2011–12.

All these programmes have quite long histories, and they were not actually introduced by the UPA government, but they were boosted during its period in office – particularly by their inclusion in the new rights agenda. All except social security pensions came to be protected either by national legislation or by orders of the Supreme Court.

The stories with regard to other parts of the rights agenda are somewhat less positive. The implementation of the Forest Rights Act has been both tardy, and subject to concerted efforts to dilute it (Menon 2016). Reporting on the first two years following the inception of the Act, Sarkar noted that 'Comparing the number of claims processed (2.7 million claims filed and 760,000 titles issued) with the estimated number of people economically dependent on forests (275 million) suggests that the FRA has done little to extend property rights' (2011: 28). Menon argued that the situation had, if anything, got worse after 2010.

Perhaps the most striking failures of the rights legislation, even beyond those associated with the Forest Rights Act, have had to do with education (which we discuss in greater depth in chapter 13). Thanks to programmes that were started in the 1990s, and continued with the Sarva Shiksha Abhiyan – the elementary education programme inaugurated in 2001, well before the RtE was passed into law – the school infrastructure across the country has been greatly improved, and enrolment in primary schools is now virtually universal, with very little difference between girls and boys, or between Scheduled Castes and Scheduled Tribes, and others. The ambitions of the old Article 45 of the Constitution have at last been realized, more than half a century after the target that was set, of 1960. But both attendance and retention remain significant problems, and there is clear evidence of steeply declining levels of attainment, both in reading and in arithmetic. It is in part for this reason that the numbers of children going to private schools increased sharply, to about one-third of the total, over the few years following the passage of the RtE. For many observers, this is a serious indictment of the failures of the public education system.

When he came to office in 2014, Narendra Modi promised to bring 'Maximum Governance, Minimum Government' and to make the government machinery work much better. Has this promise been honoured in regard to social rights?

8.4 Social Rights under the First Modi Government

It seems possible that Narendra Modi was aware of the part played by the provision of social services by non-party organizations affiliated with his party in building support for it among poor people. This is the subject of a study by Tariq Thachil (2014), who asked the broad question of why poor people vote for elite parties, such as the BJP. The party has generally been identified as one for the privileged upper castes, but it has clearly achieved more and more success among India's poorer people. Thachil found that it was the private provision of public goods – social services, primarily health care, but also education – by the affiliated organizations that had delivered votes for the BJP. Services were not provided on a clientelistic basis, and the deliberate stratagem of demonstrating apparently disinterested, committed public service was successful in winning the support of poor people for the Hindu nationalist party. The Modi government may or may not have learned from this experience. The BJP-led government of 2014–19 finally concentrated, as we go on to explain, much more on the supply of private goods such as gas cylinders, than on the provision of public services. The approach was evidently electorally successful.

It was thought possible, however, that parts of the new rights agenda – MGNREGS, Food Security and the progressive clauses of the new Land Acquisition Act, in particular – might be undone by the government that came into office in 2014. Narendra Modi once mocked the Employment Guarantee Scheme as a 'living monument' to the failure of Congress governments to tackle poverty. At the same time, however, he said 'Do you think I will put an end to the scheme? My political wisdom does not allow me to do it . . . With song and dance, and drum beat, I will continue with the scheme'. Sure enough, two years after taking office, Modi claimed that the BJP government had improved the employment guarantee scheme (*First Post*, 2016). Yet when it came to it – in the views of many careful observers – the BJP-led government of 2014–19, though it did not dismantle the rights-based programmes, undercut them fairly systematically. The undermining of MGNREGS, as they saw it, led 250 members of parliament and 'eminent citizens' to write to the prime minister in January 2019, expressing their alarm about the way the programme was being starved of funds (reported by *The Wire*, 14 January 2019). Other observers reported that unmet demand continued to grow; that back wages were allowed to mount up (in 2016–17, for example, 53 per cent NREGS payments were delayed [Aiyar 2017]; and see Narayan and Swamy 2019); and that the mechanisms in the legislation intended to ensure transparency and participation were being ignored. The government also moved only slowly in implementing the Food Security Act, seeming to try to kill it by neglect (Mathew 2015; Bathia and Negi 2016), and the requirement that was introduced, making access to food conditional on successful registration in the biometric identification system (*aadhaar*), led to the exclusion of many poor people (Sagar 2017). A particularly egregious failure was that the central government entirely ignored the provision of maternity benefits of Rs 6000 per child to all pregnant women, legislated for under the Food Security Act, until at the end of December 2016 the prime minister introduced his own maternity benefit scheme. The Pradhan Mantri Matru Vandana Yojana provided, however, for a lower level of benefit (Drèze 2019). The rights-based spirit of the laws passed under the UPA government was, in effect, whittled away. Instead, to begin with at least, the Modi government offered Indians 'empowerment'.

Empowerment, or JAM today?

Early in its tenure, the government set out ideas for improving – as it claimed – on the delivery of social welfare, by shifting from an 'entitlement' approach to one of 'empowerment'. The Government of India's *Economic Survey 2015–16* referred to 'the game-changer potential of technology enabled direct benefits transfer (DBT), namely the JAM (Jan Dhan-Aadhaar-Mobile number) trinity solution, which offers exciting possibilities to effectively target public resources to those who need them most, and include all those who have been deprived in multiple ways' (GoI 2016, volume 2: 213). This was to be the foundation of the 'empowerment' approach promised by the government. The JAM was announced as a 'revolution' by Arvind Subramanian (Chief Economic Adviser to the Government of India 2014–18) and S. George in an article in the *New York Times* (22 July 2015), looking to a cashless society in which all subsidies could be rolled into a single lump-sum cash transfer to households.

Among the elements of the 'trinity', 'Jan Dhan' refers to the *Pradhan Mantri Jan Dhan Yojana* ('Prime Minister's People Money Scheme') – also known as the National Mission for Financial Inclusion – announced by the prime minister shortly after his election, in August 2014, and aimed at ensuring that every household should have a bank account. On the inauguration day alone, 15 million new accounts were opened. Account holders were provided with accounts that required no minimum balance, and they were intended to be accessible by mobile phone. By February 2019, 347 million accounts had been opened under the scheme, though more than 20 per cent of them at that time were still zero balance (*Business Line*, 6 January 2019). *Aadhaar* refers to the twelve-digit unique identity number, associated with individual biometric and demographic data, which it is intended every Indian resident should be assigned. The programme for achieving this target was designed by the UPA government in 2009, when it set up the Unique Identification Authority of India. By March 2018, according to an answer given by the government to a question asked in the Lok Sabha, more than 89 per cent of Indians had their *aadhaar* (but see posts by Drèze and co-authors, *Ideas for India*, 2–6 May 2016, for critical discussion of *aadhaar*). The final member of the JAM trinity is the mobile phone, which has penetrated Indian society very deeply (Doron and Jeffrey 2013). Given that only 27 per cent of Indian villages have a bank within five kilometres, beneficiaries should be able to access their money without actually having to go to a bank, making and receiving payments electronically using their phones. The JAM idea is that it will be possible to target public resources to those who need support (though how they are to be identified remains unclear), transferring money directly into bank accounts, identified by the *aadhaar*. This is expected to permit the 'rationalizing' of public expenditure by 'ensuring the removal of so far undetected fake and duplicate entities from beneficiary lists, resulting in substantial savings of public money' (GoI 2016, volume 2: 213).

So there was mounting support for the expansion of direct cash transfers (or direct benefits transfer, in the terminology employed by government in India) in place of what were seen as 'leaky' welfare programmes (see Kapur et al. 2008; Panagariya 2008). This partly followed from the apparent success of such programmes in Latin America, notably in Brazil where it is thought that the *Bolsa Família*, a cash transfer scheme that was made conditional upon children's minimum school attendance, lifted many out of poverty. The attractions of such schemes are fairly obvious. They seem to be administratively much simpler than running something like the PDS, and they are less paternalistic, giving people choice, allowing them to access whatever goods and services they want in private markets – which is ideologically much to be desired on the part of economic liberals (and absolves government of the responsibility for ensuring public provision). A major flaw in this reasoning is that it assumes that there are no supply-side difficulties, particularly in regard to basic services of education, health – and food. As Jayati Ghosh put it, 'Providing small amounts of cash to allow people [for example] to visit private local quacks will hardly compensate for the absence of a reasonably well-funded public health system' (2011; and see also Drèze 2015). Substituting cash transfers for the provision of important public services by the state most certainly attenuates the idea of there being a right for citizens of the country to employment, or food, or education, or health care. As Mehta argued, the danger with direct cash transfer is that 'it is seen as a substitute for governance, rather than an instrument of governance. It gives up on the state' (2011: 15). This matters greatly, of course, in regard to the social democratic objectives of the Constitution of India, but it is precisely why direct cash transfer is so attractive to others, like those policy makers in India who are inclined to economic liberalism.

By 2018, however, the idea of direct cash transfer had begun to be questioned, even by economists who had been among its more articulate advocates. Kotwal and Ramaswami (2018), for example, who had been, according to their own self-description, 'enthusiastic cheerleaders', began to express criticism, recognizing that the way in which *aadhaar* was being used was making it an instrument of exclusion. There is ample documentation of the negative impact of *aadhaar* on welfare programmes in work by Reetika Khera (2017). As Ashok Kotwal has said, even if the application of technology in the delivery of welfare has considerable potential over the longer run, for now 'we are learning that due to the inadequacies of the technological infrastructure, costs may outweigh benefits' (Drèze and Kotwal 2018). Jean Drèze said of JAM that it looks like the pursuit of nirvana (Drèze 2015). It may realize some benefits for the mass of India's poor people, but as he argued, until such time as India invests adequately – not only in financial terms – in education and in health services, nirvana, or more prosaically, the realization of the social rights agenda, will remain elusive.

There is a coda to this discussion, however. The potential that is identified in direct cash transfers reappeared in the *Economic Survey* of the Government of India for 2016–17, the one after the edition of this important publication that proclaimed the virtues of JAM. This was in a chapter entitled 'Universal basic income: A conversation with and within the Mahatma' (Government of India 2017), where it was argued that the idea of providing a basic income to *all* citizens, as a matter of right, is one that must be taken seriously, and is not without the bounds of feasibility for India. The idea of universal basic income (UBI) is one that has been discussed quite intensively among economists (in regard to India, see Bardhan 2016, 2019), and has won significant support. The idea moved from the sphere of academic discussion, or the pages of the *Economic Survey*, into the realm of politics in the run-up to the 2019 general election when the President of the Congress Party, Rahul Gandhi, announced that if it won office the Party would ensure 'a minimum income guarantee to every poor person in the country' (*The Hindu*, 29 January 2019); and it was said that the idea was based on the chapter on UBI in the *Economic Survey 2016–17*. It was perhaps in response to this that the BJP government, just a few days later, in its Interim Budget, announced the *Pradhan Mantri Kisan Samman Nidhi*, providing for income support to small farmers. Neither scheme was quite UBI, but it was thought that they might well presage a move towards its implementation.

Welfarism, After All

In practice, after all the excitement over JAM and 'empowerment', the Modi government of 2014–19 resorted to the welfarist supply of private goods rather than either JAM or the kind of productive public services that contribute significantly to 'empowerment'. Only very late in the day did it announce significant new policies in regard to health care and education (on the delay, see Aiyar 2017). As it was, a number of schemes were set up, with much fanfare and branding in Modi's name, of a distinctly 'welfarist' kind, mostly based on a revamping of existing programmes (some of which bore the names of earlier prime ministers – Modi was certainly not the first prime minister to associate him- or herself with supposedly 'people-focused' programmes). These included the *Swachh Bharat Abhiyan*, announced in October 2014, aimed at eliminating open defecation through construction of toilets – and which, if successful, would make a significant difference to the health of Indians (discussed in chapters 3 and 4); the *Pradhan Mantri* [prime minister] *Awas Yojana*, launched initially for urban India in 2015 and a year later for rural India (as *Pradhan Mantri Awas Yojana Grameen*), intended to provide 'affordable housing for all', by 2022; *Pradhan Mantri Ujjwal Yojana*, launched in 2016 to distribute

50 million liquid propane gas (LPG) cylinders to poor women 'free of cost'. These three programmes were intended to come together with completion of the provision of electricity to all villages, access to clean drinking water, investment in rural roads and *Jan Dhan* banking facilities.

There is strong evidence that the BJP government did well in achieving ambitious numerical targets in all these areas. We mentioned the speed with which bank accounts were opened up under *Jan Dhan*; the numbers of toilets constructed have been impressive – according to the government 99 per cent of households now have a toilet, as against 33 per cent in 2014; in its first two years the rural housing scheme was reported to have doubled the number of houses built (Tewari 2018); the immediate objectives of the *Ujjwal Yojana* have been achieved; the electrification of all Indian villages was achieved in April 2018 when Modi tweeted, '28th April 2018 will be remembered as a historic day in the development journey of India . . . I am delighted that every village in India now has access to electricity'.

There are problems, no doubt, with the substance of all these achievements: a large number of the *Jan Dhan* accounts remain zero balance, and there are increasing doubts over the effectiveness of the banking system of which these accounts are a part (Dhorajiwala et al. 2019); whether toilet construction has really had a major impact in reducing open defecation is open to question (see our discussion in chapter 4, and recent findings in four north Indian states by Coffey and Spears and their associates: Gupta et al. 2019); there are many criticisms of the *PM Awas Yojana*, including doubts over the quality of the houses that are built and whether they meet people's needs, as opposed to favouring the interests of property developers (Patel 2016) – and there is a strong case for the argument that the housing problem of very poor people would be better tackled by the provision of public rental, as happened in Europe (N. C. Saxena, personal communication); it is doubtful whether the *Ujjwal Yojana* has brought about sustained change because of issues around affordability and reliability (Dabadge et al. 2018); and for all that every village has an electricity connection, large numbers of homes do not, and remain in the dark (Dutt D'Cunha 2018).

Then the first budget of the new Modi government, presented in July 2019, did little to suggest that social objectives figure very highly among the government's priorities (Narayanan 2019). Poverty was mentioned just once in the budget statement; there was no mention of rural distress or of the role of the MGNREGS; no mention of malnutrition and very little was said on health. Economists reckoned that the budget allocations fell far short of placing India on track to reach the commitment made in the National Health Policy to increase public health expenditure to 2.5 per cent of GDP (Sundararaman 2019). Much more funding was thought to be required if the health insurance scheme, *Ayushman Bharat*, was to live up to Modi's proud boast that it would be 'the world's largest healthcare programme'.

Still, the achievements of the first Modi administration seemed impressive. They led one of India's prominent businessmen, Gaurav Dalmia, to write in the London *Financial Times*, 'In a country notorious for leakages, Mr Modi has shown government can deliver services effectively' – though in the light of the hype over 'JAM' it was striking that Dalmia went on, 'Its biggest success has been the direct-to-consumer benefits in lieu of cash transfers to the poor' (Dalmia 2019). Reports show that these benefits did have some influence in winning votes for the BJP in 2019 (see Chaturvedi et al. 2019). But has Narendra Modi succeeded in overcoming historical pathologies of poor governance in India, and in making government more responsive? We develop our answer below: the 'direct-to-consumer' benefits, to which Dalmia refers, are relatively easy to deliver. Education, health care – and food security – are tougher nuts to crack.

8.5 How Government Works

In regard to many of its functions, the Indian state has performed very well indeed. What Devesh Kapur (2010) refers to as the 'macro-state', responsible for the major instruments of economic policy, has generally done very well indeed even in the period of low rates of economic growth when India at least avoided the disasters of high rates of inflation that so badly affected other 'developing' economies. This is the sphere of the often highly competent upper echelons of the Indian Administrative Service (IAS). India does well, too, in regard to some indicators of democracy. But Indian governments have not performed very well historically in regard to the delivery of services, even by comparison with their poorer and economically less dynamic neighbouring countries. The 'Fragile States Index' for 2019 shows Pakistan at 23rd (i.e. there are only twenty-two countries that do worse on this Index), Bangladesh at 36th, Nepal at 45th and Sri Lanka at 46th, while India is ranked 74th. In regard to the criterion (included in the Index) of 'state of public services', however, India does only a little better (with a score of 6.8, where 10 would mean complete breakdown) than its neighbours Pakistan (8.0) and Bangladesh (7.5), less well than Nepal (6.6) and far worse than Sri Lanka (4.5) (see www.fsi. fundforpeace.org). The 'micro-state' has, for example, launched a long series of programmes to address different dimensions of poverty but with very little to show for most of them (see chapter 3, and Kapur 2010; for an old but still penetrating account of how benefits from poverty programmes leak upwards, see Guhan 1980). What accounts for these characteristics of the Indian state – high levels of competence and performance at the centre, but a distressing inability to deliver programmes and services to the mass of the people?

The immediate causes have to do with the way the government machinery works. There are serious problems of bureaucratic capacity. For all that there are vast numbers of government employees in India, in relative terms they are few in number. In India there are 1.4 government employees for every 100 citizens, while Sri Lanka, for example, has the ratio of 4.5:100 (these data, and those that follow are from Saxena 2016). This must play some part in the superior performance of Sri Lanka in regard to delivery of public services. There are big differences, too, between Indian states, as shown in figure 8.1. It is generally considered that service provision by government in Tamil Nadu, and in states such as Punjab, Maharashtra and Kerala, is relatively good, and that service delivery is especially poor in Bihar and UP. The fact that the higher performing states have, relative to population, so many more government employees surely plays some part in the differences in performance.

The Indian bureaucracy is characterized, as well, by having relatively very large numbers of personnel in support positions – drivers, clerks and manual labourers – and too few regular employees, who do the work of service delivery in education and health care, and in policing. Then, there are, as we have said, many members of the Indian Administrative Service who are very capable, but they are hampered by some of the ways in which the bureaucracy is organized. In particular, they are subject to frequent transfers between positions, which means that many have little chance of developing professional expertise. It was reported in 2014 that 68 per cent of IAS officers had average tenure in a position of only eighteen months; and in Uttar Pradesh the average was as little as six months (*Times of India*, 1 January 2014, cited by Saxena 2016). The powers that politicians have to transfer a civil servant from one post to another, and to promote and to demote them, is one of the crucial problems in the functioning of government. These powers open up huge possibilities for securing rents, on the parts of both officials and especially of politicians

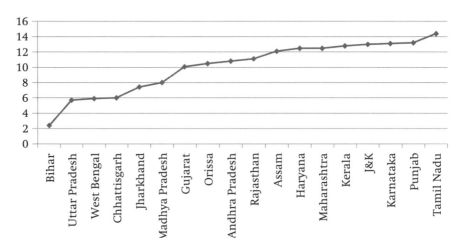

Figure 8.1 Number of State Government Employees per 1,000 of Population
SOURCE: Saxena (2016)

(Wade 1982, 1985) – as government employees seek to avoid difficult postings and to secure ones that are simply more comfortable, or in which there are significant opportunities for graft. It also means that even the most competent and uncorrupted officials – often especially them – are unlikely to remain in one position for very long. It all leads to a lack of professionalism, and to a tendency to follow procedure, so as to avoid possible censure, as opposed to commitment to problem solving and perhaps taking initiative.

Following procedure, in the context of a hierarchical and seniority-obsessed bureaucratic culture, is pervasive. A common perspective among the bureaucratic elite is that lower-ranking and frontline staff 'are corrupt, unresponsive and caught up in local political and social networks' (Mehta and Walton 2014). They are not be trusted, therefore, and have to be monitored very carefully. They are disempowered, in consequence, and are given little space for exercising discretion or initiative. They seek to avoid being noticed by following the rules, come what may – which reinforces the impression that they are merely time-servers. It is a culture that leads to what has been referred as the 'post-box' paradox in a study of education administrators at the block level across four states (Aiyar and Bhattacharya 2016). These government workers described themselves as being like post-boxes, receiving messages from above and delivering them below, simply doing the bidding of higher authorities. They have no authority themselves to take decisions and resolve problems that they unearth as they do their jobs. The deliberative culture that Mangla analysed in the education administration of Himachal Pradesh – which does unusually well in elementary education – is an exception that proves the general rule (Mangla 2015).

A bureaucracy with these characteristics, in which field-level staff have little scope for problem solving, may do well when it comes to delivering standardized services – such as building so many toilets in a given place over a given period, or houses, or schools, or (literally) delivering gas cylinders. Then rule-based bureaucratic functioning may do quite well, but it is not likely to do so well when it comes to delivering services that involve both large numbers of transactions, and the exercise of significant discretion on the part of the service providers, such as is the case in teaching, or in health care, or in policing (see Pritchett and Woolcock 2004). The successes of the first Modi administration in delivering services, as we suggested, have been relatively easy ones.

An ethnography of what the researcher, Nayanika Mathur, calls the 'Paper Tiger' that is the Indian state, based on a year-long immersion in the NREGS cell of the district administration of a part of Uttarakhand, both qualifies and complements these arguments. While Mathur disputes the argument that the critical problem of the Indian bureaucracy is that it lacks capacity, there is much in her account that does show that there are simply not enough competent people with the power to take decisions and resolve problems.

But she provides a compelling analysis of how 'it is through the production of variegated documents and through the convening and staging of meetings that the accomplishment of development by the state is said to be "done"' (2016: 169). Huge amounts of time and effort go into producing paperwork that proves that the individual bureaucrat has done his or her work. It may be recognized that what appears on paper bears little relation to what has actually happened, but the paperwork has to be done. The accent is on the 'performance' of government.

The further characteristic of government administration in India – beyond the lackadaisical time-keeping that Mathur also describes – is the problem of absenteeism, staff not being in their workplaces. It has often been found that teachers are not in their classrooms – perhaps for private reasons, but sometimes for a public reason, such as that they have been deputed to work on other government tasks. Another illustration of how crippling absentee-ism can be comes from the health sector. Studies have shown that although the country has a public system of health care, staffed by quite well trained and technically competent personnel, who can provide care more cheaply than private medical practitioners, the public system is widely distrusted by people. People, even very poor people, prefer to seek health care from private providers, even though the private practitioners whom they seek out may be technically less competent than those in the public system as well as costing more (though lesser competence isn't always the case, given evidence on the diagnostic skills of some so-called 'quacks' – see Das and Hammer 2012). An important part of the reason for the preference for private practitioners is the very high levels of absenteeism that prevail among doctors and nurses, so that people cannot rely on local health centres being open when they should be, or on actually having access to a doctor when they go to higher level primary health care centres. Research has shown that absenteeism may be institution-alized, with health service managers conniving with junior staff to sanction and so to perpetuate absenteeism (Banerjee and Duflo 2009). But there is also the problem that the poor working conditions and facilities in many public health centres cause or exacerbate the problems associated with absenteeism. In March 2018, only 12 per cent of Primary Health Centres in the country were functioning according to Indian Public Health Service standards. It is hardly surprising, then, that the fourth round of the National Family Health Survey (2015–16) should have found that 52 per cent of people in the bottom two wealth quintiles did not generally use public facilities (Kapur and Shukla 2019).

What we have described as pathologies of the Indian bureaucracy are inter-locked. The importance of the paperwork that Nayanika Mathur describes is in part because it is a way of shuffling off responsibility (2016: ch. 4, esp. 111–12). Absenteeism fosters the idea that junior staff cannot be trusted to do their jobs. But teachers or health workers may evade censure for absenteeism because of the patronage of politicians, who have the power to transfer higher-level officers who seek to ensure that staff are in their posts. Then a perverse spiral is set in motion. There is a significant inter-relationship between the ways in which politicians operate and the routines of the bureaucracy. As Saxena, a scholar-administrator, puts it:

> Efficiency in the civil services was always very narrowly defined. It meant contempt for politics and rigid adherence to rules; 'public satisfaction' was an insignificant part of the job evaluation. In such an environment, it is unfair to expect that the political processes would be totally free from populism or sectarianism. *Because of the inability of the system to deliver, politicians do not consider good governance as feasible or even important for getting votes* . . .[they] are forced to find other ways to keep alive the faith of the voter in the political system. Populism serves this purpose (Saxena 2016: 134, emphasis added).

Populism (sometimes reflected in promises such as 'rice at one rupee per kilo', or even give-aways of consumer goods) is one way in which a politician may seek to win and to maintain support, or it may be by the delivery of benefits to particular supporters, perhaps fellow caste members. From the point of view of the politicians, being able to control selective benefits through patronage using the resources of the state seems to be a more reliable way of ensuring continued support – and of realizing rents for themselves – than standing on a policy platform including promises about the delivery of *public* goods. There are very significant differences between states, however, and the states of Kerala, Tamil Nadu and Himachal Pradesh, in particular, have done fairly well in delivering public services by pursuing programmatic politics (perhaps alongside frankly populist measures, in the case of Tamil Nadu; see Wyatt 2013).

But there is still a puzzle as to why voters – who include large numbers of poor people, who would greatly benefit from better provision of public health, education and other services – do not hold politicians (and through them the frontline bureaucrats who are immediately responsible for service delivery) democratically accountable for poor public provisioning. One answer – exactly as Saxena has suggested (see above) – is that it is because of the lack of credibility of political promises to provide broad public goods. Keefer and Khemani attribute 'the differential credibility of promises related to public goods versus private transfers' (2004: 935) to three factors: the history of electoral competition, the extent of social fragmentation of voters and the limited information among voters about the quality of services. The first of these points involves an argument about historical path dependency. There are states – Keefer and Khemani give the familiar example of Kerala – where there is a history of governments being held to account because voters have been highly mobilized (in Kerala by the communist parties) over service issues. In the absence of such a history, as in Uttar Pradesh, it is difficult for any political leader or party to break from a path that has been determined by competition around selective benefits. The argument then shows up the significance of the second factor – that of social fragmentation. Public provisioning has generally been better in those states in which poorer people have been mobilized collectively, as by the communist parties in Kerala, or by the Dravidian parties in Tamil Nadu (see Harriss 2003b), or perhaps around solidaristic sentiments of sub-nationalism (Singh 2015).

The factor of collective mobilization in turn ties up with the one to do with information. The argument is made in work by Besley and Burgess (2000) on variations in government responsiveness across the major Indian states. They examined public food distribution and calamity relief expenditure as measures of government responsiveness and showed that differences between states in their regard are only weakly related to variations in economic development, but that states with historically higher electoral turnouts and more competitive politics, and those with higher newspaper circulation, are distinctly more responsive than others. It seems clear that higher levels of information among voters and higher levels of collective political mobilization are mutually supportive and inter-related. The data given by Besley and Burgess show that the most 'responsive states' according to their measures are Kerala, Maharashtra, Tamil Nadu and West Bengal, which are also the states with the highest newspaper circulation, and states in which the lower classes have historically been most highly mobilized politically.

Keefer and Khemani's argument therefore seems to point to the significance of long-run trends of political mobilization and so it poses a further question: why is it that poorer people have not been mobilized collectively to any great extent around public provisioning in most Indian states? We can turn to Kanchan Chandra's analysis of 'patronage democracy' (referred to in chapter 7). She asked how benefit-seeking voters in a patronage democracy like India select politicians to vote for, and how politicians on the other hand decide which groups of electors to pitch for. The decisions both of voters and of politicians are subject, she said, to severe information constraints, and that these 'force voters and politicians to favour co-ethnics in the delivery of benefits and votes (resulting in) a self-enforcing and reinforcing equilibrium of ethnic favouritism' (2004: 12). What matters to voters is not what a party or a political leader says, but *who* it, or she is. The basis for such ethnic favouritism may be caste, language or religion, or a sense of a 'national'/regional identity that is perhaps only rather loosely linked to linguistic difference (as was the case in the Telengana region of Andhra Pradesh, before it became a separate state in 2014), and it is always subject to reconstruction. This is the reason why, according to Chandra's analysis, ethnic voting does not lead to permanent electoral majorities, because rival politicians can reconstruct salient identities (as, for example, Rajput politicians in Gujarat – from a numerically small group – succeeded in extending the category of Kshatriya to a very wide group. See Chandra 2004: 289). Ethnic parties are likely to succeed when they have competitive rules for intra-party advancement, and so are open to elites from across the possible sub-divisions of the ethnic category around which they are organized, and when voters from the target category are sufficiently numerous to take the party to an influential position. Once the equilibrium of ethnic favouritism is established, it is not easily broken down.

With the decline of the Congress Party as an encompassing interest, embracing many different actually or potentially self-conscious groups of people (on which, see Corbridge and Harriss 2000: chs 3–6), so Indian politics became more of a field of contestation over ethnic identities – often involving claims about dignity or self-respect, as well as over resources – which has reinforced government failure. Witsoe (2013) has shown this in his study of Bihar under the leadership of Lalu Prasad Yadav, whose concern was above all to raise the sense of self-respect and dignity among those he referred to as 'his people', Yadavs and others among the OBCs. And as Banerjee and Pande showed in a test using data from Uttar Pradesh, if voters are concerned about the group identity of political candidates, then if this group has a majority in a particular political jurisdiction, the quality of the candidates can be very poor and yet they will still win. In such circumstances 'a strengthening of group identity on citizens' political preferences worsens the quality of political representation' (Banerjee and Pande 2009: 2). The two authors developed a data set, from a field survey covering a sample of 102 jurisdictions, on legislator corruption in Uttar Pradesh over the period 1980–96, when it is generally recognized that ethnic voting became increasingly significant (the standard source on this is Yadav 1996). They then demonstrate both that increased legislator corruption over this period can be attributed to legislators from the party that shared the ethnic identity of the dominant population group in a jurisdiction (Congress or BJP for upper caste voters, Samajwadi Party or Bahujan Samaj Party for lower caste voters), and that increased corruption was largely concentrated in those jurisdictions with substantial high- or low-caste domination. Jurisdictions with the more biased caste distributions showed the greatest increases in corruption.

Following the 2019 general election, however, Narendra Modi attacked opposition leaders and parties for 'doing caste-based politics', which he claimed to have overcome. He argued that his victory was a validation of his welfare programmes, which did not use caste as a determinant. 'Only two castes will remain in this country' he said, the poor, and those trying to 'free the country from poverty'. This conveniently overlooked a good deal of evidence of the effective use of caste appeals by the BJP in the election (Sagar 2019). Yet there is evidence from eastern UP, certainly, of the weakening of caste links between voters and parties. Reporting from Yogi Adityanath's old constituency of Gorakhpur, Chaturvedi et al. (2019) argue that the breaking down of the old caste dynamics, together with efficient delivery of welfare services by BJP governments, ensured the victory of the BJP. Voters made such statements as 'Largely the vote is for the lotus (BJP), who cares about the candidate?', and their satisfaction with the efficient delivery of services was reported even by people, including Muslims, who were not Modi supporters. This evidently outweighed dissatisfaction over jobs or farm incomes. Opposition based on caste considerations was ineffectual. The researchers argued, 'The liberal intelligentsia simply fails fully to appreciate these ground realities and nuances' (Chaturvedi et al. 2019).

The patterns of identity-based politics discussed by Chandra, and by Banerjee and Pande, are not yet dead, but changes are taking place, and new fault lines are emerging. What has not changed is that a high proportion of elected politicians have criminal records, many of them relating to serious crimes including kidnapping and murder. The link between crime and politics is in significant part because of the costs of financing elections. As Vaishnav says, in his study *When Crime Pays* (2017), 'parties value "muscle" . . . because of the money that comes along with it' (2017: 20). But then office, once won, turns out to be highly lucrative. One study showed that the average wealth of legislators increased by 222 per cent over just one term. As Vaishnav argues, '[M]oney serves to bankroll politics; politicians and political parties are beholden to vested interests that can organize and deploy sizeable amounts of largely undocumented cash. But while money greases the wheels of politics, political office can also generate large quantities of money' (2017: 62). And a good many of the criminal-legislators are also out-and-out thugs. Money and fear are closely aligned, and in many parts of India there is what has been described as 'mafia raj' (in a set of studies by Michelutti and other anthropologists: Michelutti et al. 2019). Voters more often return the thugs to office than other candidates at least in part because they have a reputation for getting things done – reflecting, of course, the poor state of the state in India.

The ways in which Indian democracy works, therefore, constrain the capacity of the state to deliver on the rights agenda and on public services – and the limits of state capacity, as Saxena argues (cited above), reinforce the particular ways in which democratic politics functions.

8.6 Conclusions

Jawaharlal Nehru's promise, speaking before the Constituent Assembly in January 1947, that with freedom from colonial rule India would 'feed the starving people, . . . clothe the naked masses, and . . . give every Indian the fullest opportunity to develop himself according to his capacity' (cited in chapter 1), was honoured only very imperfectly by the governments that he headed. There was an egregious failure to honour the constitutional commitment to making elementary education universal by 1960, and both education and health were never adequately funded. Neither of these sectors, so important though they are for giving Indians opportunity, became a political priority then, or under subsequent governments. In practice, the achievement of high rates of economic growth, as an end in itself, has always been paramount – though some states, such as Kerala and Tamil Nadu, have done much better than others at improving the well-being of their citizens.

We have shown in this chapter how at last, early in the twenty-first century, as a result of activism in civil society, and judicial intervention – not, primarily, because of leadership from politicians – important economic and social rights were established in India, and the interests of human development became more significant. Delivery of these rights by the state has been imperfect, but there has been progress, though more in some areas than in others, and more in some states than in others. India does now have the framework of a social security system. The most striking failure has been in regard to education. Although elementary education is at last more or less universal, the quality of that education in the public schooling system remains quite lamentable. A right to health care has yet to be established.

The first BJP government headed by Narendra Modi weakened rather than strengthened the 'new rights agenda' established under the United Progressive Alliance governments of 2004–14, and in the end – its interest in shifting to a cash transfer-based 'empowerment' approach notwithstanding – concentrated on the provision of 'direct-to-consumer' benefits, such as gas cylinders. The government did this well enough, and reaped an electoral dividend. Only towards the end of its tenure of office did the Modi government undertake a major initiative in regard to health care, with the introduction of what is intended to be a massive health insurance scheme. There were no new initiatives in regard to elementary education until the appearance of recommendations for a New Education Policy just after Modi's re-election in 2019 (see chapter 13). At the time of writing, following the first budget of the new Modi government elected in May 2019, it seems unlikely that either the health scheme or others that have to do with the delivery of economic and social rights will be given much priority.

We have argued, finally, that the failures of the Indian state in regard to social development have to do with the limits of state capacity and the ways in which the administration functions, and that these are interlinked with the ways in which India's so-called 'patronage democracy' works. Given the inability of the state system, over most if not quite all of the country, to deliver, promises related to public goods are hardly credible. It is unsurprising, then, that politicians mobilize support by other means including still the promise of patronage. But then the actions of politicians, more and more of whom are criminals or who have criminal connections, continually undermine the functioning of the bureaucracy. Breaking this vicious spiral is a major challenge for India today.

9

Is There a Countermovement against Neoliberalism in India?

9.1 Introduction: Polanyi's Idea of the 'Double Movement' and India Today

The shift in India's economic policies that is marked especially by the inception of 'economic reforms' in 1991, which we have discussed in earlier chapters, can sensibly be seen as reflecting the ascendancy of neoliberalism – even if the policy elites, more than twenty-five years later, are still struggling to implement important elements of neoliberal economic policy such as labour market 'flexibility' (see chapter 4). India has been experiencing a particular version of the market fundamentalism that has been the dominant mode of thought about economic policy across much of the world since the late 1970s, as David Harvey has explained in *A Brief History of Neoliberalism* (2005). The economy is conceptualized as an autonomous self-governing entity, and it is held that it should be left as far as possible to regulate itself. Hence the emphasis on deregulation, liberalization and privatization – all intended to limit the role of the state in the economy – in India's reforms, as in economic policy in many other countries.

The contemporary episode in which these ideas hold sway may be thought of as their 'second coming' – the first having taken place in the nineteenth and early twentieth centuries (Block and Summers 2014). That earlier era of economic liberalism is the subject of Karl Polanyi's *The Great Transformation: The Political and Economic Origins of Our Time* (1944), in which the author finds the causes of the economic and political crisis of his own times of the mid-twentieth century in the failed attempt to make a reality of the idea of the self-regulating market economy (SRM). Polanyi argues that in trying to realize this idea (which he considers utopian), labour, land and money all have to be treated as commodities, with their prices set by the forces of supply and demand. Yet none of these three vital factors of production is truly a commodity. Labour is simply human activity; land – a metaphor for the natural environment – is given to us, not produced for sale in the market; and money is a token of purchasing power that facilitates exchange. If there is to be a self-regulating market, all of these elements of the economy have to be commodified. The economy has to be 'dis-embedded' from society, as Polanyi puts it. This is what was attempted in the nineteenth century, in England first of all, from the 1830s.

But the moves to establish the SRM gave rise to a countermovement, as people resisted the treatment of their capacity for work as a commodity, ultimately through unionization and political pressure for legislation to protect workers; as others – land owners, capitalist farmers and peasants – sought to protect land from its commoditization and domestic agriculture from the effects of free trade; and, eventually, as governments intervened increasingly, to protect business from the effects of the operation of the gold standard (the commodity form of money), which tended to bring about deflationary pressures, and thus both the destruction of businesses and the rise of unemployment. States had to intervene to protect labour, land and domestic agriculture, and national currencies, though this upset the entire premise of the SRM. The conflicts that ensued underlay the mid-twentieth-century crisis, which was the time of what Polanyi calls 'the great transformation', that saw the rise of different approaches to the re-embedding of the economy into society: communism, the broadly social democratic approach of Roosevelt's New Deal, and fascism.

Polanyi argues, therefore, that the history of his own time had been defined by a 'double movement':

> the action of two organizing principles in society … The one was the principle of economic liberalism, aiming at the establishment of a self-regulating market, relying on the support of the trading classes, and using largely *laissez-faire* and free trade as its methods; the other was the principle of social protection aiming at the conservation of man and nature as well as productive organization, relying on the varying support of those most immediately affected by the deleterious action of the market (1944: 132).

The first movement is clearly recognizable in the intentions of influential Indian policy makers since 1991. But what of the countermovement? Is there a countermovement in contemporary India?

Reflecting upon developments in India's politics and society in the contemporary epoch through the lens of Polanyi's idea of the double movement, we seem to see people coming together, as they have done historically, to protect themselves from the precariousness in their lives (see chapters 3 and 4) – but in and on behalf of particular groups, and in defence of their particular privileges, rather than on behalf of society as a whole (chapter 8). Mobilizations around the Hindu identity that have become increasingly powerful in the twenty-first century (and are the subject of chapter 6) represent a particular case of a widespread trend, that has both fed into and been strengthened by the rise of authoritarian populism (which we also discuss in chapter 6). These mobilizations, in India and elsewhere in the world, can be understood in some part as being a response, not so much to increasing economic inequality, as to increasing economic insecurity in the context of neoliberalism, and the sense of powerlessness that many people feel. Jan Breman refers, for example, to the appeal of *Hindutva* among former permanently employed mill-workers in Ahmedabad, who have been forced into various forms of informal employment (2001). Only rarely has the basis of mobilization been that of class identity. The mass of the peasantry (as opposed to the rural bourgeoisie), the rural proletariat, and the unorganized working class have never been effectively represented by any political party in India, except perhaps in Kerala by the communist parties. Even in West Bengal, continuously governed by the organized left from 1977 to 2011, the Communist Party of India (Marxist) (CPI (M)) represented mainly the labour aristocracy and sections of the peasantry, generally ignoring unorganized workers (see Agarwala 2013: ch. 4). Political parties such as the Bahujan Samaj Party (BSP) have claimed to represent poorer people, but have mobilized on the basis of identity. The BSP in Uttar Pradesh identified itself originally as being a Dalit party – but even then it was seen as a party of one particular Dalit caste group, the Chamars. In other states, too, Dalit political mobilization is fractured by caste divisions.

The relationship between caste and class entails a paradox, as the writer Shashank Kela has explained: 'Caste is – and is not – class. It is class insofar as it determines class position for most Indians. It is not class insofar as it inhibits class mobilization *across* castes' (2012: 76). There is a very significant overlap between caste and class, no doubt (see chapter 11). The rural proletariat, for example, is made up disproportionately (and increasingly) by Dalits, and rural Dalits are far more likely to be casual daily paid labourers than they are to be substantial farmers. The latter, members of the rural bourgeoisie, are likely to come from locally dominant castes, like the Jats in western Uttar Pradesh (Jeffrey et al. 2008). The recent history of Tamil Brahmans is one of the formation of a middle class, according to the account given by Fuller and Narasimhan (2014). So, as Kela argues, caste exercises considerable influence on the class positions that Indians occupy. And there are circumstances in which the congruence of class and caste can encourage political mobilization, as Béteille showed, for example, with regard to agrarian social relations in Thanjavur in the 1950s and 1960s. In the eastern taluks of the district, he observed, almost all of the agricultural labourers were from the same Dalit community. The unity of the Dalit agricultural workers was reinforced by their physical isolation in separate hamlets (*cheris*), making it 'particularly easy for them to be organized into a class for the purpose of political action' (1974: 167). But more generally caste inhibits class mobilization. In northern Tamil Nadu, for instance, there is a long history of tension between the two most numerous caste communities, the Vanniyars, a historically low-ranked 'most backward' group, and the Paraiyars, the principal Dalit community, that has regularly erupted into violence. Part of the reason is that the two groups may be in competition for the same informal jobs. Latterly, there is evidence of the resentments of Vanniyars against the relative success of the Paraiyars – concerns, then, about privilege, or social status as much or more as over economic interest, but a powerful inhibitor of class mobilization. And in the same state, while there is good reason for seeing the successful political mobilization of the Dravidian parties that have ruled there since 1967, as reflecting the interests of lower castes/classes, it is also the case that Dalits have generally not been well represented by them – which helps to account for the formation of Dalit political parties (Harriss 2018).

In this context, in which Indians generally mobilize, in response to economic insecurity, on group lines, as they have done for long, what specific responses may be discerned to neoliberalism? In this chapter we discuss the response of the labour movement; mobilizations over agriculture, land and natural resources more generally, including that associated with the Maoist insurgency; and middle-class activism around social and economic rights and the claims of equal citizenship (to which we have also referred in chapter 8, and again in chapter 10). We find that there is a countermovement against neoliberalism, though one in which social democratic or socialist tendencies are outweighed politically by the claims of Hindu nationalism, which may be seen as another sort of response to market fundamentalism.

9.2 Towards Social Movement Unionism?

In the time of the 'first coming' of market fundamentalism, in the nineteenth and early twentieth centuries, very large numbers of men employed in mines and factories in the industrialized countries came to be well organized by trade unions, and succeeded in winning substantial protection for working people. Labour was, to an extent, decommodified as a result of these actions. But the circumstances of labour now are very different. Technological change and changes in industrial organization have brought about extensive informalization of work – 'labour on tap', as *The Economist* once put it – not just in India, and trade unions have much less power and influence than was the case before. The main factor in bringing this about is not so much technological change in itself, as the systematic weakening over time of labour organizations. The Indian labour movement in any case has been regarded very critically by some scholars. Trade unions have been seen as defending the special interests of a very small fraction of the labour force, against the mass of workers who, it is argued, would benefit from greater labour market flexibility. At the same time critics from the Left have regretted the lack of unity in the movement, given the divisions that are caused by the political affiliations of the major union federations and the subordination of workers' interests to party politics. They recognize, too, the failure, historically, to bring in the large numbers of workers who are informally employed. Some of these arguments have been critiqued in research by Emmanuel Teitelbaum (2006, 2011), who shows how the claims of fragmentation and political interference may have been overestimated; while Rohini Hensman (2010) has documented how the trade unions were fairly successful in staving off changes in labour law, sought by neoliberal policy makers, and promised by the Second National Labour Commission that reported to the NDA government in 2002.

The attempt to reform labour law in the interests of business was renewed after the election of the BJP government in 2014. This government has sought to create – it has claimed – a 'more friendly' atmosphere between industry and labour (*Economic Times*, 17 December 2015), through the Labour Code on Industrial Relations Bill 2015, which aims to integrate and simplify existing legislation. Its provisions are, however, strongly supportive of the rights of employers, whilst proposing such severe penalties for workers and trade unions, even for seemingly minor violations (like non-submission of returns by trade unions), as to 'deter them from raising issues against employers or putting up any form of resistance that could be declared illegal' (Bhowmik 2015: 17). The passage of the Bill into law was held up by union opposition – though this did not stop other state governments from following the example of Rajasthan in changing labour laws so as to make it easier for companies to hire and fire workers (Majumder 2017).

It was striking that trade unions in India experienced significant growth in their memberships over the years following economic liberalization – in contrast with the decline observed in many other countries (Lambert and Gillan 2013: 189). The frequency of work stoppages did go down but their duration and size increased. Data from the International Labour Office for the period 2005–08 showed that India was among the top five countries in the world for number of workdays lost per 1,000 employees. Of course it is true that the share of contract labour in total employment in the organized factory sector has increased considerably, from 13 per cent in 1992–93 to about 33 per cent in 2009–10 (see chapter 4); and tensions over the employment of contract workers have led to some of the worst labour unrest in India's recent history, such as at the Maruti Suzuki plant at Manesar in July 2012. This was over the formation of a union and the regularizing of contract employees. Such struggles have 'rocked industrial relations in many firms' in the recent past (Shyam Sundar 2015: 47).

India's trade unions are not a spent force, therefore. Eleven central trade union organizations came together to call for a massive general strike, to take place on 2 September 2015, in protest against the proposed new industrial relations legislation, and the government's unwillingness to consider union demands. The strike went ahead, marking 'the first time trade unions sought to challenge the NDA government', according to the *Economic Times* ('Labour strike hits normal life in parts of the country', 3 September 2015). The newspaper reported that 15 crores of workers (150 million) were involved but said that 'the response was mixed and evident only in pockets'. It was later reported, however, that the strike was estimated to have cost the national economy as much as Rs 25,000 crores (Sampath 2016). The action was repeated in March 2016 and again in September 2016 in protest against 'government indifference' to a fifteen-point charter of demands that the trade union organizations had submitted in January 2016. These embraced calls for 'stoppage of pro-employer labour law amendments', 'stoppage of disinvestment in central and state public sector units' and 'stoppage of FDI in railways, insurance and defence', in addition to demands about the minimum wage, pensions and social security.

The unions have, therefore, widened their agenda 'to include systemic issues [such as inflation and the efficiency of the public distribution system] in a manner not seen before' (Shyam Sundar 2015: 49), and they also seem to have recognized the importance of mobilizing among informally employed workers, so as to build a much wider social movement (what has been referred to elsewhere, notably in Brazil and South Africa, as social movement unionism). Indeed, the General Secretary of the Centre of Indian Trade Unions (CITU) claimed in a speech in 2013 that 'the largest number of members mobilized in all trade unions are from the unorganized sector' (quoted by Ramani 2013a: 13). It has been noted, too that 'many trade union federations are committed to "coalition building"' (Lambert and Gillan 2013: 191).

The potential of a much wider, inclusive labour movement is still a very long way from being realized, but there are signs of some progress, therefore. This is in line with what Rina Agarwala has reported of the significant numbers of informally employed workers who are actually 'organized', as were construction workers, and the women bidi workers in her study (2013). She thinks that the movements she has studied 'may reflect a global trend toward social movement unionism', and that 'a modern blend of class politics may now be finding a new echo in, of all places, the informal economy' (2013: 204–5).

The demands that are being made, however, such as those over the minimum wage and for an 'assured pension for the entire population', are demands made more upon the state by the workers, rather than demands made directly upon capital or for workplace rights. In some states of India competitive electoral politics (in Tamil Nadu, in Agarwala's research, as opposed to West Bengal) have made for conditions in which some groups of informally employed workers have been able to secure significant welfare benefits through state intervention. Agarwala's own assessment of these developments is distinctly nuanced. She recognizes the compromise with neoliberalism: 'Their acknowledgement and protection of informal workers have enabled populist leaders in Tamil Nadu to pursue liberal economic reforms by assuring support from the very groups most disaffected by the reforms' (2013: 113). Some scholars in Tamil Nadu are more explicitly critical, such as M. Vijayabaskar, whose views we cited earlier (see chapter 8). The state, he said, has shifted responsibility for the welfare of labour 'from the domain of capital to the domain of government (so that) capital accumulation can now proceed unencumbered by the burden of protecting workers' livelihoods' (2011: 44). And a critical response to Agarwala's arguments holds that the 'assertion that informal workers are acting as a class by seeking welfare from the state, but refraining from wage related demands from their private employers, is very troubling as [their action] fails to address the central issue of income poverty' (RoyChowdhury 2014: 81). But successful welfare states *have* protected workers' livelihoods, in just the way that Vijayabaskar argues is happening in Tamil Nadu, enhancing the productivity of labour as they have done so. There seems now to be more of a base for broad unity of working people around mobilizations aimed at securing social rights and good public services than there is around workplace issues, given uneven industrialization and the extent of informalization of labour in the Indian economy (remember that around 50 per cent of the labour force are self-employed). It may be that it will be on these foundations that a more robust countermovement will be constructed.

9.3 Rural Struggles: Agrarian Crisis, and the 'New' Land Question

The 1980s in India saw the rise of what were referred to as 'new farmers' movements', which came for a time to play a significant part in national politics. Organized and led by richer 'farmers' (the English word being used deliberately, as opposed to 'peasant', to emphasize their class character), and focused on issues of agricultural costs and prices, these movements were sometimes successful in mobilizing large numbers in support of their demands. But then, in the course of the 1990s the farmers' movements, though they did not altogether fade from view, no longer appeared to play nearly such a prominent role in Indian politics – in part because, as Pattenden argued (2005), the big farmers who had led them, had become more interested in activities outside agriculture.

In the second decade of the twenty-first century, however, and in the context of the long-running crisis of Indian agriculture (as discussed in chapter 4), there came about a resurgence of rural protest, reflected in the 'cover story' of the magazine *Frontline* for 7 July 2017 – 'Farmers' Revolts'. Journalists wrote of a prolonged demonstration in 2017 by farmers from Tamil Nadu, in New Delhi, that the last time the capital had seen such an agitation was in 1988; while of Maharashtra it was said that not since an agitation in 1982 over milk prices organized by the Shetkari Sanghatana (one of the most significant of the farmers' movements of the 1980s), 'has there been a united farmers' action on the scale that the state witnessed in early June [of 2017]' (Bavadam 2017). There were large-scale agitations in Madhya Pradesh, Punjab and Haryana, Rajasthan, Uttar Pradesh, and elsewhere. Then in March 2018 there took place a remarkable 'Long March' of 40,000 or more mainly small farmers and landless peasants, many of them adivasis, from Nasik to Mumbai, a distance of 180 km. According to journalists' reports, the march started with 25,000 but ended, in the mass meeting that took place in Mumbai, with 50,000. The demands of the marchers, largely repeating demands addressed to the Government of Maharashtra through earlier protests, and in response to which promises made by the government had not been kept, were for the waiving of farmers' bank debts, for the payment of minimum support prices at the level (one and a half times the cost of production) recommended by an official committee headed by the eminent scientist M. S. Swaminathan, and for the proper implementation of the Forest Rights Act, supporting the rights of forest dwellers (on which, see chapter 8). It seems that the class character of this movement, with its focus on land rights for adivasi farmers (Shantha 2018) was significantly different from that of the farmers' movements of the 1980s, even if others of the demands were quite similar. It was said, by the National President of the CPI(M)-linked All India Kisan Sabha, heavily involved in the organization of the march, that 'The March was directed against the anti-farmer, anti-people, pro-corporate, neoliberal policies of the BJP-led central and state governments' (reported in *Frontline*, 13 April 2018).

Indeed, it is in the Indian countryside, rather than in cities and industrial centres, that a countermovement to market fundamentalism has developed most forcefully, particularly in what Michael Levien has referred to as 'India's "new" land question'. As he says, 'The Indian state is caught between the land requirements of capitalist growth and the political compulsions of electoral democracy' – and whether, how far and for whom this contradiction is resolved constitutes the 'new' land question (as opposed to the land question of the past that had to do with the conditions of land tenure and the distribution of land ownership amongst cultivators) (Levien 2015: 146). An indication of the importance of the land question is in the estimate, reported by Levien, that in 2011 alone capital investments worth 3 per cent of GDP were stalled due to land acquisition problems. Farmers had effectively stopped the two largest proposed Special Economic Zones (SEZs) in India, all of the SEZs in Goa, and four in Maharastra (Levien 2013a).

The problems of land acquisition embrace struggles over the land that is required for industrial projects, as in the notorious cases of attempted land acquisition at Nandigram and Singur in West Bengal, in 2007 and 2008, which were the immediate triggers of the electoral defeat in 2011 of the Left Front government, headed by the CPI(M), that had ruled the state continuously for thirty-four years (Chattopadhyay 2007, 2008). The land question embraces, too, struggles over access to mineral resources, such as those that have contributed to the support won in some parts of central and eastern India by the Communist Party of India (Maoist). The Party has its origins in the Naxalite movement that started in 1967 in an armed uprising of peasants against local landlords, and that has survived the repressive violence of the Indian state for over fifty years (Banerjee 1980, 2009). The intensity and the spread of the Maoist insurgency explain the Indian prime minister's description of it, in 2006, as the most serious internal security threat that India has ever faced. The insurgency certainly did not start as a countermovement to neoliberal market fundamentalism, but there is substantial evidence showing that Maoists have built support by addressing the structural violence to which tribal people, Dalits and poor rural people more generally are subjected, and that has been exacerbated by the land question and by the mineral rush in eastern India (see chapter 5). The CPI (M) has decided, in the words of its General Secretary Ganapathy, 'to take up struggles against the SEZs which are nothing but neo-colonial enclaves on Indian territory' (Ganapathy 2007).

Struggles over land acquisition in India might be thought of in the context of the very widespread phenomenon of 'land grabbing' – the buying or leasing of large tracts of land by national and transnational companies – that has been going on, especially since the crisis of world food prices in 2007–08 (Borras et al. 2011). Such transactions are considered to be a form of what David Harvey has described as 'accumulation by dispossession', referring to the process of dispossession of their assets from people in the interests of capital accumulation. Levien argues persuasively that while the concept is a valuable one, Harvey does not sufficiently recognize the extent to which dispossession is a political process, often involving heavy reliance on state force. Why, he asks, do capitalists rely so often on states to secure land for them, rather than acquiring land through the market? In practice, extra-economic coercion is an on-going aspect of accumulation even under advanced capitalism. Levien's view is that 'dispossession is politically organised in different socio-historical contexts to serve different class interests' (2015: 149), so we may distinguish different 'regimes of dispossession', involving varying combinations of out-right coercion, compensation and normative persuasion.

India, Levien suggests, has moved from a 'regime that dispossessed land for state-led industrial and infrastructure expansion to one that dispossesses land for private and increasingly for financial capital' (2015: 150). The earlier regime was certainly not benign, and there was an almost complete disregard on the part of the state for those displaced from their homes and livelihoods by 'the march of progress'. Their misfortune was held to be a price well worth paying for the common good of irrigation water and power generation. It is significant that for a long time the Government of India had no figures for the numbers of those displaced. Well-reasoned estimates vary quite widely between 20 and 38 million (Whitehead 2003) – though there are other, higher estimates, of up to 60 million (Fernandes 2009). As we commented in chapter 5, what is certain is that members of the Scheduled Tribes – 'tribals' or *adivasis* – who make up about 8 per cent of the population of the country, are quite dispro-portionately represented among those who have been displaced, with Dalits disproportionately represented among the remainder. What is also certain is that only a very small minority of those displaced have been at all adequately compensated, and most states have lacked resettlement and rehabilitation policies. Still, there was expropriation of land for productive, public purposes, and sometimes for public sector housing. This was the case, for instance, with the establishment of big steel-making plants with associated townships, as at Bhilai in Chhattisgarh, Durgapur in West Bengal and Rourkela in Odisha – described by Nehru as 'temples' of India's industrial modernity (Parry and Struempell 2008). Levien argues of the land acquisitions of the Nehruvian state that 'social commitments . . . combined with the state-driven and productivist character of industrial areas place them squarely within a developmentalist regime of dispossession that enjoyed significant legitimacy' (2013b: 391).

It was only in the 1970s and 1980s that movements of opposition to expropriations of land for development projects gathered momentum. Among them the most important was that opposing the gigantic Sardar Sarovar Project, aimed at building more than 3,000 dams along the length of the river Narmada in western India, for irrigation, drinking water supply and power generation – but reckoned to require the displacement of 200–250,000, or even as many as 500,000 people, 60–70 per cent of them tribals. Concerns on the part of civil society groups – brought together under the banner of the Narmada Bacha Andolan (NBA) – about the benefits of the scheme and to whom they would accrue (disproportionately, it was thought, to agro-industrial elites), as well as about the sheer impossibility that all those who would be ousted would be provided with full resettlement and rehabilitation, led to very effective opposition to the completion of the project. In the end, the NBA lost its fight, when judges in the Supreme Court finally found against it in 2000, in the case that it had brought against the Government of India. But the NBA has had an indelible influence on public opinion about the rights of those displaced by projects, and subsequent judgments of the Supreme Court have reflected the view that appeal to the 'common good' does not cancel out fundamental human rights (a key part of the discourse of the NBA, see Nilsen 2010). The NBA, too, has played a significant role in mobilizing a wider social movement – through the National Alliance of People's Movements – 'to struggle for a development process that empowers people against the hegemonic, exploitative culture associated with the words "privatization" and "liberalization"' (in the words of its mission statement).

But even Narmada was a development project with at least a claim to public purpose, whereas since 1991 and the beginning of India's shift in the direction of neoliberalism, the regime of dispossession is one that involves the appropriation of land for private purposes, and has facilitated private real estate accumulation: 'Land was now being dispossessed and given to capital without the veneer of Nehruvian social justice' (Levien 2013b: 393). The setting up by states of Special Economic Zones, under an Act of 2005, has given private companies considerable powers; the Act requires only that 35 per cent (later 50 per cent) of the land acquired be used for 'processing', giving developers freedom to exploit the rest as real estate (on SEZs, see Jenkins 2011; Jenkins et al. 2014). Liberalization has also encouraged competition between states to secure private investment, both domestic and foreign (in what Jenkins once described as 'a pattern of provincial Darwinism'; cited by Corbridge 2011: 70). The competition between them requires state governments to secure land for investors. The Left Front government of West Bengal failed in the end to secure land for the Tata company so that it could construct the plant for manufacturing its new small car, the Nano, and Narendra Modi, then chief minister of Gujarat stepped in sharply to snap up the project for his state. State governments have quickly become adept at evading the provisions of the new Land Acquisition Act (The Land Acquisition, Rehabilitation and Resettlement Act 2013) that threatened to make land acquisition more difficult, and the more effective of them have built up 'land banks'. The 'transformation of India's states into land brokers for private capital', Levien argues, 'has been a necessary condition of India's neo-liberal growth model' (2015: 147). Land is now being acquired for the market, and Levien calculates a 'rate of accumulation by dispossession' (the mark-up on the sale price of land above the price paid in compensation to the original landowners) on one SEZ project in Rajasthan at 439 per cent (Levien 2015).

Dispossession, in the service of India's strategy for bringing about economic growth via support for private enterprise, is actually much less 'developmental' than it was under the earlier regime, but it has also become the site of resistance that has often been successful (as is shown in the evidence cited earlier about the stalling of capital investments and the failure of major SEZ projects). The gaps between compensation levels and subsequent market prices are becoming increasingly obvious, and so it has become harder to persuade people of 'public purpose'. There is increasing resistance, according to Levien, even to compensation – though solidarity in anti-dispossession movements may be undermined by differences between those who refuse to give up their land at any price and those who fight for higher compensation (Levien 2013a). Protesters, organized locally on an ad-hoc basis around the single issue of land acquisition, outside political parties, frequently make use of the law in their struggles against state governments and their parastatal arms. If legal strategies fail, then violence is likely to come into the open. But this is 'resistance as negotiation', as Uday Chandra has put it, rather than resistance involving the negation of power (Chandra 2015: 568). It shares characteristics with what writers on rural China have described as 'rightful resistance': 'a form of popular contention that . . . employs the rhetoric and commitments of the powerful to curb the exercise of power, hinges on locating and exploiting divisions within the state, and relies on mobilizing support from the wider public' (cited by Chandra 2015: 564).

Struggles over land acquisition have become a major political issue, and efforts by the BJP government in 2014–15 to relax provisions of the new Land Acquisition Act were met with forceful opposition, causing prime minister Modi to defend himself in one of his regular broadcasts against the charge that his government was on the side of capital rather than of the farmers (Sen 2015).

Adivasis, the 'Mineral Rush' and the Maoist Insurgency

The people who have been most affected historically by displacement from their land have been the members of the Scheduled Tribes – those people from what were thought of as backward, tribal areas who were 'scheduled' for particular protection under the Constitution of India – living in the forested hilly tracts of eastern and central India (Guha 2007a). These *adivasis* include many different tribes, but they have in common a way of life, bound up with the forest, and ritual and religion centred around village gods and spirits. They also have in common their exceptional disadvantage in regard to all the key indicators of social welfare, even by comparison with members of the Scheduled Castes (Dalits). Unlike the Dalits, too, they have until now been unable to constitute themselves as an interest group in national politics.

Adivasis have suffered from the forest policies of successive governments, which have, in effect, criminalized them, as 'encroachers' on public land, and subjected them to oppression at the hands of Forest Department officials. The state has generally championed capitalist interests in the forests of India, as against the needs and interests of those who have historically been forest dwellers. Recently, too, to the pressures upon the *adivasis* from the Forest Department and from the alienation of forest tracts for mining and industrial projects, have been added demands from wildlife conservation (Kothari 2007). Some conservationists opposed the passage in 2006 of the Scheduled Tribes and Other Traditional Forest Dwellers (Recognition of Forest Rights) Act, which at last vested in forest-dwellers inheritable rights in land, which were not alienable or transferable (Bhatia 2005; Editorial 2007; Prasad 2007). The Act was the outcome of the activism of more than 200 organizations from across the country brought together in the networking movement called the Campaign for Dignity and Survival (see chapter 8).

State governments have, however, dragged their feet over the implementation of the Forest Rights Act (as discussed in chapter 8), and the pressures upon the forests and the lands of tribal people remain intense, across large parts of central and eastern India, because of the escalating demand for the resources of the region. These include most of India's reserves of coal, iron ore, bauxite and other minerals (see chapter 5). Resistance movements have sprung up among tribal people in response to attempts to acquire land for mining or for industrial projects using the resources of the state: as at Kalinga Nagar against the expropriation of land for a Tata steel plant; against the South Korean steel firm POSCO's project to mine iron ore and build a new steel plant and port facilities near Paradeep; against the London-based Vedanta company's alumina refinery at Lajgarh; and the same company's plans to clear a huge site for a private university campus. Vedanta's projects were stopped, the first as a result of the recommendations of an official panel specially appointed by the UPA government (the work of which is discussed in chapter 5), and the second by the High Court of Orissa (*The Hindu*, 17 November 2010); the POSCO project has met with such opposition that construction had not been started more than ten years after the signing of the memorandum between the company and the state government; development did proceed, however, at Kalinga Nagar.

Kundan Kumar (2014) has provided a long list of social and environmental movements in Odisha, which gives an impression of the extent and tenacity of resistance to dispossession in the state. The list also gives an indication of the connections between India's Maoists, now organized across a swathe of the centre and east of the country, and local movements of resistance to capital and to the state. It is not, generally, that the Maoists have organized resistance to projects like that of the Tatas at Kalinga Nagar, but they have both tried to take some movements over and have sometimes won support from them. Their involvement, however, has made it easy for the state government in Odisha to paint the movements as 'Maoist' and this has allowed the state to justify its use of force against them.

The Maoist movement itself is shot through by contradictions, as such a sympathetic observer as the anthropologist Alpa Shah – who has lived among Maoists in Jharkhand, and who admires their 'long history of renunciation and sacrifice', and their humaneness in everyday social relations – has pointed out (Shah 2017). The movement is seriously constrained, Shah argues, by its dogmatic commitment to an outdated analysis of the Indian economy as 'semi-feudal and semi-colonial'; the use of arms has brought the violence of state repression, and has led the Maoists to focus on military strategy rather than working with people to realize a socially transformative agenda; and, ironically, for a movement fighting against Indian democracy, by 'expanding its reach amongst people who have been left on the margins of the state', the Maoists have 'nurtured Dalits and *adivasis*' who, in the end, 'seek not a withering away of the state' but 'a greater share of and space within Indian democracy' (2017: 55). Shah has elaborated these arguments in a remarkable book, based on her experience of participating in a 'nightmarch' – actually a series of nightmarches, spread over a week – between Bihar and Jharkhand, with a platoon of Maoist fighters (Shah 2018).

A similar hope of securing 'a greater share of and space within Indian democracy' underlies the National Alliance of People's Movements, set up in 1992, and now including over 200 affiliated organizations. This is to realize the vision expressed some years ago by a scholarly observer of Indian politics, D. L. Sheth, who argued that 'Movement politics articulates new discourse of democracy through a sustained political practice' – a practice that is critical of 'prevalent macro-structures of political representation' (2004: 56). In line with this argument, Nilsen's studies of movements in western Madhya Pradesh lead him to suggest that tribal people there experience both 'enablement' and 'constraint' as they engage with the state and the vocabularies of democratic rights and citizenship. He concludes that 'the best way for social movements in India to advance their oppositional projects is to harness the state to their attempts to deepen democracy and advance subaltern emancipation' (2012: 615), even while recognizing that operating on the terrain of the state carries with it risks and constraints. In the end, therefore, we conclude as we did in our discussion of labour politics by asking whether it is possible that the huge potential of countermovement from below, which at the moment is fragmented between different interests and different struggles, might be brought together in common struggles for the realization of social citizenship.

9.4 Middle-Class Activism

The middle-class activists and policy entrepreneurs, such as the former senior bureaucrats Aruna Roy, Harsh Mander and N. C. Saxena, and the economist Jean Drèze, whose role in establishing what we referred to as India's 'new rights agenda' is discussed in chapter 8 of this book, have sought indeed to extend, and to make a reality of, the rights of citizenship among the mass of the Indian people. The drive behind the rights agenda came originally from the movement for the right to information (formally, the National Campaign for the People's Right to Information, created in 1996), which itself had its origins in the work of the Mazdur Kisan Shakti Sangathan (MKSS, meaning 'organization for the empowerment of workers and peasants') in Rajasthan. Established first in 1990, the MKSS organized among poor people, aiming to 'strengthen democratic process and to collectively fight exploitation' (website: mkssindia.org), and it was recognized, very early on, that in order to hold the government accountable, as it should be in view of its responsibility for the welfare of the people in a democratic polity, it is necessary both that people should know what their entitlements are and have access to information about what government has done to satisfy them. The MKSS, therefore, adopted the slogan 'The Right to Know, the Right to Live'. And as one of its leaders, Nikhil Dey, has put it: 'Accountability from a citizen's point of view is inextricably tied to basic entitlements. Who can I hold accountable if I don't have any entitlement?' (cited by Aiyar and Walton 2014: 10). A well-defined entitlement is a right. It was not an accident that the campaigns over the right to food and the right to work should have had their roots in the right to information movement. And there is a clear logic to the way that the rights legislation has entailed governance reform, actively encouraging the 'mobilization of popular discontent', as Aiyar and Walton have it (2014: 4), and seeking to change the power relations between the state and citizens. In India, the pursuit of rights 'embodies both the aspiration of substantive provisioning and the deepening of citizenship' (Aiyar and Walton 2014: 10).

As the political philosopher Pratap Bhanu Mehta observed some years ago, writing in *Indian Express* (7 June 2006), the middle class in India 'is now struggling to articulate new conceptions of social justice'. This is seen very clearly in the passage of legislation concerning social and economic rights. But Mehta also noted that the middle class is not 'an unalloyed carrier of virtue'. We think of the middle class as constituted by different fractions. The dominant fraction, according to Fernandes and Heller, 'consists of those with advanced professional credentials or accumulated cultural capital who occupy positions of recognized authority in various fields' (2006: 500). They constitute what is often called the 'new middle class', a class fraction that is clearly distinct both from the numerous petty bourgeoisie of merchants and small-scale manufacturers and retailers, and from the mass of salaried 'white-collar' workers. The new middle class, to a significant extent, sets the tone for the other fractions, and there is no doubt that many of them are committed to the ideology and culture of individualism, that is encouraged by and supportive of neoliberalism, and reflected in the use of the term 'consumer-citizen' by some civil society organizations. And it is 'consumer-citizens' from the middle classes who have, for instance, made use of the instrument of public interest litigation – drawn on by the rights activists to pursue their objectives – for the purpose of moving courts to require slum clearance, never mind the homes and livelihoods of large numbers of poor people that have to be destroyed (Bhan 2009). Middle-class activism, therefore, is not always at all supportive of the countermovement against neoliberalism; it is not, in Mehta's words, always a carrier of virtue.

The antinomies of middle-class politics in India were clearly on display in the campaign India Against Corruption (IAC), mobilized around the Gandhian social worker Anna Hazare, and which was supported especially by young people from (or aspiring to be from) the new middle class (it is discussed in more depth in chapter 10). The campaign had a distinctly authoritarian tendency and it showed contempt for representative democracy, as those around Hazare proposed arrogating to themselves considerable powers – technocrats dictating to democratically elected political leaders (Mehta, *India Express*, 7 April 2011). A tendency towards illiberal democracy on the part of the new middle class, and of civil society movements supported by it – consistent, in fact, with neoliberalism (see Harvey 2005) – has to be set against the actions of the rights campaigners, who – as we have argued here – aim at the deepening of citizenship.

The IAC campaign had begun to peter out by late 2012, and it was then that one group, led by Arvind Kejriwal – as we discuss in chapter 10 – broke away to form a political party, the Aam Aadmi (or 'Common Man') Party (AAP). The party initially proposed an alternative politics – opposed to illiberal democracy – involving a much more direct relationship between people and the decision making that affects their lives, and suggesting a level and kind of participation going well beyond participation in elections every five years. It promised to 'do different', and drew in numbers of young people, some of whom gave up prosperous careers in order to work for the new party. It encouraged the idea of doing something 'extraordinary' (Roy 2014) and then achieved the extraordinary (for a political party only twelve months old) when it upset 'politics as usual' in the Delhi (state) elections of November 2013, defying all expectations by winning twenty-eight seats and preventing a resurgent BJP from securing a majority. The AAP went on to form the government, though briefly, and then proceeded on a turbulent career – to a significant extent because of what seemed to be the personal ambitions of Kejriwal, which led to the disaffection of other senior and respected figures in the party – before coming back to win what is perhaps the most astounding victory in the whole of India's electoral history, when in the 2015 Delhi elections it won sixty-seven of the seventy seats in the Delhi Assembly.

What was striking about AAP's electoral victories in 2013 and 2015 was where it won support. Though the primary activist base of the party was drawn from the middle classes – professionals, rights activists, teachers and students – it was also the case that 'constituencies with a large number of slum clusters . . . [almost] invariably voted for the party' (Ramani 2013b: fig. 4), working poor people being motivated by concerns over public services. Many professional people saw the need for a 'non-corrupt force', while members of the traditional middle class – shop-owners and small merchants – were drawn to the party over such issues as inflation and the delivery of public services. It was, Ramani says, an 'uneasy coalition', but exactly the kind of coalition that has to be built in countering neoliberalism, bringing together the masses of working poor people and substantial numbers from the middle classes. The landslide of 2015 can only have been achieved by the consolidation of such a coalition. An observer, the political scientist P. K. Datta, noted at the time that AAP's 'politics of delivery' brings together different classes through widely shared interests in the quality of government and of public services. This is politics as a 'search for public good' – or in other words, meaningful citizenship (Datta 2015).

The AAP experience also reflects, however, the difficulty of sustaining such a coalition. Srirupa Roy, who studied the AAP closely in the run-up to the 2013 elections, noted that there might be quite a gap between the mainly upper and intermediate caste men from non-working-class backgrounds who make up a lot of the rank-and-file of the party and the majority of those who voted for it. Her account of AAP in action shows that the party members have only a limited recognition of the problems of realizing 'participation' in a society marked both by sharp economic inequalities and by hierarchical social values (Roy 2014; and see our further discussion in chapter 10). More generally, there can be tensions between cosmopolitan, English-speaking rights activists and the local activists with whom they engage, as Jamie Cross notes from his ethnography of rights activism (Cross 2014). Cross found that the first could betray frustration with the second, because of the latter's inability 'to think about wider issues'; there could be tensions over money, when the local activists both looked to the 'cosmopolitans' to come up with funds, while being suspicious of them for either being from or depending on foreign-funded 'NGOs' (which are widely regarded with suspicion, as agents of neoliberalism); while Cross's account of the way in which the People's Audit of SEZs of 2009 was managed by rights activists shows how the 'cosmopolitans' were criticized by local activists: 'People like them take decisions on our behalf; people like them live off people like us'.

The problems of building and sustaining a broad-based political movement to defend society against the impacts of neoliberalism, to put it after the manner of Polanyi, are much greater than he recognized. The rise of AAP is an instance of the transformation of protest politics into a party-movement that is dedicated to realizing political change, and in a way that might challenge the dominance of neoliberalism in policy thinking. But whether the new party could sustain its transformative potential, rather than becoming just another political party, was quickly compromised by in-fighting within it, which led the *Economic and Political Weekly* to declare 'the end of AAP as a political alternative' (Editorial 2015: 8). The bold ambitions with which the party started out – symbolized by the idea, taken from Gandhi, of *swaraj*, 'where the power of governance and the rights of democracy will be in the hands of the people of India' – were reduced to quite restricted goals relating to service delivery. But it must be acknowledged, too, that the AAP government of Delhi was subjected to all manner of obstacles by the spoiling tactics of the BJP-led central government. AAP has shown what might be achieved, certainly in the cities, when alliances are built between middle and working classes (see also EPW Engage 2019).

9.5 Conclusions

There is, therefore, abundant evidence of opposition to neoliberalism in India, and it is certainly holding back labour and land-related reforms, even if it is not stopping them altogether. But equally clearly, there is no coherent countermovement. What is happening bears some resemblance to what is going on in Brazil, and perhaps in South Africa, too. In regard to Brazil, James

Holston has written about what he calls 'insurgent citizenship', entailing 'a new kind of participation in an alternative public sphere', constituted by grassroots organizations, new understandings of rights, and a transformed understanding of the relationship between state and citizens. Poor people have appropriated the 'right to have rights' (Holston 2009, quoted in Seekings 2013: 359). The 'alternative public sphere' is being created as a result of the excluded poor demanding inclusion. There are indications of a similar movement in India.

On the other hand, there are ways in which the support won for Hindu nationalism (that we discuss in chapter 6) by the appeal to many people of Narendra Modi as prime minister, may also be understood as a response to neoliberalism, and as another form of countermovement. It is complicated, of course, because Modi is close to the corporate sector and came to power promising to carry forward the economic reform agenda. This included relaxing some of the constraints on land acquisition, and 'flexibilizing' labour markets, both of which we have referred to here. But Modi has felt compelled to pull back from some of these commitments by the need to maintain electoral support amongst people who have looked to him as a 'strong man', able to supply them with the sense of security that they lack, and that for many has been exacerbated by the requirements of neoliberalism.

PART THREE

SOCIETY

10

Is India Witnessing a Social Revolution?

10.1 Introduction

One of the most remarkable but also least commented upon changes occurring across the world since the late 1990s has been the extraordinary spread of citizenship and social movements associated with a broader underlying dissemination of notions of liberal rights (see Arnot 2009). The rapid increase in people's enrolment in secondary schooling, combined with an acceleration in state and NGO efforts to inculcate core citizenship ideas – and interacting, too, with a communications revolution – has led to the proliferation of people who understand and believe in citizenship. In the 1980s and 1990s, intellectuals such as Mamdani (1996) and Chatterjee (2004) charted how colonialism had prevented people across large swathes of Africa and Asia from accepting and fully understanding norms and ideas of citizenship. In Chatterjee's terms, the masses in the Global South were imagined as 'denizens' rather than 'citizens'. But this idea, if it were ever true, is now consigned to the history books, for a growing number of people in the Global South do expect the state to work on their behalf, have absorbed the notion that the government should be impartial and come to believe that they have rights.

One of the implications of this profound shift has been an effervescence of a wide range of social movements, NGOs and everyday forms of politics across the Global South (see Jeffrey 2012). Notable examples include many of the movements associated with the Arab Spring (Bayat 2013), the Occupy movement (Schneider 2013), and World Social Forum (Fominaya 2014). At the everyday level, citizenship activists include youth engaged in environmental politics in Senegal (Ralph 2008), those involved in NGOs addressing corruption in Ethiopia (Mains 2012) and a wide range of activist groups in South-East Asia (Li 2007). The UN has also assembled a vast array of examples of active citizenship among young people across the Global South (see United Nations 2016).

Many of these references come from the period between 1995 and 2013. A key question for analysts is how far a citizenship revolution – or wider 'social revolution', to encompass the transformation in communications technologies and rising education – will last into the 2020s, and there is no more fascinating context for exploring this question than India. Various forces are arrayed against the expansion of notions of liberal citizenship. These include the destabilizing effect of rising inequalities and the desperation and anxiety caused by a glaring gap between expectations and social realities. Another is the rise of populist nationalist parties, which often have an ambivalent relationship to the rights discourse, sometimes supporting liberal citizenship and sometimes twisting it to reflect majoritarian communal concerns (see chapters 6 and 7). Yet another brake on the expansion of liberal citizenship is the sheer inertia built into many bureaucracies in the Global South, which run on the basis of institutionalized forms of patronage often reflecting sectarian concerns. All these 'brakes' on social revolution are evident in India, and the theoretical primacy given to the revolution or to the countervailing forces varies across the country.

10.2 What is the Social Revolution?

By social revolution, we refer to a shift in aspirations, values and practices related to social action in India that has been exceptionally rapid since 2000. The shift is especially evident amongst India's younger generation. There are three aspects to this revolution. The first relates to education. Although there are serious concerns regarding the quality of educational provision in India (see chapter 13), there has plainly been an increase in access to education since the turn of the century. Not only have the numbers of schools and colleges increased (see Kapur and Mehta 2017), but students from poor and socially marginal backgrounds who had once been excluded from the benefits of education – such as SC and ST youth – are completing primary and secondary education and attending college in increasing numbers. The gross enrolment ratio has steadily increased, such that by 2015–16, 56 per cent of appropriate-age students were attending higher secondary school, and studies show significant improvements in equality of access to primary and secondary education since the 1980s (Asadullah and Yalonetzky 2012). Not surprisingly, there has been a corresponding rise in literacy rates – from 52 per cent of the population in 1991 to 74 per cent in 2011, according to the Census of India. Education has become a key aspirational resource in India, seen as having both intrinsic and instrumental value – being essential not only to access employment, but also to act with confidence in civil society, politics, and engaging with the state.

The second aspect of the social revolution derives from the increased penetration and use of digital communications technologies, particularly mobile phones and the internet. Media theorists have for the past two decades observed the transformative and empowering potential of digital media. Castells (2009) posits that new media technologies – particularly the internet – have led to a 'communications revolution' that has spread throughout the world over the last two decades. This revolution has had the historically novel effect of both allowing media users to reach a global audience, but also to define their potential audience and to retrieve information in such a way as to meet their unique needs. The horizontal nature of these communication networks, wherein users are all simultaneously consumers, producers and broadcasters of content, grant significant autonomy to media users relative to established powers (see also Shirkey 2008). This revolution has been made possible not only by new technologies, but also by the growing institutional power of media corporations, who have pushed communications technologies into almost every aspect of people's lives, novel global digital cultures, and new social actors who have applied the technology to innovative social purposes. There is a dark side to the growing power of digital media corporations and the ubiquity of digital media in our lives, as was made all-too-apparent by major privacy violations by Facebook and Cambridge Analytica in early 2018. Yet, theorists such as Castells (2015) argue that the communications revolution and the social media that it has facilitated have also been implicated in a new wave of social movements, from the Arab Spring to Occupy Wall Street. These social movements began on social media, as a relatively autonomous domain of mass communication, free from censorship by the state or corporations. Social media has provided citizens with a space to share both their grievances and their hopes and has facilitated diverse people to come together, network and collaborate on projects to transform their societies. Once a movement has started, digital technology also provides the medium through which their ideas and innovations rapidly spread. Notably, incidents such as the Tahrir Square uprising in Egypt (Hussain and Howard 2013) and the Shahbagh movement in Bangladesh (Sorour and Dey 2014) were catalysed in very large part by mobile internet technology – and the use of social media in particular.

There is a body of scholarship cautioning against an overly hasty celebration of the potential of new communications technology to facilitate social and political transformation. Couldry (2015), for example, notes that while new media may make political action easier, whether it leads to sustained political action or the development of a policy agenda for meaningful institutional change remains to be seen. He adds that much of the discussion of the potential for these technologies as a tool for empowerment of the general public neglects to engage with the ways in which they are also powerful tools for states and corporations, which may seek to suppress political action. Despite such critique, however, few would contest that the ever-deeper penetration of communications technology is reducing the entry costs of historically marginalized communities to participate meaningfully in political, economic and cultural life (see Benkler 2006; Chadwick 2013).

India is a crucial site in this global communications revolution. The uptake of mobile phone technology in India has been phenomenal. From less than 2 million phone subscribers in 2000, India had more than 1.1 billion subscribers in 2018, with over 500 million of these being based in rural areas (TRAI 2018). As Doron and Jeffrey (2013) document, this rise in mobile phone usage has created unprecedented opportunities for marginalized populations to connect with each other and to powerful people in NGOs, media and government. They have also allowed poor entrepreneurs to connect directly with consumers and reduce the influence of exploitative middlemen.

Figures on internet subscriptions in India are somewhat less impressive but are growing rapidly. The Internet and Mobile Association of India reported 40.9 per cent of Indians had an internet subscription as of 2019. Although this did represent a doubling of subscriptions since 2014 and an astonishing increase from the very low figure of 0.5 per cent in 2000, India's internet penetration remained more than ten percentage points lower than all other BRICS countries. One point that is worth noting, however, is that these figures do not capture the large numbers of Indian mobile phone subscribers who also receive 'over-the-top' mobile internet services, which includes free access to applications such as WhatsApp and Facebook (Mani and Sridhar 2015). Though exact figures on the use of such services are not available, it is assumed to be very large. Qualitative studies show that Facebook and WhatsApp are very popular amongst youth from all class backgrounds in India and that they are having profound effects – both positive and negative – on the organization of social life (Venkatraman 2017).

A final aspect of the social revolution is in popular understandings of citizenship and the state. In India, as across much of the Global South, there are growing expectations, at least amongst some sections of the population, that governments and state departments should conform to liberal democratic norms. People expect adequate representation from elected officials, an impartial bureaucracy, and a fair and open legal system. This comes in part as a consequence of the rise in access to education and media discussed above – but not only this. Global institutions, such as the United Nations, have actively promoted citizenship education – particularly amongst youth – viewing an engaged global citizenry as crucial to managing the challenging social, economic and ecological conditions of the twenty-first century (Arnot and Swartz 2013).

Historically, processes of social transformation broadly associated with modernization have also been implicated in a rise in cosmopolitan, liberal citizenship ideals, including middle-class formation (Watenpaugh 2012) and urbanization (Holston and Appadurai 1996). These social dynamics have been evident in India across the last two decades and have been implicated in changes in civic values. Although India's urbanization has been slower than in comparable countries (notably China and Indonesia), it has gathered pace since the turn of the millennium, driven largely by the growth of small towns (Bhagat 2011). It must be noted, however, that the character of India's urbanization has been largely exclusionary, with segregation of richer and poorer residents (Bhattacharya and Sanyal 2011; Kundu and Saraswati 2012). Moreover, the unplanned nature of India's urbanization has created problems with inadequate infrastructure and public services (Ahluwalia et al. 2014). These factors have limited its potential to drive substantial shifts in civic values, since new urban residents do not have access to spaces in civil society nor the appropriate resources – such as quality education and media – that might enable them to become participants in a broad-based social transformation (Bobbio 2015).

Yet, there is evidence that the increase in physical mobility (particularly rural-to-urban migration) that has occurred alongside India's urbanization has led to some forms of progressive social change. Gidwani and Sivaramakrishnan (2003), for example, argue that in navigating different social and cultural environments, rural-to-urban migrants develop new capabilities and cosmopolitan dispositions. Physical mobility has also been shown to enhance people's awareness of their civic rights: Brulé (2015), for example, finds that women with experience of labour mobility feel more competent in holding local governments to account. In contemporary India, perhaps an even more decisive factor in growing civic awareness is the decentralization of governance and the suite of rights-based legislations that have been introduced over the past two decades, discussed at length in chapter 8. Devolution of democratic decision making and legislation such as the Right to Information Act make the state more accessible and accountable, facilitating greater civic participation (see Ruparelia 2013).

The changes in expectations and values that we refer to as 'social revolution' generate a kind of cultural counter-current to the trends towards reactionary nationalism, authoritarianism and cultural chauvinism that we have discussed in chapters 6 and 7 – though in some instances these two ethical and political currents may converge and co-articulate in novel ways.

10.3 Cultural Renaissance

The social revolution has stimulated a flourishing of cultural expression in India. Much of the early discussion around the projected impacts of communications technologies and the broader impacts of globalization reflected a fear that a wave of 'Americanization' would erode cultural forms in the Global South. This does not appear to have been borne out: cultural activity in India is booming.

Bollywood forms the most prominent point of reference for an explosion of cultural production. The year 1998 is commonly identified as pivotal for the Mumbai-based Hindi film industries known colloquially as 'Bollywood'. This was the year when Bollywood was granted industry status by the Government

of India, which reduced the burden of taxation and enabled foreign investment, precipitating a significant injection of capital (Ganti 2013). It was after
this point that Bollywood could consolidate itself as a film industry with truly
global reach and recognition. Yet, the transformation of Bollywood was also
attributable to the evolution of the media and communications landscape
(Punathambekar 2013). Over the past two decades, new digital technologies
have not only allowed for striking new visual effects, they have also allowed
Bollywood to converge cinema with other media. As Punathambekar (2013)
documents, films are routinely released alongside their corresponding song
and dance numbers and feed into advertising and internet platforms. Further,
Bollywood has linked with tech-savvy members of the Indian diaspora, who are
able to connect with foreign media companies to bring not only new sources
of capital to Bollywood, but also new technologies, corporate practices and
ideas. This is a major factor behind the dynamism and rapid change exhibited
in Bollywood in the 2010s. Bollywood's international commercial success has
allowed Hindi cinema to emerge with new confidence, re-making and reinventing older Hindi films in ways that draw on contemporary technologies
and sensibilities, while preserving and embracing the unique features that
make them different to the film traditions of the West (Wright 2015).

   Bollywood's influence extends beyond the realm of cinema – it has a profound impact on the cultural life of contemporary India. Although recent
years have seen Bollywood films that celebrate reactionary forms of cultural
nationalism (Banerjee 2016), there have also been films that reflect more liberal, cosmopolitan values and sensibilities – and these are influencing the
outlook of Indian youth. Recent examples of this include the films *Pink* (2016),
which drew attention to the matter of sexual violence against women and
the stigmatization of women's sexuality, and *Bombay Talkies* (2013), which
highlighted the plight of homosexual men in India and also the limiting
influence of gender stereotypes. If Bollywood's moral and cultural influence
was once confined to the urban middle class, this is no longer the case. The
widespread availability of colour television since the early 2000s, along with a
rise in the availability of cable and satellite channels, has brought Bollywood
and other forms of entertainment media into the slums and villages of India.
In a study of the way in which Bollywood is consumed amongst young Muslim
women in the slums of Kolkata, Chakraborty (2016) finds that although
the overt displays of consumerism, individualism and liberal sexuality in
Bollywood films are not always suited to young people's (often religious and
conservative) social setting, youth nonetheless draw on Bollywood as a 'guide'
to navigate the boundaries between tradition and modernity. Many youth
draw on Bollywood selectively to negotiate their position in local society – for
example, Chakraborty (2016) documents how youths' public participation in
Bollywood-inspired and overtly sexualized mixed-sex dancing in the slums of
Kolkata serves to challenge the boundaries of acceptable relations between

unmarried men and women. It may, therefore, be interpreted as a driver for progressive cultural change.

Yet it is not only the capital-intensive film industries of Bollywood that are thriving – there is also evidence that the three aspects of the social revolution are facilitating a growth in more grassroots forms of cultural expression. Manuel (2014), for example, shows how in Uttar Pradesh, traditions of religious songs known as Ghazals were profoundly revitalized by the introduction of cassette technologies in the 1990s, and then further by the introduction of MP3 formats, DVDs and the Internet in the 2000s. These technologies allowed the production of these songs to be decentralized, with a constant stream of music being produced from diverse locations and actors.

Religion in India, rather than withering away under the 'disenchanting' influence of modernity, appears to be stronger than ever. Indian television is saturated with celebrity gurus, who provide lifestyle advice on how to navigate the modern world while retaining traditional spiritual and religious commitments (Lewis et al. 2016). The Internet has allowed even deeper penetration of religious gurus into everyday life – including interactive spiritual practices such as 'cyber darshans', which provide devotees with a sense of proximity to deities and saints whom they are unable to access physically (Warrier 2013). Instances of elderly people taking pilgrimages remotely via online platforms such as Skype are no longer uncommon.

The Internet has provided a platform for a new generation of spiritual teachers to reach audiences across India's regions and to reach international audiences. This process of extending beyond the local has transformative effects on both the teachers and their message – sometimes in ways that result in the promotion of more liberal and inclusive values. Lucia (2014b) documents the emergence of 'global gurus' from India, who, while broadly inspired by Hinduism or Buddhism, pitch their message to a global audience. While in some cases this has led to the globalization of conservative religious values (Fuller and Harriss 2005), Lucia provides evidence that the process of globalizing can also stimulate a cosmopolitan transformation in religious discourse. Engaging with a diverse audience consisting of multiple cultural and religious groupings requires these gurus to adapt their message into a format that can be widely understood and embraced. They therefore tend both to engage with 'modern' discourses that transcend the particularities of the Indian setting, while simultaneously drawing on their 'Indian traditions' and references to an ancient past – whether real or imagined – as a way of creating a sense of cultural authenticity. This involves both exaggerating some of the unique features of these traditions – in order to provide a unique offering – but also rendering them in a form that is widely acceptable. Lucia suggests that these gurus, as they participate in a competitive global market, are forced to be innovative in order to offer something new. In some cases, this goes beyond building on 'Indian' traditions alone and involves active engagement with discourses that are globally dispersed and articulated through multi-ethnic and multi-faith spiritual communities. The Osho International Meditation Centre in Pune, for example, though inspired by aspects of the Indian Buddhist and Hindu traditions, ultimately lets go of its adherence to anything bound to India. It unapologetically embraces materialism, individualism, spiritual tourism, and globalized capitalism, which enables it to serve as a key node in an international network of a spiritual communities (Urban 2013).

Especially remarkable has been the rising popularity of relatively new spiritual traditions which, while broadly derived from Hinduism, attempt to break free of traditional sectarian divisions. The spiritual guru Sathya Sai Baba (1926–2011), for instance, developed a following that spread not only across India, but throughout the world. Srinivas (2010) suggests that part of Sathya Sai Baba's global appeal was the way he stripped away some of the more particularistic and esoteric aspects of Hinduism. Instead of addressing a particular caste or religious community, his message was pitched to humanity as a whole. Lucia (2014a) has made similar arguments about Sudhamani Idamannel – known as 'Amma', or 'mother' to her followers – a guru figure from South India, who is known for hugging her devotees to induce transcendent states of consciousness. Being from a low-caste background, Amma's hugs are immanently transgressive of traditional rules surrounding untouchability and caste segregation. Her message, which centres on love and selfless service, is not exclusively Hindu, and the numerous charitable activities that she funds emphasize having a positive impact on society. Her reach is global, not narrowly focused on India, and her followers have made great use of the Internet – particularly social media – to spread her message and raise awareness of her global tour dates and charitable events. Similar arguments about the rise in non-identitarian spiritual movements have been made in respect to Sri Sri Ravi Shankar's Art of Living Foundation (Jacobs 2015) and the work of the Sri Aurobindo Society (Pandya 2016).

10.4 Growing Prominence of Civil Society

The most direct expression of the social revolution is the flourishing of activity in civil society. Whether in formal NGOs, informal neighbourhood associations, or more politicized social movements, Indian citizens are taking advantage of new opportunities to improve their social, economic, political and environmental conditions. Especially prominent has been an upswing in activities in civil society aimed at improving the functioning of government.

Discussions of civil society as a distinct space of association became prominent in India in the 1970s after Indira Gandhi's imposition of Emergency Rule. Civil society – identified in the context of these discussions as being constituted by social movements, volunteer groups and NGOs – was thought to provide an important check on excessive state power (Chandhoke 2009b). There was also a view that civil society could be a domain in which the voices of those excluded from full participation in the state might find an avenue for expression (Kothari 1984). After the liberalization of India's economy, however, the emphasis in discussions of civil society began to shift. Concerns were expressed about the over-emphasis on civil society organizations in neoliberal discourse and the expectation that voluntary and privately funded charitable organizations should provide the social services from which the liberalizing state was withdrawing its responsibilities (Pattenden 2016).

In the 2000s and 2010s, however, there appears to have been yet another shift. As sustained economic growth has allowed for the extraction of greater revenue, the state has once again begun to expand its role as a provider of basic services – particularly in the domain of poverty alleviation. In this context, there has been a shift away from civil society organizations' involvement in the direct provision of services. Instead, these organizations have increasingly engaged in advocacy for the poor, guiding policy reforms, and providing accountability checks to ensure that social welfare and rights-based legislations are functioning in an effective and inclusive manner (Dubochet 2012; Chandhoke 2012; see also chapter 8). India's increasingly educated and well-connected public have become enthusiastic and engaged participants in the process through which civil society is refining and improving processes of governance in India. Digital media has been a great enabler of this. A number of NGOs have developed online apps to allow citizens to lodge reports of poorly functioning government services – making note when teachers, doctors and public servants are absent from their duties, for example.

Young people are especially important participants in this newly invigorated civil society. Young people in India today are far more educated and better connected than any previous generation and as such are better equipped to participate in the political process. Many, however, are jaded with formal, electoral politics, seeing this as a corrupted space to which they lack an entry point (Ilavarasan 2013). Civil society activities – in the form of both activism and social service – become a more attractive pathway to contribute towards India's social transformation. Mobile phones and the Internet play a major role in this, providing opportunities for youth to coordinate volunteering and protest activities with others and to network with like-minded groups (Ilavarasan 2013).

Perhaps the most prominent and dramatic example of an upsurge in civil society activity in India came in the 2011 Indians Against Corruption (IAC) campaign and its various later off-shoots. These movements began when the renowned Gandhian social worker Anna Hazare began an indefinite hunger strike in Jantar Mantar, New Delhi, in protest against a series of corruption scandals within the then Congress-led government. Hazare and his followers demanded the creation of a 'Jan Lokpal', or 'people's ombudsman', which would be an independent body with oversight over corruption in government. The movement proved immensely popular, bringing people to the streets throughout India and dominating news headlines for months to come.

The Anna Hazare movement clearly reflected the three core aspects of the social revolution. It appealed chiefly to the educated classes, those who had benefitted from increased access to education. It made skilful use of social media – not only as an arena for discussion and debate, but also to coordinate protests across the country (Harindranath and Khorana 2014). And, in its opposition to corruption, it reflected India's new civic sensibilities. If in the 1980s anthropologists could still claim corruption to be an extension of local cultural customs of patronage (e.g. Saberwal 1986), it seemed that in the 2010s this assumption no longer held. People in India were demanding that the political class behave in a responsible manner and should be held accountable for their actions. In the initial protests, leaders of farmers' movements, student organizations, sex workers' unions, and large numbers of people from marginalized groups such as Muslims and Dalits came out into the streets to show their support. This spoke to the broad spectrum of society to whom the demands for a corruption-free India appealed, even if, as subsequent analysis suggested, these groups were not able to have a meaningful impact on the evolution of the movement's demands and strategy (see Sengupta 2014).

The movement against corruption did not end with Anna Hazare's very public campaign. As Tarrow (1998) demonstrates in his classic treatise on social movements, a movement's success should not be measured only in terms of its own narrowly defined objectives, but also in the political opportunities it opens for others to participate in the political process. The most notable successor to Hazare's campaign is the Aam Aadmi Party (AAP), led by Arvind Kejriwal. From an educated, middle-class family, Kejriwal first became a prominent figure in civil society after he resigned from his position in the Delhi Income Tax Department, after witnessing widespread corruption. Kejriwal had started an NGO called *Parivartan* (Change), which worked to oppose corruption in Delhi's public life. He campaigned for the introduction of Right to Information legislation and, after the introduction of RTI laws, he made use of them in his anti-corruption campaigns. He was a leading participant in the IAC movement and formed AAP to take the issues raised by the movement into electoral politics.

Kejriwal and AAP have mobilized a compelling discourse about an out-of-touch and corrupt political elite and the need for political reform. They have also been somewhat responsive to issues raised by their constituents around the right to access basic services such as water and electricity. Given Kejriwal's unique discourse and mode of organizing, Wyatt (2015) has described him as a 'political entrepreneur', who has responded to shifts in social attitudes in India by offering innovation and creativity at the political level. He offers a style of politics based on advocacy, rather than patronage, reflecting the increased disillusionment with older styles of politics and the appeal of liberal citizenship ideals. Although the electoral success of the party on a national level remains rather limited, it has had a surprising amount of success in Punjab, Goa and – most notably – in the National Capital Region, where Kejriwal was elected chief minister in 2013 and again in 2015.

Certainly, there has been criticism of both AAP and IAC, some of which we detailed in chapter 9. In the case of IAC, many have noted that the campaign was oriented excessively towards the perspectives of the urban middle class. A diverse range of people from various class strata were a part of the IAC campaign in the sense that they participated in street-level protests – reflecting the widespread nature of frustrations with corruption throughout India. Yet, the leaders of the movement were overwhelmingly middle class and the repertoire of public action that they drew upon – candlelight vigils, Twitter campaigning, media blitzes – mostly appealed to the sensibilities of middle-class audiences (Sitapati 2011). Further, the middle-class organizers who coordinated action tended to draw on ideological assumptions that reflected middle-class interests – in particular an assumption that the corruption of the political class was the most egregious, neglecting other forms of 'everyday' corruption by police and public officials that are more salient in the lives of the lower classes (Harindranath and Khorana 2014). This, combined with a tendency towards authoritarianism and *Hindutva*-style symbology used by the movement, had the effect of alienating some potential supporters, and led to a petering out of the movement (Sengupta 2014). The movement's fixation on a narrow agenda for legislative change in instituting the Lokpal – and that too, an agenda that was not very different at all from changes the government had already proposed to undertake – tended to disappoint expectations that the movement would bring about revolutionary change in Indian society (N. Shah 2012).

Similarly, at a national level, AAP has struggled to find resonance beyond a cadre of urban middle-class supporters. It is, of course, noteworthy that the party has had remarkable success in garnering support across classes in Delhi, having organized very effectively in poor and lower middle-class neighbourhoods. However, given its dependency on new media and appeal to the sensibilities of the educated, its success in Delhi is unlikely to be replicated across other areas of the country, where media saturation is less and urban methods of social organizing are unlikely to be effective (Diwakar 2016). Further, its model of 'direct democracy', with a strong emphasis on the rights of engaged citizens and civil society organizations to intervene in the political process, is problematic in a country as diverse as India. As Palshikar (2013) persuasively argues, the party's emphasis on giving greater scope for citizens to propose new legislation and recall existing legislation will only empower the middle and upper-class sections of society who have the education, skills and social connections necessary to engage in such action. This may, in practice, limit the political power of the poor, who rely to a greater extent on their elected representatives to solve their problems (Harriss 2006). Given this somewhat elitist tendency in AAP's ideology, it is perhaps unsurprising that its evolution as a party has involved a centralization of decision making around a core group of activists – and much is centralized around Kejriwal himself (Wyatt 2015). These are unfortunate signs that despite an evident shift in public values and an appetite for change, the middle-class composition of existing organizational structures tend to slow the progress of the social revolution in transforming the lives of India's poor majority. Neither IAC nor AAP should be regarded as 'vanguards' of the social revolution taking place throughout India. Nonetheless, the support they have gained in a relatively short period reflects the expectations on the part of many Indian citizens for far greater impartiality and transparency from their political leaders, and their increased capacity and willingness to hold leaders to account.

It is not only through such high-profile, national-level campaigns that civil society actors are addressing the issue of corruption. There are numerous instances of NGOs spread throughout India which are leveraging new technology and a growing anti-corruption sentiment in the general public to launch effective campaigns and projects. In Bangalore, for example, the Jaanagraha Centre for Citizenship and Democracy in 2008 established the 'I paid a bribe' website (www.ipaidabribe.com) to allow citizens to anonymously report instances in which they paid bribes in order to access public services. Citizens can also lodge reports on instances in which they refused to pay bribes and more positive cases of non-corrupt officials. In late 2019 there were over 180,000 reports lodged from more than 1,000 cities across India. The website is used to compile data on patterns of corruption and to develop reports which are presented to the media and policy makers to raise awareness and advocate new measures. The website also allows citizens to have queries about corruption answered and provides support to individuals struggling against everyday corruption. Ang (2014) argues that the website has been successful in India not only for its effective use of the web-based platform, but also because of the existence of well-organized and relatively autonomous civil society organizations capable of coordinating the effort. Further, the website intervened in an environment in which growing numbers of Indian citizens recognized everyday forms of corruption to be a significant social problem. Ang suggests that this is why comparable efforts in China have been far less successful, as China lacks an autonomous civil society and the public are less likely to see corruption by state officials as a major issue. Although those lodging reports via the 'I paid a bribe website' may be, for the most part, relatively privileged urban middle-class citizens, there are also other instances of NGOs mobilizing some of India's poorest citizens against corruption. There are many NGOs working in rural India, making use of progressive legislation – such as the Right to Information Act – and governments' own rhetoric around anti-corruption and 'good governance' to mobilize poor, low-caste people to oppose corruption at the hands of government officials (Verma et al. 2017).

Beyond the issue of corruption, there has also been a recent rise of activism in India using digital technology to hold corporations and governments to account. For some activists, being able to reach global audiences has been tremendously beneficial. Sofia Ashraf, for example, an activist from South India, has used rap and YouTube to deliver messages about corporate negligence to worldwide audiences – putting pressure on companies such as Unilever to show greater environmental and social responsibility. NGOs in India are also making creative use of digital technologies as tools for the assertion of marginalized people's rights. Livengood and Kunte (2012) have documented how the coalition of slum-dwellers' rights NGOs known as 'the Alliance' have utilized digital mapping software to empower people living in informal settlements in Cuttack, Orissa. The Alliance developed easy-to-use applications that allowed residents of informal settlements to participate in mapping their communities, build a profile of population pressures, as well as the 'condition of roads, number of community and individual toilets, access to water, and risk of flooding or other natural disasters' (Livengood and Kunte 2012: 86). The data thereby collected was used to allow these communities to assert their land use rights and have them recognized by the state – thereby preventing forceful evictions – and to prioritize the upgrading of services and resettlement options for those whose living conditions had become unacceptable. Initiatives such as this are using new technology to put pressure on the state to develop more inclusive and responsive modes of governance.

Digital media also provide a platform for activist groups to consolidate collective identities that may be absent or transient at the local level – something which social movement theorists have long recognized as crucial for sustaining mobilizations. The 'Pink Chaddi' movement illustrates this well. This movement emerged in response to the harassment of young women by *Hindutva* activists for drinking alcohol in public and alleged 'loose' sexual behaviour. A Delhi-based activist used a Facebook page to coordinate women from around the world to send pink underwear (*chaddis*) to the *Hindutva* vigilantes as a protest and expression of women's rights. The Facebook community and subsequent blog that developed as the mouthpiece of the movement helped to construct a collective identity amongst those who believed in women's freedom of lifestyle choices. Connecting with like-minded people dispersed throughout India and abroad gave the movement fresh ideas and confidence, which may not have been possible without the communication tools to bring them together in dialogue (Chattopadhyay 2011). The Internet has also been crucial in constructing politicized collective identities amongst LGBT people in India and facilitating social action. Many LGBT people had historically suffered from isolation imposed by the risks associated with publicly expressing their sexuality and this created limits to public mobilization around the consolidation and protection of their rights. Connecting online has allowed LGBT people in India to create opportunities for socializing (both on- and offline) and to find new ways of developing and expressing their sexual identities (Dasgupta 2017). Digital activism and online networking were crucial in bringing together otherwise dispersed LGBT voices in opposition to India's colonial era anti-sodomy laws and giving a public face to queer people as citizens (Dasgupta 2017).

10.5 Constraints on India's Social Revolution

Although there are major changes evident in many domains of Indian society, India's social revolution faces at least six constraints, which broadly relate to the structure of Indian civic institutions. The first constraint relates to the suppression of dissent by the state. The Indian state has a long history of intervening to restrain activity in civil society. Nehru's government gagged trade unions in the interests of consolidating industrial capital in the newly formed state (Chibber 2005). More notably, in 1975, Indira Gandhi introduced the Foreign Contributions Regulation Act (FCRA), which required civil society organizations to obtain licences to receive any foreign financial contributions, and which allowed the state to cancel such licences should organizations receiving funds be perceived to be engaged in activity deemed 'political'. What qualifies as 'political' activity has always been ambiguous; in practice, both Congress and BJP-led governments have used the FCRA to justify the cancellation of funds to organizations that were seen to be politically threatening (Jalali 2008; Udayakumar 2012).

This tendency to restrain civil society through the regulation of funding mechanisms has been hugely amplified since the election of the Modi government. In early 2014, the Modi government froze the accounts of 8,795 NGOs – an unprecedented number – including those of high-profile organizations such as Greenpeace India. This was followed a few months later by the cancellation of foreign contributions licences to 4,470 organizations, including several universities. Even the Ford Foundation – historically a major development collaborator with the Indian state – was subject to greater monitoring of its financial contributions to development and human rights initiatives in India. Although the government cited 'financial irregularities' as the reason for this intervention, its motives were suspect, as a leaked Intelligence Bureau document showed that, in late 2013, Modi was briefed on NGO oppositional activity becoming a threat to national economic development. Civil society actors have pushed back against these moves, challenging the cancellation of licences and the freezing of accounts in the courts, re-asserting their right to express dissent in a democratic society (Bornstein and Sharma 2016). Yet, even in instances in which government actions were reversed, such interventions have a disciplining effect on civil society, encouraging civil society actors to take a more cautious, conformist and depoliticized approach to their work (Brown 2018). Such political conformity restricts the kind of free democratic expression that a 'social revolution' presupposes.

Since the liberalization of India's economy, the Indian state has shown a more pronounced tendency to use coercion in response to expressions of democratic dissent, and this is especially evident in relation to social and political activism amongst India's poor (see also chapter 9). Numerous studies conducted since 1991 have documented excessive use of coercion by the Indian state in responding to expressions of dissent, especially from those who resist forms of corporate expansion, such as those dispossessed of land to make way for large development projects or Special Economic Zones (Walker 2008; Levien 2011; Sinha 2015). In a study of informal workers' politics in Chhattisgarh, M. Nair (2016) found that mobilizations for better wages and working conditions in the period after liberalization have been met with far greater violence from the state and paramilitary forces than was the case for very similar expressions of dissent just a few decades earlier. Nair attributes this shift to a shrinking space for democratic dissent since liberalization. In the decades following India's independence, discourses of anti-colonial nationalism and socialist development prevailed and trade unions had closer relations with the state. This state–society constellation meant that even though many poorer sections of the population were not formally members of political parties or trade unions, their expressions of dissent were still recognized as legitimate. In the period since 1991, the state has been less willing to recognize such expressions of democratic dissent as legitimate, deferring to discourses of market fundamentalism, within which dissent is often perceived as a threat to economic growth. While a 'social revolution' may be bubbling away, it comes up against limits when it challenges the state – particularly in ways that may obstruct economic growth.

A second constraint on India's social revolution relates to the structure of its civil society. A constant theme in the literature on civil society in India is that it was historically 'thin', comprised largely of sections of the upper middle class and elite. The work of Chatterjee (2004, 2011) has been especially influential in this respect. Chatterjee argues that since India's independence, the upper middle classes have used their access to education and social networks to constitute civil society as their own exclusive domain, and there is now a large volume of studies supporting this idea. Harriss (2006) has identified that the upper middle classes in Chennai have developed a range of civil society institutions to bolster their power, including registered NGOs. These organizations are formally committed to notions of abstract liberal citizenship, and work with the state to offer poor people certain minimum goods, such as microcredit loans. Yet, these NGOs may also prevent marginalized communities from launching critiques of established power structures. The rich use their NGOs to put forward technocratic solutions to problems of poverty, governance and city infrastructure, rather than supporting more democratic and political contestations by poor people. Harriss (2010) argues that, by bidding successfully for grants and tenders offered by the state and international organizations, elite civil society organizations often 'crowd out' opportunities for other sections of urban society to become more involved in participatory governance (see also Kamat 2002).

Upper middle-class dominance in Indian civil society prevents the development of a 'social revolution' that reflects the perspectives and aspirations of all sections of Indian society. It implies that those with greater access to social and cultural capital have a greater capacity to build durable institutions to defend their interests. Residents' associations illustrate this well. Fernandes (2006) has described neighbourhood associations and Resident Welfare Associations (RWAs) in Mumbai that police their gated communities, build parks adjoining their homes, and celebrate religious festivals. RWAs also aim to intervene in the life of the city by improving governance, contributing to urban planning and fostering certain forms of 'development'. Yet Fernandes shows that these practices are often detrimental to the lower classes: in their efforts to make the city conform to their aesthetic standards, middle-class RWAs frequently lobby to delimit poor people's access to public space, openly contesting the right of hawkers and pavement dwellers to remain in the streets. A common theme in literature on middle-class 'urban beautification' efforts is a tendency to construct the poor as responsible for urban degradation and pollution, while ignoring the contribution of middle-class consumption (Gooptu 2011; Baviskar 2011; Taguchi 2012). This tends to marginalize the poor, not only by excluding them from public space, but also economically – there are cases of middle-class activist groups forcing the closure of small-scale industries in the informal sector in the interest of 'beautification', for example (Baviskar et al. 2006). Further, when middle-class dominated civil society organizations attempt to 'represent' the poor, they often do so in a manner that is condescending. In the interest of attracting funding and harmonizing with global development discourses, middle-class NGO leaders may represent 'poor communities' in a manner that is highly romantic, glossing over important internal differences within communities and the diversity of individual aspirations (Shah 2010; Brown 2018). While there is certainly much variation in the dispositions of India's middle classes – and some middle-class activists have clearly made positive contributions to the development of livelihood opportunities for the poor (see Kamath and Vijayabaskar 2009) – there is a demonstrated tendency for middle-class privilege to be leveraged within Indian civil society, which is not conducive to a broad-based social revolution.

Indian civil society is also limited in achieving the ends of social revolution because it is rarely organized based on norms of impartial solidarity. This is particularly true of the poor, who generally petition the state through reference to kinship, caste and religion (Chatterjee 2011). However, it is also evident in the politics of the upper middle class, such as Hindu nationalist appeals to a politicized vision of religious identity (Hansen 1996a). In both rural and urban India, caste associations are prominent and typically defend the interests of members of particular castes or subcastes (see Jeffrey 1999). There are, certainly, some historical examples of civil society organizations founded on particularistic identities that have played a positive role in the development of India's civic life. This includes the Arya Samaj, which in the early twentieth century built numerous schools, libraries and cultural associations across north India (Jones 1966).

More recently, a shared sense of low-caste identity has provided the basis for forms of civil society. For example, in many parts of Uttar Pradesh, Dalits have come together to establish libraries, schools, rotating credit associations, and other social and economic organizations (Pai 2002; Jaffrelot 2003). These institutions tend to cater only for low castes, but they draw together urban Dalit elites and the very poor, creating meaningful and lasting forms of cross-class collaboration.

There are also many examples of faith-based organizations in India that simultaneously communicate religious ideas while also providing non-religious services for some of India's poorest people, such as schooling, food distribution and basic health care (Iyer 2018). Yet, even when these organizations are successful in building Indian civic culture, critiquing the state and aiding the delivery of services, their victory often comes at the cost of entrenching particularistic principles and communal divisions. There is also the problem that many associations misrepresent their core aims. For example, the caste associations (*mahasabhas*) across India typically downplay their role in consolidating the power of urban elites, preferring to stress their work on behalf of the poor. Even caste *panchayats*, which typically engage in more aggressive forms of reactionary social practice such as punishing people for marrying across caste lines (see Kaur 2010), sometimes claim to be part of 'civil society' (see Chowdhry 2009). To a large extent, the problem arises because there is no necessary contradiction between caste and communal projects, on the one hand, and deliberative critique, on the other. Indeed, Kaviraj (2001) argues that efforts to encourage 'civil society' in India might actually work with rather than against social formations representing caste and religious goals. This is likely to militate against the development of the kinds of liberal citizenship norms that are central to our conception of 'social revolution'.

A third constraint on India's social revolution is its legal system. As of 2016, India's courts had a backlog of some 27 million cases, with many citizens waiting more than ten years for their cases to go to trial (Doshi 2016). Further, although the judiciary has been a source of many progressive developments in India in recent decades, many have questioned whether the judiciary has become overly interventionist in Indian society and politics. Legal activism has become a key domain in which the upper middle classes exert their privilege over poorer sections of society. Baviskar (2011) demonstrates this point with reference to upper middle classes' involvement in legal campaigns in Delhi. The rich in Delhi have successfully pursued their goal of 'beautifying' the city through a multi-pronged strategy. They have petitioned the courts to shut down industries allegedly responsible for pollution and filed public interest litigation aimed at cleaning up the city. The closure of these industries was detrimental to the livelihoods of Delhi's poor, while the vehicular emissions of the middle classes were unaffected.

A fourth constraint on the social revolution derives from the Indian police force. Even a charitable analysis of the Indian police force would suggest that it has failed to perform its social mandate of upholding the rule of law and protecting people's physical security. Jauregui's (2016) ethnographic study of police forces in Uttar Pradesh found that amongst the general public, the word 'police' is almost synonymous with 'corrupt'. Police in Uttar Pradesh routinely demand and accept bribes and are seen to be instruments of the powerful, rather than protectors of the poor and powerless. Jauregui demonstrates, however, that this is not due to the character flaws of individual police officers – the problem is, rather, systemic. Many new recruits are forced to pay bribes simply to obtain their position and thus enter the job indebted. As a result of this – as well as poor salaries awarded to lower-level police officers and demands for continual payment of bribes by senior members of the police administration – many ground-level police officers rely on the extraction of bribes from citizens to remain afloat. Successive governments in India have lacked the will to make the necessary reforms to the police force. Everyday exposure to police corruption undermines the confidence of Indian citizens in the state and tends to dampen the efficacy of social revolution.

A fifth constraint on India's social revolution is the mainstream media. India has a history of a strong, lively and independent press – and this has been a cornerstone of its reputation as a successful democracy. Yet, corporate influence over the Indian media is expanding. To give just one high profile example: in 2017, the *Economic and Political Weekly*, for decades a bastion of critical academic analysis of contemporary affairs in India, courted controversy by removing an article by its editor Paranjoy Guha-Thakurta. The article alleged tax evasion by the Indian multinational conglomerate, the Adani Group. Much of the analysis of this controversy – which ultimately led to Guha-Thakurta's resignation from the editorship of the publication – suggested that the article was removed due to threats of legal action by the Adani Group. Such risks to freedom of expression in India are even more prominent in regional media outlets. Regional language channels show a worrying concentration of ownership (P. Thomas 2014) and local political parties often exercise undue amounts of control over regional news – in some cases paying large donations to ensure favourable coverage (Chadha and Koliska 2016). Such developments weaken the character of public debate and thus limit the potential of the social revolution to alter the status quo.

A sixth and final constraint on India's social revolution concerns the role of international actors. Indian civil society is strongly influenced by international donors and institutions. It is not clear to what extent vertical organizational structures – for example, where international institutions work alongside small-scale NGOs – play a positive role in the development of India's civic culture. Scholarly analysis and public discourse in India suggest that the dominance of foreign-funded NGOs within Indian civil society drowns out more grassroots commentary on issues of local significance (Brown 2014; Kamat 2002). Furthermore, the saturation of civil society with globally sponsored NGOs tends to benefit the relatively privileged: the urban rich in India are enmeshed in global flows of money, know-how and cultural capital that are redefining how civil society works (Ellis 2010). For example, Webb's (2010) research shows that foreign donors have become involved in trying to sponsor particular community activists in Delhi. Institutions such as the Association for India's Development in the US offer activists fellowships and stipends – but this sponsorship comes at a price. Money and influence become concentrated in the hands of a few prominent activists at the expense of more democratic group-based forms of civic activism. At the same time, those who do obtain foreign funding increasingly imagine their work less in terms of community service and more as a form of 'social entrepreneurship' that can contribute to their curriculum vitae.

A further concern regarding the international influence on Indian civil society is that it has resulted in a proliferation of discourses that do not clearly resonate with local realities. Lerche's (2008) research on the involvement of international organizations in Dalit activism in north India illustrates this tendency. Lerche focuses on the efforts of the International Dalit Solidarity Network (IDSN) to bring Dalit activists together around the quest for a certain form of 'empowerment.' IDSN, however, has tended to draw on discourses and policies from the Global North around 'affirmative action', which in the Indian setting are only of benefit to a relatively thin layer of the Dalit middle class. Fixation on a globally influential discourse meant that opportunities to uplift the position of poorer Dalits – through improving access to services, for example – were missed. Similarly, Brown's (2018) research suggests that sustainable rural development NGOs in India have a tendency to draw on globally trending discourses, such as those surrounding 'food sovereignty', at the expense of articulating more grassroots concerns regarding the condition of the Indian countryside. While speaking in terms of global discourses enables leaders of NGOs to become well-networked in global activist and NGO networks, their appeal amongst farmers in the NGOs' target communities is often limited.

10.6 Conclusion

There is evidence from across India to suggest that a profound shift has occurred in values and civic awareness, such that dynamics in India mirror in key respects the rise of liberal citizenship in Africa (Arnot 2009), Latin America (R. Harriss 2003), and many other parts of the Global South. People in India are today less willing to tolerate corruption, and they expect greater accountability, transparency and responsiveness from their elected political leaders and bearers of public office than they did two decades ago. Increased participation in formal education and access to communications technologies have undoubtedly played a role in facilitating this shift, and they also provide new methods for social actors to organize to achieve progressive social change. In these respects, India appears to conform in broad respects to the rise of broadly liberal values identified by other accounts of the Global South (Arnot 2009; United Nations 2016).

This social revolution has evolved in tandem with an upsurge in confident forms of cultural expression evident within India and increasingly linking India to its diaspora population and other populations globally. To a much greater extent than in the 1990s, India plays a major role in defining global cultural practice, especially through film, sport, religion, and in areas such as yoga and the development of ideas of well-being.

India's social revolution faces major constraints, however (cf. Bayat 2013). These include poorly functioning civic institutions, an increasingly coercive state and a civil society that remains dominated in many respects by the upper middle class and the elite. The failure of successive government regimes to engage in police reform is also a major brake on effective civic activism in modern India. The rise of extremist forms of Hindu nationalism may also erode citizenship ideals in the 2020s, especially perhaps among India's lower middle classes (see Hansen 1996a). A key question will be the extent to which a broad belief in 'liberalism' – in the sense of a belief in equal rights and freedom of expression – continues to hold sway in the minds of India's younger generation. Equally key will be the role of institutions, especially schools and universities, in undergirding what we have described here as a 'social revolution'.

11

Does Caste Still Matter in India?

11.1 Introduction

'Caste' most closely approximates two terms common in India: *varna* or *jati*. *Varna* refers to the four sub-divisions of the Hindu hierarchy, believed – according to the *Purusa Sukta* hymn in Sanskrit scripture – to have been derived from different parts of the body of a primal being, Purush. They consist of the Brahmins, who were traditionally priests; the Kshatriyas (warriors); the Vaisyas (husbandmen); and the Sudras, who performed a broad range of other tasks. The Brahmins, Kshatriyas and Vaisyas together comprise the 'twice born' castes in which male adolescents undergo a second, spiritual birth. They are often also called the 'Forward' castes, distinct from the Shudras who are defined as 'Backward'.

A fifth category, unnamed in Hindu scriptures, lie outside the *varna* hierarchy altogether. They tended to be confined to work that other castes imagined as demeaning, such as skinning animals and performing cremation, and for this reason were subject to practices of untouchability. The social reformer and member of an 'untouchable' community, Dr. B. R. Ambedkar, used the term 'Dalits', meaning 'the oppressed', to refer to this group, a term which is now in common usage. For the purposes of developing forms of positive discrimination in relation to state representative bodies and schooling, for example, the state commonly refers to Dalits as 'Scheduled Castes' (SCs) or 'Scheduled Tribes' (STs) – terms coined in the mid-1930s to reflect the fact that certain communities were listed on 'schedules' as being deserving of positive discrimination. Some Dalits also sometimes refer to themselves as 'Harijans' (children of god) – a term coined by Gandhi that many view as patronizing. It is difficult to estimate the population of each *varna* because figures on caste have not been included in the census since 1931. But SCs constituted 16.6% of the Indian population in 2011.

Each *varna* is comprised of thousands of *jatis*: endogamous caste 'groups' that in the past were at least somewhat linked to a specialist occupation. Members of each *jati* often have a sense of how they are placed with respect to the *varna* hierarchy. But the relationship between *jati* and *varna* has never been fixed (e.g. Béteille 1992, 2001). M. N. Srinivas (1989) argued that in certain

circumstances *jatis* may try to move 'up' within the four-fold *varna* classifica-
tion, a process he termed 'sanskritization'. It is also possible for *jatis* to move
in the other direction, for example where a Forward caste tries to establish
a Backward status in order to obtain government reservations for disadvantaged castes in public-sector employment (Jeffrey et al. 2008). This has been
particularly evident since 2015. For example, Patels in Gujarat and Marathas
in Maharashtra – both numerous and relatively wealthy castes (Deshpande
and Ramachandran 2017) – have engaged in large-scale mobilizations aimed
at ensuring that they receive 'Other Backward Class' (OBC) status. The agitations over the period 2016–18 were frequently violent and reflected the
potent combination among many Marathas of a sense of their entitlement to
urban well-paid employment and their simultaneous insecurity in the context
of a shortage of work. The government caved in to Marathan pressure and
granted them OBC status only for the judiciary to overturn this decision on
the grounds that Marathas were not economically backward.

There are marked variations in how caste becomes manifest in north and
central India, on the one hand, and the four main linguistic regions of the
south. There are few indigenous Kshatriyas and Vaisyas in the south, and
thus the Sudra category is far larger there than elsewhere. There are also
relatively few Brahmins in Tamil Nadu (Harriss 2018). Moreover, *jatis* in the
south, unlike their counterparts elsewhere, were split historically between
right-hand and left-hand divisions, which derive from religious ritual and
shape social relations (e.g. Mines 2006).

Caste hierarchies have become less important over the past sixty years. Few
people think or talk about *varna* in twenty-first-century India and the term
never had any pan-Indian validity (Mosse 2018). But we will argue in this chapter that *jati* identities remain significant in the fields of politics, education,
work and marriage, and also that Dalits suffer multiple forms of disadvantage
in modern India. Recent research shows the enduring significance of hierarchy in Indian society.

11.2 Caste in Mid-Twentieth-Century India

The anthropologist Louis Dumont (1970) used ancient Hindu texts as well
as findings from ethnographic village studies to argue that the Hindu caste
system is oriented around the principles of purity and pollution. Brahmins are
at the top of the resulting hierarchy and untouchables at the bottom, and all
castes are linked together via a complex system of ritual acts that confirm and
reproduce conceptions of purity and pollution. In this vision, caste was not
based upon power, status or authority, as is the case for Western structures of
stratification, but on the purity embodied by the Brahmin.

Dumont's ideas have been roundly critiqued, as misinterpretations of Hindu texts, overly reliant on written sources, and reflecting Brahmin ideology (for a review, see Fuller 1996: 3ff.). Other scholars in the 1950s and 1960s focused on how caste is lived and practised on the ground (e.g. Srinivas 1955; Mayer 1996) – providing a 'field view' to complement Dumont's 'book view' (Béteille 1991). These scholars frequently imagined caste society at the village level as a *'jajmani* system', a term originally associated with the work of William Wiser (1936) in southern Uttar Pradesh. In the *jajmani* system, a powerful caste – or 'patron' *(jajman)* – made payments, to a range of clients *(kameen)*, usually in kind. The patrons' power was derived in part from their control over local social and economic assets. The patrons were the major landowners, usually lived in the largest houses, typically possessed the most extensive contacts outside the village, and presided over a governing council in many villages. Patrons were usually from a relatively high *jati* within the *varna* hierarchy and they commonly dominated the ritual life of the village. But patrons were not usually Brahmins. One of the most important empirical studies of the *jajmani* system, by Raheja (1988), focuses on Gujars, a caste of only middling status within the *varna* hierarchy. Raheja concentrates on symbolic aspects of the relationship between dominant Gujars and other service castes, especially Brahmins. Through giving gifts *(dan)* to Brahmin priests, the Gujars marked their own power as a dominant caste and confirmed their spiritual well-being.

The *'jajmani* system' as described by scholars such as Raheja could only capture certain elements of a complex social reality. It should also be noted that the various 'caste systems' described never reached a fully-fledged form nor became wholly taken-for granted, partly because large sections of the rural economy were already integrated into the capitalist economy in the 1950s and 1960s. For example, Scarlett Epstein (1973) notes that in the two villages she studied in the 1960s, *jajmani* systems were well-developed but coexisted with a cash economy. Fuller (1989) and Commander (1983) have critiqued work on the *jajmani* system more thoroughly.

But there were certain common features to caste in the 1950s and 1960s that together suggest the existence of localized caste systems that sometimes bore a resemblance to the *jajmani* arrangements described by scholars such as Wiser (1936) and Raheja (1988) and in which considerations of power and inequality were almost always important (see especially Mandelbaum 1970). These systems tended to have five characteristics. First, *jatis* often specialized to some extent in terms of occupation and various occupations had different connotations in terms of purity and pollution. The functions performed by particular castes within the *jajmani* system tended to be fairly stable over time and passed on inter-generationally within the family. Thus, particular *jatis* came to be associated with specific hereditary trades. For example, in large parts of Uttar Pradesh, the Dhimmars served the function of carrying water, the Chamars were leatherworkers or shoemakers, and the Dhobis washed clothes. It would be mistaken to imagine that all members of these castes

performed these tasks – as early as the 1890s, many Chamars worked in agricultural labour in western UP, for example (see Neville 1922). Yet occupational
categories were often indicative of people's work in the 1950s and 1960s.
Untouchables in most parts of India often worked as slaves until action on the
part of the colonial government to introduce reform (Viswanath 2014).

A second key feature of caste was its reproduction through rules about the
sharing of food, bodily contact and other interpersonal relations. These norms
often covered such matters as who could officiate at marriage ceremonies,
where people should sit at village feasts, and who could attend the birth of
a child, among many other aspects of everyday village life at the time (see
Mandelbaum 1970). Low-caste inequality had a marked spatial aspect, too, in
some parts of India: Dalits were forced to live in specific parts of the village
away from higher castes; they were often refused entry to temples and schools;
and they were banned from using the water pumps of the rich, for example
(see Srinivas 1955; Béteille 1965; Mayer 1996). Contraventions of these norms
often led to violent higher caste retribution and reprisals.

Third, caste shaped marriage practices. Most castes practised endogamy.
Many had further rules about marriage, for example that a member of a
specific sub-caste could not marry within their own sub-caste or that of their
paternal and maternal grandparents, to take the case of the Jats of western
UP (Pradhan 1966). Within the caste-based arranged marriage system other
norms applied, too: for example, in many parts of the plains of north India it
was usual for a woman's family to pay a dowry to a husband's family.

Fourth, notions of caste hierarchy had achieved a degree of acceptance in
rural areas. We need to enter some caveats here. Low-caste political movements aimed at raising the standing of untouchables were active in parts
of India in the late nineteenth and twentieth centuries (e.g. Gooptu 2001;
Rawat 2011). During the twentieth century activists began to mobilize around
the term 'Dalit'. In some parts of the country Dalits effectively questioned
dominant caste power (e.g. Guha 2007b: 287). Moreover, even in the areas
where Dalits were not engaged in forms of social mobilization, they had not
necessarily internalized the notion of themselves as 'defiled' in any sense (see
Berreman 1960: 127). But the weight of evidence from village ethnographies
suggests that in the 1950s and 1960s, higher castes had little compunction
about using the language of caste to explain and justify their elevated position. As Dalit biographies and autobiographies also show (Ilaiah 1991), low
castes had commonly internalized social subordination; low self-esteem came
to be reflected in their demeanour in public settings.

Fifth, higher castes were often able to translate their local economic and
political power into a wider dominance over state bureaucracies, representative government and local electoral outcomes. Marguerite Robinson (1988)
shows how dominant castes in Andhra Pradesh in the 1950s and 1960s were
able to influence the votes of lower castes, such that rural elites were able to

deliver 'vote banks' to political parties. Pradhan (1966) analyses the capacity of dominant caste Jats to control village government through the use of traditional caste councils in UP. Higher castes monopolized key posts in the district offices of the ruling Congress Party in the 1950s and 1960s (Brass 1965). Dominant castes also predominated within state legislative assemblies and the Lok Sabha (Jaffrelot and Kumar 2009). A key point here is that higher castes were actively producing notions of caste as an idea in the 1950s and 1960s rather than simply abiding by a historically predetermined 'cultural idea'.

Studies of these five dimensions of dominance in mid-twentieth-century India cannot be read as wholly accurate reflections of village power structures at the time. There was a tendency to ignore women's social practices and overplay caste to the detriment of analysis of other axes of differentiation. It is also important to note a relative lack of material on caste in urban India (see Vatuk 1972; Gooptu 2001). But the work of scholars in the 1950s and 1960s suggests that fairly rigid and stable caste hierarchies existed in many parts of India during this period. Higher castes benefitted from mutually reinforcing modes of power and their dominance tended to be reproduced inter-generationally in somewhat predictable ways.

11.3 The Decline of Caste Hierarchies

In the late 1960s, there was a shift in scholarly approaches to Indian anthropology (Singer and Cohn 1968). An old idea of the subcontinent as timeless gave way slowly over the 1970s and early 1980s to understandings of India – and caste within it – as a product of history and social and political work (see Corbridge 1988, and Clark-Deces 2011 for a review). This shift spurred academics to reconsider caste in pre-independence India. Scholars began to show how, from the early seventeenth century onwards, patterns of militarization and trade across South Asia reinforced tendencies towards caste-related forms of difference and inequality (S. Bayly 2001). One effect of this 'historical turn' in the analysis of caste was to shine a light on the role of the British in actively producing caste ideas during the nineteenth and early twentieth centuries in India, for example by including caste on the census and inducting dominant castes into the lower reaches of the colonial administration. Corbridge (2000) has traced this process in Jharkhand, India. He demonstrates how in the second half of the nineteenth century the British imposed rigid caste and tribe labels on populations that were fluid and internally differentiated. In the early twentieth century, the British policy of divide and rule meant that tribes were increasingly hived off from castes, and in the postcolonial era political parties have found it expedient to persist with the 'ST' nomenclature, in spite of its faulty sociological logic. Washbrook (1988: 83) therefore has a point when he notes that, 'much of India's ancient past may have been made in the second quarter of the nineteenth century'. But the British did not conjure caste difference from the ether. Peabody (2001) shows that pre-British rulers also used caste-wise tabulations to enumerate subjects and that the British were encouraged by sections of Indian society to continue this practice.

The relative importance of the political and social production of caste versus its erosion or diminution in the face of other forces is a key issue today. Dipankar Gupta (2005) makes a case that caste became much less important in the period between the 1960s and early 2000s in India. He claims that a former tendency for caste to reflect occupation declined. Growing urbanization and commercialization, as well as rapid economic growth in some parts of India, has allowed people from many caste backgrounds to find off-farm work or incomes (see chapter 4). This has had the wider effect of undermining 'jajmani systems' as far as they ever existed (Gupta 2005; Jodhka 2015). People formerly dependent on local landowners have been able to migrate to other parts of India or even abroad to work. Some studies emphasize the capacity of lower castes to travel every day to local urban areas to find jobs (e.g. Anandhi et al. 2002), or else to move within India on a seasonal basis (Shah 2006; and see chapter 4). Surinder Jodhka (2008, 2015) describes the rapid growth of a wide range of Dalit enterprises in western UP and Haryana in the 1990s and early 2000s that have elevated individual entrepreneurs out of poverty while also providing jobs for others. Mendelsohn (1993) maintains that by the late 1980s, the traditional system of *jajmani* relations in northern Rajasthan had become marginal to the overall economy of the village of Behror in which he worked. There appears to have been a parallel decline in awareness of caste as a religiously sanctioned institution and of traditional councils dominated by a single caste and claiming authority over other villagers. Mendelsohn links the decline of the *jajmani* system and traditional councils not only to a sharp rise in rural people's economic activity outside the village but also to increased economic differentiation among Ahirs, the erstwhile 'dominant caste'. Economic differentiation had eroded a sense of collective interest among Ahirs, such that caste solidarity had been replaced by 'pragmatic individualism or at least family-centredness' (Mendelsohn 1993, 824–5). Some recent work points in the same direction as Mendelsohn's study. A survey by Kapur et al. (2010) of two UP villages argues that the absorption of the rural area more tightly into the market economy had facilitated marked improvements in Dalits' income and assets between 1990 and 2010. A set of studies based in south India make a similar point (Anandhi 2013; Carswell and De Neve 2014). These studies also highlight local variability: the capacity of low castes to challenge systems of caste domination through economic mobility can vary within a single region, for example reflecting the relative capacity of Dalits in different villages to obtain work outside agriculture.

Reservations have also played a prominent role in delinking caste from occupation (Howard and Prakash 2012). Positive caste-based discrimination in India can be traced to the 1930s, when the British created lists of formerly Untouchable castes and tribes deemed eligible for special state assistance: 'Scheduled Castes' (SCs) and 'Scheduled Tribes' (STs), so-called because they were listed on 'schedules' by the British. The 1950 Indian Constitution offered SCs and STs legal equality and reserved places in public-sector employment, educational institutions and government representative bodies (Galanter 1984). Shortly after independence, Nehru established a Backward Classes Commission to investigate the condition of castes formally above the SCs but nonetheless suffering from social and economic disadvantages. This Commission reported in 1956 with a list of 2,399 backward caste *jatis* and suggested measures to improve their position. Nehru believed it politically impossible to implement this recommendation. But the issue of reservations for these 'Other Backward Classes' (OBCs) – as they came to be labelled – emerged again in 1977 when the Janata Party pledged to establish a new investigative body. The resulting commission under the chairmanship of B. P. Mandal reported in 1980, recommending the extension of positive discrimination to OBCs. The Mandal Report was set aside for the next ten years, but V. P. Singh promised to implement its recommendations during electoral hustings in Autumn 1989, and, as prime minister, made the actual decision to institute reforms in August 1990 (Dirks 2001: 284–5). This provoked a fierce higher caste backlash, especially among students (Balagopal 1991).

In most parts of India, the effect of OBC reservations was more symbolic than substantive. When reservations were introduced for Backward castes, competition for positions in government employment was intense. It was often only households that could afford to pay a bribe and had the right social contacts – a 'creamy layer' of relatively rich OBCs from comparatively well-placed *jatis* – who obtained quota positions (Michelutti 2007).

Similarly, a few Dalit *jatis* have tended to dominate access to reserved government jobs for SCs. Wealthier Dalits and those already possessing good links in government service have often monopolized access to public-sector jobs, becoming in some places a self-reproducing clique. Béteille (1992) notes other problems with SC reservations: since those in government employment are legally debarred from participating in politics, positive discrimination deprives low-caste communities of potential political representatives. Moreover, many SCs move out of their villages and urban neighbourhoods to work in government, robbing communities of talented individuals. Government-employed Dalits may withdraw psychologically from their origins or even refuse to acknowledge their caste peers as they become assimilated into an urban middle class. Yet, recent research suggests that access to reserved government positions has led to positive changes in the occupational choices of SC individuals, though the effect is much stronger for SCs with higher levels of education (Howard and Prakash 2012; Deshpande 2016). Reservations can also have flow-on effects. Parry (1999) points out that for every SC who enters government employment, many others in the immediate and extended family will benefit. Moreover, the entry of SCs into government employment plays an important symbolic role, instilling a measure of confidence and pride in low-caste communities. Parry contests the notion that low castes in government service disown their caste peers: they often play important roles in caste associations, social organizations and cultural festivals. Parry concludes that SC reservations have led to greater churning in local patterns of caste and class reproduction and contribute to a diminution in caste hierarchies, even while they have failed to transform society.

Corbridge's (2000) account of the cultural politics and substantive effects of Scheduled Tribe (ST) reservations in Jharkhand parallels Parry's analysis in several key respects. Corbridge shows that reservations have been important in the creation of an ST middle class in Jharkhand. Most members of this ST petty bourgeoisie now live in urban areas and come from established tribal elites. But some tribals from non-elite backgrounds have been able to take advantage of reservations. Moreover, reservations have worked in part to 'crystallize a conception of *adivasi* (tribal) identity that recognizes the exploitation/marginalization of many tribal communities and which demands compensation from the authorities' (Corbridge 2000: 65).

The debate on reservation took a new twist in 2019 when, as an electoral gambit, the BJP-led coalition introduced reservations for 10 per cent of the general castes that suffered from economic disadvantage (classified as earning less than INR 800,000 a year). This revived a similar proposal made by Congress politician Narasimha Rao in 1991. Critics have noted that the Constitution establishes a principle of positive discrimination based on named classes, such as OBCs or SCs, but does not allow for reservations within classes.

Electoral reservations for SCs and STs appear to have had positive social and economic impacts in some instances. At the micro level, reservations and corresponding increases in the representation of SCs and STs in local *panchayats* can have positive effects on the self-perceptions of the *jatis* that gain representation (Chauchard 2017). At the macro level, recent studies indicate that increases in reserved parliamentary seats for STs correlate with improvements in poverty rates (Chin and Prakash 2011), child labour rates (Kaletski and Prakash 2016), and numbers of visits by healthcare workers to villages (Kaletski and Prakash 2017).

Beyond reservations, the proliferation of government programmes catering for disadvantaged groups has contributed to a decline in low castes' dependence on higher castes (Manor 2011). During Indira Gandhi's period of rule in the 1970s, a wide range of initiatives emerged, often specifically directed towards low castes, that provided small amounts of land, grants to purchase livestock or housing, and cheap credit for the poor. Such programs offered a bulwark for some against the most extreme forms of poverty and dependence

(Krishna 2002). Since 2004, the Indian state has expanded the range, scope and size of such development efforts, under what has been called 'the new rights agenda' (see chapter 8). These are likely to be further accelerating the diminution of caste and class hierarchies in rural India (Manor 2011; Munshi 2016). In some areas, the National Rural Employment Guarantee Scheme has been particularly important in providing opportunities for Dalits to improve their bargaining power within the rural economy and shape the design of rural development projects to meet their needs (Carswell and De Neve 2014; Veeraraghavan 2017).

Across India, education has been important in challenging hierarchical ideas of caste. Dalit enrolment in education improved in many areas in the 1980s, 1990s and 2000s, especially among boys (e.g. Mendelsohn and Vicziany 1998; Gorringe 2009). Basic education provides Dalits with the numeracy and literacy skills required to manage businesses, navigate urban society and negotiate legal and government bureaucracies. It improves Dalits' ability to manage their own health and reduces their dependence on higher castes (Sen 2000). Formal education also often increases Dalits' self-confidence and sense of entitlement to equal treatment by the law and government (Wadley 1994: 222f.), especially where rising education is wedded to a strong Dalit movement for social empowerment (Gorringe 2009). In UP, educated Dalits commonly argue that people should be judged and valued on their behaviour not according to their caste, and they claim that education has instilled in them confidence, civility and self-belief (Jeffrey et al. 2008). Rising education, combined with the growing influence of the media, have also influenced the thinking of middle and upper castes in India, many of whom would claim to no longer believe in hierarchical ideas of caste (cf. Béteille 1991). Moreover, education has been important in precipitating a public culture in India in which it is no longer acceptable to speak of caste in hierarchical terms.

Education, growing urbanization, the expansion of the media, and the spread of ideas of democracy across India have also had the cumulative effect of altering what is considered acceptable in terms of the everyday practice of caste. There are many examples of different castes socializing together, often in intimate ways, in even some of India's more remote rural locations. Pinto (2008) records examples of cross-caste friendship and mutual understanding in her ethnography of birth practices in rural eastern UP. Nisbett (2007) refers to college students from different castes openly sharing snacks and cigarettes in south India. Nakassis (2014) documents how college students either refuse to use the traditional caste forms of address that were in use by their parents' generation – or in some cases invert them – in order to challenge caste as an axis of social difference.

Over this period, higher castes have also been unable to maintain their monopoly over political institutions. Jaffrelot and Kumar's (2009) analysis of the changing caste profiles of members of legislative assemblies (MLAs) across 16 states of India brings out regional variations in the extent and nature of change. The authors found that the Deccan (Maharashtra, Karnataka and Andhra Pradesh) and Communist states (Kerala and West Bengal) remain dominated by upper castes. But in the Hindi Belt (UP, MP and Bihar) and north-west (Punjab, Rajasthan and Gujarat), an upper caste majority gave way to OBC (Hindi Belt) or middle caste (north-west) administrations in the early 1990s (see also chapter 7).

Dalits and other lower castes have increasingly challenged the notion that higher castes are their natural superiors in village-level politics. Robinson (1988) describes how the rise of political parties and other institutions representing the interests of the poor, and growing political awareness as a result of media expansion and education, loosened the control of higher castes over vote banks and lessened Dalits' dependence on village notables in Andhra Pradesh. In a similar vein, rising education and political consciousness has allowed Dalits in western India to bypass established patron–client networks and set themselves up as social reformers operating between poor people and the state (Krishna 2002). Moreover, the 93rd Amendment Act to the Indian Constitution, passed in 1994, introduced reserved seats for Dalits in village-level *panchayats*. The degree to which this has empowered SCs varies geographically (compare Lieten 1996 with Ciotti 2006) and even when representation of SCs has improved, forward castes often remain 'dominant' within village *panchayats* in the sense of having the social connections and organizational power necessary to control the flow of state resources (Jeffrey 2001; Pattenden 2016). Nonetheless, Dalits have benefitted to a significant degree from this legislation, and some Dalit women have come to hold significant power (Ciotti 2006).

In sum, the link between occupation and caste has become less marked, rules around commensality have been relaxed, the taken-for-granted nature of caste is less evident, and upper caste dominance of politics has declined in some regions. Discrimination and segregation based on caste persist, however, and Indian citizens continue to 'produce' caste in multiple ways.

11.4 Caste, Identity and Politics

A primary way in which caste continues to be produced has been in the political sphere. As caste was declining as a hierarchical 'system', it was simultaneously being reinvented and redeployed as an identity in the sphere of modern competitive politics. This is a theme that has been developed in a wide range of works (e.g. Kothari 1970; Jaffrelot 2003). In a review article on caste and politics, Manor (2011: 26) uses an analysis of National Election Survey (NES) data to argue that caste continues to influence voting behaviour in India, if not at the all-India level then certainly in many states. Manor argues that individual *jatis* are less significant as political actors than *jati*-clusters, comprised often of castes that have a roughly similar standing with respect to the *varna* hierarchy. He also emphasizes the localized nature of these caste effects: it is often within specific regions at the sub-state level that influence of *jati* clusters over voting behaviour becomes apparent.

Of course, caste is only one among many bases upon which people may vote. Drawing on a survey of people's voting behaviour in three states, Gupta (2000) claims that people's individual choices at elections are a great deal more idiosyncratic than most commentators would lead us to believe. Factors other than caste – economic interest, personal links with a local politician, party loyalty, for example – are often as or more important than people's *jati* or *jati*-cluster in governing voting behaviour. But, as Chandra (2004) points out, voters often use politicians' pronouncements regarding caste as a means of intuiting their policies and priorities in office (see also chapter 8). Even in states without a strong presence of caste-based parties, attempts to capture the 'vote banks' of particular caste groups remain central to electoral strategies (Martin 2015),

Caste or coded references to caste provide a basis for politicians and political parties to utilize in the quest for power (e.g. Kothari 1970; Chandra 2004; Mosse 2018). That politicians do so has its own sociological effects: strengthening caste identities, heightening people's suspicion of other castes, and encouraging people to consult with each other in *jati* meetings in the period running up to elections. In the 1960s, OBC and middle-caste mobilization was most evident. For example, in UP in the 1960s and 1970s, Chaudhry Charan Singh, a member of the middle-ranking Jat caste, developed an alliance of Ahirs, Jats, Gujars and Rajputs (AJGAR) that served as a durable support base. Gupta (2000:143ff.) argues that AJGAR was a community of rich peasants rather than a caste-based coalition. But fears about Dalit assertion certainly contributed to AJGAR solidarity. In the late 1980s, the controversy over the report of the Mandal Commission heightened the connection between caste and politics. The OBC reservations issue polarized opinion and encouraged people to link their future prosperity to collective caste 'interests'. The political landscape changed again in the 1990s, and again caste came to the fore. During that decade and the following one, BJP defended higher castes' economic and cultural-political goals while strategically cultivating support among sections of the lower castes that had not been mobilized by other groups, such as the so-called Most Backward Castes (MBCs) – the poorest among those in the OBC category – and poorer Dalit *jatis*.

The importance of caste in processes of political mobilization spreads well beyond central and state-level elections to influence almost all processes of competitive election in India's vast democracy: union ballots, district board elections, even appointments to neighbourhood associations and voluntary groups. For example, in the period before a *panchayat* election, village homes are typically abuzz with calculations regarding how different castes are going to vote and what this means for the eventual outcome (Lieten 1996). Similarly, caste is also crucial in student politics in many parts of provincial India. Young people often hold *jati* meetings to decide on how to vote, and candidates often recruit statistically-minded peers to compute how caste might shape the election (Jeffrey 2010).

Caste has been given a fresh salience, too, by the rise of parties associated with the cultures of specific *jatis*, such as Mulayam Singh Yadav's Samajwadi Party (SP), and Laloo Prasad Yadav's Rashtriya Janata Dal (RJD) party in Bihar. These politicians garnered support through promoting Yadav and Backward Class interests while at the same time making links with Muslims and some other castes (see Witsoe 2013, on Bihar). As Michelutti (2007) argues, the SP played on notions of Yadavs as people with a democratic tradition and used symbols of Yadav identity in its campaigns. This encouraged the emergence of Yadav social associations and cultural practices. Similarly, the Bahujan Samaj Party (BSP) in UP made explicit efforts to court the votes of Dalits, especially the most important Dalit jati in UP: the Chamars. Since the 1990s there has been an effervescence of 'mytho-histories' of Dalit achievement circulated by educated politicos with links to the BSP (Narayan 2008).

11.5 Caste as Habitus: Hierarchy Revisited

Caste hierarchies continue to have great importance, too, in terms of schooling, work and marriage. Dalits remain well behind upper castes and OBCs with respect to education (see Ramachandran 2004; Shah et al. 2006: 46). In most parts of India, higher castes enter school at an earlier age, obtain admission in better institutions, follow more prestigious routes through education, and acquire relatively marketable qualifications. The main difficulty for Dalits is not access to primary school, but remaining in education in the context of discrimination, poverty and a lack of obvious incentives to study (see Vasavi 2015 and chapter 13). Desai et al. (2010) argue that a Dalit's caste identity has an importance in creating poor educational experiences independent of parent's education and income (see also Shah et al. 2006).

In higher education, Dalit students report feeling out of place in colleges that are both culturally and administratively dominated by upper castes. Notwithstanding improvements in this area, they continue to be subject to subtle and overt discrimination, which impede their academic progress and prevent their achievements from being recognized (Ovichegan 2015). The high-profile suicide of Dalit PhD student Rohith Vemula in 2016 made this only too apparent. Vemula's suicide followed months of harassment by right-wing Hindu students' groups for his pro-Dalit political views and the reported cancellation of his fellowship at the University of Hyderabad and expulsion from the university's dormitory due to his involvement in an Ambedkarite students' association. Vemula's suicide note spoke of multiple frustrations with having his destiny and aspirations tied to his caste status, and became a lightning rod for public discussion and protest surrounding the continued salience of caste-based discrimination in India's universities.

Educational inequalities have knock-on effects in terms of Dalits' and other low castes' capacities to compete for secure and well-paid work. For example, dominant castes' monopoly over the credentials and forms of comportment that confer advantage in social settings has allowed them to dominate access to secure salaried work in rural western UP (Jeffrey et al. 2008; Munshi 2016; Deshpande and Ramachandran 2017). This is all the more surprising since western UP has been an area in which low castes have achieved new forms of political representation through the rise of the BSP. Jeffrey et al. (2008) show that higher castes are able to draw upon local and regional stocks of social and cultural resources, as well as their formidable economic advantage, to 'counter-resist' low-caste political assertion. This is a point that also emerges from research among Dalits in Tamil Nadu (Gorringe 2009), where low-caste political mobilization has a longer history but where there are similar barriers to rapid low-caste mobility. Caste hierarchies are often fairly persistent even in a political context conducive to change.

A similar picture emerges in small towns and big cities. Dalits and MBCs are less successful at finding secure salaried work, and establishing successful businesses, than are higher castes in urban India. Thorat and Newman (2007) find quantitative evidence of discrimination in hiring, wages, working conditions and patterns of upward mobility within urban labour markets in India. Thorat and Newman (2010) sent mock applications for private-sector service jobs in India, using identical CVs but two sets of names, one high caste and one Dalit or Muslim. Their experiment showed that Dalit and Muslim applicants face significant discrimination in the white-collar job market. The odds of a Dalit applicant receiving a follow-up call were only 67 per cent of a high caste Hindu applicant with the same CV. Research on Delhi students' experiences of seeking white-collar work provides comparable evidence (Deshpande and Newman 2007). Dalit students were much more likely to experience searching interviews, and these often entailed being quizzed on their caste, views on reservation, and family background. Deshpande and Newman (2007) conclude that recruitment to private-sector jobs is often 'rigged' in favour of higher castes. Harriss (2018) notes that caste even shapes access to NGO work in Tamil Nadu.

Harriss-White (2003) makes similar points on the basis of long-term research in the small town of Arni, Tamil Nadu. Arni experienced rapid economic change during the 1980s and 1990s, in part through the rise of new forms of commodity production. But caste continues to shape people's capacity to participate in relatively secure and lucrative sections of the economy. Moreover, caste interests strongly influence the activities of the institutions, such as trade associations, that have emerged to adjudicate on wages, working hours and employment disputes in the town. In later research on SC- and ST-owned businesses, Harriss-White et al. (2014) found consistent patterns of discrimination within markets, and both the state and civil society preventing such businesses from generating remunerative returns. Upper castes would create obstacles to accessing prime locations and formal sources of credit, while exclusionary practices by upper castes prevented SCs and STs finding entry points to the social networks through which information, supplies and labour recruitment were organized. Dalit businesses lacked the economic group identity to pressurize key state departments to provide key resources such as licences, and access to sites and infrastructure, while established upper-caste networks maintained privileges within these departments, through methods ranging from the payment of bribes to marriage alliances. Harriss-White and Vidyarthee (2009) use economic census data to tease out how this kind of upper-caste privilege and discrimination against SCs and STs in different parts of India shapes their participation in various forms of business. Summarizing the data, they note that:

> SCs have entered mining, quarrying and construction and are most consistently prevented from entering trade, transport, hospitality and service sectors [. . .] STs have a relative disadvantage in all sectors of the non-agricultural economy but have been able, with the help of improvements in literacy, to move into services – though, it is likely, at the low end (Harriss-White and Vidyarthee 2009: 332).

Dalits' exclusion from relatively remunerative work is thus multi-layered, reflecting especially the caste stereotyping of particular occupations, referral-based systems of labour recruitment that privilege some castes over others, and the existence of higher caste networks that exclude and marginalize lower castes (Mosse 2018).

Mosse (2018) and others point to the common inability of Dalits to use entrepreneurship as a means of social mobility. Lower castes often face enormous obstacles in establishing businesses. This is in part because markets themselves are often 'ranked' such that they become associated with specific castes. For example, in parts of south India, construction and transport are coded as relatively 'low-caste' spheres and health, education and food services as higher caste arenas (Thorat and Newman 2010; Harriss-White at al. 2014). Even in spheres in which they gain entry, Dalits often face major challenges in acquiring capital, connections, premises, infrastructure and customers (see Prakash 2015). As a result, most Dalit business is 'survival-oriented [. . .] owner-occupied or reliant on family labour, without formal credit, rural and male' (Mosse 2018: 429). In this area, as in others, higher castes are able to use their caste identity to protect social privilege (Mosse 2018: 430).

In metropolitan India, caste inequalities and the production of caste by relative elites are also apparent. Fuller and Narasimhan (2007) show in their research on the IT sector in Chennai that the great majority of people in skilled jobs are from urban, upper middle class, Brahmin backgrounds. In her work in Bangalore, Carol Upadhya (2007) argues that higher castes are more likely to possess the money, social links, education and other types of cultural capital to acquire relatively good jobs in India's new economy (see also Nisbett 2007). Upadhya also explains the dominance of upper castes in Bangalore's IT sector with reference to the caste bias of engineering colleges and the industry's recruitment process, which place explicit emphasis on cultural markers of distinction. Such findings help to contextualize broader, quantitative studies of socio-economic mobility in India, which show that despite the opportunities offered by the 'new economy', prospects of upward mobility are severely curtailed for SCs and STs relative to their upper caste counterparts (Iversen et al. 2017; and chapter 3).

The marked over-representation of Brahmins in the IT sector does not necessarily imply that recruitment markets and the wider economy are caste discriminatory, however. Harriss's (2003c) examination of trust in Indian business practices points to ways in which people's attitudes to caste are changing in urban India. Drawing on research conducted in 2000 within firms in Ahmedabad, Gujarat and Chennai, Tamil Nadu, Harriss shows that, in small and medium-sized companies, people's assessment of whom to trust is based primarily on their own personal history of conducting transactions, not on their caste, class and other aspects of their background. Harriss points to a general move towards more 'modern' forms of business organization, for example through the restructuring of family business and inter-caste marriage.

Higher caste discrimination prevents low castes from obtaining high-status positions in the modern economy. This, in turn, discourages inter-caste mixing and militates against the emergence of new attitudes. In addition, low castes' efforts to accumulate economic, social and cultural capital tend to reinforce 'the rules of the game', as set by dominant castes (Bourdieu 1984). Moreover, low castes' relative exclusion from lucrative sectors of the modern economy prevents them from acquiring knowledge and the sense of entitlement that comes with inherited caste privilege. Higher castes monopolize the information and embodied assurance that comes with success while low castes commonly come to experience feelings of embarrassment and awkwardness – precisely the type of qualities that higher castes view as markers of a low-caste status.

Marriage is another sphere in which ideas of caste hierarchy remain important in contemporary India. Many commentators predicted that the spread of ideas of individual choice and romantic love through the global media would lead to a shift to Western-style marriages in India, wherein young people would arrange marriages themselves based on their own preferences and independent of caste (see Clark-Deces 2011 for a critical review). Scholarship on middle-class urbanites provides some support for this idea. Donner (2002) has written on the rise of inter-caste love marriages in urban India, and Grover (2011: 89–98) has discussed how some poor youth in Delhi have defied norms of caste endogamy. But most studies suggest that a widespread move away from a system of caste-based arranged marriages has not taken place. Banerjee et al. (2013) estimated that 70 per cent of urban middle-class Indians married broadly 'in-caste'. What appears to have emerged instead in many areas of provincial India, including among low castes in rural areas (e.g. Roulet 1996; Biao 2005), is some version of a 'dowry system' with four key characteristics: senior kin arrange the union; marriages are usually caste endogamous; socio-economic considerations are primary in the choice of partner, and dowry is used as a bargaining tool in families' efforts to secure a groom with valued qualities, such as secure work.

There are certain circumstances in which caste remains explicit within this dowry system. Advertisements for brides and grooms in newspapers and on websites are often organized by *jati* or *varna*. But euphemism is much more common. A vocabulary of codewords has emerged that serves the function of signalling caste without making it explicit. People refer to the importance of finding a match for their son or daughter who is of the right 'community' (*biradiri*) or has the right 'culture'. Without mentioning caste, people often speculate about the negotiations and misunderstandings that may ensue if two people from different *jatis* marry: whether to celebrate particular festivals, when to fast, and which deities to worship, for example (see Jehan 2009). In other circumstances, class differences act as a relatively safe idiom for talking about caste. For example, people refer to the importance of spouses' compatibility at the level of 'lifestyle'.

Caste *panchayats* continue to adjudicate on situations in which people have contravened marriage norms in many parts of north India, especially among the Jats of Haryana and western UP (Chowdhry 2009; Kaur 2010). The caste *panchayats* increasingly enrol younger men as well as elders, and they often spend a significant portion of their time meting out punishments to people perceived to have endangered caste honour. Situations in which a Dalit man elopes with a Jat woman arouse the fiercest reprisals. There are cases of dominant caste *panchayat* members terrorizing, assaulting and damaging property of entire Dalit communities in order to punish the behaviour of a single couple (Katulkar 2013), and public beatings and humiliations of inter-caste couples are commonplace. These relationships generate such a strong response because of the large gap between the hierarchical standing of the two young people and the anxieties they produce about low castes 'stealing' (and polluting) dominant caste women. Kaur's (2010) analysis of Haryanvi Jats' practices highlights the idiosyncratic manner in which norms of caste purity are invoked. Her informants make great play of abiding by caste rules but are also increasingly importing non-Jat brides from Orissa, Kerala and Assam (see also Srinivasan 2017).

In the marriage sphere, caste continues to operate on the unconscious levels of presupposition and taste. To adopt one of Bourdieu's (1984) terms, caste is imbued in the 'habitus': an embodied system of dispositions durably inscribed in people's reflexes, movements and desires. In an illuminating passage, Bourdieu (2001: 216) describes the habitus as something that is 'deposited like a spring at the deepest level of the body' – a conceptualization that is especially useful in thinking about caste. Students in UP told Jeffrey (2010) that they are often unaware of a classmate's caste when they make friends or start a relationship. If the person turns out to be from the same caste, students said that they experience a 'strange feeling of happiness welling up from within' – it is precisely at the level of pre-conscious, embodied feeling that young people experience caste most viscerally. That they refer to the feeling as 'strange' is notable. Bourdieu argues that in certain moments or conjunctures, people can become aware of their inherited habitus and problematize embodied dispositions. Students were conscious that favouring a person – in a sexual relationship or friendship – on the grounds that they are from the same caste is somehow not acceptable in modern India. At the same time, they felt helpless in the face of embodied emotion.

Such embodied feelings are linked to practices of untouchability. There are some seasoned commentators in India who argue that untouchability has entirely vanished from the subcontinent. For example, Gupta (2005) draws on research in villages in Punjab and Haryana to assert that 'untouchability has disappeared from India' (see also Deliege 1999). Shah et al. (2006) conducted a survey of 565 villages across eleven states of India to test the merits of such assertions. They found that in over half the villages they studied, Dalits were still denied entry into non-Dalit houses and prohibited from sharing food with higher castes. In over a quarter of the villages Dalits were forced to stand before upper caste men and refused employment in house construction. Practices of untouchability also mark the activities of the state. Shah et al. (2006) found that Dalits were prevented from entering police stations and ration shops in over a quarter of the villages they surveyed and excluded from electoral booths in 12 per cent. When Dalits, in mass acts of protest, have entered public spaces from which they have traditionally been forbidden for reasons of untouchability – such as temples – it is often the police who intervene to prevent this (Gorringe 2016a).

Intensive ethnographic research in different parts of rural India supports this picture. Gorringe (2009) notes continuing practices of untouchability in Tamil Nadu, as does Dube (1998) in research in UP, and Da Costa (2010) in work in West Bengal. As Harriss (1982a: 298) presciently argued with respect to social change in rural Tamil Nadu: 'Although the restrictions on commensality and interaction between castes have largely broken down, they are still maintained in relation to untouchables'.

The denigration of low castes continues in part because of how it is embedded in the higher caste habitus. For example, higher castes across parts of north India use the phrase 'Chamari-si' to refer to embarrassing and uncouth behaviour (Chamar is the name of a Dalit caste). Similarly, rural women who hitch their saris up when passing through Dalit parts of villages in western UP do so unconsciously, as a matter of habit (see Jeffrey et al. 2008). When this continuing embodied caste prejudice interacts with low-caste self-assurance, violence often results (e.g. Brass 1997). If there is a theme of contemporary caste-based violence, it is of Dalits contravening partially forgotten norms around caste and their trespass on higher caste sensibilities then triggering fierce reprisals. The resulting atrocities, in turn, become a focus of further caste-based tension and conflict, as Dalits and higher castes compete for political assistance, legal support and public sympathy.

Cases of violence against Dalits are increasing, perhaps reflecting a perceived need to police the growth in Dalit self-assertion. Reported crimes against SCs showed a steady increase throughout the 2010s. There was a sharp rise from 33,655 such crimes in 2012 to 40,401 in 2014, with similar figures reported for 2015 and 2016 (NCRB 2017). Many of these were violent crimes, including a sharp increase in reported instances of rape of SC women. It is noteworthy that this rise in crimes against Dalits has occurred at the same time as the surge of Hindu nationalism (see also chapter 6). Since the election of the Modi government in 2014, multiple cases of beatings and humiliation of Dalits for skinning cows or consuming beef have been reported. 'Beef bans', such as that introduced in BJP-ruled Maharashtra in 2015, not only serve to police the cultural practices of Muslims, but also Dalits, many of whom rely on beef as a cheap source of protein and who produce leather as a form of livelihood (G. Nair 2016).

11.6 Conclusions

There is no longer and never really was anything like a 'caste system' in India. The relatively closed economies of the 1950s and 1960s in which caste formed an interrelated social ecosystem of sorts have dissolved. The anthropological search for different 'caste structures' and arrangements – which occurred especially in the 1960s and 1970s and tended to exaggerate or falsely reify 'caste' – now seems arcane. The late 2010s was marked by a situation more complex, fluid and indeterminate, one in which castes are more commonly jostling up against each other – literally and figuratively – than marking hierarchical difference.

At the same time, however, forms of caste hierarchy mark contemporary

India, as evident in spheres as diverse as education, work, politics and marriage. In addition, caste often intersects in important ways with other axes of social difference – especially class and gender – to privilege some and markedly disadvantage many others. Moreover, caste maintains many of its hierarchical elements, with low castes continuing to face structural disadvantages in multiple spheres.

Caste persists in large part because higher castes and to some extent also low castes actively produce it as an idea. For higher castes, and again to some extent for low castes (for example when mobilizing politically), caste acts as a resource. Political parties, individuals standing for village council elections, and student political leaders running for union elections, for example, make coded references to caste in their campaigns. Beyond politics, caste remains as a type of system of dispositions or 'habitus' (Bourdieu 2001) that acts as a well-spring for judgements and actions operating as a form of unconscious or semi-conscious bias. Caste in this optic is not a residual feature of Indian society but something actively created, dynamic and closely intertwined with other forms of difference and inequality.

12

Why Does Gender Inequality Persist in India?

12.1 Introduction

In 2017, the World Economic Forum's *Global Gender Gap Report* drew attention to the persistent nature of gender inequality throughout the world (World Economic Forum 2017). It noted that while global gender disparities in educational attainment, health and survival have been greatly reduced, remarkable disparities in political empowerment remain. Moreover, its index of economic participation and opportunity showed that the trajectory over the last decade has been towards a slight widening of gender inequality. Based on this, the report's projection was that at current rates of change, it will take the world an astonishing 217 years to close the economic disparity between men and women. India performed poorly in the 2017 report – ranked 108th of 144 countries for gender equality. Its ranking was dragged down by its poor performance on economic participation. On this measure, it ranked 138th of 144 countries, one place ahead of the Islamic Republic of Iran.

Just as persistent as gender inequality itself is the view that gender inequality should – and inevitably does – reduce over time as a consequence of modernization. This view – prevalent both amongst the general public and within major development institutions – is based on two assumptions: first, that economic growth should draw more women into the workforce, providing wages and associated increases in personal autonomy; and second, that the proliferation of modern, liberal ideas should lessen the stranglehold of patriarchal ideologies. Yet, in many countries in the developing world, this has not occurred (Jayachandran 2015). In India, gender inequality on some measures has, in fact, widened in recent decades, while on other measures it has improved only at a very slow pace.

Why is this the case? As Naila Kabeer (2016) argues, studies based on aggregate global data struggle to identify clear causal pathways for the reproduction of gender disparities. She suggests there is a need to attend to local- and meso-level studies on the role of specific policy regimes and regional patriarchies. Thus, in this chapter, we draw on studies that identify some of the key social, economic and institutional mechanisms specific to the Indian setting that are implicated in the reproduction of inequalities between men and women.

We acknowledge that gender inequality is, of course, not an issue that is confined to India. Yet, following Walby (1989), we are mindful that the strength and persistence of patriarchy lies largely in its capacity to co-articulate with other systems of social relations and exploitation. The forms that gender relations and patriarchy take in India – and, indeed, across India's regions and communities – tend to be socially and culturally specific.

We understand patriarchy as the loose but nonetheless coherent systems of social relations that sustain male privilege – generally to the detriment of women and other genders. In India, patriarchy has a strong generational component. Kandiyoti (1988) observes that across much of South and East Asia, as well as the Middle East, there is a consistent pattern of patriarchy defined by the normativity of patrilocal households within which elder males have executive decision-making power. Women are expected to accept limited personal autonomy and adopt demure temperaments in exchange for economic protection. As they grow older, women who conform to culturally sanctioned ideas of womanhood may gain advantages in the form of increased authority within the household. The generational dimension of patriarchy in India means that the constraints on autonomy that it imposes on women may similarly be experienced by younger men – though generally not to the same extent as by their female peers.

Throughout India's modern history, gender inequality has been politicized and challenged in various ways. During the late colonial period, many movements and organizations emerged to promote improvements in the conditions of women. They emerged from within all religious communities and across India's diverse regions, and varied in their politics from reformist to revolutionary (Anandhi 1991; Devji 1991). In its Karachi Congress of 1931, the Indian National Congress enshrined the equality of the sexes as part of its statement of Fundamental Rights, without any significant opposition (Som 1994), and later, the Constitution of India would recognize equality of the sexes under the law as a basic right. Yet, superimposed on these abstract rights to equality were systems of 'personal laws', which applied differently to different religious communities. Within these systems, various forms of gender discrimination prevailed, placing women at a distinct disadvantage in matters such as marriage, divorce, inheritance and guardianship (see Gangoli 2007). This legal protection of patriarchal institutions – which the state continues to support – is the context in which many of the issues discussed below should be situated.

We begin this chapter with an examination of family structures. Family remains the crucial institution for understanding gender relations and gender inequality, as it is within the family that gender roles are socialized and performed. Furthermore, the ideas about gender that are normalized within the family spill out into other domains. We then go on to explore the persistence of gender inequality within education and the workforce, highlighting how patriarchal family structures interlock with other exploitative institutions to marginalize women and enhance gender inequality. Finally, we discuss the ways in which gender inequality has been politicized, both historically and in more recent years.

12.2 Gender Relations and the Family

The role of family in the reproduction of gender inequality can be a sensitive topic. As Uberoi (1993) notes, familial relations are often animated by ties of love and affection and are powerful sources of both individual and collective identity. For this reason, critique of the family can be met with resistance. Yet, families are also sites marked by unequal power, especially on the basis of gender and age, and this is reflected in norms surrounding property owner-ship and inheritance, the division of labour, marriage customs and household decision making. While individual household arrangements in India are highly diverse, certain common forms of family structure remain powerfully normative and can have major implications for gender inequality (Uberoi 1993). While the family is not the only site at which gender inequality is reproduced – education, the workplace, the state and popular culture all play their role – it nonetheless remains the primary environment within which gender roles are socialized and patriarchal control is exerted. Moreover, gender relations that are normalized in the household frequently spill over into other domains. For example, one key reason that women's labour is under-paid throughout the world is because, in the context of male bread-winner norms within the family, women's income is positioned as 'supplementary', which is used to justify wages that are sub-subsistence (Chow 2002).

The family is also particularly significant in India because, for powerful historical reasons, its role in perpetuating gender inequality has not been contested or politicized to the extent one might expect. In the context of the nationalist movement, the Indian National Congress felt the need to pre-serve aspects of what it saw as 'traditional' gender relations. Chatterjee (1989) argues that the nationalist movement inherited British binary assumptions of 'Western materialism' versus 'Eastern spiritualism', and that this influenced its stance on gender relations. Many nationalist leaders felt that while India needed to learn from the West in the material domain, it was essential to pre-serve the 'traditional' Indian spiritual domain as a matter of national identity. Women's domestic roles within the family were seen as a vital component of India's spiritual identity, not to be compromised through adopting elements of women's liberation that were taking place in the West. So strong was the force of this discursive construction that even figures like Nehru – a keen advo-cate of gender equality – felt the need to preserve personal laws, within which women were treated unfairly in matters of property, inheritance, divorce and guardianship; to have done otherwise would have been perceived as a top-down imposition on India's cultural and religious traditions (Som 1994).

There are many difficulties in generalizing about gender relations within Indian families. There are substantial regional variations. As a general rule, women in the north have less autonomy than women in the south, in the sense that they are more often confined to the family home after marriage, have less freedom of movement outside the home and have less influence over family decisions (Jejeebhoy and Sathar 2001). In the north, there is generally also a more skewed sex ratio, higher fertility rates and a younger age of marriage, all of which have negative implications for women's autonomy and well-being. Several explanations have been offered for this north–south divide. Dyson and Moore (1983) argue that much of the difference can be explained in terms of kinship systems. In the north, marriages have typically taken place between distant kin with different places of origin and are a means of building alliances between male heads of household. In the south, by contrast, marriages tend to take place between families with closer existing ties. After marriage, it is more difficult for women in the north to retain ongoing relations with their natal home, severely restricting their capabilities. This north–south divide is, however, only a generalization. Even within the same region there are major variations in family structure, based on class, caste, ethnicity and religion, and it is critical in the study of gender inequality to recognize this diversity and consider how gender intersects and comes into tension with other determinants of social difference (Kabeer 1994).

Yet, recognizing diversity should not lead us to lose sight of the fact that there are common features of gendered exploitation. Kalpana Bardhan (1986) outlines how the vast majority of women in India are restricted by patriarchal family institutions, in which female subordination to male family members – whether father, husband or son – is normalized and men exert executive control over land, money and household labour. In most parts of India, families are structured along patrilineal and patrilocal lines – meaning that women are expected to leave their family home and reside with their husband's family at the time of marriage. The personal, social and economic costs of disconnection from their local social milieu puts women at a structural disadvantage relative to men. The passage of property and family name to sons rather than daughters within most communities in India effectively means that women play little role in the continuity of family lines, and girl children are consequently devalued (CSWI 1974). Moreover, although the substance of what constitutes appropriate behaviour varies between caste, religious and ethnic groups, in almost all cases, cultural customs demand more of women, particularly in terms of how they conduct themselves in public. For upwardly mobile families, control over what female family members do or do not do is often central to making claims of a higher class or caste status. For example, withdrawal of female members from paid labour and public life may be an important family strategy of asserting increased respectability (Bardhan 1986). Some women, recognizing that they, too, stand to benefit from the upward mobility of their families, may become willing accomplices in their own subordination by accepting and performing these norms (Kandiyoti 1988).

For the most part, families in India restrict women's sexual agency by arranging their marriage partners and prohibiting or severely limiting male–female relationships – and all sexual relationships – outside of marriage. Having a daughter married at an early age can be a way of symbolically demonstrating her modesty, chastity and the value the family places on gender segregation (Desai and Andrist 2010). In communities in which Brahmanical Hinduism is or has been influential, cultural customs surrounding caste purity also serve to restrict opportunities for women. Caste purity is maintained through caste endogamous marriage practices, which require control over female sexuality to be maintained, and women from higher caste backgrounds are often subject to the tightest restrictions on their sexuality, marriage choices, mobility and behaviour (Chakravarti 1993). More broadly, the 'sexual double standard' observed throughout the world is especially prominent in India. In an extensive study of youth sexualities in Mumbai – often regarded as a bastion of sexual liberalism within India – Abraham (2001) finds that while relatively liberal attitudes are common regarding young men exploring their sexuality, female sexual activity is regarded as impure, shameful and even dangerous. After the first instance of menstruation, families and the wider community often become involved in curtailing girls' mobility and restricting their interactions with young men. Although recent cultural productions – including 2018 films *Veere di Wedding* and *Lust Stories* – were notable for challenging these cultural codes through their depictions of female sexual agency, there was much disparaging public commentary – largely from men – on the 'shameful' nature of these depictions (Tilak 2018).

The institution of dowries, whereby a bride's family makes substantial payments to that of her groom, is a major contributor to the poor position of women within Indian society. Srinivas (1984) suggests that the dowry system has its origins in the hypergamous marriage practices that were common in north India prior to the colonial period. Hypergamy involves the marriage of women to men of superior status within their own *jati*. This improved the status of the bride's family and involved payments to the family of the groom, whether in gifts or cash. These payments, however, tended to be relatively modest. Srinivas argues it was British colonialism, which introduced tremendous demand for the salaried, British-educated sons of the Indian elite, that saw dowries inflate to the astronomical levels that have since become the norm throughout much of India. Despite being technically illegal since the passage of the Dowry Prohibition Act (1961), the size of dowries continued to inflate throughout the twentieth century, reaching more than half the size of total family assets by the early 1990s (Rao 1993).

Recent years have seen not only an increase in the size of dowries, but the spread of the institution into new communities (Clark-Deces 2018). The payment of dowries is no longer confined to upper-caste Hindus in north India, as was historically the case, but has also become standard practice in communities within which bride price had been the norm, including south India (Srinivasan 2005) and amongst Muslims (Waheed 2009). The reasons for this spread are multiple, but there are some common trends. It appears that often the practice is first taken up by elite families in order to attract wealthier husbands and ensure the physical security of daughters, with lower castes and classes soon following their lead in competition for status (Srinivasan 2005). Whatever the reasons, the result is almost universally the positioning of women and girls as burdens and the impoverishment of poorer households with one or more daughters. Indeed, as women's earning power relative to that of men has declined in recent decades, along with the importance of fertility to the reproduction of families, dowry has become one of the primary measures of a woman's value (Stone and James 1995). Consequently, when dowry payments are not as expected, women are left highly vulnerable. Upwards of 10,000 women a year either commit suicide or are murdered as a result of inter-familial disputes over dowries (Babu and Babu 2011), with many more being subject to torture and abuse in perverse forms of bargaining between marital and natal families (Bloch and Rao 2002).

When matters turn awry within marriages, options for divorce are limited. Census data shows that although there have been decade-on-decade increases in the proportion of individuals recorded as separated or divorced, it still remains under 1 per cent. This partly reflects the social stigma attached to divorce, but also constraints imposed by the legal system. Divorce is covered under personal law in India, which varies according to the religious community to which one belongs. Most systems of personal law require either mutual consent or substantive fault to allow divorce, while family courts generally see their role as facilitating reconciliation within marriages, rather than the termination of marriages marked by abuse, dissatisfaction or irreconcilable differences. It is noteworthy, however, that there are substantial regional differences in divorce rates – they are much higher in the north-east and south than in the north, and this has been interpreted as a by-product of limited female agency in north India (Dommaraju 2016).

The expectation that women are responsible for the success of their marriages and the concomitant social stigma attached to divorce mean that, in many cases, women (and men) endure unhappy marriages. Escaping abusive family situations can be highly challenging when faced with the fear of social stigma and the disappointment of parents.

The normativity of these practices – and the fact that they occur in a patriarchal context – mean that if a woman exercises agency by choosing her own marriage partner (referred to in India as a 'love marriage'), the results can be even worse. As Grover's (2011) ethnographic research shows, because arranged marriages are the social ideal in most communities in India, contravention of this ideal results in reduced physical security. Women in arranged marriages are better able to retreat to the natal home if faced with mistreatment from their husbands or husbands' family. The threat of withdrawal to the natal home can be an effective bargaining strategy for women. In 'love marriages', this option is often not available, as parents are less likely to provide support to daughters who have transgressed marriage conventions.

The vulnerable position of women within the family is exacerbated by their lack of control over productive assets. Most crucial in this respect is ownership and inheritance of land. As both the means of subsistence and the primary productive asset in India's agrarian economy, ownership of land is a central determinant of well-being and autonomy (Agarwal 1994; Patel 2007). Yet the India Human Development Survey of 2005 found that land is inherited by women in less than 2 per cent of cases. Progressive legislation has sought to address the disparity in ownership. The Hindu Succession Act, for example, sought to provide equal rights to property for Hindu, Sikh, Buddhist and Jain women. The Act was introduced in 1956 and then amended in 2005 so as to further improve women's claims to the inheritance of property. Similarly, Muslim personal law contains provisions to protect women's rights to inheritance – though women are invariably entitled to less than similarly positioned men. Despite these provisions, in practice, family heads tend to circumvent these laws, chiefly by gifting land to sons, and then compensating daughters in the form of higher dowries or greater family expenditure on their education (Roy, Sanchari 2015). Families typically do not recognize women's claims to land rights as legitimate, particularly when women are positioned as guardians of family honour and making such a claim might be seen as damaging to a family's reputation (Patel 2007). The manner in which these issues play out varies between castes and regions, though highly unequal control over assets is fairly common throughout the country (Jejeebhoy and Sathar 2001). For high-caste women in the north of the country, the institution of *purdah*, which strictly limits women's activities outside of the domestic sphere as a matter of family honour, reinforces men's control over land and other productive assets (Sharma 1980). For women from more marginalized communities, such as the Santal Adivasis studied by Rao (2018), claims to land rights are often subsumed within the broader struggles of their community for recognition. Women from such communities who make claims to land ownership may be reprimanded by male activists for undermining their community's cause.

None of the above should suggest that family structures – or the gender roles that are socialized through them – are static. Women (and many men) contest them in multiple ways. The increase in practices such as 'love marriages' (Allendorf and Pandian 2016), online dating (Chakraborty 2012), same-sex relationships (Menon 2009), and the firm assertion by some poor women of their property rights (Rao 2018) all destabilize assumptions of 'normal' family structures in ways that may open spaces for greater autonomy for women. Yet, challenging gender relations at the level of the family is no straightforward task, particularly when the 'family system' and culturally constructed ideas of 'Indian womanhood' are often presented by nationalists as lynchpins of 'Indian culture'. Consequently, until relatively recently, even Indian feminists have refrained from critiquing these social and cultural institutions directly for fear of losing legitimacy (Kapur 2012).

The Family and Gendered Violence

The patriarchal norms and relations described above are upheld through economic dependency and reinforced socially and by way of religious and cultural ideologies. When they are transgressed, they are often reasserted through violence. Since at least the 1970s, feminists around the world have drawn attention to the centrality of violence against women – and the threat of such violence – to the reproduction of patriarchy (see Caputi 1989; Morgan 1989). Violence against women within the family home can diminish their capacity for agency, particularly when it is backed by societal tendencies towards disbelief and blaming of victims. The non-responsiveness of neighbours and families to persistent abuse can lead victims to perceive themselves as worthless or even deserving of abuse (Dworkin 1997).

In India, too, evidence suggests that family violence contributes to the reproduction of patriarchal dominance and gender inequality. Although there is some evidence to suggest that women who have control over immovable assets have increased security against domestic violence (Agarwal and Panda 2007), in other respects, as women's status improves, their risk of incurring violence from male spouses increases. As women become more educated and earn more as a proportion of their spouse's earnings, they are likely to experience more regular and more severe violence from male family members – and this is at least partly attributable to the perceived threat they pose to the norms of male dominance and bread-winner status (Srinivasan and Bedi 2007; Weitzman 2014). This violence, in turn, puts an additional brake on women's capacity to earn more, reinforcing their second-class status (Weitzman 2014). There is also some evidence that male violence is used to police liberal values and dispositions amongst women (Simister and Mehta 2010), for example, when fathers physically abuse daughters for exercising sexual agency (Still 2011). Perhaps of greatest concern, Indian women's options for support when they are victims of family violence are extremely limited. A study by Ragavan et al. (2015), involving interviews of 108 men and women in both rural and urban areas in Rajasthan, found that *all* respondents believed that the most appropriate response for women to violence from their husband was to endure it, provided that the violence was infrequent or was in some way 'deserved'.

There was also a strong belief that matters should be settled within the family, with appeal to the police, NGOs or divorce being seen as highly inappropriate responses. The problem of family violence is made significantly worse when there are prevailing ideologies that position male violence as a legitimate assertion of authority within the domestic sphere (Ahmed-Ghosh 2004; Dalal et al. 2012).

There are numerous challenges associated with finding reliable data on the incidence of violence against women in India. Official crime statistics only reflect the incidents of violence against women that are reported – which in India is a very low number. Moreover, India remains one of a handful of countries globally in which marital rape is not recognized as a crime, further militating against the collection of data on the scope of the problem. Surveys and qualitative studies face methodological challenges, given the sensitivity of the topic and the diversity of understandings of what constitutes 'violence'. The National Family Health Survey (NFHS) of 2015–16 estimated that 28.8 per cent of women who had ever been married had experienced domestic violence, yet this figure seems low, given that the estimate in the 2005–06 survey was 37.2 per cent. Twenty-four per cent of women surveyed reported having experienced domestic violence within the previous twelve months. A quarter of domestic violence victims reported that they had sustained serious injuries and less than 14 per cent had sought help (though see Piedalue 2015, for a critique of NFHS survey methods).

Although Indian women are most likely to experience violence in the home, public acts of violence are also highly significant, not only as harmful in themselves, but also in curtailing women's mobility. The fear of rape, violence, sexual assault and verbal harassment (often known colloquially in India as 'eve-teasing') causes women to navigate public spaces in India with far greater caution than men. For example, women may be reluctant to use public spaces late at night, or may tend to only 'pass through' public space on their way to shops or college rather than to spend extended time there, reflecting a view that only men may legitimately occupy public space (see Paul 2011). Research by Phadke et al. (2011) in Mumbai shows that women seeking enjoyment in public space are regarded with suspicion in popular discourse and the spaces that do exist in which women can engage in leisure activity are often highly sanitized or accessible only to upper- and middle-class women.

Bhattacharyya's (2015) research suggests that such patterns reflect patriarchal values that have their origins in the family. The view that women belong within the 'private' domain of the home, while the 'public' domain of the streets is for men is reinforced and policed through public harassment and violence (or the threat thereof). In interviews with 300 women across north and east India, Bhattacharyya found that not only did the vast majority of women experience some form of harassment when in public – for example, on public transport – but these acts of harassment were culturally reinforced in various ways. There is a deeply ingrained view in India that only 'bad women' are subject to harassment and that women's 'immodest' attire is a cause of sexual assault. Public acts of sexual violence and harassment against women tend to be under-reported, as women fear the stigma associated with being identified as a victim of such crimes – and may feel a need to protect perceptions of their own 'purity' in the context of patriarchal marriage customs, which prize female virginity. When women do report these crimes, they are often met with incredulity from male police officers, who may question their 'decency' (Bhattacharyya 2015).

The Family and Unequal Sex Ratios

Aspects of family structure, combined with the depreciation of women's work within the economy, lead to a devaluing of women in Indian society. One of the outcomes of this is a persistently unequal sex ratio. The low ratio of women and girls relative to men and boys in India has been evident since the earliest censuses were undertaken in India, during the colonial period. After independence, this ratio continued to decline each decade, bottoming in 1991 at 927 females for every 1,000 males. The figure rose slightly to 933 in 2001 and 940 in 2011. The declining sex ratio throughout much of the middle twentieth century has been attributed to families' relative neglect of women and girls' nutrition and health (Miller 1981), and this remains a major issue. Many studies show that parents discriminate against girl children in the allocation of food (Rajan and Morgan 2018) and in critical healthcare interventions, such as vaccinations (Borooah 2004). There is some evidence that such discrimination begins immediately after birth, with boys receiving breast milk sooner and more frequently than girls, resulting in larger numbers of girl children who are underweight, malnourished and stunted (Pandey 2009). The gender gap in infant mortality rates is higher in the north Indian states of Bihar and Uttar Pradesh than elsewhere in the country, most likely reflecting broader social conditions there that are less favourable to women (Chaudhuri 2015; Dyson and Moore 1983). Discrimination against women in matters of health continues throughout the lifespan, particularly under conditions of poverty. In times of agrarian distress, women work harder and eat less, and consequently gender disparities in health outcomes tend to widen (Vepa 2009).

It is worth noting, however, that in some key respects, women's health outcomes have improved in recent decades. For example, the maternal mortality ratio (deaths per 100,000) has declined dramatically since the beginning of the millennium – from 301 in 2001–03 to 167 in 2011–13 (MSPI 2016). This figure was below the global average for 2015, of 216 (World Bank 2016). General improvements in women's health and nutrition may explain why there has been an improvement in the sex ratio since the 1991 Census, though substantial gender inequalities in access to healthcare and adequate nutrition remain.

In more recent decades, female feticide has played a greater role in India's skewed sex ratio. From the 1980s onwards, the growing availability of ultrasound and other technologies to determine the sex of an unborn child led to a surge in sex-selective terminations, beginning in larger cities and subsequently spreading to other parts of the country. Thus, although the overall sex ratio has improved, a study by Jha et al. (2011) found continuous decreases in the sex ratio of children aged 0–6 between 1991 and 2011, with an especially marked decline in the sex ratio for second-born children when the first-born child had been a girl. Their findings led them to estimate that between 2000 and 2010, between 3 and 6 million sex-selective terminations were performed – up from between 0 and 2 million in the 1980s. This was the case notwithstanding the passing in 1994 of a Pre-Conception and Pre-Natal Diagnostic Techniques Act, which bans the use of ultrasounds and similar technologies to inform and facilitate sex-selective terminations. The reasons for this trend are undoubtedly complex, but clearly the rising costs of having a girl child are a major contributor towards the continuation of son preference in many families. These costs include an increase in dowry prices, increased expectations that women should receive higher levels of education, and the extension of the period of time that women typically spend at home before marriage (John 2014).

While some demographers had once hoped that the decline in the proportion of women in India may result in their being valued more and in a reduction in dowry prices – perhaps even the erosion of dowry payment as an institution – this does not appear to have borne out. Jeffery (2014) argues that when families are caught in status aspirations, a shortage of women is only likely to result in the continued payment of dowries for more high-status men, while men of lower status struggle to find marriage partners. One consequence of this is that in relatively wealthy regions of India, families of lower status are seeking to marry their sons to women from poorer regions of India, or from states such as Kerala, where brides are in surplus. While there is some evidence that this practice can have progressive effects, including a lessening of the practice of caste endogamy, the vast distances separating brides from their natal families makes them vulnerable to exploitation and abuse (Mishra 2013). Srinivasan's (2017) recent research on women from Kerala migrating to Tamil Nadu for marriage provides an apt illustration of how a patriarchal and caste discriminatory context foreshortens the possibility that such marriages will result in improvements in women's well-being or autonomy. The brides whom Srinivasan interviewed often came from families in Kerala with multiple daughters who could not afford the cost of dowries. While marriage to lower status men in Tamil Nadu often provided a measure of economic security that may not have been available in Kerala, there were also significant costs. Women were often victims of deceit – with men misrepresenting their earning capacity or lying about previous marriages – and would be subject to disrespect and gossip about their caste status in their new homes. Clearly, the social dynamics unleashed by a shortage of women in India has not straight-forwardly led to women being more highly valued in society.

12.3 Gender Inequality in Education and the Workplace

Participation in education and the workforce are often imagined as means by which women can work to overcome some of the disadvantages imposed upon them by patriarchal structures in the family. Qualitative research from India does indicate that under certain conditions, education can be a site at which limiting conceptions of women's potential are challenged (Klenk 2010), alternative futures are rendered possible (Patel 2017) and patriarchal mindsets contested (Unterhalter and Dutt 2001). This is particularly the case when education has an explicit focus on gender empowerment. Yet, across Asia, quantitative studies have shown that there is no straightforward, positive correlation between women's access to education and measures of social, economic and political empowerment (Jayaweera 1997). The empowering potential of education is too often constrained by the influence of the family, the labour market and other social dynamics.

In terms of access, gender inequalities in education appear to be lessening in India. Enrolments from primary education through to undergraduate university studies are approaching gender parity. Female literacy rates have improved since independence and quite strongly so since 1991, standing at 65.5 per cent as of the 2011 census. Yet, a gap of more than 16 percentage points in literacy rates for men and women remained in 2011, suggesting that although Indian women are enrolled in education in record numbers, there remain serious questions about the quality of their education, relative to that received by men. Part of the problem is that the efforts of governments, NGOs, multilateral development institutions and families to increase female enrolments have not been accompanied by a commitment to challenging women's subordinate position within Indian society. As Kamat (2014) observes, much of the push to increase female participation in education has been informed by a concern for other objectives – such as reducing the fertility rate or leveraging women as agents for promoting rural development – sidelining the question of empowerment. In the absence of more genuine efforts at empowerment, education falls short of its emancipatory potential for many Indian women and girls, who suffer from significant disadvantages and discrimination in educational settings, are consigned to inferior quality schools and colleges, and are more restricted than their male counterparts in what they can do with their education.

Even if crude enrolment rates are improving, studies suggest very large numbers of girls in India are missing out on quality education and the prospects of upward mobility that it provides. A study by Azam and Kingdon (2013) revealed continuing pro-male bias in household spending on education and a reluctance for families to provide financial support for girls into higher secondary school. Moreover, a common pattern was identified of families sending boys to private schools, while sending girls to government schools, reflecting a view that girls' education is not a worthwhile investment (see also Woodhead et al. 2013). These tendencies were significantly more pronounced in rural areas than in urban areas. Yet, as Kamat (2014) notes, this trend has also been prominent amongst upwardly mobile sections of the lower middle classes, particularly since liberalization. The development of education as an 'aspirational resource' has led to a surge in overall household spending on education and, as a consequence, parents are making more calculated decisions regarding the likely returns on investment on sons' versus daughters' education. When there is a rise in costs associated with education, girls are generally the first to be withdrawn (Kamat 2014: 283). At the college level, the high concentration of female students in the humanities and social sciences and male students in more costly – and later more remunerative – degrees such as engineering and medicine, also reflects this bias against investment in girls' education.

For poorer households, there are strong economic incentives for families to terminate girls' education prematurely – particularly when families are reliant on girls' domestic labour as part of their livelihood strategies. In an illuminating ethnographic study of predominantly ST families in rural Chhattisgarh, Froerer (2012) found that many girls would bargain with their parents to continue their education. Girls themselves valued education as crucial to escaping a life of domestic and agricultural labour and, while parents would allow daughters to continue studying, they did so on the condition that they perform additional household chores. This, in turn, tended to undermine girls' capacity to study at home and thereby achieve at school. Parents in Froerer's study were reluctant to allow daughters to continue education beyond Class 5, seeing secondary education as undermining girls' capacity to develop domestic skills and thereby weakening their marriage prospects. This provides powerful evidence of how gendered roles that are normalized within the family serve to undermine girls' and women's prospects in other domains. It is worth noting, however, that there are signs that these barriers can be overcome through decisive government action. In Bihar – a state once marked with some of India's largest gender gaps in education – a programme was launched in 2006 in which girls were given bicycles in exchange for enrolling into Class 9. This significantly reduced some of the time costs involved in girls attending school, particularly for students in rural areas in which schools are often far from home. A recent study has shown that the program has had a profound impact, reducing the gender gap in secondary school enrolments by as much as 40 per cent (Muralidharan and Prakash 2017).

Even when women have access to education, they may still be restricted in terms of what they can do with it. For many girls and young women in India, education is not primarily a resource to support their individual aspirations: rather, it is entangled in the class and status trajectories of their entire families. This is closely linked to the norms of Brahminical patriarchy, within which both female education and the withdrawal of women from non-domestic labour are signs of upper-caste status. Regrettably, while these norms were historically confined to upper castes, lower castes have increasingly emulated them in their quest for status. In an ethnographic study, Still (2011) shows that for upwardly mobile rural Dalit families, girls are educated as part of family strategies to gain status by 'marrying up' into middle class, urban Dalit families. This is seen as a crucial component of bringing respectability to the family and to escape associations with 'degrading' agricultural labour. Yet, though girls' education is seen to have strategic value for the family, it is also seen to be risky: a source of liberal ideas, expectations of autonomy, and a site at which girls may form relationships of their own choosing. The families Still spoke to had concerns that education could 'spoil' young women, ruining families' plans for their marriage, deterring potential husbands and soiling the family's reputation. Amongst the older generation – both male and female – education was associated with the excessive freedom and degenerate tendencies of modern youth. Families thus have allowed girls to attend school and college, but placed restrictions on how they participate in education and what they are able to do with it. Given that the families in Still's study had been involved in decades-long struggles for respect and recognition, their efforts to control women to assert family honour were all the more strident (see also Berreman 1993). This is by no means an experience of Dalit women alone. The fear of losing respectability and status has long been recognized as a source of similar dynamics that adversely affect women's participation in education among higher caste families (e.g. Bardhan 1986). What makes Still's findings a matter of considerable concern is that they represent the generalization of these tendencies such that they are now also evident – in some cases in intensified form – among lower caste families, in which gender relations were historically more equal.

When it comes to paid employment, the situation for women is in many ways even worse. While many may have expected women's control over their lives to have increased as more women have gained access to paid work, recent data suggests an alarming trend: women's labour force participation in India is declining. National Sample Survey data shows that in the period between 2004–05 and 2011–12, there was an increase in the percentage of women principally engaged in domestic duties in almost all age categories and in both rural and urban areas – the exceptions being women under the age of 15, and urban women aged 15–29 (NSS 2014b). Working age women's total workforce participation rates were stagnant over this period at 33.1 per cent – 37.8 per cent in rural areas and 22.2 per cent in urban areas (NSS 2013). Perhaps most surprising, there was a sharp decline in the workforce participation rate of women with high school qualifications or higher (Klasen and Pieters 2015). Klasen and Pieters (2015) suggest that taken collectively, these figures were highly unexpected, given the high rate of economic growth during the same period, substantial improvements in female educational enrolments, small improvements in women's wages and the declining birth rate. They suggest the stagnation and decline of female workforce participation can be attributed to a combination of a rise in male incomes and education, along with stigma associated with educated women entering low-skilled sectors resulting in more educated women refraining from entering the workforce. The withdrawal of women from the workforce in families experiencing upward mobility has a long pedigree in India (Chowdhury 1994) and is now especially evident across rural India (Mehrotra and Parida 2017). Another explanation offered for the decline in women's labour force participation is the profile of India's recent economic growth, which has not been labour-intensive and which has shown demand for skill sets that women generally do not possess (Lahoti and Swaminathan 2016).

Women who do enter the workforce in India are largely concentrated in informal production – particularly household-based – and their work is likely to be of low status, seasonal and with fewer hours. These factors place women at a significant disadvantage relative to men in building on their employment to overcome poverty and achieve greater autonomy (Banerjee 1985). Matters are made worse by a persistent and substantial gender pay gap. A report by Varkkey and Korde (2013) showed that formal sector wages in 2013 were 24.8 per cent lower for women than for men across India. This did represent a major improvement on figures from 2006, when the gap was as high as 44.8 per cent, but the 2013 figures remained high by global standards. There were, however, large variations between states – with just an 8 per cent gap in Uttarakhand and an alarming 63 per cent gap in Bihar. NSS (2014a) data on wages – including those in the formal and informal sectors – show the pay gap tends to decrease with educational qualifications. Gaps in wages exist between men and women at all levels of educational qualification, but are less for urban women with graduate-level qualifications. Illiterate, rural women earn less than half the wages of their male counterparts. NSS data showed an overall decrease in the wage gap of almost 10 per cent since a decade earlier, which could mostly be attributed to the impact of the National Rural Employment Guarantee Scheme. This has provided many rural women with access to a measure of secure employment (see chapter 4).

Understanding why inequalities in wages persist requires attention to the conditions in which women work and how women's work is situated within broader systems of social relations. Although the interests of capitalism and patriarchy at times diverge, in practice, historically ways have been found for reaching compromises that are to the mutual benefit of both (see Walby 1989). Rather than challenging traditional gender roles, women's involvement within the Indian economy tends rather to reconfigure gender relations in ways that serve to preserve both the power of capital over the workforce and the power of men over households. Recent studies re-affirm that decisions regarding whether and how women enter paid work are framed by their position within the domestic sphere. When women make decisions about taking on paid work, their primary consideration is often whether this work can fit in alongside a host of domestic and reproductive obligations (Carswell 2016). The fact that women take their domestic duties as primary not only ensures that their reproductive labour is always available in the household, but is also used by employers to justify providing women-only casual, temporary employment (see Banerjee 1985).

Within the precarious sectors of the economy within which women's work is clustered, employers tend to rely on patriarchal social conventions to undermine women's earning power. Women may be granted lower wages, based on the assumption that, given male bread-winner norms, women are not 'primary earners'. Agarwala's (2014) research on informally employed bidi (hand-rolled cigarette) workers illustrates this point well. Since the 1960s, when unions won several rights for formally employed bidi workers, the industry has increasingly relied on contracting work out to home-based workers, to whom regulations do not apply and who are overwhelmingly female. The work is highly intensive, often relying on the participation of multiple family members, and is precarious, as contractors can always refuse to pay for produce, claiming that it is 'poor quality'. Women bidi workers also frequently face sexual harassment from contractors. They are highly under-paid, which contractors justify through reference to patriarchal norms: they claim that because the work is home-based, it can only be considered 'part-time' work, which women undertake in between their domestic duties. These workers have also been historically neglected by (male-dominated) unions, the leaders of which have assumed that female workers lack 'fighting spirit'. Women endure such conditions partly because their husbands will not allow them to undertake other kinds of work outside the home and partly because they have internalized the conception that it is women's responsibility to remain within the home to raise children. For working class women, the dual exploitation by employers and male family members restricts any possibility that work could lead to a lessening of gender inequalities.

Within the so-called 'knowledge economy' – consisting chiefly, in India, of the information technology (IT) and business process outsourcing (BPO) industries – one might expect that women would gain substantial autonomy through increased earning capacity. Yet, qualitative and ethnographic research on women workers in these sectors suggests that both the family and the workplace continue to exert pressures that prevent many women from receiving substantially greater autonomy. This is chiefly because, within the family, women are generally not socialized to think of their engagement with work as part of a narrative of personal progress – it is rather, positioned as how they can serve their families (Belliappa 2013). The fact that women are positioned as being 'allowed' or 'permitted' to continue to work after marriage by their husband's family tends to reinforce the impression that, rather than being a right, participation in work is a privilege for women that comes with a series of attached obligations. Family constraints are a persistent theme in the literature on middle-class women's economic participation. Radhakrishnan (2011), for example, in a study of women in the IT sector, shows that not only do women continue to shoulder the burden of domestic labour even when working full-time, but they also experience limitations in their capacity to develop career ambitions, for fear of unsettling their husbands. These women were aware that they had been positioned as emblematic of India's fast-globalizing society, and were cautious of being perceived as part of an excessively rapid cultural change that would erode India's cultural identity. They carefully balanced modernity and 'Indian tradition' by maintaining their domestic responsibilities while working, thereby preserving an idealized imagine of 'Indian womanhood'. Vijayakumar's (2013) research on young, unmarried women in BPOs had similar findings. Her informants, who had often experienced a measure of upward mobility through their employment, came to develop a set of career aspirations. Yet, they were mindful that these aspirations – in contrast to those of their male colleagues – needed to be highly flexible, and that they would need to make adjustments – in some cases major adjustments – in order to meet the expectations of their future husbands' families.

   Similar issues are encountered by women who run their own businesses. Female entrepreneurs are overwhelmingly clustered in the informal sector and receive less remuneration than men. Poor women involved in small-scale entrepreneurial activity – particularly those from higher castes, and Muslims – face restrictions on their mobility and social connections that limit their exposure to profitable business opportunities (Field et al. 2010). Studies on the relatively small number of women who have risen to positions of leadership within the corporate sector have found numerous demands that make their work more difficult than that of their male counterparts. There are ongoing struggles to have their achievements recognized by male colleagues, continuing expectations that they remain involved in domestic work, and challenges in finding appropriate forms of care for children and elderly family members (Mani 2013). At both the 'top end' and 'bottom end' of the Indian economy, the family and other institutions continue to exert constraints on women's mobility and earning power.

12.4 Politicizing Gender Inequality

The problem of gender inequality has not passed by unnoticed in India. Women's movements and governments alike have attempted to politicize the issue and drive both social and legislative change. The early 1970s was an important period for mainstream recognition of gender inequality as a significant policy concern. In 1971, the Ministry of Education and Social Welfare resolved to form a 'Committee on the Status of Women in India'. The Committee was charged with assessing the impact of India's legislative framework on women and identifying problems and constraints experienced by women in Indian society and in the workplace. In 1974, the Committee released its *Towards Equality* report, which suggested that Indian women had been side-lined in efforts to achieve the goal of equality for all citizens outlined in the Constitution. The report explicitly argued that oppressive social and cultural institutions, including the family, had stymied efforts to improve the position of women. It concluded that there was an urgent need not only to improve women's wages and access to education and the workforce, but also to facilitate a widespread shift in societal attitudes towards women. The report provided women's organizations with a powerful focal point for their lobbying efforts and forced the issue of gender inequality onto the agenda of policy makers.

Since the 1980s, growing awareness of gender inequality has led to the introduction of legal and governance mechanisms aimed at improving women's position. Alongside this have been ongoing pushes to abolish different personal laws and establish a uniform civil code that would finally remove legal bases for gender discrimination. Yet, given that the struggle for a uniform civil code has been co-opted by the Hindu Right, there are concerns that if the push to establish such a code were successful, it is unlikely to operate in a manner that is unbiased, secular or genuinely concerned with mitigating gender inequalities (see Choudhury 2008). This has been evident, for example, in the Modi government's efforts to ban the Muslim practice of 'Triple Talaq' – a form of instant divorce that had led to the abandonment and impoverishment of many Muslim women – which some activists argued showed a disproportionate emphasis on regressive features of Muslim personal law and lacked a meaningful commitment to gender justice (The Wire 2019). Such disputes have contributed towards a decades-long stalling of progress on personal law reform. Notwithstanding this, there has been progress in other aspects of legislation, including the passage of the Protection of Women from Domestic Violence Act (2005), which defined domestic violence for purposes of Indian law for the first time and offered victims of domestic violence various avenues for protection and compensation. Other promising developments in the legislative sphere are efforts to bring greater consideration of the position of women into state-led development efforts. Most recently, the draft National Policy for Women (2016) has placed special emphasis on improving women's nutritional security and recommends all ministries collect gender disaggregated data to show whether women are receiving the benefits of policy interventions.

While legislative change is welcome, legislation requires committed actors to become effective. Moreover, meaningful change requires sustained action across multiple spheres to challenge the foundations of gender inequality. Yet, at first glance, the early 2020s do not appear an ideal time for feminist organizing in India. In particular, the rise of *Hindutva* politics has in some ways discouraged feminist expression. This was evident, for example, in the aftermath of the Supreme Court's 2018 ruling that the Sabarimala Temple in Kerala be forced to allow entry to women of all ages. Until 2018, women of menstruating age were banned from entering on the grounds of 'impurity', which the Supreme Court found to be in violation of both the principles of equality and the right of all citizens to free religious practice, enshrined in the Constitution. Yet, the ruling triggered a fierce response from the RSS and other Hindu nationalist organizations. Women who attempted to enter the temple were prevented from doing so by protestors, in some cases violently (BBC 2018).

Hindu nationalists have also promoted the idea that aggressive, at times militant forms of masculinity are required to defend India against its Islamic neighbours and the corrupting influences of 'Westernization' – including feminism. This was strikingly apparent in the 2014 election campaign, when the BJP party machine projected its prime ministerial candidate Narendra Modi as a strongman with a '56-inch chest'. Modi's supposedly virile characteristics – including his willingness to take firm and decisive action against both external and internal 'enemies' of India – were juxtaposed to the quieter leadership of Manmohan Singh, which was denigrated as effeminate (Srivastava 2015). Banerjee (2006) argues that neoliberal globalization has been a key underlying driver of this resurgence of aggressive, politicized masculinity. The stark rise in economic inequality along with the phenomenon of educated unemployment have left many young men feeling powerless, deprived of independence and breadwinner status. This has made them susceptible to political mobilization that encourages a reclaiming of power through the performance of hyper-masculinity and the assertion of control over female bodies through imposing virtues of female chastity. Although many women have participated in *Hindutva* politics, they have done so in ways that conform with the image of the chaste, demure Indian woman and the 'harmonious Hindu family' (Banerjee 2006: 63). Their participation is enlisted to further the political interests of their parties rather than the interests of women and is often circumscribed within the traditional gender roles that their parties seek to defend – cooking meals at political events, for example (Rai 2012).

The gendered composition of India's state and federal legislatures are also not encouraging. The unequal representation of men and women in electoral politics not only reflects gender inequalities in wider society, but also militates against the formation of policies to combat such inequalities. As Phillips' (1995) work suggests, due to their position in society, women have substantively different experiences to men, such that their presence in parliament is not only valuable in disposing them towards acting in the interests of other women, but also in introducing fresh perspectives that enrich democracy itself. Indeed, there is some evidence from India to suggest that even in reactionary political parties, female politicians introduce new political styles that not only provide a voice for women's issues, but also offer entry points to the political process for groups that historically had been excluded (Bedi 2016). It is therefore a matter of deep concern that in India's Lok Sabha, only 14.4 per cent of elected representatives were female after the 2019 election. Within India's state legislatures, matters are even worse: only 8.8 per cent of seats were occupied by women in 2017. The state legislatures of Mizoram and Nagaland had not a single female representative during this time. Women are certainly voting in greater numbers in India – in the 2014 elections the gender gap in voter turnout was less than 2 per cent – but the absence of female members of parliament limits the power of their voice. This speaks to patriarchal cultures within political parties, which are reluctant to nominate female candidates (Rai and Spary 2019).

In local government, women's representation is considerably better. This is due almost entirely to the passage of the 73rd and 74th Amendments to the Constitution in 1992. These Amendments augured the devolution of government in India, but also mandated both caste and gender-based quotas in local government. In all representative bodies of local governance, it became mandatory that at least one-third of seats be reserved for women and this was increased to half of seats in 2009. Having more women in local government has improved women's access to the benefits of development schemes, social services, and natural resources, and also to a certain extent challenged women's subordinate social position: for example, women representatives note being awarded greater respect within their community and are able to renegotiate the division of labour within their families (Jayal 2006). Nonetheless, there are constraints: women's capacity to make the most of their position in local government is limited by their relative lack of access to resources and education and the greater demands on their labour in the home (Kalaramadam 2018; Jayal 2006). In some settings, women *panchayat* members – particularly those from lower castes – are expected only to perform domestic duties for the council (Anandhi 2017). Jakimow (2017) notes that women representatives in local government face numerous challenges, including gaining the confidence necessary to perform the role of a representative and making demands on people in positions of power. She shows that although efforts at building the capacity of women representatives exist, they have often attempted to boost skills that are assumed to be useful for a representative, rather than giving women the scope to become the kind of representative that they wish to be.

Yet, literature on women's political inclusion in India has suggested it may be necessary to attend to a broader range of factors than the number of female elected representatives. This has been apparent in feminist debates surrounding electoral quotas for women, which have been ongoing since the 1990s. Several feminist authors have noted that elected officials draw upon multiple identities and the idea that female representatives will draw primarily on their identity as women and legislate according to the interests of women cannot be taken for granted (see Menon 2000; Kudva and Misra 2008). Indeed, when the established polity is chiefly structured around other identities – notably caste, religion and, to a lesser extent, class – female representatives are primed to act on behalf of these identities, rather than their gender (Rai 2012).

Similarly, the view that gender inequality can be overcome through NGO-led 'empowerment' projects has been challenged in the scholarly literature. Women's NGOs are often constrained by their institutional environment to focus on narrowly defined ideas of women's empowerment. Their donors and the state officials with whom they work tend to favour neoliberal notions of 'empowerment', focused on giving women information to improve their entrepreneurial capacity, rather than focusing on structural barriers to women's economic participation (Sharma 2006). In some instances, these kinds of 'empowerment' NGOs seek to harvest women's agency to ensure the success of development projects with little regard for the negative and potentially violent consequences that women may incur from their communities for expressing such agency (Madhok and Rai 2012). Moreover, NGOs that are led by urban middle-class professionals – often men – have not proven particularly effective in representing the perspectives of women from poor and marginalized communities (Narayanaswamy 2016).

For these reasons, feminist scholars have recently signalled a need to reject the idea that NGOs can, by themselves, challenge entrenched forms of gender inequality. NGOs should rather be seen as part of a much broader field of contestation, within which social movements and everyday struggles play vital roles (e.g. Roy, Srila 2015). Indeed, in recent years, some of the most vibrant forms of opposition to patriarchy in India have not come from formal organizations, but rather from more organic, grassroots social movements, which have mobilized women from various social strata. These forms of political action are diverse in their constituents and the issues they seek to address. To provide a complete list of these initiatives would be beyond the scope of this chapter. The examples we detail below have been selected based on their public prominence and/or their potential to politicize some of the social bases of gender inequality.

Perhaps the most publicly visible efforts to politicize gender inequality in recent years have focused on the issue of gendered violence and access to public space. On 16 December 2012, a young female physiotherapy student was raped in a particularly brutal way, and murdered on a bus in Delhi, sparking outrage across the country. The incident drew attention to the sexual harassment and violence to which women are routinely subjected in the streets of India and the impact this has on women's capacity to move about freely and without fear. In the wake of this incident – which came to be known as the *Nirbhaya* ('fearless') case – women's movements have been vociferous in fighting against claims that it is women's responsibility to behave 'modestly' to prevent public acts of violence and have attempted to reclaim women's right to public space.

These movements have also demonstrated that many of the popular expressions of opposition to sexual violence tend to reinforce patriarchal norms. One example of resistance to this is the *Pinjra Tod* ('Break the Cage') movement (see Roy 2016). In mid-2015, Jamia Millia Islamia University in Delhi issued a notice advising that female students residing at the university's college could no longer request permission to stay out of their dormitories later than 8pm. In an open letter to the university's Vice Chancellor, students questioned not only the changing of the rules, but also why women should need to request permission to stay out at night at all – why women's mobility needed to be subject to any such arbitrary restrictions. The open letter triggered an outpouring of related grievances from female students across Delhi and, in time, across the country. It was not just about curfews – women began speaking out against college dress codes that were applied to women but not men, against the non-inclusive nature of university spaces, and against the price of accommodation for female students that remains much higher than for male students – ostensibly because of the higher costs of ensuring women's physical security. In the months and years that followed, young women fought a series of campaigns to challenge patriarchal and protectionist restrictions on women's autonomy, under the *Pinjra Tod* banner. What this movement highlighted was that the dominant cultural response to the problem of public sexual assault and harassment – and that publicly endorsed by many police officers, politicians and media commentators across India – was to restrict women's mobility even further, rather than attempt to change the underlying problem, namely, men's behaviour, attitudes and privileged position.

Although the issue of gendered violence affects women from all social strata, highly mediated forms of activism against such violence, including *Pinjra Tod*, tend to be led by tertiary educated, urban women. Yet, what has been remarkable about women's activism over the last decade is the extent to which it can also be found in more historically marginalized communities. On the issue of gendered violence, one initiative that gained international media attention was the 'Gulabi Gang' (see Richards 2016). This 'gang', which formed in rural Uttar Pradesh in 2006, has responded to a lack of police responsiveness to cases of violence against rural women by taking the law into its own hands, collectively confronting perpetrators with lathis (large sticks). They have campaigned on issues such as improving women's educational outcomes and ending the practice of child marriage.

Another fairly recent example of oppressed women expressing political agency is the sex workers' rights movement. Given their deviation from normative family life, sex workers have often been stigmatized in Indian society and criminalized by governments. Matters are often made worse by the interventions of some international feminist organizations, which have tended to frame all female sex workers as victims of human trafficking and male commodification of women's bodies, leading to ongoing efforts to abolish sex work and conduct 'rescue' raids on sex workers' living quarters. These forms of intervention have too often had the effect of further marginalizing and restricting options for sex workers, whose lives are already defined by high levels of precarity. Yet, as S. P. Shah (2012) outlines, with the outbreak of HIV/AIDS in the 1980s and 1990s, governments were forced to engage more with sex workers as potential transmitters of the disease, which sex workers took as an opportunity to make their needs for better healthcare protection known. Since 2000, sex workers have become organized as a lobby group and subsequently as trade unions, through which they have asserted their needs for rights as workers. They have asserted the need for the decriminalization of their work, in order to reduce its precariousness and to allow them to secure various workplace protections.

Recent years have also seen remarkable examples of rural Indian women engaging in grassroots struggles against intersecting forms of inequality. Of particular interest is the increased incidence of political activity by rural Dalit women, who have been simultaneously marginalized by gender, caste and rural–urban hierarchies. A study by Anandhi (2017) highlighted the role of Dalit women in contesting both patriarchy and caste oppression in rural Tamil Nadu. Anandhi focuses on villages in Tamil Nadu where the debt bondage of the lowest strata of Dalits has allowed the continuation of a brutal tradition, whereby young Dalit women and girls are dedicated by their families to the goddess Mathimmar. After their dedication, these women are enlisted to perform sexual services and free agricultural and domestic labour for upper-caste men. Alarmingly, until relatively recently, this practice had been ignored and silenced by men within the Dalit movement, who saw it as a poor reflection on their caste's honour. The victims of this practice thus found themselves doubly oppressed by traditional caste practices and the patriarchal attitudes of men of their own castes. Recently, however, women belonging to Dalit castes of slightly higher status and with greater economic mobility have emerged as political leaders in the region. Unlike more established Dalit politicians, who have typically only mobilized for the interests of their sub-caste, these women have emphasized building solidarity with other women across varying oppressed classes, and this has extended to representing the women who had been dedicated to Mathimmar and struggling for their liberation. Although the entrenched attitudes of established Dalit politicians have meant that, to date, the Dalit women's movement's efforts to draw attention to this issue have largely fallen on deaf ears, Anandhi emphasizes the potential of this form of activism to create 'spaces for new forms of women's collectivization against caste discrimination and oppression – in other words, they can become the matrix of an alternative politics' (Anandhi 2017: 121). This is especially important in a context where historically, not only has the Dalit movement tended to ignore women's issues, but equally, upper-caste feminists have ignored the plight of Dalits.

These examples are not isolated. Across India, women facing multiple forms of inequality are finding new opportunities to express their discontent with the current gendered order. Indeed, many are rising to positions of leadership within social movements and trade unions, and are proving effective at drawing attention to how gender inequality intersects with other forms of social disadvantage (e.g. Agarwala 2014; Kabeer 2018). Issues that had historically been ignored – often because of the stated need to protect 'Indian culture' and its 'traditional family system' – are being brought to the table. While many NGO workers and politicians may still shy away from direct politicization of gender inequality, the diversity of contemporary women's movements offers reason for hope.

12.5 Conclusion

Gender inequality remains a significant issue in India. There are substantial wage gaps for women of all education levels. The female workforce participation rate appears to be stagnant or declining, contrary to the expectations of economists. In the post-Green Revolution rural societies of north-west India, women find themselves increasingly confined to the domestic sphere, ironically, as a biproduct of their families' upward mobility. Women continue to experience violence and sexual harassment, both at home and in the streets. And although women vote more today than in generations past, the number of elected female political representatives rarely exceeds 10 per cent and is particularly low in state legislatures. The fact that gender gaps have not closed more substantially points to the constraining effects of patriarchy on women's opportunities, both in the home and outside.

It is encouraging that in some domains gender inequalities are lessening in India. Enrolments of young men and women in higher education, for example, have almost reached parity – though issues persist with the *quality* of education that young men and women receive. In many other domains, however, inequalities remain stark, and in some – such as educated women's labour force participation rates – inequalities have *widened*. So why do gender inequalities persist? There are numerous reasons, many of which have their origins in the constructions of gender identities, roles and relations, which have their origins, in turn, within the family structure. Though education may be a crucial domain in which girls and young women struggle to achieve greater autonomy and upward mobility, other factors – such as expectations of domestic duties, or the neglect of girls' health and nutrition – mean that they do not compete with boys and young men on a level playing field. Social conventions also place greater limitations on what women can do with their education – for many, education can be at best a marriage asset: families do not intend it as a resource to meet women's personal or professional aspirations. When women do enter the workforce, capitalist and patriarchal institutions conspire together to 'super-exploit' them, such that prospects of wage earnings leading to greater autonomy or mobility are curtailed from the outset. Finally, in formal politics, women are woefully under-represented in India, partly a reflection of the patriarchal norms within mainstream political parties. Women's movements, however, have done much in recent years to bring issues of gender inequality into public discourse, and, at a day-to-day level, women are challenging patriarchal conventions in many aspects of their lives. Notwithstanding the recent resurgence of aggressive Hindu nationalist masculinities defending traditional family institutions, we have reason to be hopeful that women's movements will be able to facilitate significant shifts in India in the coming decades to further mitigate gender inequality.

13

Can Youth Transform India?

13.1 Introduction: Ideas about 'Youth'

Young people in India typically have high aspirations, participate actively in civic life, and in many cases have skills and capacities as a result of their education and technological knowledge that their parents and grandparents do not possess. Yet young people also face problems in acquiring quality education and obtaining secure work. Young women or young people belonging to minority groups often face particular obstacles. It is perhaps unsurprising in this context that young people have started to exhibit disenchantment, even as many are wont to ask: Can youth transform India?

'Youth' is a contested term. In India, the official definition of youth is typically someone aged between 16 and 35. It is, according to some social scientists, an extended period of post-adolescence. But youth is a flexible term (Durham 2008), and in India it has been stretched to enormous lengths. There are people in their fifties who trade on being youth politicians (Jeffrey 2010).

The term 'youth' is a moral category as well as a sociological one. In various contexts, 'youth' is ascribed with either the positive virtues of innocence, vitality and an uncorrupted mind, or linked to negative tropes: risk, threat and danger. The German sociologist Karl Mannheim (1972) argued that young people have a type of 'fresh contact' with their inherited social and environmental setting. Youth are able to rethink approaches to the economy, society, culture and politics, in part because they are less invested in the status quo and in part because their proximity to childhood gives them a type of spirited inventiveness. Mannheim was careful not to romanticize youth, but he did argue that human society advances, in part, because of the constant emergence of new generations into society.

Such ideas have re-emerged during the twenty-first century. Young people were in the vanguard of a number of major global democratic movements in the first 15 years of the current century, including the Occupy Movement, World Social Forum and various uprisings that formed part of the so-called 'Arab Spring'. These movements and agitations, while diverse in their nature and effects, had the general impact of changing global discourses on rights and the economy, and they sometimes played a major role in political change.

At the policy and scholarly level, there have been several major reports noting the capacity of youth to push for global change, including the UN's World Youth Report (2018) and a welter of publications produced by the United Nations Development Programme.

Economists have developed similar ideas in positing the potential for countries to gain from a 'demographic dividend' (Bloom 2011). There were 422 million people aged between 15 and 34 in India in 2011. By 2025, the average age in India will be 29, compared to 37 in China and 45 in Japan. Economists have argued that a substantial young adult population relative to the number of old people is likely to boost economic productivity and also means that the state does not have to spend as much on welfare, which typically goes towards young children and the elderly.

The notion of youth as harbingers of change also has a venerable history in India. Young people were central to the anti-British demonstrations of the early twentieth century – Nehru himself was a 'youth' when he joined the struggle in 1919. In the post-independence period, the image of the young person on a bicycle was frequently invoked in the process of nation building. More recently still, the Indian nation has looked to youth, especially educated youth, as engines of development. In this optic, India is poised to reap the rewards of a demographic dividend, just as East Asia benefitted from its dividend in the 1970s and 1980s. Modi has made exactly this point.

But the capacity of youth – even educated youth with good access to technology – to transform Indian society in positive ways depends to a large extent on their social circumstances. At the very least, it depends upon them having access to good education and some prospect of acquiring decent work. Globally, a neoliberal turn in the policy environment has often had the effect of undermining state support for quality education, training and healthcare.

What, then, of India's capacity to provide a conducive environment for the flourishing of its young population?

13.2 School Education

Educational enrolment has certainly increased rapidly in recent years in India. The percentage of children in upper primary (10–13 years), rose from 71 per cent in 2005–06 to 91.2 per cent in 2014–15, and the equivalent figures at secondary level (14–15 years) are 52 per cent and 78 per cent. Girls' increased enrolment accounts for the majority of the gains over this period (Saha and Saha 2018; Gilbertson 2019). Gross enrolment rates for SCs, STs and Muslims have also increased markedly. In India young people are roughly three times as likely to go to secondary school as they were in 1994.

Government development programmes have played a major role in this process. In 2001, the government established a large-scale development initiative, the 'Education For All Programme' (*Sarva Shiksha Abhiyan*) that aimed to improve enrolment and standards in schools. The government has also established residential schools for girls from marginalized communities (*Kasturba Gandhi Valika Vidhyalaya*) and provided girls with bicycles to get to school (*Balika Cycle Yojana*) (Gilbertson 2019). More recently, the Right to Education (RtE) Act (2009) obligates the central and state government to provide all children with free education up to the age of 14 and makes education to this age compulsory across India. The act also stipulates a range of measures to improve school curricula and guarantee minimal standards. The RtE Act mandates that 25 per cent of seats in private schools are open to children from 'economically weaker' families, free of cost. Stricter conditions have been imposed on private schools in an attempt to drive up standards.

There has been an increase in the amount of NGO activity aimed at improving the quality of government and private schools, enhancing students' participation in school, and preventing them from dropping out. Moreover, NGOs are increasingly working with government to achieve change. For example, Pratham India Education Institute (Pratham), an NGO based in Mumbai, tries to improve educational governance and provides tutoring of at-risk children. Studies suggest that Pratham has had limited effect on educational governance but more success in improving children's reading skills (Jowett and Dyer 2012). Esther Duflo and colleagues at MIT have used research with Pratham to help develop the Jameel Abdul Latif Poverty Action Lab (JPAL). JPAL has raised teacher attendance, enhanced tuition and played an important role in monitoring education in several parts of India (Dhaliwal et al. 2013).

Yet policy and NGO initiatives have not yet had a significant overall impact on school quality. Dramatic increases in school enrolments mask chronic problems of low attendance and poor educational outcomes. The state of government schools is especially concerning. The *Annual Status of Education Report* – based on a comprehensive survey of more than half a million students across almost all districts of India – found that, in 2018, the proportion of 5th Grade (upper primary) students in rural government schools who could read was 44.2 per cent, compared to 53.1 per cent in 2008, while those who could do division was 22.7 per cent compared to 34.4 per cent in 2008 (ASER 2019). Overall, the percentage of students with basic literacy and numeracy skills in government schools declined substantially between 2008 and 2012 and levelled off thereafter, picking up slightly between 2016 and 2018, but still below 2010 levels. Private schools, including ones that charge very low fees, consistently perform better in terms of numeracy and literacy than their government counterparts (Kingdon 2017). Partly as a consequence, student numbers in private schools have increased rapidly since the early 2000s (Kingdon 2017). This includes a large number of elite schools, such as boarding schools modelled on UK public schools as well as a much larger number of modest institutions, some of them run by individuals, some by charitable or religious organizations.

The state's investment in education since 1990 has been low, hovering around 3 per cent of GDP and considerably less than the 6 per cent often mentioned as the desirable figure in planning reports (see chapter 3). Most expenditure on education is provided by state governments, and it is therefore important to note that Bose et al. (2017) found that many of the twelve states that they surveyed were investing far less in education than required to meet the minimum standards and enrolment targets laid down in the RtE Act. Moreover, the central government did not increase its transfer of education funding to states between 2013 and 2017; indeed, it may have actually declined, in spite of the rhetoric around implementing the RtE Act and improving education (see Bose et al. 2017). This underinvestment means that teacher/student ratios in government schools are poor in many areas. Recent survey evidence in UP and Bihar suggests that average class sizes in these states remain at over 60 (The Economic Times 2018).

There is rather limited public pressure to improve education. Davies (2018) has found that teacher absenteeism is lower around election time in India relative to other periods, a point he links to low interest in education during periods in which candidates are not vying for attention. Even during elections, education often receives short thrift in India. It is notable that education was hardly mentioned in the public pronouncements of major parties in the lead up to the 2019 Indian election.

The governance of schooling is also a major difficulty. Many of the teachers who are formally registered within government schools do not turn up on any given day (Muralidharan and Prakash 2017). Teachers can bribe or mobilize networks of influence to obtain transfers to favoured districts, leaving schools in remote, rural or high-minority population areas starved of instructors (Jeffery et al. 2006; Béteille 2009; Vasavi 2015). Even where they are in school, teachers often have to perform a range of duties not directly related to their formal educational responsibilities. Government teachers are paid between four and eight times their counterparts in China, yet Indian problems of accountability and governance mean that Chinese learning outcomes are much better (Kingdon 2017).

In addition to the problem of financing and governance, the teaching delivered in schools in India is often narrow. Institutional pressure to improve India's standing in key indices of global development – such as literacy and numeracy indicators – have led to an emphasis on examination success in core disciplines to the exclusion of enquiry-based and active learning opportunities (Vasavi 2015). There is also a problem of political interference in the development of school curricula. School textbooks in Indian states ruled by the BJP governments are being rewritten to erase India's 'Muslim past' and glorify Hindu traditions (see Bénéï 2008).

Poor quality education has generated a shadow economy of private coaching and tuition, which sometimes prey on poor people's lack of information (see Faust and Nagar 2001; McGuire 2013). McGuire (2013) has described the manner in which 'personality centres' in north India often exploit youth aspirations through cultivating false hopes. Jayadeva's (2019) work on English coaching in south India likewise pays close attention to the relationship between informal tutorials and the reproduction of class and gender inequalities.

Forced to study in poor-quality institutions, many young people drop out of school. Bose et al. (2017) found 12 per cent of children in Uttar Pradesh were out of school in 2016 and 10 per cent in Bihar. It is often the need to receive assistance from children in household or paid employment that, in combination with a perception that school education is of poor quality, leads parents to remove children from school (Jeffrey et al. 2008; Dyson 2018). The problem of high dropout rates is especially marked among girls, whose education is often devalued relative to that of boys and who are more likely to be withdrawn from school to assist with housework (see Chaudhury et al. 2006; Dyson 2019).

Research on school dropouts also underlines the connection between educational malaise and problems in India's health sector (see especially Krishna 2013). The Expanded Programme of Immunization introduced in India in 1978 has gone a long way towards reducing child deaths from many major diseases. Moreover, the past fifty years has witnessed a considerable expansion of health facilities and some improvements in sanitation and water supply in most parts of India, especially the south. But healthcare spending in India has remained under 1 per cent of GDP in spite of repeated calls for it to be raised to 2 per cent (Mooij 2014; and see chapter 3). Access to health care has become rapidly privatized since the early 1990s. In most parts of rural and small-town India, as well as in poorer areas of big cities, people are unable to acquire cheap and rapid access to medical facilities (Drèze and Sen 2013). Health care is typically expensive and acquiring the assistance of a nurse or doctor often involves the expenditure of money and time as well as the mobilization of social networks. The absence of a good-quality primary healthcare system means that children often have to leave school to care for ill family members or as an economizing measure in the face of exorbitant and unexpected health expenditure (Alex 2008; Krishna 2013). This is often especially the case within minority populations. For example, Husain and Chatterjee (2009) note that primary school completion rates of Muslims in West Bengal are substantially lower than those of Hindus – indeed, their data suggest that the gap increased during the 2000s. SCs and STs are often especially likely to drop out of school (Shah 2009; Patel 2017).

The draft National Education Policy (DNEP), prepared by a committee chaired by Dr. K. Kasturirangan and released while we were writing this book, is an important attempt to address this malaise. It is the first comprehensive policy statement on education in India since 1986. The DNEP is impressive in many respects and steers well clear of the type of incrementalism often associated with such reports. It recommends a doubling of funding for public education from 10 per cent of total public expenditure to 20 per cent (roughly 6 per cent of total GDP) by 2025. This is hitched to a vision of comprehensive change. At the school level, the DNEP recommends extending the Right to Education Act to all young people aged between 3 and 18 as well as a new structure for the school education of three pre-school years, two primary, three preparatory, three middle school years, and four high school years.

Among a large number of accompanying school reforms, the DNEP suggests introducing breakfasts in addition to the established 'midday meals scheme' at all pre-primary and primary schools across India – a key initiative in a country where child undernourishment is a pressing public concern (see chapter 8). It also suggests countering the problem of the fragmentation of government primary school education by gathering schools together in 'school complexes'.

The DNEP suggests promoting a 'liberal education' encompassing creativity, collaboration, social responsibility, multilingualism and digital learning. Distinctions between different streams of study in schools – such as Arts, Science and Commerce – would be abolished and compulsory courses would be established on topics such as ethical reasoning, current affairs and 'critical issues', such as climate change.

The DNEP recommends professionalizing school teaching. Schemes of appointing temporary, part-time 'para-teachers' would be abandoned, and all teachers would now be required to qualify in large multidisciplinary universities rather than the small, low-quality 'B.Ed. Colleges' that absorb many trainee teachers at present. At the same time, the structure of winner takes all, high stakes 10th grade and 12th grade board examinations would be replaced by a modular system throughout grades 9 to 12. As the report points out, this would relieve pressure on youth and stem the growth of India's parasitic coaching culture of the type described by Jayadeva (2019) and McGuire (2013).

The draft NEP's recommendations in relation to schooling have come in for criticism (e.g. Bhushan 2019). A key point is that the draft NEP may be unimplementable. Not enough consideration is given to the relationship between the centre and India's constituent states, which have primary responsibility for education. Much of the additional public expenditure that is forecast will need to be raised by the states (see Bhushan 2019). There is a risk that the DNEP may be easiest to implement in the better-run, wealthier (mainly southern) states that are in least need of reform.

But the vision of school restructuring and the decision to endorse broad visions of school education are welcome. The attempt to tackle the exam culture is laudable as is the forecast improvement in teacher training. The DNEP is also significant for what it is not: it is not an effort to enforce a Hindu nationalist vision of education, even if some see the references in the document to India's educational traditions as an attempt to prepare the ground for such a move. As a paean to the benefits of public education and an open, critical approach to pedagogy, the document is also impressive. We will have to wait to see whether this promise is fulfilled.

13.3 Higher Education

The higher education picture broadly mirrors that of school education – a picture of decline with some evidence of a new determination to achieve change. There has been a sixtyfold increase in university and college enrolments in India since independence, and most of this increase has occurred since 2000 (Kapur and Mehta 2017). In 1950–51, India had 27 universities, 370 colleges for general education and 208 colleges for professional education (engineering, medicine, education). In 2016–17, India had 895 universities and just over 42,000 colleges. Approximately a thousand new colleges are opened in India each year.

But higher education is in an even more profound crisis than school education. There were only seven institutions in India in the top 400 in the QS World Rankings in 2016 and none in the top 100. The world ranking tables are problematic, but India's performance in the Times Higher Education rankings released in September 2019 shows that Indian universities are not improving. Indeed, India's rankings have been getting worse since 2014. India arguably does not contain a single world-class general university. India and China were producing roughly the same number of research publications per year in the 1980s. By 2013, China was producing more than three times the number of research publications as India, reflecting large-scale Chinese investment in research funding without any parallel initiative in India (Panat 2014).

Government spending on higher education remains at only about 0.5 per cent of GDP, well below the level in most countries. A third of teaching posts are currently vacant in India's central universities due to a lack of funds, and contract teachers are increasingly taking the place of permanent faculty. To take just one example, Gujarat College, widely known in the early twentieth century for its teaching, had over 100 faculty for roughly 1,500 students in 1960. By 2015, the student population had increased to 2,500 but the number of faculty had declined to just 26.

India has some good higher educational institutions. The Indian Institutes of Technology and Indian Institute of Science in Bangalore are globally competitive. But these absorb a miniscule proportion of the overall university population. The vast major of students, over 90 per cent by some estimates, study in universities or colleges run by India's states, and most of these students are in colleges affiliated to a state university, where they are very rarely taught by research-active faculty.

Within most colleges and universities, the curricula are outdated, there is little continuous assessment or careers advice, and research productivity is extremely low. In many parts of India, faculty frequently skip classes in favour of giving tutorials to students outside class for additional fees. A recent NDTV sting showed that many universities lacked basic facilities. One institution – Baba Bhimrao Ambedkar University in Bihar which has 200,000 students – has not held examinations since 2015.

One result of this underinvestment and malaise has been to encourage elites in India to send their children abroad to acquire university degrees. Another result is privatization of colleges and universities. In order to meet soaring demand for higher education, the government's University Grants Commission (UGC) has approved a huge number of private higher educational institutions. Most do not conduct research, have under-qualified faculty, and are usually small in size, preventing the benefits of economies of scale (Kapur and Mehta 2017). At the same time, there are numerous state functionaries and private brokers who extract money from the system of regulations imposed on higher education by the state and who therefore have an interest in the maintenance of the status quo (see Gould 1972; Jeffrey 2010). The growth in private colleges has also led to an increase in self-financing students and a corresponding ballooning of student debt.

These problems affect minorities and women especially adversely. The ratio of men to women in higher education in India moved from 8:1 in 1950 to 1.2:1 in 2014 and of general caste students to SC/ST students from 12:1 in the late 1950s to 6:1 in 2004. But the vast majority of those from relatively marginalized groups attend poorer quality universities and colleges. Moreover, social inequalities are pronounced within higher education. SCs, STs, Muslims and also OBCs remain seriously under-represented in India's colleges and universities relative to their population share, and less than 3 per cent of faculty at IITs are SC or ST (Dutta 2019). Dalit students often find it difficult to acquire PhD supervisors (Jeffrey 2010), and there remain many separated 'Dalit hostels' in higher educational institutions across India. The suicide in 2016 of Rohith Vemula, a PhD student at the University of Hyderabad (see chapter 11), led to the exposure of many examples of caste prejudice in colleges and universities. University education is also strongly gendered. For example, young women have historically been concentrated in non-professional courses that offer relatively few opportunities for lucrative employment (Chanana 2007).

The Government of India is aware of many of these problems. The Twelfth Five Year Plan of 2012 established a National Higher Education Council which offered states increased funding, especially for higher educational infrastructure. But this funding was too small to make any significant difference. The Modi administration's recent attempts to reform higher education have been largely ineffective to date. It has designated twenty universities as 'Institutes of Eminence' (IoE) marked out for special funding. But this programme is piecemeal and lacks any vision for the IoEs that will catalyse wider educational change. The Indian government has also granted some autonomy to sixty other universities and colleges, freeing them somewhat from the stultifying regulatory regime imposed by the University Grants Commission. But, again, this shift is small and divorced from the obvious requirement for very large-scale investment in higher education. Across both the IoE scheme and the move to grant greater autonomy to institutions, the Government of India's rhetoric and action around higher education reform has been entirely framed in terms of 'excellence' with almost no attention paid to questions of equity.

Over and above these problems, the Modi administration has tried to limit the public function of universities as bases for critique, for example in well-publicized attempts to discipline Jawaharlal Nehru University (JNU). These started with a government crackdown on student protestors in early 2016 in which the leader of the JNU student's union was arrested, but later extended to a much wider range of actions to change the culture at the historically left-wing university. There have been allegations, for example, that the university's Vice Chancellor has made biased appointments of new faculty with links to the Sangh Parivar (Mahaprashasta 2018). Regrettably, the incidents at JNU were not isolated. They form part of a long-standing effort by sections of the Sangh Parivar to oppose the culture of dissent on university campuses; there are even instances of BJP-led state governments issuing threats to use the Sedition Act against student politicians for making statements critical of the government (Bajpai 2016).

When it comes to India's vocational education and training system, the situation is even worse. Since 1988, students have been able to opt for vocational streams in some senior secondary schools, though only a small percentage of students do so, as most would prefer either 'general' (i.e. academic) education, or dropping out of school prior to the senior secondary level to pursue work (Rao et al. 2014). At the post-secondary level, there is a somewhat more established coterie of (government) Industrial Training Institutes (ITIs), and (private) Industrial Training Centres (now referred to as private ITIs). Yet, historically, these have been marked by severe government neglect, and often disengaged from both the skills needs of industry and more 'traditional' systems of skill development, such as craft-based apprenticeships (Singh 2001). As a consequence of this, and the low social status awarded to vocational qualifications, the number of workers who receive training from these centres (or through government-recognized apprenticeship programmes) is exceptionally low – less than 2 per cent of the workforce in 2008, and still significantly less than 10 per cent in the mid-2010s (Rao et al. 2014).

Criticisms of India's vocational education system are legion. Curricula in ITIs are often outdated and do not reflect industry demand (Pilz 2016). The majority of teachers in ITIs lack both industry experience or any form of pedagogical training (Ajithkumar 2016; Pilz and Gengaiah 2019). A pervasive issue is that teachers in India's vocational training institutions present materials in an overly theoretical manner, lacking either the capacity or the inclination to foster the development of skills through more practical, 'hands-on' pedagogical strategies (Pilz 2018; Zenner et al. 2017). Youth who pass through India's vocational education system thus leave without the confidence of having acquired the practical skills necessary to work in their chosen fields – and this is reflected in poor employment outcomes (Agrawal 2014). Many graduates of ITIs feel frustrated when, despite their qualifications, they are only able to obtain (at best) low-skilled, poorly paid and insecure jobs (Cross 2009).

The government has recognized the need to transform its vocational education sector, seeing vocational skills as necessary to drive India's future industrial growth. In 2006, the UPA government included in the 11th Five Year Plan an agenda for expanding India's existing set of ITIs, such that the percentage of India's skilled workforce would increase from 2 per cent to 50 per cent by 2022 (King 2012). The Modi government gave an additional boost to this policy agenda – which it deftly rebranded as 'Skill India' in 2015 – by forming a separate Ministry of Skill Development and Entrepreneurship (MSDE). The MSDE has driven curriculum reform in vocational education in India, including the development of a National Skills Qualifications Framework. Industry and foreign vocational providers have been involved in the process. Partly as a result of the very weak base of vocational training institutes in the country, however, progress has been disappointing. Recruitment has been a major challenge – given that vocational qualifications and careers do not align with most Indian youths' aspirations – and labour market outcomes have been poor, often reflecting a lack of industry recognition of the value of formal skills qualifications.

It is into this situation of crisis that the drafting committee pitched the new Draft National Education Policy (DNEP). The report places particular emphasis on higher education. In a marked shift from its former focus on only elite Indian universities and the aim of making these 'world class', the report takes a dispassionate look at provincial higher education. DNEP sets the target of 50 per cent of youth being enrolled in universities by 2035 but notes the widespread decay or underdevelopment of higher education across India, especially the state-run universities and college where 93 per cent of students study. This is partly a problem of fragmentation: 20 per cent of degree colleges nationally have fewer than 100 students. But it also relates to the curriculum; the report notes that 40 per cent of tertiary-level colleges in India teach a single subject. The DNEP also reports that, 'Even within multidisciplinary universities, there is currently little interaction among different disciplines' (Government of India 2019: 203).

More broadly, the DNEP notes that research in India is concentrated in specialist institutes, central universities and a small number of elite state universities, thus leaving the vast majority of students with no opportunities to be taught by research-active faculty. In addition, senior leaders and faculty at universities and colleges – who, the report notes, have typically been selected via arbitrary measures rather than on merit – are characterized by a 'severe lack of motivation and innovation' (Government of India 2019: 204). The DNEP argues that in many degree colleges there is almost no teaching occurring at all.

The existing higher education system is characterized by the 'widespread prevalence of vested/commercial interests' and 'a mechanistic and disempowering regulatory system' (Government of India 2019: 205). The report could have added other issues: woefully poor library and general infrastructural facilities (Kapur and Mehta 2017) and an atmosphere among students of cynicism and disappointment (Jeffrey 2010; Jha 2017).

In response, the DNEP recommends dismantling the current system of universities and non-degree granting private and public colleges. These would be replaced by a smaller number of institutions – between 10,000 and 15,000. All of the institutions in the new system would have the capacity to grant degrees but would be organized into three tiers: Tier 1 universities would focus on research and teach the gamut of undergraduates through to PhD students. In a move to spread a research culture broadly across India, Tier 2 institutions – while teaching-focused – would also carry out research. Tier 3 institutions would be teaching-only undergraduate colleges.

There are three other notable innovations. The DNEP critiques instrumentalist visions of higher education. It makes the repeated case for universities as sites for broad-based, interdisciplinary enquiry: 'Higher education must develop good, well-rounded, creative individuals with intellectual curiosity, a spirit of service, and a strong ethical compass' (Government of India 2019: 203). The DNEP recognizes that interdisciplinarity rests on mutual respect for different disciplines, and humanities and social sciences are championed. In an unexpected pivot away from an overwhelming focus on STEM (Science, Technology, Engineering and Mathematics), the DNEP views Liberal Arts as important in its own right and in terms of a person's personal and social development, even if there remain concerns over how 'Liberal Arts' is conceptualized and whether it encompasses the type of critical social science perspectives that provide much of the source material for our book.

The DNEP also recommends a largely new regulatory structure, with a new National Education Commission, chaired by the prime minister, at the apex. Under this body, a new National Higher Regulatory Authority will regulate higher education, a revamped National Assessment and Accreditation Council will develop an accreditation ecosystem, and the University Grants Commission will be renamed as the Higher Education Grants Commission. In addition, a new National Research Fund will be established charged with developing a research culture, with an annual budget of 200 billion rupees. The Union Budget of India released on 5 July has initiated the process of creating these institutions.

Whether it will be possible to implement the DNEP in its current form is doubtful. There are enormous practical difficulties that will accompany any effort to 'convert' a system of a central university affiliating a plethora of surrounding colleges into autonomous degree-granting institutions at different tiers. Most obviously, it will be very difficult to compel private educational entrepreneurs running specialist colleges into transforming their institutions into multidisciplinary enterprises. More broadly, many regional players and local elites benefit from the higher education system and school education system as currently constituted, for example profiting from the process through which affiliations are disbursed (see Jeffrey 2010). The political influence of educational leaders and teachers, the strength of teaching unions, and the nexus that links educationalists to politicians at local and regional levels are all left undiscussed.

Aside from the issue of implementation, the draft NEP's approach to higher education requires some revision and further work. There is repeated reference made to 'autonomy', but this is not the same as ensuring that the university is a democratic, safe and critical space. This is especially important in the light of recent concern over government interference in the work of key universities in India, as previously discussed.

In addition, the DNEP needs to pay greater attention to questions of social equality. The document is committed to improving the participation of under-represented groups in universities. But this stops short of the wholesale effort required to address gender, caste and class inequalities and processes of marginalization. People with disabilities are severely under-represented in universities, as are Muslims. Caste discrimination remains a major problem in many institutions. Talk of inclusion and 'upliftment' – a common trope in the document – is not enough. Greater attention must be paid to the role of individual forms of inequality in shaping people's access to education, experience of school/university, and trajectories post-education.

There are two other significant issues that require some reflection. First, the idea of mentorship is discussed in the DNEP but unconvincingly. On the one hand, the draft NEP notes the importance of senior educationalists in mentoring universities in the new scenario envisaged. On the other hand, it notes that many senior educationalists in India have been promoted through 'arbitrary means' and without enough emphasis on merit. This does not add up. In addition, attention needs to be paid to the specific connotations of 'mentorship', which has somewhat paternalistic overtones.

Second, the government needs to pay careful attention to how to enrol young people and students in the finalization and implementation of the DNEP. Students are already demonstrating in Delhi against the draft policy, partly on the grounds that it may result in an increase in fees. Listening to young people and channelling youth critique in such a way that it can contribute to policy development is crucial.

There are still other smaller issues associated with the DNEP's approach to higher education: there is little indication of how the DNEP relates to some earlier schemes such as India's efforts to identify 'Institutes of Eminence'; there is a lack of focus on the rural and agriculture; at the school level the abandonment of the system of recognition for private schools needs a better rationale; some of the educational terminology employed in discussing curricular change is confusing and used inconsistently (see Dhanka 2019); and the decision to make education compulsory up to 18 looks expensive and perhaps unworkable.

All of these criticisms should be read in context, however. The DNEP represents at last an open acknowledgement of the largely moribund state of university education ('the picture beyond the IITs') and an effort to think through radical change comprehensively in a relatively non-partisan manner. It is a document that contains a wealth of useful ideas and which makes an attempt to develop these with a broadly plausible overarching ideological and structural framework. Many of the critiques of the DNEP to date appear to rely on arguments of bad faith. For example, it is asserted that DNEP's references to 'autonomy' are code for the rapid neoliberalization of universities, that the National Research Foundation will not fund social sciences and humanities, and that the prime minister's position at the apex will lead to wholesale government interference, but all of these assertions are based on a questionable cynicism. Alternatively, the critiques rely on nit-picking about details. Ultimately, the DNEP is a pretty good first go, will lead to many improvements and is very unlikely to worsen the current state of play.

13.4 Unemployment

There is one critique of the DNEP that has certainly hit the mark. The focus on enrolling 50 per cent of the population in university is unhelpful in an environment in which graduate unemployment is high and in which manual and craft labour is often stigmatized. Focusing more on vocational education and informal learning occurring outside institutional contexts would be more appropriate.

Unemployment has become a critical issue in India in the 2010s. It is true that a thin upper stratum of young people has moved quickly and successfully into well-paid, secure salaried work, often in the IT sector and allied employment. But this elite is small and almost entirely from upper castes and classes. Fuller and Narasimhan (2007) have described how upper middle-class youth in Chennai have used their social connections and cultural confidence to dominate access to IT jobs, and Nisbett (2007) makes similar arguments based on data from south India (see also Gooptu 2013).

Another much larger section of educated youth – those from the 'middle middle', 'lower middle' or poorer classes – has typically faced disappointing occupational outcomes. Educated unemployment is not new in India. The colonial state often encouraged large numbers of young people to enter formal education, and not all of these men acquired salaried work (see Coleman 1965). Complaints about 'semi-educated' young men 'hanging about' around government offices surface in the reports of colonial officials at least as far back as the mid-1850s in India (Dore 1976: 53). Moreover, Ronald Dore (1976) argued over forty years ago that a combination of population growth, a lack of expansion in manufacturing and service industries, and increased enrolment in education had created a large cohort of unemployed young people in many parts of India.

Yet educated unemployment has become especially pronounced since the 1970s in India and in many other post-colonial settings, as well as in the West (see Kaplinsky 2005). Substantial numbers of people in India, especially those from lower middle classes and upwardly mobile formerly disadvantaged groups, have looked to formal schooling as a means of social mobility since 1970, and they have been exposed via this education and media or development institutions to images of progress through education and entry into white-collar work. At the same time, global economic changes since 1970 have often failed to generate sufficient numbers of permanent white-collar jobs to meet this growing demand (and see chapter 4 regarding economic liberalization and employment generation in India). The result has been the emergence of a surplus population of people who, unlike those in the 'reserve army of labour' discussed by Marx in the nineteenth century, possess educational qualifications and are sometimes highly skilled (see Kaplinsky 2005). Indeed, many in this group perceive themselves to be 'underemployed' rather than wholly without work. They are dependent on involuntary part-time work, engaged in intermittent unemployment and/or involved in poorly remunerated labour (Prause and Dooley 1997: 245). In many parts of India, educated unemployment bears most pressingly on men in their twenties or early thirties. But young women are also experiencing increased unemployment, and they are often exposed to reinforcing modes of subordination, as young people excluded by economic structures from salaried work and as women seeking to challenge entrenched gendered ideas (Miles 2002; Dyson 2019).

Unemployment and underemployment seemed likely to become key issues in the run up to the Indian elections in early 2019. This partly reflected a sharp increase in open unemployment in the 2010s. National Sample Survey Office (NSSO) data leaked to the media early in 2019 suggested that unemployment for rural male youth stood at 5 per cent in 2011 and jumped to 17 per cent in 2018. The parallel figures for young women were 5 per cent and 14 per cent.

Some have cast doubt on the NSSO's methodology. There are other reasons for questioning the gloom that may accompany the figures. Unemployment may reflect increased participation in education or even greater prosperity since families can temporarily 'afford' to keep their children in unemployment. But Mehrotra (2019) has challenged both those quibbling with the data and the argument that unemployment may be 'positive'. Mehrotra demonstrates that the number of 15–29-year-olds in India who are 'Not in Employment, Education or Training' (NEET) rose from 70 million in 2004 to 116 million in 2018. The proportion of NEETs grew at roughly 2 million a year between 2004 and 2012 and by 5 million a year between 2012 and 2016. Numerous stories circulate of there being over 500 applications for every open government post in India.

Despite sustained economic growth in the 2000s and 2010s, India's economy is clearly not creating enough jobs to cater for the estimated 1 million young people who emerge onto the job market every month in the country. Service sector job growth is weak and there has been an absolute fall in the number of manufacturing jobs in India (Mehrotra 2019). The figures on agricultural work are particularly alarming. During the 2000s the number of young people in agriculture declined, as would be expected in a modernizing economy. But in the 2010s there has been a substantial increase in the number of youth employed in farming (Mehrotra 2019). Many of these young people feel in some sense underemployed in agriculture and did not expect to return to the land.

Educated young people are not only unable to acquire secure salaried work, they also commonly lack the skills, aptitudes and contacts required to migrate in search of work or establish successful businesses (Jeffrey et al. 2008). This partly reflects the institutional environment in many parts of India, where high levels of crime, endemic corruption, and the poor physical infrastructure act as blocks to new forms of entrepreneurship (see Harriss-White 2003). In addition, the school, university and vocational training systems ill-prepare young people for establishing new ventures: they typically lack the necessary skills and motivation. In a recent India-wide survey, young people listed 'unemployment' as the most important challenge facing the country (see De Souza et al. 2009). In 2018 and 2019, there were numerous regional as well as metropolitan protests by young people on the issue of unemployment, including an especially vocal protest in Delhi in February 2019.

Scholars employing ethnographic methods have started to uncover the anxieties of educated unemployed youth in the 1990s, 2000s and 2010s in India. Jamie Cross (2009) focuses on lower middle-class youth unable to acquire prestigious jobs in a Special Economic Zone (SEZ) in Andhra Pradesh. Cross tracks the fortunes of unemployed young people who entered 'fallback work' in a diamond manufacturing plant. The work in the plant offered a measure of respect and an income higher than manual wage labour. Yet it also locked young people into hierarchical relationships within the company and prevented them from achieving further upward mobility. Cross writes of a generalized atmosphere of 'blighted hope' among these youth. Cross's work is more broadly indicative of research with educated unemployed youth in India, who are often unable to marry (see Chowdhry 2009), find it difficult to leave home and purchase or rent independent living space, and are commonly dogged by a sense of not having achieved locally salient notions of gendered success (Dyson and Jeffrey 2018).

Economists writing on the demographic dividend stress the capacity of young people to invest judiciously in their families and futures. But educated unemployed youth often appear to occupy a type of limbo in which the whole issue of planning a 'future' is rendered open to doubt. Jeffrey (2010) describes educated Jat young men in western UP who have acquired prolonged formal education but have been unable to obtain secure salaried work. Many of these men have responded by remaining in education, where they imagine themselves as people 'just passing the time' (doing 'timepass'). Timepass simultaneously conveys young men's sense of being detached from their education, plagued by feelings of surplus time, and left behind by Indian modernity. Many young men told Jeffrey that they are just 'waiting for their lives to change'. This haunting vision of youth frustration is reflected, too, in other writing. The author Pankaj Mishra (2006) has discussed towns in north India where young people appear to be waiting, and his novel on youth politics in Benares is full of images of youth in limbo (Mishra 2004). More recently, Morrow (2015) has described a widespread sense of limbo and ennui among youth in Andhra Pradesh.

The state aggravates problems of youth ennui. On the one hand, governmental agencies perceive jobless youth as threats to the state and civil society. In many places the state has resorted to strong-arm tactics and intimidation to police the behaviour of educated unemployed young people, especially men (see Jeffrey 2010). On the other hand, the state and other powerful organizations often identify young people as sources of hope and enjoin them to craft their own futures (see Gooptu 2007). The educated unemployed are 'responsibilized' – charged with finding their own, individual solutions to the problem of prolonged joblessness – at the same time as they are denigrated and disciplined by sections of the state.

Among those facing educated unemployment in India, SCs and STs are often especially disadvantaged (see also chapter 11). Chakravarthy and Somanathan (2008) have used an analysis of the occupational outcomes for college-leavers in Ahmedabad, Gujarat, to demonstrate that graduates belonging to SCs or STs receive significantly lower wages than those in the general category. Likewise, Deshpande and Newman (2007) found that university-educated Dalits' relatively scarce social and cultural capital relative to higher castes places them at a marked disadvantage in markets for graduate-level private-sector jobs.

Moodie's (2015) recent research with a small ST group in Rajasthan gives a sense of the challenges affecting many SCs and STs in an era of highly intense competition for white-collar work (see also Parry 2001). Moodie shows that Dhanka men in Jaipur City were able to use reservations to acquire government posts in the 1970s and 1980s. But the increasing privatization of utilities in the city means that younger men of the community are unable to obtain government positions. Vasavi (2019) has used long-term research with a single Dalit young man seeking government employment to explore in detail the obstacles that many Dalits face in pursuit of white-collar work in modern India (see also Patel 2017). Vasavi writes that reservations and related schemes aimed at empowerment, 'fail to address the embedded nature of discrimination, disadvantage, and internalized structures of inequality'.

Moodie (2015) also emphasizes the gendered nature of any upward mobility that has occurred: women and girls have rarely been encouraged to pursue education or employment via reservations in her Jaipur study area. There is a paucity of good recent research on young women's experience of educated unemployment, but the picture Moodie provides is likely to hold true for large sections of the youth population in provincial India, especially in the north. For example, Patel (2017) has described a growing number of educated underemployed young women in rural Gujarat. Educated unemployment among men may also have indirect negative effects on women's autonomy. For example, Chowdhry (2009) argues that parents' increased concern over young men's public behaviour in contemporary Haryana has sometimes led them to discipline young women more tightly within the household.

13.5 The Politics of Youth Unemployment

The emergence of a large cohort of frustrated educated unemployed youth in India raises pressing questions about the political future of the country. In the absence of a propitious institutional and infrastructural environment, the apparent advantage to a country of a large adult population may turn into a negative risk. A large unemployed youth population in postcolonial countries may lead to rising crime (e.g. Roitman 2004) and pose a security threat (Cincotta et al. 2003) – a 'demographic timebomb'. This is an argument that also comes across strongly in the 2011 *World Development Report*. The World Bank (2011: 81) uses a selection of surveys to argue that the main motivations for young people to become rebels or gang members have to do with unemployment rather than any type of ideological commitment. In an accompanying bar chart, the World Bank shows unemployment towering above two alternative motivations – 'revenge and a sense of injustice' or 'belief in the cause' – as triggers to violent gang activity and rebel activity.

The problems with the World Bank's report are legion: it conflates gang and rebel activity with violence, fails to specify how different grievances such as unemployment and injustice can be teased apart in a survey, and does not examine how unemployment is shaping politics in regions not affected by widespread violence. But the timebomb thesis deserves careful scrutiny. There are several more serious and careful studies that emphasize the reactionary, self-serving nature of educated unemployed young people's mobilization. For example, Hansen (1996a) describes how widespread exclusion from secure employment led lower middle-class young men in Bombay in the early 1990s to develop identities as Hindu nationalist political bosses. These men reconstructed a sense of masculine prowess through assuming roles as brokers between the urban poor and government officials. They also acted as provocateurs during anti-Muslim agitations and as 'hard men' capable of intervening violently to assist their friends (see also Heuzé 1992; chapter 10). Paralleling Hansen's account, Prem Chowdhry (2009) has studied unemployed young men in Haryana, north India, who channelled frustration into work in all-male caste *panchayats* (caste associations). These young men used the *panchayats* to engage in illegal reactionary political practices, for example violently punishing those who marry across caste boundaries.

The reactionary nature of unemployed young men's politics is also evident in journalist Snigdha Poonam's (2018) recent book, which documents how upper-caste Hindu men in their late teens and early twenties find solace from the disappointments of globalization in Hindu nationalist discourses. Her interviewees had come to expect much from life, given their exposure to discourses on youths' entrepreneurial potential from global media and the internet, yet were angered by their bleak prospects for secure employment when entering the job market. They have directed their anger at reservation policies for SC/ST youth and the 'old politics' of the Indian National Congress, including its commitments to secularism and democracy. They are drawn to *Hindutva* discourses – abundantly available on the internet – that tell them of the glories of India's past, which has been stolen from them by outsiders and is waiting to be reclaimed. Modi, in particular, is a source of inspiration, as he is seen as a break from the status quo and often speaks of the potential of youth to reclaim India's greatness. A post-poll survey found strong swings to the BJP amongst young Hindu voters in the 2019 election, particularly amongst those aged 18–27, and this was largely attributed to Modi's personal popularity (Mishra and Negi 2019).

Yet there is now evidence from many parts of the world that unemployed youth may also play a key role in progressive social and political change. Unemployed or underemployed young people were central to the success of many democratic anti-globalization movements in the period between the late 1990s and mid-2010s, including the Occupy Movement (see Schneider 2013) and World Social Forum (Fominaya 2010). There is also evidence of democratic activity among unemployed youth in India. Webb (2013) describes the importance of educated un/under-employed young people in the Right to Information movement in Delhi in the late 2000s. Likewise, Jeffrey (2010) has discussed the rise of higher caste and low-caste youth in western UP who style themselves as 'social reformers'. In addition to assisting the poor in their dealings with the state, they are often concerned to change society for the better, for example through campaigning on labour issues, dowry and education. In other parts of north India, unemployed youth have become involved in 'prefigurative politics' – embodying an ideal for the future in their present action – for example, by engaging in the construction and repair of civic infrastructure and developing sports clubs and facilities for children (Jeffrey and Dyson 2016). Youth recognize these activities as ultimately being the responsibility of the state, yet, in the absence of effective state action, they have chosen to undertake them themselves.

Another way in which unemployed or underemployed young people may contribute to wider society is via the role they commonly play as educators or advisors to children (see Klenk 2010; Dyson and Jeffrey 2018). Youth in India have often responded to joblessness by working as tutors or establishing private schools. Even where they do not act as educators, they may help younger children with homework, advise them on schooling decisions and guide them with regard to employment. The rapid pace of socio-economic change in many parts of India means that parents are sometimes poorly positioned with respect to advising children in these areas. Youth in their late teens, twenties and early thirties act as a type of 'interstitial generation', mentoring and guiding younger children. As Mannheim (1972) argued in his classic writing on generations, particular age cohorts, because they have experienced similar social forces at the same stages of life, may feel a sense of generational solidarity, and in certain circumstances they may act on these bonds to try to change society. This is a type of 'demographic dividend', if not the one anticipated by economists.

13.6 Conclusions

The reasons for India's failure to take more immediate advantage of its large youth population are multiple. Corruption, poor physical infrastructure, educational decay and inadequate health services are all well-known impediments to broad-based social development, as we have noted in other chapters of this book. In this chapter we have focused on two of the most pressing difficulties that young people face in developing their own human capital: the poor quality of mass education in India and the absence of secure salaried jobs in many parts of the country.

China provides something of a counterpoint to India. China was able to take advantage of its demographic dividend in the 1980s and 1990s because it was relatively successful in ensuring that children receive a meaningful elementary education and in guaranteeing some degree of healthcare to the mass of the population (Drèze and Sen 2013). Compared to India's northern states, China had a relatively good infrastructure and lower levels of corruption.

There are nevertheless at least three signs of hope in India. First, the state is expending increasing effort on trying to improve the prospects for people in their late teens and twenties in the country. The recent government efforts to craft a new education policy to widen access to education are indicative of this trend, as is the rapid expansion of public development projects (see chapter 4). Second, NGO activity in the realms of education, and to a lesser extent unemployment, is burgeoning. Third, young people themselves, including the educated unemployed, are becoming involved in public action. As the recent proliferation of youth-led social movements around the world would attest, a youth generation hardened by dispiriting experiences may emerge as agents of change.

AFTERWORD

14

Afterword:
Is India Now a 'Leading Power'?

14.1 Introduction: India's Transformations and the
International Arena

The story that we have told through the chapters of this book is one of the transformations of India over the final years of the twentieth century and the first two decades of the twenty-first. In this period India has been reinvented, social continuities and elements of path dependency in economic development notwithstanding. We argued in the first chapter that modern, independent India was subject to particular acts of invention, mainly through the Constitution that was drawn up between 1946 and 1950. India was to be a democracy, with a broadly 'socialist' economic orientation. It was to be secular in the distinctive sense that all faiths were to be treated with equal respect. And it was to be a federation of states, though one with a strong central government. All four of these founding myths have been supplanted – or at least, in the case of federalism, called into question.

Through the first four decades of independence, India's mixed economy, in which the state played a leading role, and which was very little integrated into the international economy, saw generally low and always erratic rates of growth. India was known internationally as the archetypal poor developing country. The 'socialist' pattern was modified in the 1980s, and was finally overturned with the 'economic reforms' that began to be implemented in 1991. Since then, India's economy has been increasingly integrated into the global economy; the country has experienced generally high and much less variable rates of economic growth; and India has become the third largest economy in the world. While concerns about the poverty of many Indians remain pressing, the country is known as much for its fabulously wealthy businessmen and apparently thriving middle class. It has been quite a transformation, even if doubts remain about its sustainability – and not least its environmental sustainability, with ever mounting evidence of environmental degradation and of the exhaustion of critical resources. Even of water. India resembles rather the Gilded Age of late nineteenth-century American capitalism – the age of the 'Robber Barons' – than any kind of socialism. The 'Gilded Age' was a period in which there came about both rapid economic growth and concentration of wealth, in a context of extensive relationships between big business and government. This seems to many observers also to describe India in the early twenty-first century (Walton 2020).

We have argued that while India has sustained its electoral democracy remarkably well, its achievements in regard to substantive democracy have been much more limited. Large numbers of Indians, especially those from the Scheduled Castes and Tribes, and Muslims, are subject to different forms of exclusion. Caste and hierarchy are remarkably enduring features of Indian society. But we also believe that the electoral dominance that has been established by the Hindu nationalist party, the BJP, in the second decade of this century has brought about a serious weakening of the institutions of liberal democracy. India is becoming the Hindu rashtra long sought by Hindu nationalists. It is a majoritarian state, in which civil liberties and the rights of minorities are circumscribed, and the fundamental freedoms of expression, of association and of religion are in jeopardy. The state has arrogated to itself arbitrary powers, generally in the name of 'security', that can be used to suppress democratic dissent. There is opposition, on the parts of labour and agrarian classes, and from some among the middle classes. There are contrary trends in society, no doubt, but the ruling party is able to use its claims that it is acting on the part of 'the people' as a very effective counter. The Modi-led BJP regime used its powers to undercut the constitutional conventions of Indian federalism when it intervened in Kashmir in August 2019. As the Varieties of Democracy (V-Dem) Report that we referred to in chapter 7 shows, India is one of several countries now at risk of 'autocratization'.

In this final chapter we take up the question of the implications of the transformations that India has experienced for its place in the world. In doing so we must, of course, take account as well of the changes that have taken place in international relations over the period from the late twentieth century: notably, of the end of the Cold War, and its implications; of the rise of China and of multi-polarity; and latterly, of the uncertainty introduced into international relations by the behaviour of the US President, Donald Trump.

Indian elites have always thought that their country must be a major power, by virtue of its size, its history as a great civilization, and – for some of them, anyway – because of the values and principles for which they believe it stands. These elites have very often been frustrated by the ways in which India, as they have seen it, has been disregarded in international affairs. But Indians have not been alone in having high expectations regarding their country's place in the world. Such international authorities as the former US Secretary of State, Henry Kissinger, and an eminent Harvard professor, the late Samuel Huntington, have, at different times expressed the view that India must join the ranks of the great powers (Nayar and Paul 2003: 10). There is an arc represented, perhaps, in the titles of books written in this century. In 2003 Baldev Raj Nayar and T. V. Paul published their book *India in the World Order: Searching for Major Power Status*, the sub-title suggesting that India still had a way to go. Fifteen years later, in 2018, a book by Alyssa Ayres, an American specialist and sometime Deputy Assistant Secretary of State for South Asia, carried the title *Our Time Has Come: How India is Making its Place in the World*. Ayres took the first part of her title from statements made both by Manmohan Singh and then later by Narendra Modi, as prime ministers of India. In 2007 Singh said in a speech, 'I am confident that our time has come. India is all set to regain its due place in the comity of nations'. In 2015 Narendra Modi said something very similar: 'Now it is India's turn. And we know that our time has come' (cited by Ayres 2018: 9). Has India's 'time come'? Is India *searching* no more for major power status? Is there now confidence among elites about India's place in the world?

Dr S. Jaishankar, then the Foreign Secretary of India (that is, the senior-most civil servant in the Ministry of External Affairs), and later (from May 2019) India's Foreign Minister, certainly reflected confidence in a speech in Singapore in 2015, when he said that over the last year, since the election of Narendra Modi, there had come about 'the emergence of a very differ-ent global sentiment in regard to this nation [India]' (Jaishankar 2015). And indeed Modi – who had never before shown much interest in foreign affairs – had surprised almost everyone in India by the energy he had displayed in regard to international affairs from the very beginning of his premiership. He had invited the heads of all the countries in the South Asian Association for Regional Cooperation (SAARC), including the then prime minister of Pakistan, Nawaz Sharif, to his swearing-in ceremony. This was a controversial move, but evidently intended to re-launch negotiations with Pakistan. Modi proceeded to make trips to many countries, some of them, such as his visit to France in the spring of 2015, very high profile. In his maiden speech before the UN General Assembly in September 2014, he had asked world leaders to recognize and observe an international Yoga Day – and this was subsequently agreed by the UN, and first celebrated on 21 June 2015. There was justification, therefore, for his claim, in a speech made in Silicon Valley later in the year, that 'The whole world, that until yesterday saw India at the margins, today sees India as a focal point' (cited by Ayres 2018: 32). There is no doubt that the wishes of very many Indians that their country be respected in the world, go a good way to accounting for the support that Modi has commanded.

Modi went on to visit more than 50 countries in his first period in office – not actually all that many more than his predecessors, but many of the visits attracted massive public attention in a way that was unprecedented. The ques-tion may be asked, however, as to what resulted from these visits. Jaishankar, in the Singapore speech of 2015, after describing the early achievements of the Modi administration, concluded: 'The transition in India is an expression of greater self-confidence. Its foreign policy dimension is to *aspire* to be a leading power, rather than just a balancing power' (Jaishankar 2015, emphasis added).

The argument of this chapter is that India has indeed become a much more significant player in international affairs since the end of the twentieth century, and taken on a more visible leadership role. But the country remains 'a cautious power' (Ayres' words, though they echo the views of other scholars). Though Narendra Modi, as prime minister, has taken some initiatives, he has not introduced any radical departures from previous policies, except perhaps in regard to Pakistan. India's responses to terrorist attacks, such as that on the Indian army base at Uri, in Kashmir, in January 2016, and most strikingly following the attack on security forces at Pulwama, also in Kashmir, in February 2019 – when, in response, India launched an air strike into Pakistan – have been much sharper and have marked 'a new Indian willingness to call Pakistan's bluff on the threat of nuclear weapons' (Ayres 2018: 131). Indian ambitions to become a leading power are still constrained by structural weaknesses and by the country's continuing need to manage relationships with the United States and China, which are complicated by the threat from Pakistan. India's room for manoeuvre is still effectively contained by the United States, China and Pakistan. On the one hand, there is the danger that India becomes a junior partner to the United States. On the other, there is a serious threat from China. And there is always Pakistan at India's back, complicating relationships with the two great powers, and diverting manpower and resources – even if, as Ayres suggests, 'Pakistan does not existentially challenge India's rise' (2018: 132), India now being in a different league in terms of economic strength and military capability.

14.2 Coming in from the Margins: India in the World in the Late Twentieth Century

Following the achievement of independence from colonial rule in 1947, India was effectively the pre-eminent power in Asia, and the country enjoyed significant prestige internationally. India's influence was, to a significant extent, due to the personal stature of Jawaharlal Nehru, who became recognized as perhaps the most significant leader of the countries in what came to be described as the 'Third World'. The idea of 'non-alignment', formulated by Nehru – who held the External Affairs portfolio in government, as well as the position of prime minister, until his death in May 1964 – later became identified with hostility to the West, but this was not Nehru's conception of it. Understandably, given the experience of the long struggle to achieve freedom from colonial rule, Nehru sought to ensure that India remained fully independent. This was one of the drivers of the economic policies that were pursued by the governments that he headed. India must be self-reliant, and policies of import substitution industrialization were intended to achieve this objective. In international affairs India should avoid alignment with either of the contending superpowers, and stand outside international regimes in which it had no real say. But non-alignment meant more than this. Nehru had a vision of a world that was not divided into contending blocs, which he saw as inevitably perpetuating the cycle of war. Unlike his mentor, Gandhi, Nehru was not a pacifist, though he sought to avoid war. His was a value-driven foreign policy, and India was able to exercise a good deal of 'soft power' because of it, and in spite of its relative lack of conventional power.

Nehru's approach has continued to influence Indian foreign policy over the decades following his death. Even in 2019, C. Raja Mohan – an influential writer on Indian foreign policy – argued (in an article in *The Indian Express*, 15 January 2019) that non-alignment remains 'a continuing preoccupation' of the Indian foreign policy establishment, in theory if not in practice. Non-alignment, too, has a kind of avatar in the more recent concept of 'strategic autonomy', described by Raja Mohan as 'at once vague and central to Indian foreign policy after the Cold War' (*The Indian Express*, 18 September 2018). It was reaffirmed by Narendra Modi in a speech in 2018. It seems to mean in practice that India seeks equivalent relationships with the United States, China and Russia ('multiple alignment'), as a way of trying to ensure independence in matters of foreign policy and security.

Indian neutrality in the 1950s and 1960s gave the country some leverage in regard to the two superpowers, and sometimes played to its advantage in regard to development assistance (Engerman 2018). But India was generally regarded negatively by policy makers in the United States, and seen as being implicitly hostile. In 1954 the US launched a programme of military aid to Pakistan, and though this was represented by American spokesmen (and later, by American scholars) as being a move intended to contain the Soviet Union, there is good evidence that US support for Pakistan was a deliberate move aimed at balancing against Indian power in the subcontinent (Nayar and Paul 2003: 146–9). It led Nehru to look to developing diplomatic relationships with the Soviet Union and with China. India and China held, by this time, what was in many ways, a comparable position in Asia and in the world, both being potentially significant powers by virtue of their physical size and the numbers of their peoples, and because of their histories as major civilizations. But China had been deemed a 'great power' as one of the victors in the Second World War, and had become one of the five members of the United Nations Security Council. This had happened, of course, before the Communist Party of China secured victory in the civil war in 1949. Nehru aimed to achieve a kind of balance of power with Communist China through the principles of peaceful coexistence that were contained in the Panchsheel Agreement, concluded with China in 1954. The late 1950s saw what was apparently a developing friendship between India and China ('Hindi-Chini *bhai bhai*' – 'India China brothers' – as it was called). But Nehru underestimated the Chinese, and in 1962 India suffered a crushing defeat in a border war with China (there is a border of over 4,000 kilometres between the countries, and a big stretch of it is still disputed). This event reduced India's standing in the world, exposed the idealism of a foreign policy based on the principles of non-alignment, and brought about a gradual shift in India's defence and foreign policy orientation. There was a recognition that the country had to build its conventional power and strengthen the armed forces. The United States sought to use the moment to force India to make concessions to Pakistan over Kashmir, in return for military assistance. This India stoutly resisted. The Soviet Union, meanwhile, proved very willing to help India, and the two countries embarked on an arms-acquisition relationship that went on, unbroken, until 1991, and has subsequently been continued with Russia. Indian policy makers continued to state loyalty to the principles of non-alignment, but in practice, given the American position, they had little choice but to tilt to the other superpower.

Following the China War, India became of rather marginal significance in international affairs. Some commentators are critical of India's leaders over the succeeding thirty years for what they see as failure to formulate a coherent strategy and unwillingness to adopt a more forceful stance in international affairs. Nayar and Paul, however, are more sympathetic, and argue that Shastri, after Nehru, and then Indira Gandhi and her son Rajiv, through their long periods in office, never lost sight of the aspiration for India to achieve the status of a major power. There was, they say, a 'long march for capabilities, 1964–1990' (Nayar and Paul 2003: ch. 5). These leaders succeeded, the two authors suggest, in building up India's conventional power, in spite of severe constraints. They were constrained by the failures of India's economic development, which compromised Indian independence in the 1950s and 1960s because of the need both for financial assistance and for food aid. These made India dependent upon the West and particularly on the United States, which sometimes exercised influence on Indian government policy, particularly through its control over the supply of food aid to the country. This dependence was a factor in encouraging Indian governments to adopt the New Agricultural Strategy in the 1960s, and to pursue food security through the green revolution (see chapter 4). The state of the Indian economy and domestic political problems, as well as regional conflicts in South Asia, constrained India's leaders in the international sphere. At the same time, they had to contend with encirclement because of US support for Pakistan, and the rising power of China, which carried out its first nuclear test in October 1964. Then, from the early 1970s the developing friendship between the United States and China (President Richard Nixon made his famous visit to Beijing to talk to Chairman Mao Zedong in February 1972), and China's continuing support for Pakistan, made the encirclement more or less complete. Both the United States and China focused on support for Pakistan as part of a larger strategy against the Soviet Union. India, even as a middle power, was effectively marginalized by these great powers. How was India to break out of this containment?

Indian Nuclear Policy

Jawaharlal Nehru abhorred the atomic bomb and was a strong supporter of nuclear disarmament, but at the same time he was deeply concerned that India should not be left behind in nuclear technology. For him, the building up of capabilities in science and technology was essential for India's modernization and for her independence: 'there is a special importance', he said, 'for science in a country which is not to be wholly dependent on other countries, and which has to build some capacity for self-growth, self-reliance'. While he was adamant that India would not 'go in for making atomic bombs . . . we are equally determined not be left behind in the advance in the use of this new power' (quotes from Nehru's speeches, cited by Nayar and Paul 2003: 155). The Constituent Assembly debated atomic energy in 1948, and the Indian Atomic Energy Commission was established in the same year. For all his opposition to nuclear weapons, Nehru sought the development of India's nuclear capabilities to the point where the country would be able to exercise the nuclear option, if it had to (Nayar and Paul 2003: 157; and Abraham 1999).

The China War of 1962 and then the Chinese nuclear test of 1964 became the stimuli for India's active pursuit of this option, and Lal Bahadur Shastri, in his brief period in office as prime minister, before his death in 1966, ordered Indian scientists to work on the preparation of what was described as a 'peaceful nuclear explosion'. This was in a context in which the United States actively sought to prevent India's acquisition of nuclear and space capabilities. Together with the Soviet Union, the United States pushed for a Nuclear Non-Proliferation Treaty (NNPT), to be based on the principle of containing the possession of nuclear weapons to the five countries that had conducted nuclear tests by 1 January 1967 (the US, USSR, UK, France and China – defined as Nuclear Weapons States [NWS]). Other countries were to commit not to acquire nuclear weapons in exchange for the commitment on the part of the NWS to the sharing of the benefits of nuclear technology, and to working to bring about nuclear disarmament. Indian policy makers may have been forgiven for thinking that the NNPT was directed particularly against India, as the country that, at the time, was outstanding in having both a strong incentive for developing nuclear weapons and the capability of doing it. They argued, in return, against the Treaty because of its fundamentally discriminatory nature – threatening to ensure the continuation of the existing distribution of power that was unfavourable to India – and India refused to sign in 1968, formally on moral and political grounds but with the underlying objective of keeping its options open.

Shortly afterwards, in 1971, when India went to war again with Pakistan and was instrumental in securing the independence of Bangladesh, the country confronted the outright opposition of the United States. India was accused at one point of being the aggressor, and a US naval task force was dispatched to the Bay of Bengal – though only after India had achieved its war aims. Indian suspicions of the United States inevitably hardened; and the country's reliance on a formal security relationship with the USSR, following the signing of the Indo-Soviet Treaty of Peace, Friendship and Cooperation in August 1971, was further deepened. Mrs Gandhi took the important step of renouncing the purchase of food from the US on a concessional basis – an important marker of India's independence. The United States' action in the Bangladesh war was also the provocation for India's 'peaceful nuclear explosion' of May 1974 – while being, at the same time, a show of independence in regard to the USSR. A keen critic of the government, Raj Thapar, wrote in her memoirs, 'Hate as I did every bit of nuclear experimentation, convinced that it was a sad and cruel waste for starving countries such as ours, I couldn't escape the current of glee that streaked through me at the thought of what other nations would say – they wouldn't be able to kick us around as before' (Raj Thapar, cited by Abraham 1999: 1).

India did not proceed any further, however, toward the development of nuclear weapons capability until the 1980s. Then, given the need of the United States for the support of Pakistan against the Soviet army that had invaded Afghanistan in 1979 (following not long after the US had lost what had been hitherto an important ally in the region, in Iran, after the fall of the Shah), the Americans relaxed their concerns about Pakistan's nuclear programme. It was in response to evidence of the inaction of the Americans in regard to the Pakistani programme that Rajiv Gandhi, as India's prime minister – in spite of his own earlier forcefully stated opposition to nuclear weapons – in 1988 gave the go-ahead to the Indian nuclear establishment to build India's bomb. The needs of national security required that India go for the nuclear option, exactly as Jawaharlal Nehru had thought – even if with regret – might one day be necessary. India's nuclear tests did not take place, however, for another ten years. This was in a context in which India again confronted containment, this time by the Clinton administration's efforts to secure the adoption by the United Nations of the Comprehensive Test Ban Treaty (CTBT) (which took place in September 1996). Nonetheless, Nayar and Paul are justified in arguing that 'The nuclear Rubicon was in reality . . . crossed in the 1980s' (Nayar and Paul 2003: 200). When they finally came, the tests of May 1998 marked an important shift in India's position in geopolitics. They were greeted with euphoria across the country, for exactly the same sorts of reasons as those expressed by Raj Thapar in 1974 – 'they wouldn't be able to kick us around' any more. Raja Mohan put it, more sedately, that the tests 'redefined India's approach to the question of power' (2004: xv). The country had emphatically come in from the margins.

14.3 After the Cold War: An 'Emerging and Responsible Power'?

A great deal had changed in South Asia before the nuclear tests of 1998. The end of the Cold War changed geopolitics, and – for a time – the world experienced a unipolar moment, with the United States as the only great power. Major changes in India coincided with this event, with the shift in economic policy in 1991 that took much further the process of integrating India more than before into the international, or now 'global economy' (see chapter 2). The new economic policy, and integration into the global economy, in the unipolar moment that followed the disappearance of the Soviet Union, made for a powerful set of incentives for India to seek a new engagement with the West, and with the United States in particular, as the most important economic and technological power. India now needed trade and foreign investment, not aid, and had new needs in relation to commercial diplomacy, as well as confronting the necessity of dealing with the remaining superpower. But India's improved economic performance – that, as we saw in chapter 2, started somewhat before the 'economic reforms' – also brought both new opportunities and incentives for rethinking foreign policy. Raja Mohan, in a study of Indian foreign policy after 1990, argues that in this time, 'The absolute increase in its military and economic resources began to compel India to think less like a developing, non-aligned country and more like an emerging and responsible power' (2015: 131). There was, necessarily, rethinking in regard to foreign policy, though Raja Mohan emphasizes that it generally involved incremental change, and built on initiatives that were undertaken in the 1980s.

Both Indira and Rajiv Gandhi had sought in the 1980s to reach out to the United States, but with little success, and India still remained of little account in the calculations of the Clinton administration in the early to mid-1990s. There was very little geopolitical reason for the United States to respond to Indian approaches; there were concerns in the West, where there was an emerging humanitarian agenda, about human rights violations in Kashmir and elsewhere in India; and in the aftermath of the Gulf War of 1990–91 there was a renewed focus on the proliferation of nuclear weapons, with concerns focused especially, at this point, on India and Pakistan. But the Indian nuclear tests of 1998 (followed immediately by tests by Pakistan), though they were met immediately with international condemnation and the imposition of sanctions, had the effect of bringing about an intensive engagement between India and the United States. The United States failed to isolate India partly because of the support that India won from both Russia and France – both looking towards a multipolar world – and so turned to 'strategic dialogue rather than marginalizing (India) as it had done before' (Nayar and Paul 2003: 248). India could be ignored no longer. Another factor was that an Indian government headed by the BJP was much more comfortable with a close relationship with the United States than Congress governments had been, given both their inheritance of the experience of being pushed around by American presidents, and the continuing influence upon them of the concept of non-alignment.

President Clinton made a successful visit to India in 2000 – the first visit by an American president for twenty-two years. But friction remained over nuclear weapons. George W. Bush, however, as President sought to achieve greater cooperation with India as a means of balancing the inexorable rise of Chinese power in Asia – recognizing that on this vital strategic matter the national interests of India and the United States coincided (Blackwill and Tellis 2019). In response to an initiative made by Bush in 2005, Manmohan Singh, as India's prime minister, agreed to separate India's civil and military nuclear programmes. The two countries eventually reached an agreement in 2008 under which they resumed cooperation on civilian nuclear energy, and the United States gave up its long-standing insistence that India must relinquish its nuclear weapons. Manmohan Singh had to invest a great deal of political capital to secure the deal on the Indian side, confronting heavy domestic criticism for what was represented as Indian subservience to US imperialism. The agreement opened the way, however, to greatly increased US investments in India and to much more liberal access for India to military technology.

Barack Obama as US President followed the line of the Bush administration in regard to India, albeit with less enthusiasm, but the relationship marked time after Obama's visit in 2010, when the second UPA government ran into increasing difficulties domestically over corruption charges. These badly affected its confidence in regard to foreign policy. Subsequently it was evidently a priority of Narendra Modi's, following his election in 2014, to reinvigorate ties with the US. His invitation to Obama to participate in India's Republic Day celebration in January 2015 was followed by the publication of the 'US–India Joint Strategic Vision for Asia-Pacific and the Indian Ocean', in which Indian policy makers, breaking with the past, supported the US goal of 'ensuring freedom of navigation and over flight throughout the region, especially in the South China Sea'. In August 2016 the two countries further consolidated their strategic relationship with the Logistics Exchange Memorandum of Agreement (LEMOA). This has made for increased military cooperation, including the expansion of joint military exercises and intelligence sharing.

American strategists recognize that a strong India is in the interests of the United States, and regret the fact that Donald Trump, as President, has generally ignored the importance of American alliances in Asia in the face of the rise of China, showing concern only with trade issues. In regard to India, Trump has focused on what he sees as an unbalanced trade relationship, describing Modi on one occasion as 'the tariff king'. He greeted Modi's inauguration for the second time in 2019, churlishly, by withdrawing India's privileged trade access to the United States. India has been constrained, too, following Trump's withdrawal of the United States from the 2015 nuclear agreement with Iran – which India had strongly supported – to reduce its oil imports from the country, though partnership with Iran has long been important for India. It was thought that an Indian deal with Russia for the purchase of an air defence system, concluded in 2018, might lead to the imposition of further sanctions by Washington (Blackwill and Tellis 2019).

On the Indian side, ties with the United States, though they stop short of formal alliance – and must stop short of formal alliance in view of India's long-standing concerns regarding its independence and sovereignty – are still a top priority. They interlink with India's determination to become the leading provider of security in the Indian Ocean region, laid out in the National Maritime Security Strategy of 2015, and in the service of which there are ambitious plans for building the strength of the Indian navy (Ayres 2018: 105–6). As the country has become increasingly connected with the world economically and as the economy has grown, further increasing dependence on imported supplies of energy and raw materials, so, in the words of the 'Foreword' to the Maritime Strategy, India's 'dependence on her maritime environment [has expanded] substantially ... and her national security imperatives and political interests stretched gradually beyond the Indian Ocean Region'. An important instance of the latter – of India's interests stretching beyond the Indian Ocean – is the support that India has given to Vietnam in its dispute with China in the South China Sea, also motivated by the quest for energy resources in the coastal areas of Vietnam.

India's drive to build naval strength and to become the 'net security provider in the Indian Ocean and beyond' – in words used by US Secretaries of Defense (Ayres 2019; but see also Raja Mohan 2015: 138) – has been spurred as well by the way in which China has been expanding its power across the region, developing ties with Bangladesh, Sri Lanka and the Maldives, as well as with Pakistan, as part of a network of military and commercial facilities on the seaways between mainland China and the Horn of Africa. This 'String of Pearls' strategy includes big infrastructural investments by China in port facilities at Gwadar in Pakistan; in Colombo and at Hambantota, in southern Sri Lanka; and at Chittagong in Bangladesh. Though these are all said to have only commercial objectives, the ports are financed through loans and may be financially unviable, and in this case, because of debt, countries may make significant concessions on sovereignty (Mullen 2018). Such 'debt-trap diplomacy' led the Government of Sri Lanka to conclude a deal under which control of commercial activity in the loss-making Hambantota port, together with 15,000 acres of land, were handed over to a Chinese company on a 99-year lease (*New York Times*, 25 June 2018). Visits of Chinese naval vessels to some of these facilities have confirmed Indian suspicions that they also have a military intent, while the investments at Gwadar connect with Chinese investment, as well, in the China Pakistan Economic Corridor (CPEC) that runs through the Gilgit-Balistan part of Kashmir that is claimed by India. The CPEC is a part of China's Belt and Road Initiative that is aimed ultimately at connecting China with Europe. India has steadfastly refused to participate, principally because of the CPEC – and has sought to counter the Chinese initiative through collaboration with Japan in infrastructural investments elsewhere in South Asia and in South-East Asia and Africa. India, faced as well with ongoing tensions on the border with China – there was a prolonged confrontation at Doklam, in a disputed part of Bhutan, in 2017 – and the possibility that dams constructed in Tibet can limit the flow of water into India, understandably fears encirclement by China.

India's relationship with China is complicated by the fact that trade and economic ties between the countries have greatly expanded, with China having become India's largest trade partner in goods in 2006. Though the balance of trade is greatly in China's favour, Indian governments have 'used economic ties as a positive offset for unresolved security problems' (Ayres 2018: 129), and, as fellow BRICS, the two Asian giants have sometimes made common cause. The grouping of the 'emerging economies' of Brazil, Russia, India, China and South Africa started to take on an organizational shape in 2006, following the coinage of the term 'BRIC' by a Goldman Sachs economist, Jim O'Neill, in 2003, recognizing the emerging economic clout of these big countries. India has made a strong commitment to the BRICS as a coordinated group, including giving strong support to the New Development Bank, set up by the BRICS and described as 'an alternative to the existing US-dominated World Bank and International Monetary Fund' (Ayres 2018: 170). India has been somewhat supportive too, of the Asian Infrastructure Investment Bank, which is led by China. But India has to tread with great caution in regard to China.

Still, Raja Mohan's argument that after 1990 India has no longer been a 'non-aligned developing country' is incontrovertible, and the country unquestionably has a more significant presence in international affairs. It has sought to improve relationships within South Asia – it being recognized by India's leaders that 'a peaceful neighbourhood was crucial to achieving a larger Indian role in the world' (Raja Mohan 2015: 138) – and has rebuilt relationships outside its immediate region, in the Middle East, in South-East Asia and in Africa. These had become weakened in the years of the Cold War, but are ever more important for India's energy security, for raw materials, and as markets. India has developed close ties with ASEAN (the Association of Southeast Asian Nations), strong links with Japan, and has become a full member (as has Pakistan) of the Shanghai Cooperation Organization, founded in 1996 by China and Russia with the erstwhile Soviet Central Asian states (Kazakhstan, Kyrgyz, Tajikistan and Uzbekistan). The country has done something to invigorate the Indian Ocean Rim Association for Regional Cooperation, and created the Indian Ocean Naval Symposium (in 2008) to bring together the navies from across the region. It has injected more energy into the Bay of Bengal Initiative for Multi-Sectoral Technical and Economic Cooperation (BIMSTEC). An India–Africa Forum was started by the UPA government in 2008, and has been expanded by the Modi government, along with a stepping up of development assistance to Africa.

How Much Difference Has Modi Made?

Dr S. Jaishankar's speech in Singapore in 2015 made a strong claim for the impact of Narendra Modi on India's foreign policy and the country's international relations, yet much of what Jaishankar referred to represented the continuation of the policies pursued by Modi's predecessors. Certainly Modi's invitation to the leaders of the other South Asian countries to the swearing-in of his government was a bold move, and his promises of greater connectivity and cooperation were followed up – as, for example, with the final settlement of a long-running boundary dispute with Bangladesh. But this was really about bringing more energy into the policies of earlier administrations. Modi's initiative in reaching out to Nawaz Sharif soon foundered, as had many previous Indian attempts at entering into dialogue with Pakistan, with further cross-border incidents, and then a meeting between the Pakistani High Commissioner in India and Kashmiri separatist leaders – which led to the cancellation by India of scheduled talks between the Foreign Secretaries of the two countries. Conciliatory gestures towards Pakistan failed again, running up against the continuing hostility of the Pakistan military, and the provocations of terrorist attacks on Indian bases. Subsequently, as we noted earlier, there has been a shift in policy in regard to Pakistan, as the Modi government has been ready to adopt a more assertive response to cross-border terrorism.

The announcement of the 'US–India Joint Strategic Vision for Asia-Pacific and the Indian Ocean' at the time of Obama's visit in January 2015 was a significant event, as Jaishankar argued, but built on improvements in India–US relations from the time of the premiership of Manmohan Singh. Modi has strengthened relationships with Japan, especially, and with Australia – and the three countries, India, Japan and Australia, responded favourably to the attempt of the Trump administration in 2017 to revive the Quadrilateral Security Dialogue, between them and the United States. This had been initiated in 2007 but then lapsed. Its renewal is clearly a move to counter China. And India's relationships with China have not changed in a meaningful way, the agreement between Narendra Modi and Xi Jinping at the time of their first meeting, 'to pursue national development goals and security interests in a mutually supportive manner', and India's participation in institutions sponsored by China, notwithstanding. This has not prevented the continuation and even escalation of tensions in the disputed border areas, and India's naval strategy continues to confront China's expansion.

One way in which Modi has gone beyond the efforts of previous prime ministers has been in regard to the Indian diaspora – which now numbers around 30 million people around the world. India has long recognized the significance of the diaspora and aimed both to make use especially of the wealthier and more powerful people within it, and to celebrate their achievements. Modi has sought them out on his visits overseas, and has on occasion addressed rapturous crowds. He seems to have aimed deliberately to make them an instrument of India's foreign policy – and to make them also into a significant base of support. This may have realized a dividend for him in the 2019 election (Smyth and Findlay 2019).

Overall, though, we find convincing the conclusion reached by the members of a panel of specialists that considered India's foreign policy under Modi. Policy has seen incremental change rather than sharp breaks – so it is not 'a new brand' (Gupta et al. 2019).

14.4 Conclusion: Still an Aspirant as a 'Leading Power'

India has been playing a more assertive role in international affairs since the 1990s, when the country finally crossed the nuclear Rubicon, though its foreign policy has continued to be informed by the doctrine of 'strategic autonomy' (Raja Mohan 2015; Bhatia 2019). The country has at least some of the capabilities of a major power. India's more assertive role has been based upon, and in part required by, the country's rapid and sustained economic growth (even if not sustained at the high levels that are required for it to enter the ranks of the higher income countries over the medium term), and upon the fact that it is now one of the three biggest economies in the world. It is a nuclear power, albeit still a small one, and in the Agni V, it has a missile that is capable of reaching targets over most of Asia (NDTV 2016). It has significant naval strength, and it has extended its naval reach into the South China Sea. It has a large – though (at the time of writing) still poorly equipped – air force, and a big army. It has advanced space technology, even if, in September 2019, the attempt to land a vehicle on the moon was a partial failure. But economic size does not automatically translate into power, and India continues to be constrained by particular weaknesses. Though some segments of Indian industry are internationally competitive, the country is not an industrial innovator. It enjoys the doubtful distinction of being the world's biggest arms importer – a doubtful distinction because it follows from the fact that India depends upon imports of arms. Foreign content accounted for 70 per cent of India's weaponry in 2013 (Ganguly 2015). Building up the defence industries calls not only for foreign investment for the transfer of technology but also for a major effort in local research and development to absorb and indigenize the technology. And India is heavily dependent upon imports of energy and other resources. We have emphasized, too, the extent of environmental degradation in India, and the probability that economic growth will very soon confront severe shortage of water. All these points are elaborated by Sridharan (2015), who also emphasizes that China does much better than India on every indicator of power. China is a 'system-shaping' economic power. India is certainly not – though it may be, in the future.

India is still constrained from achieving 'strategic influence', to use Raja Mohan's (2015) term – which is surely the qualification for becoming a 'leading power' – by the need to maintain a strong relationship with the United States, while still keeping up ties, especially over defence procurement, with Russia, in order to contain the growing influence of China even within the Indian Ocean region. 'Strategic autonomy', fuzzy term though it is, perhaps does quite well describe India's positioning in a multi-polar world. And though much more powerful than Pakistan, India continues to be constrained even within its own region by its neighbour to the West. It may be that the transformation of India into the majoritarian Hindu rashtra will drive the country to be more aggressive in regard to Pakistan, with consequences that there is every reason to fear.

Glossary

Adivasi	indigenous people; Scheduled Tribes
Bhagavad Gita	Hindu scriptural text (part of the *Mahabharata*); seen as a 'manual for mankind'
biradiri	'brotherhood'; a local kinship group
Brahman	the castes of priests and literati of the *varna* scheme
Dalit	Marathi word for Untouchable; the 'oppressed'
Dan	gift
Dharma	religious duty, law, and custom
gau raksha, gau rakshak	cow protection; cow protection volunteer
ghar wapsi	'homecoming'
gram panchayat	village council
gram sabha	village meeting
Harijan	'children of God': term used by Gandhi for 'unclean' or 'Untouchable' castes
Hindu rashtra	the Hindu nation, or state
Hindutva	literally, 'Hindu-ness', the idea of Hinduism as India's national faith
Jai Shri Ram	religious chant meaning 'Victory to Lord Rama' or 'Hail Lord Rama'
Jajmani	term for the traditional relationships among castes in a locality
jati	caste in the sense of a named 'birth group'
kar sevak	a volunteer in the movement to build a temple for Ram at Ayodhya
khap	a clan or group of clans, esp. among Jats of northern India
Kshatriya	the castes of princes and warriors of the *varna* scheme
Lok Sabha	'House of the People', the lower house of the Indian parliament
Mahant	chief priest of a Hindu temple or monastery
Mandir	Hindu temple
Masjid	mosque
Mutt	Hindu monastery
Naxalites	name for Indian Maoists, from the name of the place in

	West Bengal, Naxalbari, where the movement started in 1967
Notebandi	popular name for the demonetization of all Rs 500 and Rs 1000 banknotes announced by prime minister Modi on November 8 2016
Other Backward Classes (sometimes Castes) (OBCs)	socially and educationally deprived communities (not including Scheduled Castes and Tribes) for whom remedial actions are authorized by the Constitution
panchayat	council, institution of local government
panchayati Raj	official system of local self-government
pracharak	full-time organizers of the RSS (Rashtriya Swayamsevak Sangh)
Ramayana	Sanskrit epic about Prince Rama's struggle to rescue his wife Sita
Ryotwari/ raiyatwari	system of land revenue administration in which cultivators paid tax directly to government
Sangh parivar	the 'family' of Hindu nationalist organizations around the RSS
Scheduled Castes (SCs)	in effect, the official term for the 'Untouchable'castes, those castes recognized by the Constitution as deserving special assistance in respect of education, employment and political representation (other than the OBCs)
Scheduled Tribes (STs)	in effect, the official term for India's tribal or adivasi populations; those recognized by the Constitution as deserving special assistance in respect of education, employment and political representation (other than the OBCs and SCs)
shakha	local cell/organization of the RSS
shuddhi	purification and (re-)conversion to Hinduism
Shudras	the castes of workers of the *varna* scheme
Vaishyas	the castes of husbandmen and traders of the *varna* scheme
Vande Mataram	Bengali poem written by Bankim Chaandra Chatterjee, of which the first two verses were adopted as the National Song of India
varna	the four categories (or colours) which traditionally define and divide Hindu society (*Brahmans; Kshatriyas; Vaidhya; Shudras*)
Vikaas	development
zamindari	system of land revenue administration under which the *zamindar* landlord collected rent from cultivators for payment to the (colonial) government

References

Note: We have referred on a good many occasions to on-line sources. The following are websites of particularly important sources that we have referred to fairly frequently:

The Hindu (leading English language newspaper, based in Chennai, but now publishing all over India) www.thehindu.com (with an excellent Archive function).

Frontline (news magazine, published fortnightly by The Hindu Group of Newspapers) https://frontline.thehindu.com (with an Archive on the site that is easy to use).

Ideas for India (www.ideasforindia.in) is an independent website-based publication to which many Indian and other researchers, especially economists, contribute. Articles referred to are best found through the authors' names.

We have also referred to another independent on-line publication, started in 2019, *India Forum*. The website https://www.theindiaforum.in allows for downloading of PDF versions of the articles published on the site.

Abraham, I. (1999), *The Making of the Indian Atomic Bomb: Science, Secrecy and the Postcolonial State* (Hyderabad: Orient Longman).
Abraham, L. (2001), 'Redrawing the Lakshman Rekha: Gender differences and cultural constructions in youth sexuality in urban India', *South Asia: Journal of South Asian Studies*, 24 (s1): 133–56.
Abraham, V. (2017), 'Stagnant employment growth: The last three years may have been the worst', *Economic and Political Weekly*, 52(38): 13–17.
Acemoglu, D., S. Johnson and J. Robinson (2005), 'Institutions as a fundamental cause of long-run growth', in P. Aghion and S. Durlauf (eds) *Handbook of Economic Growth*, Vol. 1, Part A, 385–472 (Amsterdam: Elsevier).
Adeney, K. and A. Wyatt (2004), 'Democracy in south Asia: Getting beyond the structure-agency dichotomy', *Political Studies*, 52(3): 1–18.
Agarwal, B. (1992), 'The gender and environment debate', *Feminist Studies*, 18(1): 119–58.
Agarwal, B. (1994), *A Field of One's Own: Gender and Land Rights in South Asia* (Cambridge: Cambridge University Press).

Agarwal, B. and P. Panda (2007), 'Toward freedom from domestic violence: The neglected obvious', *Journal of Human Development*, 8(3): 359–88.

Agarwala, R. (2013), *Informal Labor, Formal Politics, and Dignified Discontent in India* (Cambridge: Cambridge University Press).

Agarwala, R. (2014), 'An intersection of Marxism and feminism among India's informal workers: A second marriage?', in L. Fernandes (ed.) *Routledge Handbook of Gender in South Asia* (London: Routledge).

Aggarwal, A. (2016), 'The MGNREGA crisis', *Economic and Political Weekly*, 51(22): 38–43.

Agrawal, A. and S. Narain (1991), *Global Warming in an Unequal World*. New Delhi: Centre for Science and Environment.

Agrawal, T. (2014), 'Skill development in India: An examination', *Journal of Education and Work*, 27(6): 629–50.

Ahluwalia, I. J., R. Kanbur and P. K. Mohanty (2014), 'Challenges of urbanisation in India: An overview', in I. J. Ahluwalia, R. Kanbur, and P. K. Mohanty (eds) *Urbanisation in India: Challenges, Opportunities and the Way Forward* (Delhi: Sage).

Ahmad, J. K., F. Blum, P. Gupta and D. Jain (2018), 'India's growth story', World Bank Policy Research Working Paper No. 8599 (Washington, DC: The World Bank).

Ahmed-Ghosh, H. (2004), 'Chattels of society: Domestic violence in India', *Violence against Women*, 10(1): 94–118.

Aiyar, Y. (2017), 'Three years on the Modi government still has gaping holes in its social policy', *The Wire*, 1 February. Available at https://thewire.in/102937/social-policy-three-years-modi-government.

Aiyar, Y. and M. Walton (2014), 'Rights, accountability and citizenship: Examining India's emerging welfare state', Working Paper (New Delhi: Centre for Policy Research).

Aiyar, Y. and S. Bhattacharya (2016), 'The Post Office paradox: A case study of block level education bureaucracy', *Economic and Political Weekly*, 51(11): 61–9.

Ajithkumar, M. U. (2016), 'Training of teachers: Institutionalising training and development of academic faculty of TVET institutions for realising excellence', in M. Pilz (ed.) *India: Preparation for the World of Work* (Wiesbaden: Springer).

Alam, J. (2004), *Who Wants Democracy?* (Delhi: Orient Longman).

Alex, G. (2008), 'Work versus education: children's everyday life in rural Tamil Nadu', in D. Behera (ed.) *Childhoods in South Asia* (Delhi: Pearson).

Alkire, S. and S. Seth (2015), 'Multidimensional poverty reduction in India between 1999 and 2006: Where and how?', *World Development*, 72: 93–108.

Allendorf, K. and R. K. Pandian (2016), 'The decline of arranged marriage? Marital change and continuity in India', *Population and Development Review*, 42(3): 435–64.

Amirapu, A. and A. Subramanian (2014), 'India must reverse its deindustriali-
sation', *Business Standard*, 9 May.

Anand, N. (2017), *Hydraulic City* (Durham, NC: Duke University Press).

Anandhi, S. (1991), 'Women's question and the Dravidian movement, c. 1925–
1948', *Social Scientist*, 19(5–6): 24–41.

Anandhi, S. (2013), 'The Mathammas: Gender, caste and the politics of
intersectionality in rural Tamil Nadu', *Economic and Political Weekly*, 48:
64–71.

Anandhi, S. (2017), 'Gendered negotiations of caste identity: Dalit women's
activism in rural Tamil Nadu', in S. Anandhi and K. Kapadia (eds) *Dalit
Women: Vanguard of an Alternative Politics in India* (London: Routledge).

Anandhi, S., J. Jeyaranjan and R. Krishnan (2002), 'Work, caste and competing masculinities: Notes from a Tamil village', *Economic and Political Weekly*,
37(43): 4403–14.

Ang, Y. Y. (2014), 'Authoritarian restraints on online activism revisited: Why
"I-paid-a-bribe" worked in India but failed in China', *Comparative Politics*,
47(1): 21–40.

Appadurai, A. (2002), 'Deep democracy: Urban governmentality and the hori-
zon of politics', *Public Culture*, 14(1): 21–47.

Appadurai, A. (2004), 'The capacity to aspire: culture and the terms of recognition', in V. Rao and M. Walton (eds) *Culture and Public Action* (Stanford, CA:
Stanford University Press).

Arnot, M. (2009), *Educating the Gendered Citizen: Sociological Engagements with
National and Global Agendas* (London: Routledge).

Arnot, M. and S. Swartz (2013), 'Youth citizenship and the politics of belonging: Introducing contexts, voices, imaginaries', in S. Swartz and M. Arnot
(eds) *Youth Citizenship and the Politics of Belonging* (London: Routledge).

Arrow, K., P. Dasgupta, L. Goulder, K. Mumford and K. Oleson (2012),
'Sustainability and the measure of wealth', *Environment and Development
Economics*, 17(3): 317–53.

Asadullah, M. N., and G. Yalonetzky (2012), 'Inequality of educational opportunity in India: Changes over time and across states', *World Development*, 40(6):
1151–63.

ASER (2019) *Annual Status of Education Report (Rural) 2018* (New Delhi: ASER).
Available at http://img.asercentre.org/docs/ASER%202018/Release%20
Material/aserreport2018.pdf.

Aslany, M. (2019), 'The Indian middle class, its size, and urban-rural variations', *Contemporary South Asia*, 27(1): 196–213.

Ayres, A. (2018), *Our Time Has Come: How India is Making its Place in the World*
(New York: Oxford University).

Ayres, A. (2019), 'Trump's South Asia policy', Seminar Number 715, March.
Available at www.india-seminar.com.

Azam, M. and G. G. Kingdon (2013), 'Are girls the fairer sex in India? Revisiting intra-household allocation of education expenditure', *World Development*, 42: 143–64.

Babu, G. R. and B. V. Babu (2011), 'Dowry deaths: A neglected public health issue in India', *International Health*, 3(1): 35–43.

Bailey, F. G. (1957), *Caste and the Economic Frontier: A Village in Highland Orissa* (Manchester: Manchester University Press).

Bailey, F. G. (1963), *Politics and Change: Orissa in 1959* (Berkeley, CA: University of California Press).

Bajpai, V. (2016), 'Deconstructing saffron nationalism: Defeat the campaign to vilify JNU', *Economic and Political Weekly*, 51(7): web exclusive.

Balagopal, K. (1991), 'Post-Chundur and other Chundurs', *Economic and Political Weekly*, 26(42), 2399–405.

Banerjee, A. and E. Duflo (2009), 'Improving health care delivery'. Available at https://economics.mit.edu/faculty/banerjee/papers.

Banerjee, A. and L. Iyer (2005), 'History, institutions and economic performance: The legacy of colonial land tenure systems in India', *American Economic Review*, 95: 1190–213.

Banerjee, A. and R. Pande (2009), 'Parochial politics, ethnic preferences and politician corruption'. Available at https://economics.mit.edu/faculty/banerjee/papers.

Banerjee, A., E. Duflo, M. Ghatak and J. Lafortune (2013), 'Marry for what? Caste and mate selection in modern India', *American Economic Journal: Microeconomics*, 5(2): 33–72.

Banerjee, M. (2014), *Why India Votes?* (Delhi: Routledge).

Banerjee, N. (1985), 'Women's work and discrimination', in D. Jain and N. Banerjee (eds) *Tyranny of the Household: Investigative Essays on Women's Work* (New Delhi: Shakti Books).

Banerjee, S. (1980), *In the Wake of Naxalbari: A History of the Naxalite Movement in India* (Calcutta: Subarnrekha).

Banerjee, S. (2006), 'Armed masculinity, Hindu nationalism and female political participation in India', *International Feminist Journal of Politics*, 8(1): 62–83.

Banerjee, S. (2009), 'Reflections of a one-time Maoist activist', *Dialectical Anthropology*, 33(3–4): 253–69.

Banerjee, S. (2015), 'Chaos in reforms', *Down To Earth*, 16–31 March, 34–7.

Banerjee, S. (2016), *Gender, Nation, and Popular Film in India: Globalizing Muscular Nationalism* (London: Routledge).

Bardhan, K. (1986), 'Women: work, welfare and status: Forces of tradition and change in India', *South Asia Bulletin*, 6(1): 3–16.

Bardhan, P. (1998 [1984]), *The Political Economy of Development in India*, 2nd edn (Oxford: Oxford University Press).

Bardhan, P. (2009), 'Notes on the political economy of India's tortuous transition', *Economic and Political Weekly*, 44(49): 31–6.

Bardhan, P. (2015), *Globalisation, Democracy and Corruption: An Indian Perspective* (Kolkata and London: Frontpage)

Bardhan, P. (2016), 'Basic income in a poor country', *Ideas for India*, 26 September.

Bardhan, P. (2018), 'Reflections on Kalyan Sanyal's Rethinking Capitalist Development', *Economic and Political Weekly*, 53(21): 19–22.

Bardhan, P. (2019), 'Yes, universal basic income. No, targeted income schemes', *The Quint*, 31 January.

Basole, A. and D. Basu (2011), 'Relations of production and modes of surplus extraction in India: Part 1 – Agriculture', *Economic and Political Weekly*, 46(14): 41–58.

Basu, A. (2015), *Violent Conjunctures in Democratic India* (New York: Cambridge University Press).

Bathia, S. and B. K. Negi (2016), 'Linking food and nutrition security', *The Hindu*, 8 November.

Bavadam, L. (2017), 'United action', *Frontline*, 34(15), 7 July.

Baviskar, A. (2011), 'Cows, cars and cycle-rickshaws: Bourgeois environmentalists and the battle for Delhi's streets', in A. Baviskar and R. Ray (eds) *Elite and Everyman: The Cultural Politics of India's Middle Classes* (New Delhi: Routledge).

Baviskar, A. and N. Sundar (2008), 'Democracy versus economic transformation? A response to Partha Chatterjee's democracy and economic transformation in India', *Economic and Political Weekly*, 43(46): 87–9.

Baviskar, A., S. Sinha and K. Phillip (2006), 'Rethinking Indian environmentalism: Industrial pollution in Delhi and fisheries in Kerala', in J. Bauer (ed.) *Forging Environmentalism: Justice, Livelihood and Contested Environments* (London: M. E. Sharpe).

Bayat, A. (2013), 'The Arab Spring and its surprises', *Development and Change*, 44: 587–601.

Bayly, C. A. (1998), *Origins of Nationality in South Asia: Patriotism and Ethical Government in the Making of Modern India* (Oxford: Oxford University Press).

Bayly, C. A. (2008), 'Indigenous and colonial origins of comparative economic development: The case of colonial India and Africa', World Bank Policy Research Working Paper No. 4474 (Washington, DC: The World Bank).

Bayly, C. A. (2012), *Recovering Liberties: Indian Thought in the Age of Liberalism and Empire* (Cambridge: Cambridge University Press).

Bayly, S. (2001), *Caste, Society and Politics in India from the Eighteenth Century to the Modern Age* (Cambridge: Cambridge University Press).

BBC (2018), 'Sabarimala: Mobs attack women near India Hindu temple', *BBC*, 17 October. Available at https://www.bbc.com/news/world-asia-india-45885996.

Bedi, T. (2016), *The Dashing Ladies of Shiv Sena: Political Matronage in Urbanizing India* (New York: State University of New York Press).

Belliappa, J. (2013), *Gender, Class and Reflexive Modernity in India* (New York: Palgrave Macmillan).

Bénéï, V. (2001), 'Teaching nationalism in Maharashtra schools', in C. J. Fuller and V. Bénéï (eds) *The Everyday State and Society in Modern India* (Delhi: Social Science Press).

Bénéï, V. (2008), *Schooling Passions: Nation, History and Language in Contemporary Western India* (Stanford, CA: Stanford University Press).

Benkler, Y. (2006), *The Wealth of Networks: How Social Production Transforms Markets* (New Haven, CT: Yale University Press).

Bennett Institute (2019), *Measuring Wealth, Delivering Prosperity: The Wealth Economy Project on Natural and Social Capital* (Cambridge: Bennett Institute of Public Policy, University of Cambridge).

Berreman, G. D. (1960), 'Caste in India and the United States', *American Journal of Sociology*, 66(2): 120–7.

Berreman, G. D. (1993), 'Sanskritization as female oppression in India', in B. D. Miller (ed.) *Sex and Gender Hierarchies* (Cambridge: Cambridge University Press).

Besley, T. and R. Burgess (2000), 'The political economy of government responsiveness: theory and evidence from India', *STICERD Development Economics Discussion Paper Series Number 28*, London School of Economics.

Béteille, A. (1965), *Caste, Class and Power: Changing Patterns of Stratification in a Tanjore Village* (Berkeley, CA: California University Press).

Béteille, A. (1974), 'Agrarian relations in Tanjore District', in *Studies in Agrarian Social Structure*, 142–70 (Delhi: Oxford University Press).

Béteille, A. (1991), *Society and Politics in India: Essays in a Comparative Perspective* (London: Athlone Press).

Béteille, A. (1992), *The Backward Classes in Contemporary India* (Delhi: Oxford University Press).

Béteille, A. (2001), 'Race and caste', *The Hindu*, 10 March.

Béteille, T. (2009), *Absenteeism, Transfers and Patronage: The Political Economy of Teacher Labour Markets in India* (Stanford, CA: Stanford University Press).

Bhagat, R. B. (2011), 'Emerging pattern of urbanisation in India', *Economic and Political Weekly*, 46(34): 10–12.

Bhagwati, J. and P. Desai (1970), *India: Planning for Industrialisation* (Oxford: Oxford University Press).

Bhagwati, J. and T. N. Srinivasan (1975), *Foreign Trade Regimes and Economic Development: India* (New York: Columbia University Press).

Bhalla, G. S. and G. Singh (2009), 'Economic liberalization and Indian agriculture: a statewise analysis', *Economic and Political Weekly*, 44(52): 34–44.

Bhan, G. (2009), '"This is no longer the city I once knew". Evictions, the urban poor and the right to the city in millennial Delhi', *Environment and Urbanization*, 21(1): 127–42.

Bharadwaj, K. (1982), 'Regional differentiation in India: A note', *Economic and Political Weekly*, 17(14–16): 605–14.

Bhatia, B. (2005), 'Competing concerns', *Economic and Political Weekly*, 40(47): 4890–3.

Bhatia, R. (2019), 'India and strategic autonomy', Speech of 7 February 2019. Available at https://www.gatewayhouse.in/india-strategic-autonomy/.

Bhattacharya, P. (2016), 'One in three households in India owns a two-wheeler', *LiveMint*, 12 December. Available at https://www.livemint.com/Politics/Yd2EAFIupVHDX0EbUdecsO/One-in-three-households-in-India-owns-a-twowheeler.html.

Bhattacharyya, R. (2015), 'Understanding the spatialities of sexual assault against Indian women in India', *Gender, Place and Culture*, 22(9): 1340–56.

Bhattacharya, R. and K. Sanyal (2011), 'Bypassing the squalor: New towns, immaterial labour and exclusion in post-colonial urbanisation', *Economic and Political Weekly*, 46(31): 41–8.

Bhowmik, S. (2015), 'Protecting employers against workers and trade unions', *Economic and Political Weekly*, 50(29): 15–18.

Bhushan, S. (2019), 'A dithering higher education policy', *Economic and Political Weekly*, 54(24): 12–14.

Bhuyan, A. (2017), 'India's health story is one of "Nations within a nation", says new study', *The Wire*, 14 November. Available at https://thewire.in/health/every-state-distinct-health-story-need-individualise-policy-intervention-finds-study.

Biao, X. (2005), 'Gender, dowry and the migration system of Indian information technology professionals', *Indian Journal of Gender Studies*, 12(2–3): 357–80.

Binswanger-Mkhize, H. (2013), 'The stunted structural transformation of the Indian economy: Agriculture, manufacturing and the rural non-farm sector', *Economic and Political Weekly*, 48(26–27): 5–13.

Birchfield, L. and J. Corsi (2010), 'Between starvation and globalization: Realizing the right to food in India', *Michigan Journal of International Law*, 31(1): 691–764.

Bjorkman, L. (2015) *Pipe Politics, Contested Waters: Embedded Infrastructure of Millennial Mumbai* (Durham, NC: Duke University Press).

Blackwill, R. and A. Tellis (2019), 'The India dividend: New Delhi remains Washington's best hope in Asia', *Foreign Affairs*, September.

Bloch, F. and V. Rao (2002), 'Terror as a bargaining instrument: A case study of dowry violence in rural India', *American Economic Review*, 92(4): 1029–43.

Block, F. and M. Summers (2014), *The Power of Market Fundamentalism* (Cambridge, MA: Harvard University Press).

Bloom, D. E. (2011), 'India's baby boomers: Dividend or disaster?' *Current History*, 110(735): 143–9.

Bobbio, T. (2015), *Urbanisation, Citizenship and Conflict in India: Ahmedabad 1900–2000* (London: Routledge).

Bonner, A. (1990), *Averting the Apocalypse: Social Movements in India Today* (Durham, NC: Duke University Press).

Bornstein, E. and A. Sharma (2016), 'The righteous and the rightful: The technomoral politics of NGOs, social movements, and the state in India', *American Ethnologist*, 43(1): 76–90.

Borooah, V. K. (2004), 'Gender bias among children in India in their diet and immunisation against disease', *Social Science and Medicine*, 58(9): 1719–31.

Borras, S. M., R. Hall, I. Scoones, B. White and W. Wolford (2011), 'Towards a better understanding of global land grabbing: An editorial introduction', *Journal of Peasant Studies*, 38(2): 209–16.

Bose, I. (2010), 'How did the Indian Forest Rights Act, 2006, emerge?', Discussion Paper Series No. 39, Research Programme Consortium for Improving Institutions for Pro-Poor Growth.

Bose, S. (2013), *Transforming India: Challenges to the World's Largest Democracy* (Cambridge, MA: Harvard University Press).

Bose, S., P. Ghosh and A. Sardana (2017), 'Resource requirements for Right to Education (RTE): Normative and the real', Working Paper No. 201 (New Delhi: National Institute of Public Finance and Policy).

Bosworth, B. and S. M. Collins (2015), 'India's growth slowdown: End of an era?', *India Review*, 14(1): 8–25.

Bourdieu, P. (1984), *Distinction: A Social Critique of the Judgement of Taste* (London: Routledge and Kegan Paul).

Bourdieu, P. (2001), *Masculine Domination* (Stanford, CA: Stanford University Press).

Brass, P. (1965), *Factional Politics in an Indian State: The Congress Party in Uttar Pradesh* (Berkeley, CA: University of California Press).

Brass, P. (1997), *Theft of an Idol: Text and Context in the Representation of Collective Violence* (Princeton, NJ: Princeton University Press).

Brass, P. (2003a), *The Production of Hindu-Muslim Violence in Contemporary India* (Delhi: Oxford University Press).

Brass, P. (2003b), 'Response to Ashutosh Varshney'. Available at https://lists.h-net.org/cgi-bin/logbrowse.pl?trx=vx&list=h-asia&month=0312&week=a&msg=GYe3Ceqh4IYJ2GJ2INF4nw&user=&pw.

Brass, P. (2011), 'Development and the peasantry: Land acquisition in Ghaziabad and the cultivators (1950–2009)', in P. Brass, *An Indian Political Life: Charan Singh and Congress Politics* (Delhi: Sage).

Breman, J. (1993), *Beyond Patronage and Exploitation* (New Delhi: Oxford University Press).

Breman, J. (2001), 'An informalized labour system', *Economic and Political Weekly*, 36(52): 4804–21.

Breman, J. (2008), 'On labour bondage, old and new', *Indian Journal of Labour Economics*, 51(1): 83–90.

Breman, J., I. Guerin and A. Prakash (2009), *India's Unfree Workforce: Of Bondage Old and New* (Delhi: Oxford University Press).

Brown, T. (2014), 'Negotiating the NGO-social movement dichotomy: Evidence from Punjab, India', *Voluntas*, 25(1): 46–66.

Brown, T. (2018), *Farmers, Subalterns, and Activists: Social Politics of Sustainable Agriculture in India* (Cambridge: Cambridge University Press).

Brulé, R. (2015), 'Accountability in rural India: Local government and social equality', *Asian Survey*, 55(5): 909–41.

CAD [Constituent Assembly Debates]. Available at www.goodgovernanceindia.com/pdf/Constituent-Assembly-Debates.pdf

Caputi, J. (1989), 'The sexual politics of murder', *Gender and Society*, 3(4): 437–56.

Carswell, G. (2016), 'Struggles over work take place at home: Women's decisions, choices and constraints in the Tiruppur textile industry, India', *Geoforum*, 77: 134–45.

Carswell, G. and G. De Neve (2014), 'MGNREGA in Tamil Nadu: A story of success and transformation?', *Journal of Agrarian Change*, 14(4): 564–85.

Carter, A. T. (1974), *Elite Politics in India: Political Stratification and Political Alliances in Western Maharashtra* (Cambridge: Cambridge University Press).

Castells, M. (1996), *The Rise of the Network Society* (Oxford: Blackwell).

Castells, M. (2009), *Communication Power* (Oxford: Oxford University Press).

Castells, M. (2015), *Networks of Outrage and Hope: Social Movements in the Internet Age* (Cambridge: Polity Press).

Chacko, P. (2018), 'The right turn in India: Authoritarianism, populism and neoliberalisation', *Journal of Contemporary Asia*, 48(4): 541–65.

Chadha, K. and M. Koliska (2016), 'Playing by a different set of rules: Journalistic values in India's regional television newsrooms', *Journalism Practice*, 10(5): 608–25.

Chadwick, A. (2013), *The Hybrid Media System: Politics and Power* (New York: Oxford University Press).

Chakraborty, K. (2012), 'Virtual mate-seeking in the urban slums of Kolkata, India', *South Asian Popular Culture*, 10(2): 197–216.

Chakraborty, K. (2016), *Young Muslim Women in India: Bollywood, Identity and Changing Youth Culture* (London: Routledge).

Chakravarthy, S. and E. Somanathan (2008), 'Discrimination in an elite labour market? Job placements at IIM-Ahmedabad', *Economic and Political Weekly*, 43(44), 45–50.

Chakravarti, U. (1993), 'Conceptualising Brahmanical patriarchy in Early India: Gender, caste, class and state', *Economic and Political Weekly*, 28(14): 579–85.

Chanana, K. (2007), 'Globalisation, higher education and gender: Changing subject choices of Indian women', *Economic and Political Weekly*, 42(7): 590–8.

Chancel, L. and T. Piketty (2017), *Indian Income Inequality, 1922–2015: From British Raj to Billionaire Raj*. WID.world Working Paper Series No. 2017/11. Available at https://wid.world/document/chancelpiketty2017widworld/

Chand, R. and S. Parappurathu (2012), 'Temporal and spatial variation in agricultural growth and its determinants', *Economic and Political Weekly*, 47(26–27): 55–64.

Chand, R., S. K. Srivastava and J. Singh (2017), 'Changes in rural economy of India, 1971–2012: Lessons for job-led growth', *Economic and Political Weekly*, 52(52): 64–71.

Chandhoke, N. (2009a), 'Civil society in conflict cities', *Economic and Political Weekly*, 44(44): 99–108.

Chandhoke, N. (2009b), 'Putting civil society in its place', *Economic and Political Weekly*, 44(7): 12–16.

Chandhoke, N. (2012), 'Whatever has happened to civil society?' *Economic and Political Weekly*, 47(23): 39–45.

Chandhoke, N. (2016), 'The chequered history of social rights in India', in O. Tornquist and J. Harriss (eds) *Reinventing Social Democratic Development: Insights from Indian and Scandinavian Comparisons*, 189–211 (Copenhagen: NIAS Press).

Chandhoke, N., P. Priyadarshi, S. Tyagi and K. Neha (2007), 'The displaced of Ahmedabad', *Economic and Political Weekly*, 42(43): 10–14.

Chandra, K. (2004), *Why Ethnic Parties Succeed: Patronage and Ethnic Head Counts in India* (New York: Cambridge University Press).

Chandra, K. (ed.) (2016), *Democratic Dynasties: State, Family and Party in Contemporary Indian Politics* (New York: Cambridge University Press).

Chandra, K. (2017), 'Who is Narendra Modi? The two sides of India's Prime Minister', *Foreign Affairs*, 29 March.

Chandra, U. (2015), 'Rethinking subaltern resistance', *Journal of Contemporary Asia*, 45(4): 563–73.

Chandrasekhar, C. P. (2007), 'The progress of "reform" and the retrogression of agriculture', *Macroscan*. Available at http://www.macroscan.org/anl/apr07/anl250407Agriculture.htm.

Chatterjee, M. (2017), 'The impunity effect: Majoritarian rule, everyday legality, and state formation in India', *American Ethnologist*, 44(1): 118–30.

Chatterjee, P. (1989), 'Colonialism, nationalism, and colonised women: The contest in India', *American Ethnologist*, 16(4): 622–33.

Chatterjee, P. (2004), *The Politics of the Governed: Reflections on Popular Politics in Most of the World* (New York: Columbia University Press; and New Delhi: Permanent Black).

Chatterjee, P. (2008), 'Democracy and economic transformation in India', *Economic and Political Weekly*, 43(16): 53–62.

Chatterjee, P. (2011), *Lineages of Political Society: Studies in Postcolonial Democracy* (New York: Colombia University Press).

Chattopadhyay, S. (2011) 'Online activism for a heterogeneous time: The Pink Chaddi campaign and the social media in India', *Proteus: A Journal of Ideas*, 27(1): 63–8.

Chattopadhyay, S. S. (2007), 'Another land row', *Frontline*, 24(1), 26 January.

Chattopadhyay, S. S. (2008), 'Singur's loss', *Frontline*, 25(22), 7 November.

Chaturvedi, S., S. K. Pandey, and D. Gellner (2019), 'The new Modi wave as seen from Eastern UP', *The India Forum*, 2 August.

Chauchard, S. (2017), *Why Representation Matters: The Meaning of Ethnic Quotas in Rural India* (Cambridge: Cambridge University Press).

Chaudhuri, S. (2015), 'Excess female infant mortality and the gender gap in infant care in Bihar, India', *Feminist Economics*, 21(2): 131–61.

Chaudhury, N., J. Hammer, M. Kremer, K. Muralidharan and H. Rogers (2006), 'Missing in action: Teacher and health worker absence in developing countries', *Journal of Economic Perspectives*, 20(1): 91–116.

Chibber, V. (2003), *Locked in Place: State Building and Late Industrialisation in India* (Princeton, NJ: Princeton University Press).

Chibber, V. (2005), 'From class compromise to class accommodation. Labor's incorporation into the Indian political economy', in R. Ray and M. F. Katzenstein (eds) *Social Movements in India: Poverty, Power and Politics* (New York: Rowman & Littlefield).

Chin, A. and N. Prakash (2011), 'The redistributive effects of political reservation for minorities: Evidence from India', *Journal of Development Economics*, 96(2): 265–77.

Chopra, D. (2011), 'Policy making in India: A dynamic process of statecraft', *Pacific Affairs*, 84(1): 89–107.

Chopra, K. (2017), *Development and Environment Policy in India: The last few decades* (New York: Springer).

Choudhury, C. A. (2008), '(Mis)appropriated liberty: Identity, gender justice and Muslim personal law reform in India', *Columbia Journal of Gender and Law*, 17(1): 45–110.

Chow, E. N. (2002), 'Globalisation, East Asian development and gender', in E. N. Chow (ed.) *Transforming Gender and Development in East Asia* (London: Routledge).

Chowdhry, P. (2009), '"First our jobs then our girls": The dominant caste perception on the "rising" Dalits', *Modern Asian Studies*, 43(2): 437–79.

Chowdhury, P. (1994), *The Veiled Woman: Shifting Gender Relations in Rural Haryana, 1880–1990* (New Delhi: Oxford University Press).

Cincotta, R. P., R. Engelman and D. Anastasion (2003), *The Security Demographic: Population and Civil Conflict after the Cold War* (Washington, DC: Population Action International).

Ciotti, M. (2006), 'In the past we were a bit "Chamar": Education as a self- and community engineering process in northern India', *Journal of the Royal Anthropological Institute*, 12(4): 899–916.

Ciotti, M. (2010), 'Futurity in words: Low-caste women political activists' self-representation and post-Dalit scenarios in north India', *Contemporary South Asia*, 18(1): 43–56.

Clark-Deces, I. (2011), 'The decline of the Dravidian kinship in local perspectives', in I. Clark-Deces (ed.) *A Companion to the Anthropology of India* (Oxford: Blackwell).

Clark-Deces, I. (2018), 'Towards an anthropology of exchange in Tamil Nadu', *International Journal of Hindu Studies*, 22(2): 197–215.

Coffey, D. and D. Spears (2017), *Where India Goes: Abandoned Toilets, Stunted Development and the Costs of Caste* (Noida: HarperCollins India).

Coleman, J.S. (1965), *Education and Political Development* (Princeton, NJ: Princeton University Press).

Comaroff, J. (2008), 'Uncool passion: Nietzsche meets the Pentecostals', Max Weber Lecture Series, European University Institute.

Commander, S. (1983), 'The jajmani system in North India: An examination of its logic and status across two centuries', *Modern Asian Studies*, 17(2): 283–311.

Corbridge, S. (1988), 'The ideology of tribal economy and society: Politics in the Jharkhand, 1950–1980', *Modern Asian Studies*, 22(1): 1–42.

Corbridge, S. (2000), 'Competing inequalities: The scheduled tribes and the reservations system in India's Jharkhand', *Journal of Asian Studies*, 59(1): 63–85.

Corbridge, S. (2011), 'The contested geographies of federalism in post-reform India', in S. Ruparelia, S. Reddy, J. Harriss and S. Corbridge (eds) *Understanding India's New Political Economy: A Great Transformation?* (London: Routledge).

Corbridge, S. and J. Harriss (2000), *Reinventing India: Economic Liberalization, Hindu Nationalism and Popular Democracy* (Cambridge: Polity Press).

Couldry, N. (2015), 'The myth of "us": Digital networks, political change and the production of collectivity', *Information, Communication and Society*, 18(6), 608–26.

Cross, J. (2009), 'From dreams to discontent: Educated young men and the politics of work at a special economic zone in Andhra Pradesh', *Contributions to Indian Sociology*, 43(3): 351–79.

Cross, J. (2014), *Dream Zones: Anticipating Capitalism and Development in India* (London: Pluto Press).

CSWI [Committee on the Status of Women in India] (1974), *Towards Equality: Report of the Committee on the Status of Women in India* (Ministry of Education & Social Welfare, Department of Social Welfare).

Currie, B. (1998), 'Public action and its limits: Re-examining the politics of hunger alleviation in eastern India', *Third World Quarterly*, 19(5): 873–92.

Da Costa, D. (2010), *Development Dramas: Reimagining Rural Political Action in Eastern India* (London: Routledge).

Dabadge, A., A. Sreenivas and A. Josey (2018), 'What has the PM Ujjwal Yojana achieved so far?', *Economic and Political Weekly*, 53(20): 69–75.

Dalal, K., M. S. Lee and M. Gifford (2012), 'Male adolescents' attitudes toward wife beating: A multi-country study in South Asia', *Journal of Adolescent Health*, 50(5): 437–42.

Dalmia, G. (2019), 'Narendra Modi has the support to build on his bold first term', *Financial Times*, 29 July.

Damodaran, H. (2008), *India's New Capitalists: Caste, Business and Industry in a Modern Nation* (Ranikhet: Permanent Black).

Dang, H.-A. and P. Lanjouw (2015), 'Poverty dynamics in India between 2004 and 2012', World Bank Policy Research Paper No. 7270 (Washington, DC: The World Bank).

Das, J. and J. Hammer (2012), 'Health and health care policy in India: The case for quality of care', in C. Ghate (ed.) *The Oxford Handbook of the Indian Economy* (New York: Oxford University Press).

Dasgupta, P. (2013), 'Getting India wrong', *Ideas for India*, 12 August.

Dasgupta, R. K. (2017), *Digital Queer Cultures in India: Politics, Intimacies and Belonging* (London: Routledge).

Datt, G. and M. Ravallion (1998), 'Why have some Indian states done better than others at reducing rural poverty?', *Economica*, 65(257): 17–38.

Datt, G., R. Murgai and M. Ravallion (2016a), 'Poverty reduction in India: Revisiting debates with sixty years of data', *Ideas for India*, 10 October.

Datt, G., R. Murgai and M. Ravallion (2016b), 'Growth, urbanization and poverty reduction in India', World Bank Policy Research Paper No. 7568 (Washington, DC: The World Bank).

Datta, P. K. (2015), 'The obvious and not-so-obvious reasons for AAP victory', *The Hindu*, 10 February.

Davies, E. (2018), 'Absence: Electoral cycles and teacher absenteeism in India', Paper prepared for the Workshop on the Political Economy of Education at Nuffield College, University of Oxford. Available at http://barrett.dyson.cornell.edu/NEUDC/paper_90.pdf.

Davies, W. (2018), *Nervous States: How Feeling Took Over the World* (London: Jonathan Cape).

De Long, B. (2003), 'India Since Independence: An analytic growth narrative', in D. Rodrik (ed.) *In Search of Prosperity: Analytic Narratives on Economic Growth* (Princeton, NJ: Princeton University Press).

De Souza, P. R., S. Kumar and S. Sandeep (2009), *Indian Youth in a Transforming World* (New Delhi: Sage).

Deliege, R. (1999), *The Untouchables of India* (Oxford: Berg).

Deokar, B. K. and S. L. Shetty (2014), 'Growth in Indian agriculture: Responding to policy initiatives since 2004–05', *Economic and Political Weekly*, 49(26–27): 101–4.

Desai, S. and L. Andrist (2010), 'Gender scripts and age at marriage in India', *Demography*, 47(3): 667–87.

Desai, S., C. Adams and A. Dubey (2010) 'Segmented schooling: Inequalities in primary education', in S. Thorat and K. S. Newman (eds) *Blocked by Caste: Economic Discrimination in Modern India*, 230–52 (New Delhi: Oxford University Press).

Deshpande, A. (2016), 'Double jeopardy? Caste, affirmative action, and stigma', WIDER Working Paper No. 2016/71. Available at www.econstor.eu/handle/10419/146265.

Deshpande, A. and K. Newman (2007), 'Where the path leads: The role of caste in post-university employment expectations', *Economic and Political Weekly*, 42(41): 4133–40.

Deshpande, A. and R. Ramachandran (2017), 'Dominant or backward? Political economy of demand for quotas by Jats, Patels, and Marathas', *Economic and Political Weekly*, 52(19): 81–92.

Dev, M. (2008), *Inclusive Growth in India: Agriculture, Poverty and Human Development* (Delhi: Oxford University Press).

Devji, F. F. (1991), 'Gender and the politics of space: The movement for women's reform in Muslim India, 1857–1900', *South Asia*, 14(1): 141–53.

Dhaliwal, I., I. Duflo, R. Glennerster and C. Tulloch (2013), 'Comparative cost-effectiveness analysis to inform policy in developing countries', in P. Glewwe (ed.) *Education Policy in Developing Countries* (Chicago, IL: University of Chicago Press).

Dhanka, R. (2019), 'A case of confused thinking: On the draft National Education Policy', *The Hindu*, 12 July.

Dhorajiwala, S., J. Drèze and N. Wagner (2019), 'A bridge to nowhere', *The Hindu*, 27 March.

Dirks, N. (2001), *Castes of Mind: Colonialism and the Making of Modern India* (Princeton, NJ: Princeton University Press; and New Delhi: Permanent Black).

Diwakar, R. (2016), 'Local contest, national impact: Understanding the success of India's Aam Aadmi Party in 2015 Delhi Assembly election', *Representation*, 52(1): 71–80.

Dommaraju, P. (2016), Divorce and separation in India', *Population and Development Review*, 42(2): 195–223.

Donner, H. (2002), 'One's own marriage: Love marriages in a Calcutta neighbourhood', *South Asia Research*, 22(1): 79–94.

Dore, R. (1976), *The Diploma Disease: Education, Qualification and Development* (Berkeley, CA: University of California Press).

Doron, A. (2010), 'Caste away: Subaltern engagement with the modern Indian state', *Modern Asian Studies*, 44(4): 753–83.

Doron, A. and R. Jeffrey (2013), *The Great Indian Phone Book: How the Cheap Cell Phone Changes Business, Politics and Daily Life* (Cambridge, MA: Harvard University Press).

Doshi, V. (2016), 'India's long wait for justice: 27m cases trapped in legal logjam', *The Guardian*, 6 May.

Drèze, J. (2015), 'JAM and the pursuit of nirvana', *Ideas for India*, 13 November.

Drèze, J. (2019), 'The mother of non-issues: On maternity entitlements', *The Hindu*, 19 November.

Drèze, J. and R. Khera (2009), 'The battle for employment guarantee', *Frontline*, 26(1), 16 January.

Drèze, J. and R. Khera (2017), 'Recent social security initiatives in India', *World Development*, 98: 555–72.

Drèze, J. and A. Kotwal (2018), 'Ashok Kotwal speaks with Jean Drèze', *Ideas for India*, 28 March.

Drèze, J. and A. Sen (1991), *Hunger and Public Action* (Oxford: Oxford University Press).

Drèze, J. and A. Sen (2002), 'Democratic practice and social inequality in India', *Journal of Asian and African Studies*, 37(2): 6–37.

Drèze, J. and A. Sen (2013), *An Uncertain Glory: India and its Contradictions* (Princeton, NJ: Princeton University Press).

Drèze, J., P. Gupta, R. Khera and I. Pimenta (2016), 'Food Security Act: How are India's poorest states faring?', *Ideas for India*, 29 June.

Drèze, J., P. Gupta, R. Khera and I. Pimenta (2019), 'Casting the net: India's PDS after the National Food Security Act', *Economic and Political Weekly*, 54(6): 36–47.

Dube, S. (1998), *In the Land of Poverty: Memoirs of an Indian family 1947–1997* (London: Zed Books).

Dubochet, L. (2012), 'Civil society in a middle-income country: Evolutions and challenges in India', *Journal of International Development*, 24: 714–27.

Dumont, L. (1970), *Homo Hierarchicus: The Caste System and Its Implications* (London: Weidenfeld & Nicholson).

Duncan, I. (1997), 'Agricultural innovation and political change in north India: The Lok Dal in Uttar Pradesh', *Journal of Peasant Studies*, 24(4): 246–68.

Duncan, I. (1999), 'Dalits and politics in rural north India: The Bahujan Samaj Party in Uttar Pradesh', *Journal of Peasant Studies*, 27(1): 35–60.

Durham, D. (2008), 'Apathy and agency: The romance of agency and youth in Botswana', in J. Cole and D. Durham (eds) *Figuring the Future: Globalisation and the Temporalities of Children and Youth* (Santa Fe: School for Advanced Research Press).

Dutt D'Cunha, S. (2018), 'Modi announces "100 per cent village electrification". But 31 million homes are still in the dark', *Forbes*. Available at https://www.forbes.com/sites/suparnadutt/2018/05/07/modi-announces-100-village-electrification-but-31-million-homes-are-still-in-the-dark/.

Dutta, P., R. Murgai, M. Ravallion and D. van de Walle (2012), 'Does India's employment guarantee scheme guarantee employment?', *Economic and Political Weekly*, 47(16): 55–64.

Dutta, S. S. (2019), 'Not even 3% of faculty at IITS are Dalits, Tribals'. *The New Indian Express*, 1 January.

Dworkin, A. (1997), *Life and Death* (New York: Free Press).

Dyson, J. (2018), 'Love actually: Youth mediators and advisors in North India', *Annals of the American Association of Geographers*, 108(4): 974–88.

Dyson, J. (2019), 'Rethinking education as a contradictory resource: Girls' education in the Indian Himalayas', *Geoforum*, 103: 66–74.

Dyson, J. and C. Jeffrey (2018), 'Everyday prefiguration: Youth social action in north India', *Transactions of the Institute of British Geographers*, 43(4): 573–85.

Dyson, T. and M. Moore (1983), 'On kinship structure, female autonomy, and demographic behavior in India', *Population and Development Review*, 9(1): 35–60.

Editorial (2002), 'Coming to terms with Gujarat', *Frontline*, 19(26), 21 December.

Editorial (2007), 'Restoring rights', *Economic and Political Weekly*, 42(1): 4–5.

Editorial (2010), 'Jobless growth', *Economic and Political Weekly*, 45(39): 7–8.

Editorial (2013), 'The problem with poverty numbers', *Economic and Political Weekly*, 48(33): 7–8.

Editorial (2015), 'An avoidable tragicomedy', *Economic and Political Weekly*, 50(14): 7–8.

Editorial Board (2019), 'The raid on the RBI is risky', *Financial Times*, 21 January.

Ellis, R. (2010), 'Civil society, savage space: Spaces of urban governance in Chennai, India', unpublished PhD Dissertation (Department of Geography, University of Washington).

Engerman, D. (2018), *The Price of Aid: The Economic Cold War in India* (Cambridge, MA: Harvard University Press).

Engineer, A. A. (ed.) (1984), *Communal Riots in Post-independence India* (Hyderabad: Sangam Books).

Epstein, T. S. (1973), *South India: Yesterday, Today and Tomorrow* (London: Macmillan).

EPW [Economic and Political Weekly] (2018), 'Conspiracy mongering', *Economic and Political Weekly*, 53(24): 7–8.

EPW [Economic and Political Weekly] Engage (2019), 'The AAP audit: Can "alternate politics" work?', *EPW Engage*, 2 April.

Faust, D. and R. Nagar (2001), 'English-medium education, social fracturing and the politics of development in postcolonial India', *Economic and Political Weekly*, 36(30): 2878–83.

Fernandes, L. (2006), *India's New Middle Class* (Minneapolis, MN: University of Minnesota Press).

Fernandes, L. and P. Heller (2006), 'Hegemonic aspirations: New middle class politics and India's democracy in comparative perspective', *Critical Asian Studies*, 38(4): 495–521.

Fernandes, W. (2009), 'Background note – Statement against Government of India's planned military offensive in Adivasi-populated regions: National and international signatories', *Sanhati*, 12 October. Available at http://sanhati.com/excerpted/1824/#4.

Field, E., S. Jayachandran and R. Pande (2010), 'Do traditional institutions constrain female entrepreneurship? A field experiment on business training in India', *American Economic Review*, 100(2): 125–9.

Findlay, S. (2019), 'No end to crisis in sight as drought grips India's Chennai', *Financial Times*, 3 August.

First Post (2016), 'Now Modi government praises MGNREGA', *First Post*, 2 February. Available at https://www.firstpost.com/india/u-turn-on-mgnrega-now-nda-govt-terms-scheme-cause-of-national-pride-2606330.html.

Fominaya, C. F. (2010), 'Creating cohesion from diversity: The challenge of collective identity formation in the global justice movement', *Sociological Inquiry*, 80(3): 377–404.

Fominaya, C. F. (2014), *Social Movements and Globalization: How Protests, Occupations and Uprisings Are Changing the World* (London: Macmillan).

Frank, A. G. (1967), *Capitalism and Underdevelopment in Latin America* (New York: Monthly Review Press).

Frankel, F. (1978), *India's Political Economy, 1947–1977* (Delhi: Oxford University Press).

Froerer, P. (2007), *Religious Division and Social Conflict: The Emergence of Hindu Nationalism in Rural India* (Delhi: Social Science Press).

Froerer, P. (2012), 'Learning, livelihoods, and social mobility: Valuing girls' education in Central India', *Anthropology and Education Quarterly*, 43(4): 344–57.

Frøystad, K. (2005), *Blended Boundaries: Caste, Class and Shifting Faces of 'Hinduness' in a North Indian City* (New Delhi: Oxford University Press).

Fuller, C. J. (1989), 'Misconceiving the grain heap: A critique of the concept of the Indian jajmani system', in J. Parry and M. Bloch (eds) *Money and the Morality of Exchange*, 33–63 (Cambridge: Cambridge University Press).

Fuller, C. J. (1996), 'Introduction: caste today', in C. J. Fuller (ed.) *Caste Today*, 1–31 (New Delhi: Oxford University Press).

Fuller, C. J. and J. Harriss (2005), 'Globalizing Hinduism: The 'traditional' teaching of Swami Dayananda Saraswati and modern business in Chennai', in J. Assayag and C. J. Fuller (eds) *Globalization and India* (London: Anthem Press).

Fuller, C. J. and H. Narasimhan (2007), 'Information technology professionals and the new-rich middle class in Chennai (Madras)', *Modern Asian Studies*, 41(1): 121–50.

Fuller, C. J. and H. Narasimhan (2014), *Tamil Brahmans: The Making of a Middle Class Caste* (Chicago, IL: University of Chicago Press).

Gadgil, M. and R. Guha (1995), *Ecology and Equity: The Use and Abuse of Nature in Contemporary India* (New York: Routledge).

Galanter, M. (1984), *Competing Equalities: Law and the Backward Classes in India* (New Delhi: Oxford University Press).

Ganapathy (2007), 'Interview with Ganapathy, General Secretary, CPI-Maoist'. Available at https://www.satp.org/satporgtp/countries/india/maoist/documents/papers/interview_ganapathy.htm.

Gandhi, A. and M. Walton (2012), 'Where do India's billionaires get their wealth?', *Economic and Political Weekly*, 47(40): 10–14.

Gangoli, G. (2007), *Indian Feminisms: Law, Patriarchies and Violence in India* (London: Routledge).

Ganguly, S. (2015), 'India's national security', in D. M. Malone, C. Raja Mohan and S. Raghavan (eds) *The Oxford Handbook of Indian Foreign Policy* (New York: Oxford University Press).

Ganti, T. (2013), *Bollywood: A Guidebook to Popular Hindi Cinema* (London: Routledge).

Gauba, K. and A. Singh (2017), 'Voter, citizen, enemy', *Economic and Political Weekly*, 52(23): 12–14.

Geevan C. P. (2004), 'National environment policy', *Economic and Political Weekly*, 39(43): 4686–9.

Ghatak, M. (2016), 'Is India ready for a universal basic income scheme', *Ideas for India*, 28 September.

Ghatak, M. and U. Mukherjee (2019), 'The mirage of Modinomics', *The India Forum*, March.

Ghose, A. (2016), *Indian Employment Report 2016: Challenges and Imperative of Manufacturing-Led Growth* (Delhi: Oxford University Press).

Ghosh, J. (2011), 'The cash option', *Frontline*, 28(5), 11 March.

Ghosh, J. (2014), 'Can employment schemes work? The case of the rural employment guarantee in India', in D. Papadimitriou (ed.) *Contributions to Economic Theory, Policy, Development and Finance* (Basingstoke: Palgrave Macmillan).

Gidwani, V. and K. Sivaramakrishnan (2003), 'Circular migration and rural cosmopolitanism in India', *Contributions to Indian Sociology*, 37: 339–67.

Gilbertson, A. (2019), 'Deepening connections between Australian schools and India: A very short policy brief'. Available at https://www.aii.unimelb.edu.au/wp-content/uploads/2019/06/VSPB-Vol-12-1.pdf.

Gooptu, N. (2001), *The Politics of the Urban Poor in Early Twentieth-century India* (Cambridge: Cambridge University Press).

Gooptu, N. (2007), 'Economic liberalization, work and democracy: Industrial decline and urban politics in Kolkata', *Economic and Political Weekly*, 42(25): 1922–33.

Gooptu, N. (2011), 'Economic liberalization, urban politics and the poor', in S. Ruparelia, S. Reddy, J. Harriss and S. Corbridge (eds) *Understanding India's New Political Economy: A Great Transformation?* (London: Routledge).

Gooptu, N. (2013), *Enterprise Culture in Neoliberal India: Studies in Youth, Class, Work and Media* (London: Routledge).

Gorringe, H. (2009), 'Shifting the grindstone of caste? Decreasing dependency amongst Dalit labourers in Tamilnadu', in B. Harriss-White and J. Heyer (eds) *The Comparative Political Economy of Development: Africa and South Asia*, 248–66 (London: Routledge).

Gorringe, H. (2016a), 'Drumming out oppression, or drumming it in? Identity, culture and contention in Dalit politics', *Contributions to Indian Sociology*, 50(1): 1–26.

Gorringe, H. (2016b), 'Out of the *cheris*: Dalits contesting and creating public space in Tamil Nadu', *Space and Culture*, 19(2): 164–76.

Gorringe, H. (2017), *Panthers in Parliament: Dalits, Caste, and Political Power in South India* (Oxford: Oxford University Press).

Gould, H. (1972), 'Educational structures and political processes in Faizabad district, Uttar Pradesh', in S. H. Rudolph and L. I. Rudolph (eds) *Education and Politics in India*, 94–120 (Cambridge, MA: Harvard University Press).

Government of India (GoI) (2009), *Report of the National Commission for Enterprises in the Informal Sector* (New Delhi: National Commission for Enterprises in the Informal Sector).

Government of India (GoI), Ministry of Finance (2016), *Economic Survey 2015–16*, Vols 1 and 2 (New Delhi: Government of India).

Government of India (GoI), Ministry of Finance (2017), *Economic Survey 2016–17*, Vols 1 and 2 (New Delhi: Government of India).

Government of India (GoI), Ministry of Finance (2018), *Economic Survey 2017–18*, Vols 1 and 2 (New Delhi: Government of India).

Government of India (GoI) (2019), *Draft National Education Policy* (Delhi: Government of India).

Greenstone, M. and R. Hanna (2014), 'Environmental regulations, air and water pollution, and infant mortality in India', *American Economic Review*, 104 (10): 3038–72.

Griffin, K. (1999), *Alternative Strategies for Economic Development*, 2nd edn (Basingstoke: Macmillan in association with the OECD Development Centre).

Grover, S. (2011), *Marriage, Love, Caste and Kinship Support* (New Delhi: Social Science Press).

Guha, R. (2007a), 'Adivasis, Naxalites and Indian democracy', *Economic and Political Weekly*, 42(32): 3305–12.

Guha, R. (2007b), *India after Gandhi: The History of the World's Largest Democracy* (London: Macmillan).

Guhan, S. (1980), 'Rural poverty: Policy and play acting', *Economic and Political Weekly*, 15(47): 1975–82.

Gupta, A., N. Khalid, D. Deshpande, P. Hathi, A. Kapur, N. Srivastav, S, Vyas, D. Spears and D. Coffey (2019), 'Changes in open defecation in rural North India, 2014–18', Discussion Paper 12065 (Bonn: IZA Institute of Labour Economics).

Gupta, D. (2000), *Interrogating Caste: Understanding Hierarchy and Difference in Indian Society* (New Delhi: Penguin).

Gupta, D. (2005), 'Whither the Indian village: Culture and agriculture in "rural" India', *Economic and Political Weekly*, 40(8): 751–8.

Gupta, D. (2007), 'Citizens versus people: The politics of majoritarianism and marginalization in democratic India', *Sociology of Religion*, 68(1), 27–44.

Gupta, S., R. Mullen, R. Basrur, I. Hall, N. Blarel, M. Pardesi and S. Ganguly

(2019), 'Indian foreign policy under Modi: A new brand or just repackaging?', *International Studies Perspectives*, 20: 1–45.

Hall, S. (1985), 'Authoritarian populism: A reply', *New Left Review*, 1/151: 115–24.

Hansen, T. B. (1996a), 'Globalisation and nationalist imaginations: Hindutva's promise of equality through difference', *Economic and Political Weekly*, 31(10): 603–16.

Hansen, T. B. (1996b), 'Recuperating masculinity: Hindu nationalism, violence, and the exorcism of the Muslim "other"', *Critique of Anthropology*, 16(22): 137–72.

Hansen, T. B. (1999), *The Saffron Wave: Democracy and Hindu Nationalism in Modern India* (Princeton, NJ: Princeton University Press).

Hansen, T. B. (2017), 'Babri Masjid and its aftermath changed India forever', *The Wire*, 7 December. Available at https://thewire.in/communalism/babri-masjid-aftermath-changed-india-forever.

Hanson, A. H. (1966), *The Process of Planning: A Study of India's Five Year Plans* (Oxford: Oxford University Press).

Harindranath, R. and S. Khorana (2014), 'Civil society movements and the "twittering classes" in the postcolony: An Indian case study', *South Asia: Journal of South Asian Studies*, 37(1): 60–71.

Harriss, J. (1982a), *Capitalism and Peasant Farming: Agrarian Structure and Ideology in Northern Tamil Nadu* (New Delhi: Oxford University Press).

Harriss, J. (1982b), *Rural Development: Theories of Peasant Economy and Agrarian Change* (London: Hutchinson).

Harriss, J. (1987), 'The state in retreat? Why has India experienced such half-hearted liberalization in the 1980s?', *IDS Bulletin*, 18(4): 31–8.

Harriss, J. (2003a), 'The great tradition globalizes: Reflections on two studies of "the industrial leaders" of Madras', *Modern Asian Studies*, 7(2): 327–62.

Harriss, J. (2003b), 'Do political regimes matter? Poverty reduction and regime differences across India', in P. Houtzager and M. Moore (eds) *Changing Paths: International Development and the New Politics of Inclusion*, 204–32 (Ann Arbor: University of Michigan Press).

Harriss, J. (2003c), '"Widening the radius of trust": Ethnographic explorations of trust and Indian business', *Journal of the Royal Anthropological Institute*, 9(4): 755–73.

Harriss, J. (2006), 'Middle-class activism and the politics of the informal working class', *Critical Asian Studies*, 38(4): 445–65.

Harriss, J. (2010), 'Participation and contestation in urban governance in India', Simons Working Paper No. 2 (Vancouver: School for International Studies, Simon Fraser University).

Harriss, J. (2014), 'Development theory', in B. Currie-Alder, R. Kanbur, D. M. Malone and R. Medhora (eds) *International Development: Ideas, Experience and Prospects*, 35–49 (Oxford: Oxford University Press).

Harriss, J. (2017), 'New directions in social policy in India: Universalizing elementary education in India – Achievements and challenges', Working Paper (Geneva: United Nations Research Institute for Social Development).

Harriss, J. (2018) 'Privilege in dispute: Economic and political change and caste relations in Tamil Nadu early in the 21st century', in S. Jodhka and J. Manor (eds) *Contested Hierarchies, Persisting Influences: Caste and Power in India Today* (Delhi: Orient Blackswan).

Harriss, J., J. Jeyaranjan and K. Nagaraj (2010), 'Land, labour and caste politics in rural Tamil Nadu in the 20th century: Iruvelpattu (1916–2008)', *Economic and Political Weekly*, 45(31): 47–61.

Harriss, R. (2003), 'Popular resistance to globalization and neoliberalism in Latin America', *Journal of Development Studies*, 19: 365–426.

Harriss-White, B. (2003), *India Working: Essays on Economy and Society* (Cambridge: Cambridge University Press).

Harriss-White, B. and S. Janakarajan (eds) (2004), *Rural India Faces the 21st Century* (London: Anthem Press).

Harriss-White, B. and K. Vidhyarthee (2009), 'Stigma and regions of accumulation: Mapping Dalit and Adivasi capital in the 1990s', in B. Harriss-White and J. Heyer (eds) *The Comparative Political Economy of Development: Africa and South Asia*, 317–49 (London: Routledge).

Harriss-White, B., E. Basile, A. Dixit, P. Joddar, A. Prakash and K. Vidyarthee (2014), *Dalits and Adivasis in India's Business Economy: Three Essays and an Atlas* (Gurgaon: Three Essays Collective).

Harvey, D. (2005), *A Brief History of Neoliberalism* (Oxford: Oxford University Press).

Heller, P. (2000), 'Degrees of democracy: Some comparative lessons from India', *World Politics*, 52(4): 484–519.

Heller, P. (2009), 'Democratic deepening in India and South Africa', *Journal of Asian and African Studies*, 44(1): 123–49.

Hensman, R. (2010), 'Labour and globalization: Union responses in India', in P. Bowles and J. Harriss (eds) *Globalization and Labour in China and India* (Basingstoke: Palgrave Macmillan).

Heuzé, G. (1992), 'Shiv Sena and national Hinduism', *Economic and Political Weekly*, 27(41): 2253–61.

Himanshu (2007), 'Recent trends in poverty and inequality: Some preliminary results', *Economic and Political Weekly*, 42(6): 497–508.

Himanshu (2011), 'Employment trends in India: A re-examination', *Economic and Political Weekly*, 46(37): 43–59.

Himanshu and A. Sen (2011), 'Why not a universal food security legislation?', *Economic and Political Weekly*, 46(12): 38–47.

Himanshu and K. Sen (2014), 'Measurement, patterns and determinants of poverty', in N. Gooptu and J. Parry (eds) *Persistence of Poverty in India* (Delhi: Social Science Press).

Himanshu, P. Lanjouw, A. Mukhopadhyay and R. Murgai (2011), 'Non-farm diversification and rural poverty decline: A perspective from Indian sample survey and village study data', Working Paper No. 44 (London: London School of Economics Asia Research Centre).

Holston, J. and A. Appadurai (1996), 'Cities and citizenship', *Public Culture*, 8(2): 187–204.

Hopkins, V. (2019), 'Hungary's Viktor Orban and the rewriting of history', *Financial Times*, 25 July.

Howard, L. L. and N. Prakash (2012), 'Do employment quotas explain the occupational choices of disadvantaged minorities in India?', *International Review of Applied Economics*, 26(4): 489–513.

Huber, E., D. Rueschemeyer and J. D. Stephens (1997), 'The paradoxes of contemporary democracy: Formal, participatory, and social dimensions', *Comparative Politics*, 23(3): 323–42.

Husain, Z. and A. Chatterjee (2009), 'Primary completion rates across socio-religious communities in India', *Economic and Political Weekly*, 44(15): 59–67.

Hussain, M. M. and P. N. Howard (2013), 'What best explains successful protest cascades? ICTs and the fuzzy causes of the Arab Spring', *International Studies Review*, 15(1): 48–66.

Ilaiah, K. (1991), 'Upper caste violence: Study of Chunduru carnage', *Economic and Political Weekly*, 26(37): 2079–84.

Ilavarasan, P. V. (2013), 'Community work and limited online activism among Indian youth', *The International Communication Gazette*, 75(3): 284–99.

Inden, R. (1990), *Imagining India* (Oxford: Blackwell).

India Today (2019), 'NRC will be implemented in whole country, can't disclose timeline: Amit Shah', *India Today*, 14 October. Available at https://www.indiatoday.in/india/story/nrc-in-whole-country-cant-disclose-timeline-amit-shah-1609338-2019-10-14.

Internet Desk (2016), 'JNU row: What is the outrage all about?', *The Hindu*, 16 February.

Isaksen, K.-A. and K. Stokke (2014) 'Changing climate discourse and politics in India: Climate change as challenge and opportunity for diplomacy and development', *Geoforum*, 57: 110–19.

Iversen, V., R. Palmer-Jones and K. Sen (2013), 'On the colonial origins of agricultural development in India: A re-examination of Banerjee and Iyer "History, institutions and economic performance"', *Journal of Development Studies*, 49(12): 1631–46.

Iversen, V., A. Krishna and K. Sen (2017), 'Rags to riches? Intergenerational occupational mobility', *Economic and Political Weekly*, 52(44): 107–14.

Iyer, S. (2018), *The Economics of Religion in India* (Cambridge, MA: Harvard University Press).

Jacobs, S. (2015), *The Art of Living Foundation: Spirituality and Wellbeing in the Global Context* (London: Routledge).

Jaffrelot, C. (2003), *India's Silent Revolution: The Rise of the Lower Castes in North India* (London: Hurst and Co).

Jaffrelot, C. (2010), 'The Hindu Nationalists and power', in N. G. Jayal and P. B. Mehta (eds) *The Oxford Companion to Politics in India* (Delhi: Oxford University Press).

Jaffrelot, C. (2014), 'The other saffron', *Indian Express*, 6 October.

Jaffrelot, C. (2017), 'India's democracy at 70: Towards a Hindu state?' *Journal of Democracy*, 28(3), 52–63.

Jaffrelot, C. (2018), 'Business-friendly Gujarat under Narendra Modi: The implications of a new political economy', in C. Jaffrelot, A. Kohli and K. Murali (eds) *Business and Politics in India* (New York: Oxford University Press).

Jaffrelot, C. and S. Kumar (2009), *Rise of the Plebeians? The Changing Face of Indian Legislative Assemblies* (New Delhi: Routledge).

Jaishankar, S. (2015), 21st Fullerton Lecture of the International Institute of Strategic Studies, delivered in Singapore, 20 July. Available at https://www.mea.gov.in/Speeches-Statements.htm?dtl/25493/iiss+fullerton+lecture+by+dr+s+jaishankar+foreign+secretary+in+singapore.

Jakimow, T. (2017), Empowering women parshads in Dehradun municipal council, *Economic and Political Weekly*, 52(23): 120–6.

Jalal, A. (1995), *Democracy and Authoritarianism in South Asia* (Cambridge: Cambridge University Press).

Jalali, R. (2008), 'International funding of NGOs in India: Bringing the state back in', *Voluntas*, 19: 161–88.

Jaoul, N. (2007), 'Political and "non-political" means in the Dalit movement', in S. Pai (ed.) *Political Process in Uttar Pradesh: Identity, Economic Reform and Governance* (New Delhi: Pearson).

Jaoul, N. (2009), 'Naxalism in Bihar: From bullet to ballot', in L. Gayer and C. Jaffrelot (eds) *Armed Militias of South Asia: Fundamentalists, Maoists and Separatists* (London: Hurst and Co.).

Jaoul, N. (2015), 'A strong law for the weak: Dalit activism in a District Court of Uttar Pradesh', in D. Berti and D. Bordia (eds) *Regimes of Legality: Ethnography of Criminal Cases in South Asia* (New Delhi: Oxford University Press).

Jauregui, B. (2014), 'Provisional agency in India: Jugaad and legitimation of corruption', *American Ethnologist*, 41(1), 76–91.

Jauregui, B. (2016), *Provisional Authority: Police, Order, and Security in India* (Chicago, IL: University of Chicago Press).

Jayachandran, S. (2015), 'The roots of gender inequality in developing countries', *Annual Review of Economics*, 7(1): 63–88.

Jayadeva, S. (2019), 'English-medium: Schooling, social mobility, and inequality in Bangalore, India', *Anthropology & Education Quarterly*, 50(2): 151–69.

Jayal, N. G. (2006), 'Engendering local democracy: The impact of quotas for women in India's panchayats', *Democratisation*, 13(1): 15–35.

Jayal, N. G. (2013), *Citizenship and its Discontents: An Indian History* (Cambridge, MA: Harvard University Press).

Jayal, N. G. (2014), 'Indian citizenship: A century of disagreement', in E. F. Isin and P. Nyers (eds) *Routledge Handbook of Global Citizenship Studies* (London: Routledge).

Jayal, N. G. (2019), 'Faith-based citizenship', *The India Forum*, 1 November.

Jayaweera, S. (1997), 'Women, education and empowerment in Asia', *Gender and Education*, 9(4): 411–24.

Jeffery, P. (2014), 'Supply-and-demand demographics: Dowry, daughter aversion and marriage markets in contemporary north India', *Contemporary South Asia*, 22(2): 171–88.

Jeffery, R., P. Jeffery and C. Jeffrey (2006), '*Parhāī ka māhaul*? An educational environment in Bijnor, UP', in G. de Neve and H. Donner (eds.) *The Meaning of the Local: Politics of Place in Urban India*, 116–40 (London: Routledge).

Jeffrey, C. (1999), 'Reproducing difference: The accumulation strategies of richer Jat farmers in Western Uttar Pradesh, India', PhD dissertation (Cambridge: University of Cambridge).

Jeffrey, C. (2000), 'Democratisation without representation? The power and political strategies of a rural elite in North India', *Political Geography*, 19(8): 1013–36.

Jeffrey, C. (2001), 'A fist is stronger the five fingers: Caste and dominance in rural North India', *Transactions of the Institute of British Geographers*, 25(2): 1–30.

Jeffrey, C. (2010), *Timepass: Youth, Class and the Politics of Waiting* (Stanford, CA: Stanford University Press).

Jeffrey, C. (2012), 'Geographies of children and youth II: Global youth agency', *Progress in Human Geography*, 36(2): 245–53.

Jeffrey, C. (2019), 'What role will "generation timepass" play in the 2019 Lok Sabha elections?', *The Wire*, 18 February. Available at https://thewire.in/labour/what-role-will-generation-timepass-play-in-the-2019-lok-sabha-elections.

Jeffrey, C. and J. Dyson (2016), 'Now: Prefigurative politics through a north Indian lens', *Economy and Society*, 45(1): 77–100.

Jeffrey, C. and S. Young (2012), 'Waiting for change: youth, caste and politics in India', *Economy and Society*, 41(4), 638–61.

Jeffrey, C., P. Jeffery and R. Jeffery (2008), *Degrees without Freedom? Education, Masculinities, and Unemployment in North India* (Stanford, CA: Stanford University Press).

Jehan, K. (2009), 'Heroes or Hondas? Analysing men's dowry narratives in a time of rapid social change', in T. E. Bradley and M. Subramaniam (eds) *Dowry: Bridging the Gap between Theory and Practice* (New Delhi: Women Unlimited).

Jejeebhoy, S. J. and Z. A. Sathar (2001), 'Women's autonomy in India and Pakistan: The influence of religion and region', *Population and Development Review*, 27(4): 687–712.

Jenkins, R. (2011), 'The politics of India's special economic zones', in S. Ruparelia, S. Reddy, J. Harriss and S. Corbridge (eds) *Understanding India's New Political Economy: A Great Transformation?* (London: Routledge).

Jenkins, R. (2013), 'Land, rights and reform in India', *Pacific Affairs*, 86(3): 591–612

Jenkins, R. (2019), 'India 2019: A transformative election?', *Pacific Affairs*, 92(3): 475–97.

Jenkins, R. and A.-M. Goetz (1999), 'Accounts and accountability: Theoretical implications of the right to information movement in India', *Third World Quarterly*, 20(3): 589–608.

Jenkins, R. and J. Manor (2017), *Politics and the Right to Work: India's National Rural Employment Guarantee* (London: Hurst and Co.).

Jenkins, R., L. Kennedy and P. Mukhopadhay (2014), *Power, Policy and Protest: The Politics of India's Special Economic Zones* (Delhi: Oxford University Press).

Jha, A. (2017), 'A college in search of a "saga"', in D. Kapur and P. B. Mehta (eds) *Navigating the Labyrinth: Perspectives on India's Higher Education*, 39–69 (New Delhi: Orient Black Swan).

Jha, P., M. A. Kesler, R. Kumar, F. Ram, U. Ram, L. Aleksandrowicz, D. G. Bassani, S. Chandra and J. K. Banthia (2011), 'Trends in selective abortions of girls in India: Analysis of nationally representative birth histories from 1990 to 2005 and census data from 1991 to 2011', *The Lancet*, 377(9781): 1921–8.

Jha, V. (2010), 'Evidence-based research mobilising action for policy-influencing in two provinces: Policy changes under the Right to Information Act in India', *Overseas Development Network* (London: Overseas Development Institute).

Jodhka, S. S. (2008), 'Caste and the corporate sector', *The Indian Journal of Industrial Relations*, 44(2): 185–93.

Jodhka, S. S. (2015), *Caste in Contemporary India* (London: Routledge).

John, M. E. (2014), Sex ratios and sex selection in India: History and the present', in L. Fernandes (ed.) *Routledge Handbook of Gender in South Asia* (London: Routledge).

Jones, K. W. (1966), *The Arya Samaj in the Punjab: A study of Social Reform and Religious Revivalism 1877–1902* (Berkeley, CA: University of California Press).

Jones, R. (2009), 'Geopolitical boundary narratives, the global war on terror and border fencing in India', *Transactions of the Institute of British Geographers*, 34(3): 290–304.

Joshi, V. (2017), *India's Long Road: The Search for Prosperity* (Oxford: Oxford University Press).

Joshi, Y. (2018), 'The real status of rural sanitation', *Economic and Political Weekly*, 53(28): 100–1.

Jowett, A. and C. Dyer (2012), 'Scaling-up successfully: Pathways to replication for educational NGOs', *International Journal of Educational Development*, 32(6): 733–42.

Kabeer, N. (1994), *Reversed Realities: Gender Hierarchies in Development Thought* (London: Verso).

Kabeer, N. (2016), 'Gender equality, economic growth, and women's agency: The "endless variety" and "monotonous similarity" of patriarchal constraints', *Feminist Economics*, 22(1): 295–321.

Kabeer, N. (2018), 'Women workers and the politics of claims making: The local and the global', *Development and Change*, 49(3): 759–89.

Kalaramadam, S. (2018), 'Presence into participation and representation: Gender quotas in local governance in India', *Journal of South Asian Development*, 13(1): 1–23.

Kaletski, E. and N. Prakash (2016), 'Does political reservation for minorities affect child labor? Evidence from India', *World Development*, 87: 50–69.

Kaletski, E. and N. Prakash (2017), 'Can elected minority representatives affect health worker visits? Evidence from India', *Review of Development Economics*, 21(1): 67–102.

Kamat, S. (2002), *Development Hegemony: NGOs and the State in India* (New Delhi: Oxford University Press).

Kamat, S. (2014), 'Gender and education in South Asia', in L. Fernandes (ed.) *Routledge Handbook of Gender in South Asia* (London: Routledge).

Kamath, L. and M. Vijayabaskar (2009), 'Limits and possibilities of middle class associations as urban collective actors', *Economic and Political Weekly*, 44(26–27): 368–76.

Kandiyoti, D. (1988), 'Bargaining with patriarchy', *Gender and Society*, 2(3): 274–90.

Kannan, K. P. (2018), 'Macro-economic aspects of inequality and poverty in India', in A. Shah, J. Lerche, R. Axelby, D. Benbabali, B. Donegan, J. Raj and V. Tharkur (eds), *Ground Down by Growth: Tribe, Caste, Class and Inequality in Twenty-First Century India* (London: Pluto Press).

Kannan, K. P. and G. Raveendran (2019), 'From jobless to job-loss growth: Gainers and losers during 2012–18', *Economic and Political Weekly*, 54(44): 38–44.

Kaplinsky, R. (2005), *Globalization, Poverty and Inequality: Between a Rock and a Hard Place* (Cambridge: Polity).

Kapur, A. and R. Shukla (2019), 'Budget 2019 is ambitious in health care. But more can be done', *The Wire*, 6 July. Available at https://thewire.in/health/budget-2019-healthcare-infrastructure-ayushman-bharat.

Kapur, D. (2010), 'The political economy of the state', in N. G. Jayal and P. B. Mehta (eds) *The Oxford Companion to Politics in India*, 387–407 (Delhi: Oxford University Press).

Kapur, D. (2018), 'The battle between India's central bank and the government has deep roots', *Financial Times*, 4 November.

Kapur, D. and P. B. Mehta (2017), 'Introduction', in D. Kapur and P. B. Mehta (eds) *Navigating the Labyrinth: Perspectives on India's Higher Education*, 1–31 (Hyderabad: Orient Blackswan).

Kapur, D., P. Mukhopadhyay and A. Subramanian (2008), 'More on direct cash transfers', *Economic and Political Weekly*, 43(47): 85–7.

Kapur, D., C. B. Prasad, L. Pritchett and S. D. Babu (2010), 'Rethinking inequality: Dalits in Uttar Pradesh in the market reform era', *Economic and Political Weekly*, 45(35): 39–49.

Kapur, R. (2012), 'Hecklers to power: The waning of liberal rights and challenges to feminism in India', in A. Loomba and R. Lukose (eds) *South Asian Feminisms* (Durham, NC: Duke University Press).

Kar, S. and K. Sen (2016), *The Political Economy of India's Growth Episodes* (London: Palgrave Macmillan).

Katju, M. (2017), 'Yogi Adityanath as UP CM: The fringe goes mainstream', *The Hindu*, 21 March.

Katulkar, R. (2013), 'Atrocities against Dalits: the Pavnava incident', *Economic and Political Weekly*, 48(28), 13 July.

Kaur, R. (2010), 'Khap panchayats, sex ratio and female agency', *Economic and Political Weekly*, 45(23): 14–16.

Kaviraj, S. (1991), 'On state, society and discourse in India', in J. Manor (ed.), *Rethinking Third World Politics* (Harlow: Longman).

Kaviraj, S. (2001), 'In search of civil society', in S. Kaviraj and S. Khilnani (eds) *Civil Society: History and Possibilities* (Cambridge: Cambridge University Press).

Kazmin, A. (2018a), 'Clouds gather over India's solar energy sector', *Financial Times*, 11 March.

Kazmin, A. (2018b), 'India: Narendra Modi hunts for more economic "firepower"', *Financial Times*, 24 June.

Kazmin, A. (2018c), 'Modi government in public spat with Reserve Bank of India', *Financial Times*, 30 October.

Kazmin, A. (2019a), 'India revises growth data as concern over official statistics mounts', *Financial Times*, 31 January.

Kazmin, A. (2019b), 'India's election: Will Narendra Modi's "giveaways" woo voters?', *Financial Times*, 8 February.

Kazmin, A. (2019c), 'Indian business presses Modi to speed up economic reforms', *Financial Times*, 4 June.

Kazmin, A. (2019d), 'India's rich party under a growing cloud of gloom', *Financial Times*, 7 August.

Kazmin, A. (2019e), 'India's economic growth rate drops to slowest in six years', *Financial Times*, 30 August.

Keefer, P. and S. Khemani (2004), 'Why do the poor receive poor services?', *Economic and Political Weekly*, 39(9): 935–43.

Kela, S. (2012), 'A party of the poor?', *Seminar*, 633: 72–6.

Kenny, C. and D. Williams (2001), 'What do we know about economic growth? Or, why don't we know very much?', *World Development*, 29(1): 1–22.

Khan, Y. (2007), *The Great Partition: The Making of India and Pakistan* (New Haven, CT: Yale University Press).

Khera, R. (ed.) (2011), *The Battle for Employment Guarantee* (Delhi: Oxford University Press).

Khera, R. (2017), 'Impact of Aadhaar on welfare programmes', *Economic and Political Weekly*, 52(50): 61–70.

Khilnani, S. (1997), *The Idea of India* (London: Hamish Hamilton).

King, K. (2012), 'The geopolitics and meanings of India's massive skills development ambitions', *International Journal of Educational Development*, 32(5): 665–73.

Kingdon, G. G. (2017), 'The private schooling phenomenon in India: A review', IZA Discussion Paper No. 10612 (Bonn: Institute of Labor Economics).

Klasen, S. and J. Pieters (2015), 'What explains the stagnation of female labor force participation in urban India?', World Bank Policy Research Working Paper, No. 7222.

Klenk, R. M. (2010), *Educating Activists: Development and Gender in the Making of Modern Gandhians* (New York: Lexington Books).

Kochhar, K., U. Kumar, R. Raghuram, A. Subramanian and I. Tokatlidis (2006), 'India's pattern of development: What happened, what follows?', IMF Working Paper (Washington, DC: International Monetary Fund).

Kohli, A. (1990), *Democracy and Discontent: India's Growing Crisis of Governability* (Cambridge: Cambridge University Press).

Kohli, A. (2001), 'Introduction', in A. Kohli (ed.) *The Success of India's Democracy* (Cambridge: Cambridge University Press).

Kohli, A. (2006a), 'Politics of economic growth in India, 1980–2005: part 1, the 1980s', *Economic and Political Weekly*, 41(13): 1251–65.

Kohli, A. (2006b), 'Politics of economic growth in India, 1980–2005: part 2, the 1990s and beyond', *Economic and Political Weekly*, 41(14): 1361–70.

Kohli, A. (2012), *Poverty Amid Plenty in the New India* (New York: Cambridge University Press).

Kothari, R. (ed.) (1970), *Caste in Indian Politics* (London: Sangam).

Kothari, R. (1984), 'The non-party political process', *Economic and Political Weekly*, 19(5): 216–24.

Kothari, A. (2004), 'Draft National Environment Plan 2004', *Economic and Political Weekly*, 39(43).

Kothari, A. (2007), 'For lasting rights', *Frontline*, 23(26).

Kotwal, A. (2017), 'The challenge of job creation', *Ideas for India*, 15 December.

Kotwal, A. and B. Ramaswami (2018) 'Aadhaar that doesn't exclude', *Ideas for India*, 11 April.

Kotwal, A., B. Ramaswami and W. Wadhwa (2011), 'Economic liberalisation and Indian economic growth: What's the evidence?', *Journal of Economic Literature*, 49(4): 1152–99.

Krishna, A. (2002), *Active Social Capital: Tracing the Roots of Development and Democracy* (New York: Columbia University Press).

Krishna, A. (2013), 'Making it in India', *Economic and Political Weekly*, 48(49): 38–49.

Krishna, A. (2017), *The Broken Ladder: The Paradox and the Potential of India's One Billion* (Delhi: Penguin Random House India).

Krishnaji, N. (2012), 'Abolish the poverty line', *Economic and Political Weekly*, 47(15): 10–11.

Kudva, N. and K. Misra (2008), 'Gender quotas, the politics of presence, and the feminist project: What does the Indian experience tell us?', *Signs: Journal of Women in Culture and Society*, 34(1): 49–73.

Kumar, A. P. (2019), 'The true dangers of the RTI (Amendment) Bill', *Economic and Political Weekly*, 54(30), 10–11.

Kumar, K. (1993), 'Hindu revivalism and education in north central India', in M. Marty and R. Appleby (eds) *Fundamentalisms and Society* (Chicago, IL: University of Chicago Press).

Kumar, K. (2014), 'Confronting extractive capital: Social and environmental movements in Odisha', *Economic and Political Weekly*, 49(14): 66–73.

Kumar, K. and J. M. Kerr (2012), 'Democratic assertions: The making of India's Forest Rights Act', *Development and Change*, 43(3): 751–71.

Kundu, A., and L. R. Saraswati (2012), 'Migration and exclusionary urbanisation in India', *Economic and Political Weekly*, 47(26–27): 219–27.

Lahoti, R. and H. Swaminathan (2016), 'Economic development and women's labor force participation in India', *Feminist Economics*, 22(2): 168–95.

Lal, V. (2014), 'State, civil society, and the right to dissent: Some thoughts on censorship in contemporary India', *India Review*, 13(3): 277–82.

Lambert, R. and M. Gillan (2013), 'Labour movements and the age of crisis: Scale, form and repertoires of action in India and beyond', *South Asia*, 36(2): 180–98.

Landes, D. (1998), *The Wealth and Poverty of Nations* (New York: W.W. Norton).

Lather, V. (2017), '"We beat teachers too" – True confessions of an ABVP footsoldier', *The Wire*, 27 February. Available at https://thewire.in/111843/we-beat-teachers-too-true-confessions-of-an-abvp-footsoldier/.

Lerche, J. (1995), 'Is bonded labour a bound category? Reconceptualising agrarian conflict in India', *Journal of Peasant Studies*, 22(3): 484–515.

Lerche, J. (1999), 'Politics of the poor: Agricultural labourers and political transformations in Uttar Pradesh', *Journal of Peasant Studies*, 26(2–3): 182–241.

Lerche, J. (2008), 'Transnational advocacy networks and affirmative action for Dalits in India', *Development and Change*, 39(2): 239–61.

Lerche, J. (2010), 'From "rural labour" to "classes of labour": class fragmentation, caste and class struggle at the bottom of the Indian labour hierarchy', in B. Harriss-White and J. Heyer (eds) *The Comparative Political Economy of Development* (New York: Routledge).

Levien, M. (2011), 'Special economic zones and accumulation by dispossession in India', *Journal of Agrarian Change*, 11(4): 454–83.

Levien, M. (2013a), 'The politics of dispossession: Theorizing India's land wars', *Politics and Society*, 31(2): 193–261.

Levien, M. (2013b), 'Regimes of dispossession: From steel towns to special economic zones', *Development and Change*, 44(2): 381–407.

Levien, M. (2015), 'From primitive accumulation to regimes of dispossession: Six theses on India's land question', *Economic and Political Weekly*, 50(22): 146–57.

Lewis, T., F. Martin and W. Sun (2016), *Telemodernities: Television and Transforming Lives in Asia* (Durham, NC: Duke University Press).

Li, T. (2007), *The Will to Improve: Governmentality, Development and the Practice of Politics* (Durham, NC: Duke University Press).

Lieten, G. K. (1996), 'Panchayats in Western Uttar Pradesh: "Namesake' members", *Economic and Political Weekly*, 31(39): 2700–5.

Linz, J. and A. Stepan (1996), 'Toward consolidated democracies', *Journal of Democracy*, 7(2): 14–33.

Lipset, S. M. (1994), 'The social requisites of democracy revisited', *American Sociological Review*, 59(1): 1–22.

Lipton, M. (1974), 'Towards a theory of agrarian reform', in D. Lehmann (ed.) *Agrarian Reform and Agrarian Reformism: Studies of Peru, Chile, China and India* (London: Faber).

Little, D. (2003), *The Paradox of Wealth and Poverty: Mapping the Ethical Dilemmas of Global Development* (Boulder, CO: Westview Press).

Livengood, A. and K. Kunte (2012), 'Enabling participatory planning with GIS: A case study of settlement mapping in Cuttack, India', *Environment and Urbanization*, 24(1): 77–97.

Lucia, A. J. (2014a), *Reflections of Amma: Devotees in a Global Embrace* (Berkeley, CA: University of California Press).

Lucia, A. J. (2014b), 'Innovative gurus: Tradition and change in contemporary Hinduism', *International Journal of Hindu Studies*, 18(2): 221–63.

McCarthy, T. (2019), 'Faith and freedom: Why evangelicals profess unwavering love for Donald Trump', *The Guardian*, 7 July.

McGuire, M. L. (2013), 'The embodiment of professionalism: Personality-development programmes in New Delhi', in N. Gooptu (ed.) *Enterprise Culture in Neoliberal India: Studies in Youth, Class, Work and Media* (London: Routledge).

Maclean, K. (2015), *A Revolutionary History of Interwar India: Violence, Image, Voice and Text* (Oxford: Oxford University Press).

Madan, T. N. (1997), *Modern Myths, Locked Minds: Secularism and Fundamentalism in India* (Delhi: Oxford University Press).

Madhok, S. and S. M. Rai (2012), 'Agency, injury, and transgressive politics in neoliberal times', *Signs*, 37(3): 645–69.

Madsen, S. T. (1998), 'The decline of the BKU', European Conference of Modern Asian Studies, Charles University, Prague.

Mahaprashasta, A. (2017), 'In Sinha's criticism of Modi's economic policies an echo of discontent within RSS's foot soldiers', *The Wire*, 30 September. Available at https://thewire.in/182963/modi-government-yashwant-sinha-rss/.

Mahaprashasta, A. (2018), 'Allegations of political bias in faculty hiring the latest battleline in JNU', *The Wire*, 18 January. Available at https://thewire.in/education/allegations-political-bias-faculty-hiring-latest-battleline-jnu.

Mains, D. (2012), *Hope is Cut: Youth, Unemployment, and the Future in Urban Ethiopia* (Philadelphia, PA: Temple University Press).

Majumder, A. (2017), 'Labour reforms in India may get going, finally', *Rediff. com*, 20 March. Available at https://www.rediff.com/business/report/labour-reforms-in-india-may-get-going-finally/20170320.htm.

Mamdani, M. (1996), *Citizen and Subject: Contemporary Africa and the Legacy of Late Colonialism* (Princeton, NJ: Princeton University Press).

Mandelbaum, D. G. (1970), *Society in India*, Vols 1 and 2 (Berkeley, CA: University of California Press).

Mangla, A. (2015), 'Bureaucratic norms and state capacity in India: Implementing primary education in the Himalayan region', *Asian Survey*, 55(5): 882–908.

Mani, M. (2014), *Greening India's Growth: Costs, Valuations and Trade-Offs* (New York: Routledge for the World Bank).

Mani, S. and V. Sridhar (2015), 'Diffusion of broadband internet in India', *Economic and Political Weekly*, 50(51), 19 December.

Mani, V. (2013), 'Work life balance and women professionals', *Global Journal of Management and Business Research*, 13(5): 35–41.

Mannheim, K. (1972), 'The problem of generations', in P. Altbach and R. Laufer (eds) *The New Pilgrims: Youth Protest in Transition*, 101–38 (New York: David McKay and Co.).

Manor, J. (1988), 'Parties and the party system', in A. Kohli (ed.) *India's Democracy: An Analysis of Changing State-Society Relations* (Princeton, NJ: Princeton University Press).

Manor, J. (2010a), 'What do they know of India who only India know? The uses of comparative politics', *Commonwealth and Comparative Politics*, 48(4): 505–16.

Manor, J. (2010b), 'Beyond clientelism: Digvijay Singh's participatory, pro-poor strategy in Madhya Pradesh', in P. Price and A. Ruud (eds) *Power and Influence in India: Bosses, Lords and Captains* (London: Routledge).

Manor, J. (2010c), 'Local governance', in N. G. Jayal and P. B. Mehta (eds.) *The Oxford Companion to Politics in India* (Delhi: Oxford University Press).

Manor, J. (2011), 'Epilogue: Caste and politics in recent times', in R. Kothari (ed.) *Caste in Indian Politics* (Delhi: Oxford University Press).

Manuel, P. (1993), *Cassette Culture: Popular Music and Technology in North India* (Chicago, IL: University of Chicago Press).

Manuel, P. (2014), 'The regional North Indian popular music industry in 2014: From cassette culture to cyberculture', *Popular Music*, 33(3): 389–412.

Marcesse, T. (2018), 'Public policy reform and informal institutions: The political articulation of the demand for work in rural India', *World Development*, 103: 284–96.

Martin, N. (2015), 'Rural elites and the limits of Scheduled Caste assertiveness in rural Malwa, Punjab', *Economic and Political Weekly*, 50(52): 37–44.

Martinez-Alier, J. (2016), 'Global environmental justice and the environmentalism of the poor', in T. Gabrielson, C. Hall, J. M. Meyer and D. Schlosberg (eds) *The Oxford Handbook of Environmental Political Theory* (New York: Oxford University Press).

Martinez-Alier, J., L. Temper and F. Demaria (2014), 'Social metabolism and environmental conflict in India', *Indi@logs*, 1: 51–83 (on-line journal).

Marx, K. (1852), *The Eighteenth Brumaire of Louis Napoleon* (available in various editions of Marx's work).

Marx, K. (1853), 'The British rule in India', *New York Daily Tribune*, 25 June (available in various editions of Marx's work).

Mathew, C. K. (2015), 'Food Security Act in sleep mode', *Economic and Political Weekly*, 50(43): 20–2.

Mathur, N. (2016), *Paper Tiger: Law, Bureaucracy and the Developmental State in Himalayan India* (Delhi: Cambridge University Press).

Matto, M. (2019), 'India's water crisis: The clock is ticking', *Down to Earth*, blog, July. Available at https://www.downtoearth.org.in/blog/water/india-s-water-crisis-the-clock-is-ticking-65217.

Mawdsley, E. and G. Williams (2006), 'Post-colonial environmental justice: Government and governance', *Geoforum*, 37: 660–7.

Mayer, A. (1996), 'Caste in an Indian village: Change and continuity 1954–1992', in C. J. Fuller (ed.) *Caste Today* (New Delhi: Oxford University Press).

Mazumdar, R. (2007), *Bombay Cinema: An Archive of the City* (Minneapolis, MN: University of Minnesota Press).

Mehrotra, S. (2019), 'India does have a real employment crisis – and it's worsening', *The Wire*, 6 February. Available at https://thewire.in/economy/india-worsening-employment-crisis.

Mehrotra, S. and J. K. Parida (2017), 'Why is the labour force participation of women declining in India?' *World Development*, 98: 360–80.

Mehrotra, S., J. K. Parida, S. Sinha and A. Gandhi (2014), 'Explaining employment trends in the Indian economy: 1993–94 to 2011–12', *Economic and Political Weekly*, 49(32): 49–57.

Mehta, P. B. (2007), 'The rise of juridical sovereignty', *Journal of Democracy*, 18(2): 70–83.

Mehta, P. B. (2011), 'The politics of social justice', *Business Standard India 2011* (Delhi: BS Books).

Mehta, P. B. and M. Walton (2014), 'Ideas, interests and the politics of development change in India: Capitalism, inclusion and the state', Working Paper 36/2014, ESID, University of Manchester.

Mendelsohn, O. (1993), 'The transformation of authority in rural India', *Modern Asian Studies*, 27(4): 805–42.

Mendelsohn, O. and M. Vicziany (1998), *The Untouchables: Subordination, Poverty and the State in Modern India* (Cambridge: Cambridge University Press).

Menon, M. (2016), 'The unmaking of the Forest Rights Act', *Economic and Political Weekly*, 51(44–45): 15–18.

Menon, M. and K. Kohli (2014), 'Executive's environmental dilemmas: Unpacking a committee's report', *Economic and Political Weekly*, 49(50): 10–13.

Menon, M. and K. Kohli (2015), 'Environmental regulation in India: Moving "forward" in the old direction', *Economic and Political Weekly*, 50(50): 20–23.

Menon, N. (2000), 'Elusive "woman": Feminism and Women's Reservation Bill', *Economic and Political Weekly*, 35(43–44). 3835–44.

Menon, N. (2009), 'Sexuality, caste, governmentality: Contests over "gender" in India', *Feminist Review*, 91(1): 94–112.

Michelutti, L. (2007), 'The vernacularization of democracy: Political participation and popular politics in north India', *Journal of the Royal Anthropological Institute*, 13(3): 639–56.

Michelutti, L. (2008), *The Vernacularization of Democracy: Politics, Caste and Religion in India* (New Delhi: Routledge).

Michelutti, L., A. Hoque, N. Martin, D. Picherit, P. Rollier, A. Ruud and C. Still (2019), *Mafia Raj: The Rule of Bosses in South Asia* (Stanford, CA: Stanford University Press).

Micklethwait, J. and A. Wooldridge (2009), *God Is Back: How the Global Revival of Faith Is Changing the World* (New York: Penguin Press).

Miles, R. (2002), 'Employment and unemployment in Jordan: The importance of the gender system', *World Development*, 30(3): 413–27.

Miller, B. (1981), *The Endangered Sex: Neglect of Female Children in Rural North India* (Ithaca, NY: Cornell University Press).

Mines, M., (2006), 'Temples and charity: The neighbourhood styles of Komari and Beeri Chettiar merchants of Madras City', in G. de Neve and H. Donner (eds) *The Meaning of the Local: Politics of Place in Urban India* (London: Routledge).

Ministry of Human Resources Development, Government of India (MoHRD) (2016), *National Policy on Education 2016: Report of the Committee for Evolution of the New Education Policy* (New Delhi: MoHRD).

Mishra, J. and A. Negi (2019), 'Post-poll survey: BJP the most preferred party of young India', *The Hindu*, 29 May.

Mishra, P. (2004), *The Romantics* (New York: Random House).

Mishra, P. (2006), *Butter Chicken in Ludhiana: Travels in Small Town India* (London: Picador).

Mishra, P. (2013), 'Sex ratios, cross-region marriages and the challenge to caste endogamy in Haryana', *Economic and Political Weekly*, 48(35): 70–8.

Mokyr, J. (2016), *A Culture of Growth: The Origins of the Modern Economy* (Princeton, NJ: Princeton University Press).

Moodie, M. (2015), *We Were Advasis: Aspiration in an Indian Scheduled Tribe* (Chicago, IL: University of Chicago Press).

Mooij, J. (2014), 'Redressing poverty and enhancing social development: Trends in India's welfare regime', in N. Gooptu and J. Parry (eds) *Persistence of Poverty in India* (New Delhi: Social Science Press).

Moore, B. Jr. (1966), *The Social Origins of Dictatorship and Democracy: Lord and Peasant in the Making of the Modern World* (Boston, MA: Beacon Press).

Morgan, R. (1989), *The Demon Lover: On the Sexuality of Terrorism* (New York: Norton).

Morrow, V. (2015), 'Social justice and youth transitions: Understanding young people's lives in Andhra Pradesh, India and Ethiopia', in J. Wyn and H. Cahill (eds) *Handbook of Children and Youth Studies* (London: Springer).

Mosse, D. (2010), 'A relational approach to durable poverty, inequality and power', *Journal of Development Studies*, 46(7): 1–23.

Mosse, D. (2018), 'Caste and development: Contemporary perspectives on a structure of discrimination and advantage', *World Development*, 110: 422–36.

MSPI [Ministry of Statistics and Programme Implementation] (2016), 'Men and women in India – 2016'. Available at http://mospi.nic.in/publication/women-and-men-india-2016.

Mukherji, R. (2013), 'Ideas, interests and the tipping point: Economic change in India', *Review of International Political Economy*, 20(2): 363–89.

Mullen R. (2018), 'The new great game in the Indo-Pacific', Working Paper No. 297 (Singapore: Institute for South Asian Studies, National University of Singapore).

Mundy, S. (2018), 'India's economic statistics bureau drawn into political row', *Financial Times*, 29 November.

Munshi, K. (2016), 'Caste networks in the modern Indian economy', in S. Mahindra Dev and P. Babu (eds) *Development in India: Micro and Macro Perspectives* (New Delhi: Springer India).

Murali, D. and R. Vijay (2017) 'Revival of agriculture sector and increase of tenancy in India', *Economic and Political Weekly*, 52(31).

Muralidharan, K. and N. Prakash (2017), 'Cycling to school: Increasing secondary school enrollment for girls in India', *American Economic Journal: Applied Economics*, 9(3): 321–50.

Muralidharan, S. (2003), 'A new phase of adventurism', *Frontline*, 20(15), 1 August.

Myrdal, G. (1968), *Asian Drama: An Inquiry into the Poverty of Nations* (New York: Twentieth Century Fund).

Nagaraj, K., P. Sainath, R. Rukmani and R. Gopinath (2014), 'Farmers' suicides in India: Magnitudes, trends and spatial patterns, 1997–2012', *Review of Agrarian Studies*, 4(2): 53–83.

Nair, G. (2016), 'The bitter aftertaste of beef ban: 'Choice', caste and consumption', *Economic and Political Weekly*, 51(10): 7–8.

Nair, M. (2016), *Undervalued Dissent: Informal Workers' Politics in India* (Albany, NY: State University of New York Press).

Nakassis, C. V. (2014), 'Suspended kinship and youth sociality in Tamil Nadu, India', *Current Anthropology*, 55(2): 175–99.

Nanda, M. (2009), *The God Market: How Globalization Is Making India more Hindu* (Delhi: Random House).

Narayan, A. and R. Murgai (2016), 'Looking back on two decades of poverty and well-being in India', World Bank Policy Research Paper No. 7626 (Washington, DC: The World Bank).

Narayan, B. (2008), 'Demarginalisation and history: Dalit re-invention of the past', *South Asia Research*, 28(2): 169–84.

Narayan, R. and R. Swamy (2019), 'Six reasons why the Economic Survey's presentation of MGNREGA is misleading', *The Hindu*, 23 July.

Narayanan, S. (2019), 'Social protection in the Union budget 2019', *Ideas for India*, 10 July.

Narayanaswamy, L. (2016), 'Whose feminism counts? Gender(ed) knowledge and professionalisation in development', *Third World Quarterly*, 37(12): 2156–75.

Nayar, B. R. and T. V. Paul (2003), *India in the World Order: Searching for Major Power Status* (Cambridge: Cambridge University Press).

NCRB (National Crime Records Bureau) (2017), *Crime in India – 2016*. Ministry of Home Affairs.

NCEUS (National Commission for Enterprises in the Unorganised Sector) (2007), *Report on Conditions of Work and Promotion of Livelihoods in the Unorganised Sector*. http://dcmsme.gov.in/Condition_of_workers_sep_2007.pdf.

NDTV (2016), 'Agni V, India's longest range nuclear capable missile, successfully test fired', 26 December. Available at https://www.ndtv.com/india-news/india-to-test-its-longest-range-agni-5-missile-1641785.

NEP (2006), *National Environment Policy* (Delhi: Ministry of Environment and Forests).

Neville, H. H. (1922), *Meerut – A Gazetteer* (Lucknow: Government Branch Press).

Nilsen, A. G. (2010), *Dispossession and Resistance in India: The River and the Rage* (New York: Routledge).

Nilsen, A. G. (2012), 'Adivasi mobilizations in contemporary India: Democratizing the local state?', *Critical Sociology*, 39(4): 615–33.

Nisbett, N. (2007), 'Friendship, consumption, morality: Practising identity, negotiating hierarchy in middle-class Bangalore', *Journal of the Royal Anthropological Institute*, 13(4): 935–50.

Noorani, A. G. (2015), 'Conversion to Hindu Raj', *Frontline*, 32(1), 23 January.

NSS (National Sample Survey) (2013), 'Key indicators of employment and unemployment in India (Ministry of Statistics and Programme Implementation: Government of India).

NSS (National Sample Survey) (2014a), 'Employment and unemployment situation in India' (Ministry of Statistics and Programme Implementation: Government of India).

NSS (National Sample Survey) (2014b), 'Participation of women in specified activities along with domestic duties' (Ministry of Statistics and Programme Implementation: Government of India).

Nunn, N. (2009), 'The importance of history for economic development', *Annual Review of Economics*, 1(1): 65–92.

Ohm, B. (2015), 'Organizing popular discourse with and against the media: Notes on the making of Narendra Modi and Recep Tayyip Erdoğan as leaders-without-alternative', *Television & New Media*, 16(4): 370–7.

Omvedt, G. (2003), *Buddhism in India: Challenging Brahminism and Caste* (New Delhi: Sage).

Ovichegan, S. (2015), *Faces of Discrimination in Higher Education in India: Quota Policy, Social Justice and the Dalits* (London: Routledge).

Padel, F. and S. Das (2010), *Out of this Earth: East India Adivasis and the Aluminium Cartel* (Hyderabad: Orient Black Swan).

Pai, S. (2002), *Dalit Assertion and the Unfinished Democratic Revolution: The Bahujan Samaj Party in Uttar Pradesh* (New Delhi: Sage).

Pai, S. (2010), *Developmental State and the Dalit Question in Madhya Pradesh: Congress Response* (New Delhi: Routledge).

Pal, J., P. Chandra and V. Vydiswaran (2016), 'Twitter and the rebranding of Narendra Modi', *Economic and Political Weekly*, 51(8): 52–60.

Palshikar, S. (2013), 'Of radical democracy and anti-partyism', *Economic and Political Weekly*, 48(10): 10–13.

Palshikar, S. (2015), 'The BJP and Hindu nationalism: Centrist politics and majoritarian impulses', *South Asia: Journal of South Asian Studies*, 38(4): 719–35.

Palshikar, S. (2017), 'India's second dominant party system', *Economic and Political Weekly*, 52(12): 12–15.

Panagariya, A. (2008), *India: The Emerging Giant* (Oxford: Oxford University Press).

Panagariya, A., P. Chakraborty and M. Govinda Rao (2014), *State Level Reforms, Growth, and Development in Indian States* (Oxford: Oxford University Press).

Panat, R. (2014), 'On the data and analysis of the research output of India and China: India has significantly fallen behind China', *Scientometrics*, 100(2), 471–81.

Pande, V. (2013), 'Getting to a greener picture of India's growth story', *Ideas for India*, 8 May.

Pandey, A. (2009), 'Gender differences in early childhood feeding practices: Rural West Bengal', in M. Pal, P. Bharati, B. Ghosh and T. S. Vasulu (eds) *Gender and Discrimination: Health, Nutritional Status, and Role of Women in India* (Oxford: Oxford University Press).

Pandey, G. (1982), 'Peasant revolt and Indian nationalism: The peasant movements in Awadh, 1919–1922', in R. Guha (ed.) *Subaltern Studies 1: Writings on South Asian History and Society* (Delhi: Oxford University Press).

Pandya, S. (2016), '"Our aim is to link humanity to the divine": Social philosophy and social service of Sri Aurobindo Society', *Humanity & Society*, 40(3): 254–77.

Panikkar, K. N. (2001), 'Outsider as enemy: The politics of rewriting history in India', *Frontline*, 18(1), 19 January.

Parkin, B. (2019a), 'Indian car sales fall 31% as sector faces prolonged decline', *Financial Times*, 13 August.

Parkin, B. (2019b), 'Narendra Modi recast as a rugged environmentalist with Bear Grylls', *Financial Times*, 13 August.

Parry, J. (1999), 'Two cheers for reservation: The satnamis and the steel plant', In R. Guha and J. Parry (eds) *Institutions and Inequalities*, 128–69 (New Delhi. Oxford University Press).

Parry, J. (2001), 'Ankalu's errant wife – Sex, marriage and industry in contemporary Chhattisgarh', *Modern Asian Studies*, 35(4): 783–820.

Parry, J. and C. Struempell (2008), 'On the desecration of Nehru's 'temples': Bhilai and Rourkela compared', *Economic and Political Weekly*, 43(19): 47–57.

Patel, R. (2007), *Hindu Women's Property Rights in Rural India: Law, Labour, and Culture in Action* (Aldershot: Ashgate).

Patel, S. B. (2016), '"Housing for all by 2022": Assignment delivered, accountability nil', *Economic and Political Weekly*, 51(10): 38–42.

Patel, V. (2017), 'Parents, permission, and possibility: Young women, college, and imagined futures in Gujarat, India', *Geoforum*, 80: 39–48.

Pattenden, J. (2005), 'Trickle down solidarity, globalization and dynamics of social transformation in a south Indian village', *Economic and Political Weekly*, 40(19): 1975–85.

Pattenden, J. (2016), *Labour, State and Society in Rural India: A Class-Relational Approach* (Manchester: Manchester University Press).

Paul, S. (2016), 'Does good governance reduce food grain diversion in the PDS?', *Ideas for India*, 24 July.

Paul, T. (2011), 'Public spaces and everyday lives: Gendered encounters in the metro city of Kolkata', in S. Raju and K. Lahiri-Dutt (eds) *Doing Gender, Doing Geography: Emerging Research in India* (London: Routledge).

Peabody, N. (2001), 'Cents, sense, census: Human inventories in late precolonial and early colonial India', *Comparative Studies in Society and History*, 43(4): 819–50.

Phadke, S., S. Khan and S. Ranade (2011), *Why Loiter? Women and Risk on Mumbai Streets* (New Delhi: Penguin).

Phillips, A. (1995), *The Politics of Presence* (Oxford: Clarendon).

Piedalue, A. (2015), 'Understanding violence in place: Travelling knowledge paradigms and measuring domestic violence in India', *Indian Journal of Gender Studies*, 22(1): 63–91.

Pilz, M. (2016), 'A view from the outside: India's school to work transition challenge – Strengths and weakness', in M. Pilz (ed.) *India: Preparation for the World of Work* (Wiesbaden: Springer).

Pilz, M. (2018), 'Opportunities and obstacles: India's school to work transition', *RDWU Journal of Social Sciences and Humanities*, 3: 83–97.

Pilz, M. and U. Gengaiah (2019), 'Teacher training education for VET teachers in India', in S. McGrath, M. Mulder, P. Papier and R. Suart (eds) *Handbook of Vocational Education and Training: Developments in the Changing World of Work* (Dordrecht: Springer).

Pinto, S. (2008), *Where there is no Midwife: Birth and Loss in Rural India* (New York: Berghahn).

Planning Commission (2008), *Eleventh Five Year Plan 2007–12. Volume 1: Inclusive Growth* (Delhi: Oxford University Press).

Planning Commission (2013), *Twelfth Five Year Plan (2012–2017). Volume 1: Faster, More Inclusive and Sustainable Growth* (Delhi: Sage).

Planning Commission (2014), *The Final Report of the Expert Group on Low-Carbon Strategies for Inclusive Growth* (New Delhi: Planning Commission, Government of India).

Polanyi, K. (1944), *The Great Transformation: The Political and Economic Origins of Our Time* (Boston, MA: The Beacon Press).

Pomerantz, K. (2000), *The Great Divergence: Europe, China and the Making of the Modern World Economy* (Princeton, NJ: Princeton University Press).

Poonam, S. (2018), *Dreamers: How Young Indians are Changing the World* (London: Hurst and Co.).

Potter, D. (1986), *India's Political Administrators: From ICS to IAS* (Delhi: Oxford University Press).

Pradhan, M. C. (1966), *The Political System of the Jats of Northern India* (Bombay: Oxford University Press).

Prakash, A. (2015), *Dalit Capital: State, Markets and Civil Society in Urban India* (New Delhi: Routledge).

Prasad, A. (2007), 'Survival at stake', *Frontline*, 23(26), 12 January.

Prause, J. and D. Dooley (1997), 'Effects of underemployment on "school-leavers" self-esteem', *Journal of Adolescence*, 20(1): 243–60.

Pritchett, L. and L. Summers (2014), 'Asiaphoria meets regression to the mean', Working Paper No. 20573 (Cambridge, MA: National Bureau of Economic Research).

Pritchett, L. and E. Werker (2012), 'Developing the guts of a GUT (Grand Unified Theory): Elite commitment and inclusive growth', Working Paper 16/12 (Manchester: University of Manchester Effective States and Inclusive Development Research Centre).

Pritchett, L. and M. Woolcock (2004), 'Solutions when the solution is the problem: Arraying the disarray in development', *World Development*, 32(2): 191–212.

Przeworski, A., M. Alvarez, J. Cheibub and L. Fernando (1996), 'What makes democracies endure?', *Journal of Democracy*, 7(1): 39–55.

Punathambekar, A. (2013), *From Bombay to Bollywood: The Making of a Global Media Industry* (New York: New York University Press).

Radhakrishna, R. (2015), 'Wellbeing, inequality, poverty and pathways out of poverty', *Economic and Political Weekly*, 50(41): 59–71.

Radhakrishnan, S. (2011), *Appropriately Indian: Gender and Culture in a New Transnational Class* (Durham, NC: Duke University Press).

Ragavan, M., K. Iyengar and R. Wurtz (2015), 'Perceptions of options available for victims of physical intimate partner violence in northern India', *Violence against Women*, 21(5): 652–75.

Raheja, G. G. (1988), *The Poison in the Gift: Ritual Prestation, and the Dominant Caste in a North Indian Village* (Chicago, IL: University of Chicago Press).

Rai, S. M. (2012), 'The politics of access: Narratives of women MPs in the Indian Parliament', *Political Studies*, 60(1): 195–212.

Rai, S. M. and C. Spary (2019), *Performing Representation: Women Members in the Indian Parliament* (Oxford: Oxford University Press).

Raja Mohan, C. (2004), *Crossing the Rubicon: The Shaping of India's New Foreign Policy* (Basingstoke: Palgrave Macmillan).

Raja Mohan, C. (2015) 'Foreign policy after 1990: Transformation through incremental adaptation', in D. M. Malone, C. Raja Mohan and S. Raghavan (eds) *The Oxford Handbook of Indian Foreign Policy* (New York: Oxford University Press).

Rajan, R. (2018), 'Raghuram Rajan explains the origins of India's NPA crisis', *The Wire*, 12 September. Available at https://thewire.in/banking/raghuram-rajan-npa-parliamentary-committee-modi-government.

Rajan, S. and S. P. Morgan (2018), 'Selective versus generalized gender bias in childhood health and nutrition: Evidence from India', *Population and Development Review*, 44(2): 231–55.

Ralph, M. (2008), 'Killing time', *Social Text*, 26(4): 1–29.

Ramachandran, V. (ed.) (2004), *Gender and Social Equity in Primary Education: Hierarchies of Access* (New Delhi: Sage).

Ramachandran, V. K. and V. Rawal (2010), 'The impact of liberalization and globalization on India's agrarian economy', *Global Labour Journal*, 1(1): 56–91.

Ramachandran, V. K., V. Rawal and M. Swaminathan (2012), *Socio-Economic Surveys of Three Villages in Andhra Pradesh: A study of agrarian relations* (Delhi: Tulika Books).

Ramakrishnan, V. (2015a), 'Project Hindutva', *Frontline*, 32(1), 9 January.

Ramakrishnan, V. (2015b), 'The lynch mob', *Frontline*, 32(21), 30 October.

Ramakumar, R. (2014), 'Economic reforms and agricultural policy in India', Foundation for Agrarian Studies, Tenth Anniversary Conference, Kochi, 9–12 January.

Ramakumar, R. and P. Chavan (2014), 'Bank credit to agriculture in the 2000s: Dissecting the revival', *Review of Agrarian Studies*, 4(1): 40–79.

Ramani (2013a), 'For a minimum living wage: Workers' march to Parliament', *Economic and Political Weekly*, 48(52): 12–14.

Ramani (2013b), 'The Aam Aadmi Party's win in Delhi: Dissecting it through geographical information systems', *Economic and Political Weekly*, 48(52), 28 December.

Ramdas, S. (2017), 'The beef ban effect', *The Wire*, 6 April. Available at https://thewire.in/politics/beef-ban-cattle-market.

Rao, K. S., B. K. Sahoo and D. Ghosh (2014), 'The Indian vocational education and training system', in S. Mehrotra (ed.) *India's Skills Challenge: Reforming Vocational Education and Training to Harness the Demographic Dividend* (Oxford: Oxford University Press).

Rao, N. (2018), *'Good Women do not Inherit Land': Politics of Land and Gender in India* (London: Routledge).

Rao, O. (2017), 'Despite available funds, 571 million in these nine states have to endure India's worst healthcare', *The Wire*, 3 July. Available at https://staging.thewire.in/health/despite-funds-581-million-in-these-nine-states-have-to-endure-indias-worst-healthcare.

Rao, V. (1993), 'The rising price of husbands: A hedonic analysis of dowry increases in rural India', *Journal of Political Economy*, 101(4): 666–77.

Ravallion, M. (2012), 'Understanding the differing fortunes of poor people in India and China', *Ideas for India*, 18 July.

Rawal, V. (2008), 'Ownership holdings of land in rural India: Putting the record straight', *Economic and Political Weekly*, 43(10): 43–7.

Rawat, R. (2011), *Reconsidering Untouchability: Chamars and Dalit History in North India* (Bloomington, IN: Indiana University Press).

Reddy, S. and T. Pogge (2009), 'How not to count the poor', Initiative for Policy Dialogue, Working Paper Series (New York: Columbia University).

Reporters without Borders (2019a), 'Media ownership monitor: Who owns the media in India?' Available at https://rsf.org/en/news/media-ownership-monitor-who-owns-media-india.

Reporters without Borders (2019b), World Press Freedom Index, 2019. Available at https://rsf.org/en/ranking.

Richards, M. S. (2016), 'The Gulabi Gang, violence, and the articulation of counterpublicity', *Communication, Culture & Critique*, 9(4): 558–76.

Robinson, M. (1988), *Local Politics: The Law of the Fishes – Development through Political Change in Medak District, Andhra Pradesh (South India)* (New Delhi: Oxford University Press).

Rodrik, D. (2015), 'Premature deindustrialization', Working Paper No. 20935 (Cambridge, MA: National Bureau of Economic Research).

Rodrik, D. and A. Subramanian (2005), 'From "Hindu growth" to productivity surge: The mystery of the Indian growth transition', *IMF Staff Working Papers*, 52(2): 1–42.

Roitman, J. (2004), *Fiscal Disobedience: An Anthropology of Economic Regulation in Central Africa* (Princeton, NJ: Princeton University Press).

Romei, V. and J. Reed (2019), 'The Asian century is set to begin', *Financial Times*, 26 March.

Romig, R. (2019), 'Railing against India's right-wing nationalism was a calling. It was also a death sentence', *New York Times Magazine*, 14 March.

Rosencranz, A. and S. Lele (2008), 'Supreme Court and India's forests', *Economic and Political Weekly*, 43(5): 11–14.

Roulet, M. (1996), 'Dowry and prestige in north India', *Contributions to Indian Sociology*, 30(1): 89–107.

Roy, S. (2014), 'Being the change: the Aam Aadmi Party and the politics of the extraordinary in Indian democracy', *Economic and Political Weekly*, 49(15): 45–54.

Roy, Sanchari (2015), 'Empowering women? Inheritance rights, female education and dowry payments in India', *Journal of Development Economics*, 114: 233–51.

Roy, Srila (2015), 'The Indian women's movement: Within and beyond NGOization', *Journal of South Asian Development*, 10(1): 96–117.

Roy, Srila (2016), 'Breaking the cage', *Dissent Magazine*, Fall.

Roy, T. (2018), *A Business History of India: Enterprise and the Emergence of Capitalism from 1700* (Cambridge: Cambridge University Press).

RoyChowdhury, S. (2014), 'Bringing class back in: Informality in Bangalore', *Socialist Register 2015: Transforming Classes*, 51: 73–92.

Rudolph, L. I. and S. H. Rudolph (1967), *The Modernity of Tradition* (Chicago, IL: Chicago University Press).

Rudolph, L. I. and S. H. Rudolph (1987), *In Pursuit of Lakshmi: The Political Economy of the Indian State* (Chicago, IL: University of Chicago Press).

Rudolph, L. I. and S. H. Rudolph (2001), 'Iconisation of Chandrababu: Sharing sovereignty in India's federal market economy', *Economic and Political Weekly*, 26(18): 541–52.

Rueschemeyer, D., E. Stephens and J. Stephens (1992), *Capitalist Development and Democracy* (Cambridge: Polity Press).

Ruparelia, S. (2013), 'India's new rights agenda: Genesis, promises, risks', *Pacific Affairs*, 86(3): 569–90.

Ruparelia, S. (2015), '"Minimum government, maximum governance": The restructuring of power in Modi's India', *South Asia: Journal of South Asian Studies*, 38(4): 755–75.

Saberwal, S. (1986), *India, the Roots of Crisis* (New Delhi: Oxford University Press).

Safi, M. (2016), 'On patrol with the Hindu vigilantes who would kill to protect India's cows', *The Guardian*, 27 October. Available at https://www.theguardian.com/world/2016/oct/27/on-patrol-hindu-vigilantes-smuggling-protect-india-cows-kill.

Safi, M. (2018), 'India's top judges issue unprecedented warning over integrity of Supreme Court', *The Guardian*, 13 January. Available at https://www.the-guardian.com/world/2018/jan/12/india-supreme-court-judges-integrity-dip ak-misra.

Sagar (2017), 'How Aadhaar and digitisation compounded problems of corruption, leakages and exclusion plaguing the PDS in Jharkhand', *The Caravan*, 31 July.

Sagar (2019), 'Narendra Modi's "two-caste society" is a facade to hide the BJP's casteist politics', *The Caravan*, 21 June.

Saha, B. and S. Saha (2018), 'Failing to learn: India's schools and teachers', in R. Kanungo, C. Rowley and A. Banerjee (eds) *Changing the Indian Economy* (Amsterdam: Elsevier).

Sampath, G. (2016), 'Labour in the 21st Century', *The Hindu*, 20 February.

Sanyal, K. and R. Bhattacharyya (2009), 'Beyond the factory: Globalisation, informalisation of production and the new locations of labour', *Economic and Political Weekly*, 44(22): 35–44.

Sardesai, S. and V. Attri (2019), 'Post-poll survey: The 2019 verdict is a manifestation of the deepening religious divide in India', *The Hindu*, 30 May.

Sarkar, D. (2011), 'The implementation of the Forest Rights Act in India: Critical issues', *Economic Affairs*, 31(2): 25–9.

Sarkar, S. (1996), 'Indian nationalism and the politics of Hindutva', in D. Ludden (ed.), *Contesting the Nation: Religion, Community, and the Politics of Democracy in India* (Philadelphia, PA: University of Pennsylvania Press).

Sarkar, S. (2001), 'India democracy: The historical inheritance', in A. Kohli (ed.), *The Success of India's Democracy* (Cambridge: Cambridge University Press).

Savarkar, V. D. (2003 [1923]), *Hindutva: Who is a Hindu?* (Delhi: Hindi Sahitya Sadan).

Saxena, N. C. (2016), 'Governance reforms in India', in O. Tornquist and J. Harriss (eds) *Reinventing Social Democratic Development: Insights from Indian and Scandinavian Comparisons*, 131–67 (Copenhagen: NIAS Press).

Saxena, N. C., S. Parasuraman, P. Kant and A. Baviskar (2010), 'Report of the Four Member Committee for Investigation into the Proposal Submitted by the Orissa Mining Company for Bauxite Mining in Niyamgiri'. Available at http://www.rlarrdc.org.in/images/Saxena%20Vedanta%20Report.pdf.

Saxena, R. P. (1990), 'Governance of Indian universities: From decay to dynamism?', *Higher Education*, 20(1): 91–111.

Schneider, N. (2013), *Thank you, Anarchy: Notes from the Occupy Apocalypse* (Oakland, CA: University of California Press).

Scoones, I., M. Edelman, S. M. Borras, R. Hall, W. Wolford and B. White (2018), 'Emancipatory rural politics: Confronting authoritarian populism', *Journal of Peasant Studies*, 45(1): 1–20.

Seekings, J. (2013), 'Is the south "Brazilian"? The public realm in urban Brazil through a comparative lens', *Policy and Politics*, 43(3): 351–70.

Sen, A. (1999), *Development as Freedom* (New York: Knopf).

Sen, A. (2000), 'Estimates of consumer expenditure and its distribution: Statistical priorities after NSS 55th round', *Economic and Political Weekly*, 35(51): 4499–518.

Sen, K. (2007), 'Why did the elephant start to trot? India's growth acceleration re-examined', *Economic and Political Weekly*, 42(43): 37–49.

Sen, K. (2014), 'The Indian economy in the post-reform period: Growth without structural transformation', in D. Davin and B. Harriss-White (eds) *China–India: Pathways of Economic and Social Development*, 47–62 (Oxford: Oxford University Press).

Sen, R. (2015), 'House matters: the BJP, Modi and Parliament', *South Asia: Journal of South Asian Studies*, 38(4): 776–90.

Sengupta, M. (2014), 'Anna Hazare's anti-corruption movement and the limits of mass mobilization in India', *Social Movement Studies*, 13(3): 406–13.

Seth, D. (2019), 'GDP data: Investment growth at 19-quarter low despite Modi government's stimulus measures', *The Wire*, 30 November. Available at https://thewire.in/economy/gdp-data-investment-growth-at-19-quarter-low-despite-modi-govts-stimulus-measures.

Shah, A. (2006), 'The labour of love: Seasonal migration from Jharkhand to the brick-kilns in other states of India', *Contributions to Indian Sociology*, 40(1): 91–116.

Shah, A. (2009), 'In search of certainty in revolutionary India', *Dialectical Anthropology*, 33(3–4): 271–86.

Shah, A. (2010), *In the Shadows of the State: Indigenous Politics, Environmentalism, and Insurgency in Jharkhand, India* (Durham, NC: Duke University Press).

Shah, A. (2017), 'Humaneness and contradictions: India's Maoist inspired Naxalites', *Economic and Political Weekly*, 52(21): 52–6.

Shah, A. (2018), *Nightmarch: Among India's Revolutionary Guerillas* (London: Hurst and Co.).

Shah, A. and J. Lerche (2018), 'Tribe, caste and class – new mechanisms of exploitation and oppression', in A. Shah et al., *Ground Down by Growth: Tribe, Caste, Class and Inequality in Twenty-First Century India* (London: Pluto Press), pp. 1–31.

Shah, A., J. Lerche, R. Axelby, D. Benbabali, B. Donegan, J. Raj and V. Thankur (2018), *Ground Down by Growth: Tribe, Caste, Class and Inequality in Twenty-First Century India* (London: Pluto Press).

Shah, G., H. Mander, S. Thorat, S. Deshpande and A. Baviskar (2006), *Untouchability in Rural India* (New Delhi: Sage).

Shah, M. B. (2012), Shah Commission Report, 'Illegal Mining in the State of Goa'. Available at http://www.indiaenvironmentportal.org.in/files/file/M_B_Shah_Report_on_illegal_mining6.pdf

Shah, N. (2012), 'Resisting revolutions: Questioning the radical potential of citizen action', *Development*, 55(2): 173–80.

Shah, S. P. (2012), 'Sex workers' rights and women's movements in India: A very brief genealogy', in S. Roy (ed.), *New South Asian Feminisms: Paradoxes and Possibilities* (London: Zed Books).

Shani, O. (2018), *How India Became Democratic: Citizenship and the Making of the Universal Franchise* (Cambridge: Cambridge University Press).

Shantha, S. (2018), 'A month after the Long March have farmers' demands been fulfilled?', *The Wire*, 12 April. Available at https://thewire.in/ agriculture/a-month-after-long-march-have-farmers-demands-been-fulfilled.

Shantha, S. (2019), 'Bhima Koregaon case: Of 230 required copies of evidence, only 4 made in 2 months', *The Wire*, 22 July. Available at https://thewire.in/ rights/bhima-koregaon-case-activists-bail-hearing-delay.

Sharma, A. (2006), 'Crossbreeding institutions, breeding struggle: Women's employment, neoliberal governmentality, and state (re)formation in India', *Cultural Anthropology*, 21(1): 60–95.

Sharma, N. (2019), 'Five reasons why the credibility of India's election commission was questioned this year', *Quartz India*, 23 May. Available at https://qz.com/india/1625877/evm-controversy-other-incidents-mar-indi an-general-election-2019.

Sharma, U. (1980), *Women, Work, and Property in North-West India* (London: Tavistock Publications).

Shastri, S. (2019), 'Leadership sweepstakes and the Modi factor', *The Hindu*, 20 May.

Sheth, D. L. (2004), 'Globalisation and the new politics of micro-movements', *Economic and Political Weekly*, 39(1): 45–58.

Shirkey, C. (2008), *Here Comes Everybody: The Power of Organising without Organisations* (London: Penguin).

Shrikanth, S. (2019), 'India set to lower "normal rain" baseline as droughts bite', *Financial Times*, 19 July.

Shrivastava, A. and A. Kothari (2012), *Churning the Earth: The Making of Global India* (Delhi: Viking by Penguin Books).

Shukla, S. (1992), *Raag Darbari: A Novel* (G. Wright, trans.) (New Delhi: Penguin).

Shyam Sundar, K. R. (2015), 'Industrial conflict in India in the post-reform period: Who said all is quiet on the industrial front?', *Economic and Political Weekly*, 50(3): 43–53.

Simister, J. and P. S. Mehta (2010), 'Gender-based violence in India: Long-term trends', *Journal of Interpersonal violence*, 25(9): 1594–611.

Singer, M. (1972), *When a Great Tradition Modernizes: An Anthropological Approach to Indian Civilization* (New York: Praeger).

Singer, M. and B. Cohn (eds) (1968), *Structure and Change in Indian Society* (Chicago, IL: Aldine).

Singh, J. (1992), *Capitalism and Dependence: Agrarian Politics in Western Uttar Pradesh 1951–1991* (Delhi: Manohar).

Singh, M. (2001), 'Reflections on colonial legacy and dependency in Indian vocational education and training (VET): A societal and cultural perspective', *Journal of Education and Work*, 14(2): 209–25.

Singh, P. (2015), *How Solidarity Works for Welfare: Sub-nationalism and Social Development in India* (New York: Cambridge University Press).

Sinha, S. (2015), 'On the edge of civil society in contemporary India', in A. G. Nilsen and S. Roy (eds) *New Subaltern Politics: Reconceptualizing Hegemony and Resistance in Contemporary India* (Oxford: Oxford University Press).

Sitapati, V. (2011), 'What Anna Hazare's Movement and India's new middle classes say about each other', *Economic and Political Weekly*, 46(30): 39–44.

Smyth, J. and S. Findlay (2019), 'Narendra Modi's BJP leans on diaspora to sway voters', *Financial Times*, 12 May.

Som, R. (1994), 'Jawaharlal Nehru and the Hindu Code: A victory of symbol over substance?' *Modern Asian Studies*, 28(1): 165–94.

Sorour, M. K. and B. L. Dey (2014), 'Energising the political movements in developing countries: The role of social media', *Capital & Class*, 38(3): 508–15.

Sridharan, E. (1999), 'Toward state funding of elections in India? A comparative perspective on possible options', *Journal of Policy Reform*, 3(3): 229–54.

Sridharan, E. (2015), 'Rising or constrained power?', in D. M. Malone, C. Raja Mohan and S. Raghavan (eds) *The Oxford Handbook of Indian Foreign Policy* (New York: Oxford University Press).

Srinivas, M. N. (1955), 'The social system of a Mysore village', in M. Marriott (ed.) *Village India* (Chicago, IL: Chicago University Press).

Srinivas, M. N. (1984), *Some Reflections on Dowry* (Delhi: Oxford University Press).

Srinivas, M. N. (1989), *The Cohesive Role of Sanskritization and Other Essays* (Oxford: Oxford University Press).

Srinivas, T. (2010), *Winged Faith: Rethinking Globalization and Religious Pluralism through the Sathya Sai Movement* (New York: Columbia University Press).

Srinivasan, S. (2005), 'Daughters or dowries? The changing nature of dowry practices in South India', *World Development*, 33(4): 593–615.

Srinivasan, S. (2017), 'Cross-region migration of brides and gender relations in a daughter deficit context', *Migration and Development*, 6(1): 123–43.

Srinivasan, S. and A. S. Bedi (2007), 'Domestic violence and dowry: Evidence from a South Indian village', *World Development*, 35(5): 857–80.

Srivastava, S. (2015), 'Modi-masculinity: Media, manhood, and "traditions" in a time of consumerism', *Television & New Media*, 16(4): 331–8.

Stacey, K. (2018), 'India defends solar panel makers from Chinese rivals', *Financial Times*, 22 January.

Stacey, K. and S. Mundy (2018), 'India: The creation of a mobile juggernaut', *Financial Times*, 1 October.

Stern, D. (2004), 'The rise and fall of the environmental Kuznets curve', *World Development*, 32(8): 1419–39.

Still, C. (2011), 'Spoiled brides and the fear of education: Honour and social mobility among Dalits in South India', *Modern Asian Studies*, 45(5): 1119–46.

Stone, L. and C. James (1995), 'Dowry, bride-burning, and female power in India', *Women's Studies International Forum*, 18(2): 125–34.

Streeten, P. and M. Lipton (eds) (1968), *The Crisis of Indian Planning* (Oxford: Oxford University Press).

Subrahmaniam, V. (2009), 'Violence and threats bring a government to its knees', and 'The system strikes back', *The Hindu*, 16–17 December.

Subramanian, A. (2018), 'Climate change and automation threaten economic convergence', *Financial Times*, 19 April.

Subramanian, A. (2019), 'India's GDP mis-estimation: Likelihood, magnitudes, mechanisms and implications', Working Paper No. 354 (Cambridge, MA: Centre for International Development at Harvard University).

Subramanian, S. (2014), 'The poverty line', *Economic and Political Weekly*, 49(47): 66–70.

Subramanian, S. (2016), 'The "poverty line" – III', *Ideas for India*, 27 May.

Subramanian, S. (2019), 'What is happening to rural welfare, poverty and inequality in India?', *The India Forum*, 6 December.

Sundararaman, T. (2019), 'Why the boost to health care in budget 2019 should be viewed with caution', *The Wire*, 6 July. Available at https://thewire.in/economy/why-the-boost-to-healthcare-in-budget-2019-should-be-viewed-with-caution.

Taguchi, Y. (2012), 'Aesthetics of civil society: "Fight the Filth" campaign in Mumbai', *Economic and Political Weekly*, 47(20): 13–16.

Tarrow, S. (1998), *Power in Movement: Social Movements and Contentious Politics*, 2nd edn (Cambridge: Cambridge University Press).

Taylor, M. (2014), 'Hindu activism and academic censorship in India' *South Asia: Journal of South Asian Studies*, 37(4): 717–25.

Taylor, M. (2018), 'Hybrid realities: Making a new green revolution for rice in south India', *Journal of Peasant Studies*, https://doi.org/10.1080/03066150.2019.1568246.

Taylor, A. (2019), 'Modi's Kashmir move proves his fiercest critics right', *The Washington Post*, 8 August.

TEEB Foundation (2008), *The Economics of Ecosystems and Biodiversity: An Interim Report* (Brussels: European Commission).

Teitelbaum, E. (2006), 'Was the Indian labor movement ever co-opted? Evaluating standard accounts', *Critical Asian Studies*, 38(4): 389–417.

Teitelbaum, E. (2011), *Mobilizing Restraint: Democracy and Industrial Conflict in Post-Reform South Asia* (Ithaca, NY: Cornell University Press).

Temper, L. and J. Martinez-Alier (2007), 'Is India too poor to be green?', *Economic and Political Weekly*, 42(17): 1489–92.

Temper, L. and J. Martinez-Alier (2013), 'The God of the Mountain and Godavarman: Net present value, indigenous territorial rights and sacredness in a bauxite mining conflict in India', *Ecological Economics*, 96: 79–87.

Tewari, R (2018), 'In two years of overhaul Modi government's rural housing scheme has doubled the number of houses built', *The Print*, 3 April.

Thachil, T. (2014), *Elite Parties, Poor Voters: How Social Services Win Votes in India* (New York: Cambridge University Press).

Thakur, S. and B. Moharana (2018), 'Bhima Koregaon and politics of the subaltern', *Economic and Political Weekly*, 53(7): 12–14.

The Economic Times (2018), 'India improves student-classroom, pupil-teacher ratios: Survey', *The Economic Times*, 29 January.

The Economist (2003), 'A tiger, falling behind a dragon', *The Economist*, 21 June.

The Economist (2012), 'Asia's next revolution', *The Economist*, 8 September.

The Economist (2017), 'Many rupee returns', *The Economist*, 7 January.

The Economist (2018a), 'The humbling of India's tycoons', *The Economist*, 21 April.

The Economist (2018b), 'India's middle class: The elephant in the room', *The Economist*, 13 January.

The Economist (2019a), 'India's justice system does far too little to protect witnesses', *The Economist*, 22 August.

The Economist (2019b), 'India's toxic smog is a common affliction in middle income countries', *The Economist*, 9 November.

The Lancet (2017), 'Nations within a nation: Variations in epidemiological transition across the states of India, 1990–2016 in the Global Burden of Disease Study', *The Lancet*, 14 November.

The Wire Staff (2017), 'NTPC washes hands of contractual jobs offered to 15 accused in Dadr lynching', *The Wire*, 14 October. Available at https://thewire. in/caste/dadri-accused-jobs-ntpc.

The Wire Staff (2018), 'When economist Surjit Bhalla was accused of "inventing" employment data', *The Wire*, 11 December. Available at https://thewire. in/labour/member-of-pms-economic-advisory-council-accused-of-inventing-employment-data.

The Wire Staff (2019), '"Complete charade": Activists, civil society groups condemn Triple Talaq Bill', 31 July. Available at https://thewire.in/communalism/triple-talaq-bill-muslim-women.

Thomas, J. J. (2014), 'The demographic challenge and employment growth in India', *Economic and Political Weekly*, 49(6): 15–17.

Thomas, P. (2014), 'The ambivalent state and the media in India: Between corporate compulsions and the public interest', *International Journal of Communication*, 8: 17.

Thorat, S. and K. Newman (2007), 'Caste and economic discrimination: Causes, consequences and remedies', *Economic and Political Weekly*, 42(41): 4121–4.

Thorat, S. and K. Newman (eds) (2010), *Blocked by Caste: Economic Discrimination in Modern India* (New Delhi: Oxford University Press).

Tilak, S. G. (2018), 'Storm over India film on women who "smoke, drink and have sex"', *BBC News*, 6 June.

Tillin, L. (2019), 'The fragility of India's federalism', *The Hindu*, 8 August.

Tilly, C. (1998), *Durable Inequality* (Berkeley, CA: University of California Press).

Timmer, C. P. (2009), *A World Without Agriculture: The Structural Transformation in Historical Perspective* (Washington, DC: AEI Press).

Topolova, P. (2008), 'India: Is the rising tide lifting all boats?', IMF Working Paper 08/54 (Washington, DC: International Monetary Fund).

TRAI (2018), 'Highlights of telecom subscription data as on 31st January, 2018' (Government of India).

Truelove, Y. (2019), 'Gray zones: The everyday practices and governance of water beyond the network', *Annals of the Association of American Geographers*, 109(6): 1758–74.

Uberoi, P. (1993), *Family, Kinship, and Marriage in India* (Delhi: Oxford University Press).

Udayakumar, S. P. (2012), 'The Koodankulam struggle and the "foreign hand"', *Economic and Political Weekly*, 47(12): 11–14.

United Nations (2016), *World Youth Report, 2016* (New York: United Nations).

United Nations (2018), *World Youth Report* (New York: United Nations).

Unni, J. and G. Raveendran (2007), 'Growth of employment (1993–4 to 2004–5): Illusion of inclusiveness', *Economic and Political Weekly*, 42(3): 196–9.

Unterhalter, E. and S. Dutt (2001), 'Gender, education and women's power: Indian state and civil society intersections in DPEP (District Primary Education Programme) and Mahila Samakhya', *Compare: A Journal of Comparative and International Education*, 31(1): 57–73.

Upadhya, C. (2007), 'Employment, exclusion and "merit" in the Indian IT industry', *Economic and Political Weekly*, 42(20), 1863–8.

Urban, H. B. (2013), 'Zorba the Buddha: The body, sacred space, and late capitalism in the Osho International Meditation Resort', *Southeast Review of Asian Studies*, 35: 32–49.

V-Dem (2019), *Democracy Facing Global Challenges. V-Dem Annual Democracy Report 2019*. Available at https://www.v-dem.net/en/.

Vachani, L. (2017), 'The Babri Masjid demolition was impossible without RSS foot-soldiers like these', *The Wire*, 8 December. Available at https://thewire.in/communalism/rss-sangh-parivar-babri-masjid.

Vaidyanathan, A. (2006), 'Farmers' suicides and the agrarian crisis', *Economic and Political Weekly*, 41(38): 4009–13.

Vaidyanathan, A. (2010), *Agricultural Growth in India: Role of Technology, Incentives and Institutions* (Delhi: Oxford University Press).

Vaidyanathan, A. (2013), 'Use and abuse of the poverty line', *Economic and Political Weekly*, 48(44): 37–42.

Vaishnav, M. (2017), *When Crime Pays: Money and Muscle in Indian Politics* (New Haven, CT: Yale University Press).

Vakulabharanam, V. (2005), 'Growth and distress in a south Indian peasant economy during the era of economic liberalisation', *Journal of Development Studies*, 41(6): 971–97.

Varadarajan, S. (2010), 'Supreme Court should not go into the realms of policy formulation', *The Hindu*, 7 September.

Varkkey, B. and R. Korde (2013), *Gender Pay Gap in the Formal Sector in India 2006–2013* (Delhi: Wage Indicator Data Report).

Varshney, A. (2017), 'Is Narendra Modi a populist?', *Indian Express*, 23 October.

Vasavi, A. R. (2015), 'Culture and life of government elementary schools', *Economic and Political Weekly*, 50(33): 36–50.

Vasavi, A. R. (2019), '"Government Brahmin": Caste, the educated unemployed, and the reproduction of inequities', in H. Ullrich (eds) *The Impact of Education in South Asia* (London: Palgrave Macmillan).

Vatuk, S. (1972), *Kinship and Urbanization: White Collar Workers in North India* (Berkeley, CA: University of California Press).

Veeraraghavan, R. (2017), 'Strategies for synergy in a high modernist project: Two community responses to India's NREGA rural work program', *World Development*, 99: 203–13.

Venkatesan, V. (2003), 'A secular veneer', *Frontline*, 20(2), 31 January.

Venkatraman, S. (2017), *Social Media in South India* (London: UCL Press).

Venu, M. K. (2017), 'RSS chief's call for National Cow Protection Law echoes a familiar pattern', *The Wire*, 10 April. (Last accessed at https://thewire.in/%22politics%22/mohan-bhagwat-cow-protection-law-bjp-rss on April 11 2017).

Vepa, S. S. (2009), *Bearing the Brunt: Impact of Rural Distress on Women* (London: Sage).

Verma, R., S. Gupta and R. Birner (2017), 'Can grassroots mobilization of the poorest reduce corruption? A tale of governance reforms and struggle against petty corruption in Bihar, India', *Development and Change*, 48(2): 339–63.

Veron, R. (2006), 'Remaking urban environments: Political ecology of air pollution in Delhi', *Environment and Planning A*, 38(11): 2092–109.

Vijayabaskar, M. (2011), 'Global crises, welfare provision and coping strategies of labour in Tiruppur', *Economic and Political Weekly*, 45(22): 38–46.

Vijayakumar, G. (2013), '"I'll be like water": Gender, class, and flexible aspirations at edge of India's knowledge economy', *Gender and Society*, 27(6): 777–98.

Viswanath, R. (2014), *The Pariah Problem: Caste, Religion and the Social in Modern India* (New York: Columbia University Press).

Wade, R. (1982), 'The system of administrative and political corruption: Canal irrigation in south India', *Journal of Development Studies*, 18(3): 287–328.

Wade, R. (1985), 'The market for public office: Why the Indian state is not better at development', *World Development*, 13(4): 467–97.

Wade, R. (1988), 'Politics and graft: Recruitment, appointment and promotions to public office in India', in P. Ward (ed.) *Corruption, Development and Inequality: Soft Touch or Hard Graft?* (London: Routledge).

Wadley, S. S. (1994), *Struggling with Destiny in Karimpur, 1925–1984* (New Delhi: Vistaar Publications).

Waheed, A. (2009), 'Dowry among Indian Muslims: Ideals and practices', *Indian Journal of Gender Studies*, 16(1): 47–75.

Walby, S. (1989), 'Theorising patriarchy', *Sociology*, 23(2): 213–34.

Walker, K. (2008), 'Neoliberalism on the ground in rural India: Predatory growth, agrarian crisis, internal colonisation and the intensification of class struggle', *Journal of Peasant Studies*, 35(4): 557–620.

Walker, S. (2019), 'Orban deploys Christianity with a twist to tighten grip on Hungary', *The Observer*, 14 July.

Walton, M. (2020) 'An Indian gilded age? Continuity and change in the political economy of Indian development', in E. Chatterjee and M. McCartney (eds) *Class and Conflict: Revisiting Pranab Bardhan's Political Economy of India* (Delhi: Oxford University Press).

Warrier, M. (2013), 'Online bhakti in a modern guru organisation', in M. Singleton and E. Goldberg (eds) *Gurus of Modern Yoga* (Oxford: Oxford University Press).

Washbrook, D. (1988), 'Progress and problems: South Asian economic and social history c. 1720–1860', *Modern Asian Studies*, 22(1): 57–96.

Washbrook, D. (1997), 'The rhetoric and democracy and development in late colonial India', in S. Bose and A. Jalal (eds) *Nationalism, Democracy and Development: State and Politics in India* (Delhi: Oxford University Press).

Watenpaugh, K. D. (2012), *Being Modern in the Middle East: Revolution, Nationalism, Colonialism, and the Arab Middle Class* (Princeton, NJ: Princeton University Press).

Webb, M. (2010), 'Boundary paradoxes: The social life of transparency and accountability activism in Delhi', unpublished PhD dissertation (Brighton: University of Sussex).

Webb, M. (2013), 'Disciplining the everyday state and society? Anti-corruption and right to information activism in Delhi', *Contributions to Indian Sociology*, 47(3): 363–93.

Weiner, M. (1991), *The Child and the State in India* (Princeton, NJ: Princeton University Press).

Weitzman, A. (2014), 'Women's and men's relative status and intimate partner violence in India', *Population and Development Review*, 40(1): 55–75.

Whitehead, J. (2003), 'Place, space and primitive accumulation in the Narmada valley and beyond', *Economic and Political Weekly*, 38(4): 4224–6.

Wilkinson, S. (2004), *Votes and Violence: Electoral Competition and Ethnic Riots in India* (Cambridge: Cambridge University Press).

Wilkinson, S. (ed.) (2005), *Religious Politics and Communal Violence* (Delhi: Oxford University Press).

Wilkinson, S. (2007), 'Reading the election results', in S. Ganguly, L. Diamond and M. Plattner (eds) *The State of India's Democracy* (Oxford: Oxford University Press).

Williams, P. (2007), 'Hindu-Muslim brotherhood: Exploring the dynamics of communal relations in Varanasi, north India', *Journal of South Asian Development*, 2(2): 153–76.

Wilson, J. (2016), *India Conquered: Britain's Raj and the Chaos of Empire* (London: Simon and Schuster).

Wiser, W. H. (1936), *The Hindu Jajmani System: A Socio-economic System Interrelating Members of a Hindu Village Community in Services* (Lucknow: Lucknow Publishing House).

Witsoe, J. (2013), *Democracy Against Development: Lower-Caste Politics and Political Modernity in Postcolonial India* (Chicago, IL: University of Chicago Press).

Woodhead, M., M. Frost and Z. James (2013), 'Does growth in private schooling contribute to Education for All? Evidence from a longitudinal, two cohort study in Andhra Pradesh, India', *International Journal of Educational Development*, 33(1): 65–73.

World Bank (2011), *Conflict, Security and Development: World Development Report* (Washington, DC: World Bank).

World Bank (2016), 'Maternal mortality ratio'. Available at https://data.worldbank.org/indicator/sh.sta.mmrt.

World Economic Forum (2017), *The Global Gender Gap Report, 2017*. Available at https://www.weforum.org/reports/the-global-gender-gap-report-2017.

Wright, N. S. (2015), *Bollywood and Postmodernism: Popular Indian Cinema in the 21st Century* (Edinburgh: Edinburgh University Press).

Wyatt, A. (2013), 'Combining clientelist and programmatic politics in Tamil Nadu, south India', *Commonwealth and Comparative Politics*, 51(1): 27–55.

Wyatt, A. (2015), 'Arvind Kejriwal's leadership of the Aam Aadmi Party', *Contemporary South Asia*, 23(2): 167–80.

Yadav, Y. (1996), 'Reconfiguration in Indian politics: State assembly elections 1993–1995', *Economic and Political Weekly*, 31(2–3): 95–104.

Yadav, Y. (1999), 'Electoral politics in the time of change: India's third electoral system: 1998–99', *Economic and Political Weekly*, 34(34–35): 2393–9.

Yadav, Y. and S. Palshikar (2009), 'Between fortuna and virtu: Explaining the Congress' ambiguous victory in 2009', *Economic and Political Weekly*, 44(39): 33–46.

Yagnik, A. and S. Sheth (2005), *The Shaping of Modern Gujarat: Plurality, Hindutva and Beyond* (Delhi: Penguin Books).

Yusuf, S. (2014), 'Fifty years of growth economics', in B. Currie-Alder, R. Kanbur and D. M. Malone (eds) *International Development: Ideas, Experience and Prospects*, 50–64 (Oxford: Oxford University Press).

Zavos, J. (2000), *The Emergence of Hindu Nationalism in India* (Delhi: Oxford University Press).

Zenner, L., K. Kumar and M. Pilz (2017), 'Entrepreneurship education at Indian industrial training institutes – A case study of the prescribed, adopted and enacted curriculum in and around Bangalore', *International Journal for Research in Vocational Education and Training*, 4(1): 69–94.

Index